IC SEA

(Free City)

Danzig

East Prussia

Pomerania

POLAND

Silesia

N

D1714727

LOVAKIA

Vienna

A

GERMANY and AUSTRIA

━━━ NATIONAL BORDERS

─── *Land* Borders

─·─· Provincial Borders (inside Prussia)

▭ PRUSSIA

Smaller *Laender*

▤ THURINGIA

▥ ANHALT

▨ BRUNSWICK

▧ LIPPE

▦ SCHAUMBURG-LIPPE

Foundations of the
Nazi Police State

Foundations OF THE Nazi Police State

The Formation of Sipo and SD

GEORGE C. BROWDER

THE UNIVERSITY PRESS OF KENTUCKY

Library of Congress Cataloging-in-Publication Data
Browder, George, C., 1939-
    Foundations of the Nazi police state : the foundation of Sipo and
SD / George C. Browder.
        p. cm.
    Includes bibliographical references.
    ISBN 0-8131-1697-X :
    1. Nationalsozialistische Deutsche Arbeiter-Partei.
Schutzstaffel. Sicherheitspolizei—History.
2. Nationalsozialistische Deutsche Arbeiter-Partei. Schutzstaffel.
Sicherheitsdienst—History. 3. Nationalsozialistische Deutsche
Arbeiter-Partei. Schutzstaffel—History. 4. Himmler, Heinrich,
1900-1945. 5. Germany—Politics and government—1933-1945.
I. Title.
DD253.6.B78 1989
363.2'83'094309043—dc20   89-22618

This book is printed on acid-free paper meeting
the requirements of the American National Standard
for Permanence of Paper for Printed Library Materials. ∞

To my MENTORS
without whom this would never have been begun.

To ETTA
without whom it could never have been finished.

Contents

[Illustrations follow pages 20 and 116]

Figures

Acknowledgments

With a work that has taken so long and led to so many places, the list of indebtedness becomes so great that there is some hesitation to publish it, out of fear of omission. If I have omitted someone, I hope he or she will be as forgiving as he or she was helpful, and understand that I am in no way ungrateful. For the numerous archivists who so generously hosted me, tolerated my rapacious demands, and then waited endless years to see any results, it seems hardly fair to be acknowledged merely in the collective, but space simply does not allow a listing of all their names.

The list of indebtedness must begin with Robert L. Koehl, who introduced me to the subject and nursed me through the initial trauma of negotiating a sea of microfilmed documents. His manuscript, which he generously made available long before its publication, was an indispensable thread through the labyrinth of primary and secondary sources.

Not only is the work of Shlomo Aronson a major contribution to high-quality scholarship in the field, but he has also been most generous in providing copies of correspondence and other materials from surviving members of Sipo and SD. The same is true of David Kahn and Peter Black.

Of course, no work of this nature would be possible without the full support and the diligent work of Robert Wolfe and his staff at the National Archives. The vast facilities and the services of the Bundesarchiv, its various branches, and the many *Land* archives in the Federal Republic of Germany made possible years of work in mere weeks or months. No scholar of modern German history need be told of the quality of their contribution, but I feel a special debt for both their patience and their professional dedication. In addition to the federal archives, specific mention is due the Geheime Staatsarchiv Berlin-Dahlem; the Politisches Archiv des Auswaertigen Amtes; the Bayerisches Hauptstaatsarchiv, Munich; the Bayerisches Staatsarchiv, Munich; the Staatsarchiv, Bremen; the Niedersaechsische Staatsarchive in Wolfenbuettel, Oldenburg, Hannover, and Bueckeburg; the Hessisches Hauptstaatsarchiv Wiesbaden and Staatsarchiv, Darmstadt; Staatsarchiv Detmold; Hauptstaatsarchiv Stuttgart; and Staatsarchiv Ludwigsburg. The staffs of the Institut fuer Zeitgeschichte, the Generalstaatsanwaltschaft bei dem Kammergericht Berlin, and the Polizei-Fuehrungsakademie Hiltrup gave assistance that was most appreciated. The late Richard Bauer and his successor, Daniel Simon, and the staff of the U.S. Document Center in Berlin made it possible to locate and review the files of hundreds of former members of Sipo and SD. Their patient and friendly service made pleasant the otherwise interminable periods of monotony between discoveries.

It is no longer possible to construct a complete list of the libraries to which the author is indebted. Most central, however, have been the services of the library of the University of Wisconsin at Madison and the Reed Library of the State University of New York, College at Fredonia. Special thanks must go to the staff working on interlibrary loans at both institutions.

Without financial backing, no scholar can manage the expenses of research across the oceans, far from home. In this respect, I am especially indebted to the National Endowment for the Humanities and to the Research Foundation of the State University of New York, both of which contributed significantly to foreign travel and extensive stays abroad. The Committee on Research and Creativity, the Department of History, and the administration of the College at Fredonia also came through to fill the innumerable cracks that are a drain on resources.

The late Harold Gordon and Charles Sydnor, Jr. deserve special mention for having waded through the entire manuscript in its earlier draft and for providing invaluable criticism. Patrick Courts's reading and suggestions at intermediate stages inspired much-improved clarity. David Kahn and George Stein read one or more chapters and applied their special knowledge to the improvement of each. Douglas Shepard helped refine the final drafts. The invaluable editorial assistance of Sharon Ihnen provided the finishing touches. Needless to say, what is good in this book owes much to their assistance, but they have no responsibilities for its problems, shortcomings, or errors. I was unable to incorporate all of their advice or solve all of the problems they uncovered.

I must also thank my colleagues for their patience and confidence over the many years that they have awaited a finished product. To those innumerable friends, students, and professional staff members of so many agencies who helped with the many little but essential details, thank you. And finally, for good measure, one libation each to Clio and to the god whose name we do not know.

Introduction

The abbreviation "Nazi," the acronym "Gestapo," and the initials "SS" have become resonant elements of our vocabulary. Less known is "SD," and hardly anyone recognizes the combination "Sipo and SD." Although Sipo and SD formed the heart of the National Socialist police state, the phrase carries none of the ominous impact that it should.

Sipo and SD was a conglomerate, formed in the summer of 1936 when Heinrich Himmler, Reichfuehrer SS, became chief of the German Police. He fused the Criminal Investigative Police (Kripo) and the Gestapo (the political police) to form the Security Police (Sicherheitspolizei or Sipo) under the command of SS General Reinhard Heydrich. Since Heydrich was also chief of the SD, the Security Service of the SS, his joint command over Sipo and SD and the exchange of personnel between the two produced an amalgam of party and state agencies that became central to the execution of most of the terror and mass murder of the Third Reich. Sipo and SD demands to be better known.

Since Sipo and SD amalgamated agencies of the state with those of the NS Movement, its origins lie in the separate histories of the police and of Nazism. By way of introduction, the first chapters of this book fill in the backgrounds of all participating organizations. From the conspiratorial environment of the NS Movement emerged the SS, the SD, and their leaders. The contest into which they entered focused first on control of the police.

Although no single organization carries full responsibility for the evils of the Third Reich, the SS-police system was the executor of terrorism and "population policy" in the same way that the military carried out the Reich's imperialistic aggression. Within the police state, even the concentration camps could not rival the impact of Sipo and SD. It was the source not only of the "desk murderers" who administered terror and genocide by assigning victims to the camps, but also of the police executives for identification and arrest, and of the command and staff for a major instrument of execution, the Einsatzgruppen. Despite its power, no serious study has been devoted to the Sipo and SD conglomperate—how it came to be and why its particular components were drawn together.

A study of Sipo and SD in the existing literature leads into a labyrinth of both popular and scholarly misconceptions. The reliable literature provides only enough descriptive narrative and substantive analysis to piece together an organizational history of the Gestapo or the SD for certain limited periods. Since there is little that deals with Kripo or with Sipo and SD as an entity,[1] construction of a political-organizational narrative is an indispensable first step. This study provides that narrative, along with an analysis of the power struggles that created the conglomerate and of the participants' competing and complementary goals, which shaped the final product. While there is some repetition of accounts found elsewhere, these accounts are tested against available evidence and woven together with new interpretations to produce a more accurate history of Sipo and SD. Unraveling the complexities of organization and development should contribute to our understanding of the Nazi regime and lay the foundations for even more significant insights.

Since Sipo and SD was so central to many of the more controversial developments in the Third Reich—the totalitarian efforts to achieve conformity and to end opposition, the race and resettlement programs, the development and implementation of imperialistic expansion—its evolution is a case study relevant to the major debates among scholars over the nature of the Nazi regime.[2]

Central to all these debates is a controversy that divides most scholars into two broad camps: the traditionalist interpretation, also known as Hitlercentrist, monocratic, totalitarian, intentionalist, or programmatic, versus the "revisionist" theories, sometimes labeled polycentrist, structuralist, functionalist, or evolutionist.[3]

The older[4] and more broadly influential Hitlercentrist-intentionalist schools generally agree that most aspects of the Nazi experience were products of a consensus of intentions among the NS leadership, fully dominated by Hitler, who orchestrated all major developments of the Third Reich and turned his ideological fixations into government policy.[5] In contrast, the polycentrist-functionalist schools, while not denying the major importance of either Hitler or the ideological consensus, argue that Hitler's style of leadership, which avoided decision making, produced an administrative chaos of competitive power centers. These in turn often made policy that Hitler sometimes accepted, sometimes modified, and only in extreme cases overruled. Furthermore, in contrast to extreme ideal images of totalitarian autocracy, the Fuehrer had to respect significant social and economic pressures and power centers, even outside his Movement, not just temporarily, but for all or most of his thirteen-year reign. In such chaos, functional pressures helped shape policy, while the ideology, rather than offering clear objectives, functioned instead to bring forward those more negative, often self-defeating goals that demanded increasingly extreme solutions.[6]

This study of Sipo and SD generally supports that polycentric-functionalist interpretation. My perspective grew from many years of immersion in the primary sources, was constantly reinforced by the emerging scholarship of the past two decades, and serves as the context in which I now read the sources. Focusing as it does on developments usually below Hitler's level of interest, yet occasionally requiring his attention and ultimately some decisions by him, the story of the formation of Sipo and SD affords many bases of dissatisfaction with most Hitlercentric, intentionalist analyses.

Much of the debate over monocraty versus polycraty centers on the question of whether or not Hitler's famous "divide and rule" strategy was as Machiavellian as traditionally believed, or more the result of his procrastinating character and his need to skirt decisions, to place himself above factional politics and association with mistakes and unpopular policies. Unfortunately, from the perspective of this study little light can be shed directly on this debate, but the latter analysis seems more consistent with his observable behavior vis-à-vis the evolution of Sipo and SD.

More concrete support for the polycratic view emerges from the great number of developments in the evolution of Sipo and SD that occurred without any evidence of Hitler's involvement or concern. Even the decisions that he did make were often ignored or so diluted or deflected in implementation that they did not hinder the participants in pursuing their own versions of the ideological consensus. When his decisions did have an effect on Sipo and SD—especially the ultimate acceptance of Himmler's consolidation of SS and police—the decisions were determined less by any long-range intentions about a police state than by pressures unleashed in pursuit of other major ideological goals. The entire process of decision making was inconsistent with intentionalist-monocratic models.

Particularly in the evolution of the Final Solution, however, functional analysis allegedly has failed to convince that the system did anything more than modify "the speed or dynamic of the intentionalist program."[7] If this were true, functionalists would have to admit that the intentionalist argument was the more powerful model. Consequently, this study and its sequel, in particular, must confront the question of intentionalism and the Final Solution. The creation of a totalitarian police state as an essential step toward the Final Solution provides one specific perspective for this study. The *self-actuating* machinery of destruction described so vividly by Raul Hilberg begs for an explanation of its origins.[8] How and why the machine was actually built is central to the intentionalist-vs.-functionalist debate.

On the other hand, this book and its sequel will add little to the debate over foreign policy, another field where intentionalism has prevailed, for a significant role for Sipo and SD in NS foreign policy postdates 1936. Here, however, early developments indicate clearly a synthesis of intentions and functional forces.

This potential synthesis encourages my hope to rise above any one-sided contribution to the ongoing debate. All of the truly significant representatives of either monocratic-intentionalism or polycratic-functionalism already present sophisticated syntheses of the other side's arguments. The monocratic-intentionalists have even added to the image of administrative anarchy in the NS regime. The polycratic-functionalists concede Hitler's central role and the ideological consensus among not only key NS leaders but non-NS allies as well. Despite their closeness to a synthesis, however, when intentionalists charge functionalists with trivializing the Nazi experience and obscuring moral issues, whole functionalists contend that intentionalists devise alibis that obscure the broader questions of responsibility, they refute the hope that either side has achieved higher-order synthesis. The moral tone of attack indicates an unabridged ideological gap.[9]

The polycratic-functionalist approach is not as "revisionist" as its detractors would argue. It seeks merely to revise the extreme implications of attributing all major developments ultimately to Hitler, or to the control of a few. Such a view gets in the way of discovering how a modern industrial society of such cultural prestige as Germany could be twisted to Hitler's ends, how so many thousands of functionaries—more ordinary Germans than Nazi extremists or sadists—could be found to execute Hitler's will. When the Nazi experience becomes a product of the will of the Fuehrer—an aberration of German history, a unique phenomenon in modern Western history—the result is both an alibi that deflects further probing and a smokescreen that obscures insights into how similarly extreme developments might reoccur, perhaps without a Hitler or a Nazi ideology or a German *Sonderweg*.

The polycratic-functionalist analysis appeals to me because it promises to cut through such smokescreens as those the Nazis themselves threw up via their propaganda about a triumph of the will. If the analyst can avoid becoming lost among the trees of Nazi infighting and the diffusion of responsibility in institutional labyrinths, and lead his reader out to view the forest of ideological conjunction, then he avoids the potential of either school to obscure moral issues. On this note, I hope to pursue a transcendent synthesis that neither minimizes the importance of Hitler or his ideology (or of other leaders such as Himmler or Heydrich) nor elevates these leaders to levels that put them in total control or that raise their intentions to the level of unchanging elements powerful enough to predetermine developments over decades. Perhaps no one can express the problem with more dialectical sophistication than did Ian Kershaw in his analysis of reactions to the debate:

> They point . . . to the need to look for a synthesis of "intention" and "structure," rather than seeing them as polarized opposites. It seems, indeed, clear that Hitler's intentions and the socio-economic "structural determinants" of Nazi rule were not antagonistic poles, pushing in opposite directions, but acted in a dialectical relationship which pushed in the same direction. Consequently, it is as good as impossible to separate as a causal factor "intention" from the impersonal conditions which shape the framework within which intentions can become "operational." At the same time, it seems important to recognize that an "intention" is not an autonomous force, but is affected in its implementation by circumstances which it may itself have been instrumental in creating, but which have developed a momentum of their own.[10]

Accordingly, one must avoid portraying Hitler or his ideas, or any major subordinate or ally or their ideas, or any member of Sipo and SD or the component agencies themselves, as monads (unchanging beings or elements) interacting with other monads. They must instead emerge as individuals and ideas involved in an ongoing process of change and / or becoming. Through interaction, each constantly modified itself and the others. To the extent that an individual mind like Hitler's suffered from an immunity to reality (a tendency to deflect cognitive dissonance), it could lock onto rigid ideas. Someone like Hitler or Himmler could thus be a more rigid component in the interactions, but his efforts to implement his ideas could not escape that reality of interaction.[11]

In such a way, this book and its sequel strive to contribute insights into how such a respectable, modern society as Germany produced the monstrous crimes of the NS regime. Sipo and SD as a case study offers an ideal perspective. As indicated, this book will explore the creation of the SS-police system without assuming that it was simply created (or ordered up) by Hitler with its ultimate role in mind. Yet it is hard to imagine the extremes of Hitler's racial policies being pursued successfully without an instrument like Himmler's system. This book will show that many other authoritarian and/or Nazi-dominated police systems might have triumphed instead, with significant differences in what might have been. Any course of development other than Himmler's triumph in the struggle for police power could have altered Hitler's ability to execute genocide and might therefore have reduced the scope of his racial destruction to more conventional forms of persecution. In support of Kershaw's previously quoted appeal for a synthesis, most psychologists argue that no matter what our inclinations, our actions are also shaped by opportunities or the lack of opportunities to act on those inclinations. No leader can execute his programs without suitable instruments.

In this light, even subtle differences in the plans and goals of Himmler's competitors, like Frick and Goering, become significant. Scholars have rightly argued that since all competitors (even many non-Nazi collaborators) sought an authoritarian police state, thay all contributed to the ultimate system; this book certainly confirms that interpretation. However, those who argue that this commonality of goal negates any significance in the variations[12] obscure a significant component of the puzzle.

From the point of view of preserving civil liberties, all police states pose the same evil potential, no matter what they propose to achieve or defend us against. History, however, offers many examples of differences among police states in action. They have served different ends, and they have indulged in various degrees of repression and inhumanity. From that viewpoint, police states are not all the same. One must consider the possibility that, regardless of the inclinations of the regime, some police state machinery does not offer its leaders the same opportunities or degree of oppportunity as do others. In some police states, the opportunities are widely at variance from what their leaders might ever have anticipated, shaping the histories of the police states as much as have the inclinations of the leaders. A Frick, or even a Goering, as police chief might not have made it possible for Hitler to do what he did, certainly not to the extent that he did it. One need look only at the failure of the Luftwaffe to see the seriousness of this possibility.

In such a light, the differences among Frick, Goering, and Himmler become most significant, demanding not only an exploration of the struggle among the contenders and the alternatives they offered, but also an attempt to determine how their struggle shaped the ultimate Himmlerian system.

Historians have long agreed that a key element of Himmler's system was the fusion of the SS, a "revolutionary" instrument of force from the NS Movement, with the legitimate police force of the state. Himmler intended an eventual, complete fusion of SS and police and, therefore, of Sipo and SD. Although this never happened de jure, it was clearly a de facto reality by the 1939 creation of the Reichssicherheitshauptamt. From its inception in 1936, Sipo and SD was a de facto entity for shaping the attitudes and actions of its members, police and SS alike. I intend to develop further in a sequel the role of Sipo and SD in moving its members toward their ultimate roles in police terror and genocide. That should, in turn, contribute to later studies of the role of Sipo and SD in converting general ideological conjunctions into a more clear consensus, then into intentions, and finally into plans and actions.

The reader of this book may feel dissatisfied because there is little or no coverage of the internal structure, operations, or personnel of the Gestapo, Kripo, or SD. Obviously, however, the narrative and analysis of the "external" struggle that created Sipo and SD needs an entire book to itself. The "internal developments"—the evolution of each organization and its operations and ethos, relations and tensions among the different branches, the personnel and how they came to play their roles in NS terror—deserve their own narrative and analysis. But such an undertaking would be risky without the context of this study. This book, in short, is offered as a preface to other work intended by me, in the hope that it will focus critical, scholarly attention on Sipo and SD.

Terminology and Style

Both the SS and the state bureaucracy employed elaborate titles and designations. This study makes constant use of such terms, which can become confusing to anyone but the specialist. Whenever possible, German titles and official designations have been translated into English for clarity, except for commonly used, anglicized German words like fuehrer. When first used, the translated title is followed in parentheses by the German original. Since translation may cause some confusion or inconvenience for the specialist, who must pursue the titles into original sources, the notes employ German language designations and spellings.

German designations, especially under the Nazis, were often lengthy. Consequently, standardized German abbreviations for offices, titles, archives, and such are employed in the notes and occasionally in the text. Frequently used, lengthy journal titles are treated in the same manner. The reader will find a list of abbreviations on pages 252-54.

As noted, Sipo and SD formed an amalgam, so it is referred to in the singular throughout the text wherever the entire organization is intended. Although Sipo and SD never formed a singular corporation like Sears and Roebuck, commonly referred to in the singular, it must be seen as a singular entity if its role is to be understood.

Throughout the text, capitalization is used consistently for words like Party and Movement when they stand for the Nazi or NS Party or Movement. In this way frequent reference to these groups can be made without repetitive use of full titles, yet they are clearly distinguished from other parties or movements and from the generic concepts. On a similar note, proper nouns like Party Leadership are translations of titles like Partei Reichsleitung, a branch of the Party structure, and are not generic references.

1

Factionalism in Pursuit of Power
The Nazi Movement to 1931

The struggle for police power at the higher levels of the Nazi Party culminated in 1936 with Himmler's triumph: the addition of the title chief of the German Police to his National Socialist power base as Reichsfuehrer of the SS. It was in June 1936 that he created Sipo—the German Reichs Security Police—and added it to Reinhard Heydrich's command over the SD, the SS Security Service of the NS Movement. At that point, the foundations of the Nazi police state were firmly laid, and the agencies for controlled police terror, and ultimately genocide, were in place. Until then, however, neither Himmler's triumph nor the nature and structure of the Nazi police state were foregone conclusions. Its ultimate missions of totalitarian terror and genocide exceeded the imaginations of even its creators. The developments that culminated in Himmler's triumph began several years before Hitler became chancellor in 1933.

The early National Socialist Movement was neither monolithic nor disciplined. By 1930, when the Nazis first became a significant political party, the Movement contained diverse, competitive, contradictory groups with one thing in common: a bond of powerful loyalty to their Fuehrer, Adolf Hitler. Each member and each faction of the Movement adhered to some variant of the Nazi Idea, or Weltanschauung, and each thought his version most closely followed Hitler's. No one ever knew for sure, however, for, unlike an ideology, his Weltanschauung was almost deliberately vague, with only one ideological certainty: the existence of the Fuehrer, the one leader who embodied the Weltanschauung and the true will of the people.[1]

To exert the widest popular appeal and to maintain his personal power, Hitler kept the Nazi Idea vague and all-encompassing, allowing each faction some leeway to push its own preferences. As conditions

changed, the propaganda themes shifted to attract those groups temporarily more susceptible to the promises of Nazism. Parallel to its clearly
conservative, anti communist appeal, National Socialism could be both
elitist and egalitarian, and ambivalent about private property. But always
there was the safe appeal to nationalism, usually chauvinistic and xenophobic, interwoven with virulently anti-Semitic theories. Even this anti-
Semitism, however, could vary greatly in both emphasis and intensity.

In juxtaposition to its vaguely defined socialism, National Socialism
called for the restoration of selected old values, traditions, and institutions, including the authority of German society. While this was basically
a reactionary attitude, for many only a radical revolutionary restructuring
of society could restore those lost values. Thus reactionaries and radicals
came together in common focus on a strong personal leader as the source
of authority in society.

The vague NS Idea fused contradictory factions into a Movement
that gave Hitler power as the ultimate authority on the Idea, never to
be clearly defined. Generally, he stood above factional disputes and
power struggles, committing himself to a position only when absolutely
forced to—and then adroitly managing to leave all parties with some—
hope, some pittance, preserving his position as the ultimate arbiter. Only
when a follower inadvertently tried to crystallize the Weltanschauung
into a reality that would limit Hitler's freedom and authority would he
bring such a man down.

Ideological ambiguity as a basis for personal authority related closely
to Hitler's tactic of divide and conquer. Just as he avoided identification
with the position of any one faction, he also restricted the development
of any clear chains of command or order of rank within the Movement,
never favoring any one leader or faction without counterbalance. Frequently he created overlapping or conflicting responsibilities and refused
to delineate spheres of influence. How much of this was a calculated
tactic and how much merely a product of his reluctance to make decisions
remains unclear, but the effect was the same. Each in his command vied
with the other for the favor and support of a man who always stood
above, withholding the ultimate favor and thus rarely having to fear an
alliance of subordinates against him. Because each lieutenant, with his
own interpretation of what Hitler had said, built agencies and organizations that he thought would best fulfill the goals of the Movement,
Hitler always had a wide variety of instruments to use and courses to
pursue, usually maintaining several alternatives simultaneously.[2]

The pecking order within the Movement resulted from whatever
personal power a lieutenant might be able to muster, and his momentary
suitability or indispensability to Hitler's quest. Consequently power re-

lationships among the Nazis have been aptly compared to feudalism,[3] being based on individual strengths and complex interpersonal relationships. Because most of Hitler's vassals were lords or little fuehrers in their own domains, each having his own personal following, the Movement and the Third Reich were neither rational nor monolithic, but became instead confusing webs of personal power and loyalty systems. Unlike the feudal lord, however, Hitler always maintained the right to interfere if he saw fit.

Although such intraparty relationships were nurtured by Hitler's character and methods, they also reflected the coalescent growth of the Movement. Even after July 1921, when he had become the almost undisputed leader of the National Socialist German Workers' Party, or NSDAP, Hitler's supporters remained indistinct from the amorphous, *voelkisch* right wing of Bavarian politics. Also part of this right wing were the ubiquitous paramilitary groups, some of which fused into the Storm Troopers, or Brown Shirts (Sturmabteilung, known as the SA).

The SA, born in the summer of 1921 as the paramilitary wing of the Party, would become one of Hitler's first factional problems. Its allegiances were unclear, and many of its members—former soldiers and their youthful followers—visualized the creation of a military society based on a new national army that would replace the decadent Prussian traditions with the spirit of trench camaraderie. Since a new order built by the SA would simply bring Hitler along with it rather than vice versa, he insisted that his new order must be built before the national army could emerge. Until then, the paramilitary wing had to remain an instrument of the political mission and subordinate to the Party, that is, to Hitler.

In addition to the SA, other factions emerged as problems. After the 1923 putsch, the outlawed Nazi Party had fragmented into groups operating under camouflaged names, becoming a national force in northeastern and western Germany, where Nazism had previously been weak. One offspring was the so-called Northern Faction, a group centered around the Strasser brothers, Otto and Gregor, Joseph Goebbels, and others. Most of them leaned much more toward anticapitalism than did the more conservative Bavarian-centered branch.[4]

Such divisiveness face Hitler in 1925 when he left Landsburg Prison and began to reorganize the NSDAP. His efforts were twofold. First, he reestablished his personal contacts and power, welding the Movement together by emphasizing the common themes of nationalism, anti-Semitism, and the beloved but absolute Fuehrer. Second, he mandated a complete reorganization and centralization of the Party from its Munich headquarters down to the local Pary organizations. In his major thrust against divided loyalties, he terminated all overlapping links with other *voelkisch* and paramilitary groups.

By dividing and conquering and by wooing many recalcitrants with a mixture of overwhelming showmanship, flattery, and unyielding insistence on his preeminence, Hitler adroitly patched over the cracks while denying the radicals a hard-line position. Nevertheless, he did not deny the specific ideological views of the Northern Faction, and left the future so vague that the faction and its leaders remained almost intact. Anything could still be read between the lines of the Party program and Hitler's statements.

Meanwhile, the SA reemerged as a rebel. During the reorganization, local Party leaders had established their own SA units. The numerous independent SA leaders and local units tended to act autonomously, and the SA attracted an increasingly rowdy and uncontrollable element. To centralize command, Hitler appointed Franz von Pfeffer Supreme SA Fuehrer in October 1926. Although Pfeffer developed a national command structure for the SA, provincial leadership prevailed over efforts to establish a military hierarchy. The SA remained diverse in membership and perhaps more untrustworthy than any of the other factions, often becoming synonymous with the more radically anitcapitalist, anti-establishment elements in the Movement. Aggravating the situation, Pfeffer favored an autonomous military force over subordination to the Party.[5]

The result of the evolution was an ever-increasing diversity that was essential to building the mass-based party that Hitler would ride to power. The central Party bureaucracy sought to impose Party discipline for its Fuehrer, but even the bureaucracy was factionalized under lieutenants who built personal structures for executing their own interpretations of the Fuehrer's will. Below them, at every level across Germany, local fuehrers emerged, each equally sure that his approach embodied the true NS Idea and the Fuehrer's will. Each resented either the bureaucratic inflexibility or the undisciplined willfulness of the other.

Ironically, this tension did not produce a badly factionalized party, but instead a flexible, dynamic Movement, bound together in xenophobic nationalism and a powerful focus on common enemies. An outward show of discipline and comradely unity in the face of those enemies became the proper NS stance. Above all, Party members united behind their Fuehrer, who could convert their tension into political power. This capacity made the Movement and Adolf Hitler synonymous, but has left open the question of when and how much he controlled the Movement, or it drove him.

Himmler and the SS

Into this context of factionalism and questionable reliability of large branches of the Movement came the SS. Hitler's chauffeur, Julius Schreck, created the first true SS prototype in April 1925, when he formed the eight-man Staff Guard for the Fuehrer, who was then uncertain about his ability to keep the SA as a subordinate wing of the Party.[6] Hitler, just released from prison and finding the Party in turmoil and the SA uncontrolled, needed personal protection and a disciplined, absolutely reliable Party police force. The eight-man Staff Guard became the model for many such units at local Party offices, soon designated Schutzstaffeln (Protection Squadrons), known as the SS.

From the beginning, the SS units resembled an elite formation: small, handpicked teams, not to exceed ten men—allegedly the best and most reliable Party members. To guard against disorderly, insubordinate elements, the screening process required of each SS candidate two sponsors and registration with the police as a resident of the local area for at least five years. Increasingly stringent physical requirements also added to the image of eliteness.

During its first years, the SS developed its mission as a security service, protecting Party leaders and speakers and, beyond that, policing within the Movement. To perform this mission, the SS soon developed its first intelligence function by requiring its members to forward to SS headquarters all newspaper and magazine clippings referring to the Movement, as well as information on undesirables and spies in the Party.[7]

No sooner had the SS begun to develop, however, than it lost its initial preeminence. When Pfeffer reorganized the SA in the fall of 1926, the nascent SS had to take a back seat. Not only did the newly designated Reichsfuehrer SS become subordinate to the Supreme SA Fuehrer, but the local SS units drew increasingly menial assignments as the SA re-emerged.[8] The little SS remained insignificant until it came under the command of Heinrich Himmler.

Himmler had joined the SS in 1925, as member number 168. At that time, as secretary and general assistant to Gregor Strasser, head of the Party District, or Gau, of Lower Bavaria, his duties included organizing and commanding the local protection squadrons. A diligent worker, he rose rapidly in the Party, and during the next year, when Strasser became propaganda chief at Party central headquarters, Himmler became deputy chief. In this position, he developed a closer relationship with the SS, which as an intelligence agency collaborated with him in propaganda and as a protection force guarded the speakers whom he furnished. In

September 1927, Himmler consequently became second in command of the SS.[9]

Immediately, he strengthened the intelligence functions of the SS by requiring that intelligence reports from the local squadrons be forwarded regularly to his central headquarters. He expanded the scope of these reports to include unusual news about (1) opponents, especially their leaders; (2) known Freemasons and Jewish leaders; (3) special political or state events; (4) important clippings, especially any about National Socialism; and (5) any orders of the opposition that might be acquired. Not to overlook home territory, he ordered the SS to report on improprieties in the SA.[10]

By this time, Himmler had already manifested most of the characteristics and preoccupations that would shape his infamous SS. He had identified the major "enemies"—Marxists, Jews, and Freemasons. He was equally preoccupied with ferreting out the internal or camouflaged enemies in German society and in the Movement, focusing his attention on the SA.

Himmler's complexity frustrates efforts to describe him. He cut such a contradictory figure that most contemporaries painted discordant pictures of him. He led an exemplary personal life, so rigidly middle-class in moralistic standards that he was absolutely priggish. He was not simply cold, however, for he often displayed genuine compassion for the unfortunate, and he sought to maintain warm personal relations with everyone around him. Many knew him as a congenial companion with a pleasant sense of humor. On the other hand, this child-loving, clerkish man became the veritable executioner of over twelve million human beings, including children. As early as 1933, selective killings and random terror were the order of the day. By 1941, murder by the millions had become a "necessary" although "un-Germanic" thing for Himmler. Even so, he reportedly became depressed when the "final solution" of the Jewish question was devised, and he was visibly shaken when he witnessed a mass execution. Although such descriptions seem totally contradictory, recent studies have drawn a more coherent picture.[11]

For instance, Peter Loewenberg employed the concept of "unsuccessful adolescence" to explain Himmler's character. Although the resultant picture was monochromatic, it laid bare significant aspects of the total man. Young Heinrich was the archetype of the good, obedient, respectful child. He identified so totally with his father, a pedantic and conscientious gymnasium professor who tutored Prince Heinrich of Bavaria, that he never developed his own independent character. Rather than acquiring an assertive personality of his own, Himmler simply expressed what he thought he should be. His image of masculine strength, which he was impelled to manifest, was one of extremely repressive self-control. Under the direction of his father, he developed many compulsive habits of orderliness and self-discipline, becoming a man who craved absolute authority for a guide. He was extremely insecure whenever he felt the loss of complete control over himself and his responsibilities. He hid his confused and tortured reactions to real-life relations behind a mask of propriety of the sort that he believed bourgeois standards dictated.

The bourgeois environment in which young Himmler developed was not only rigidly defined in terms of place and propriety, but also rich in romantic images of the heroic ancient and medieval Germans. Although he felt destined for a military career, he had been too young to be more than a cadet during World War I. Unable to make his way into the postwar Reichswehr, and with action in the Free Corps offering no career, he turned in frustration to his second love, farming. In the fall of 1919, he matriculated in agricultural studies at a *Technische Hochschule* and began a few pleasant years of student life and apprenticeship.

During his youth, Himmler had displayed few symptoms of his ultimately extreme ideas. As a typically conservative nationalist and a devout Catholic, he expressed only the sort of nonvirulent anti-Semitism then much in vogue. His two most persistent characteristics were the pursuit of security by fitting in completely, and the quest for an absolute, all-encompassing set of certainties to assure his conformity.

His intermittent involvement in things military made him a follower of Ernst Roehm, a leader in many of the Munich area paramilitary formations. In one of these units, Himmler participated in the November 1923 putsch. After this taste of dramatic political action, he gravitated to the National-Socialist Freedom Movement, one of the post-coup factions of the then illegal Party. In this way he became involved with Gregor Strasser as a propagandist in the Reichstag election of 1924. Carried away by inflammatory attacks on Liberalism, Jews, Freemasonry, and bolshevism, Himmler completed his gravitation to a radical rightist view that held an interrelated set of enemies responsible for the plight of Germany. Even so, the factionalism of the Movement disturbed him, because it had no ideological consensus. Only when Hitler emerged from prison and rebuilt the Movement around himself did Himmler find the absolute certainty to which he would cling: the Fuehrer as interpreter of the Nazi Idea with unquestionable authority.[12]

Between 1924 and 1929, while he climbed from the regional to the central offices of the Party and the SS, Himmler developed his absolutist ideology after the Hitlerian model. While fleshing out his own details, he fell under the influence of Richard Walter Darre, one of the many racist ideologues who argued that everything of greatness in human history had been done by men of Nordic blood. The greatness of Germany hinged upon promotion of its Nordic blood and culture and the destruction of anyone who opposed them. Since the chief characteristic of Nordic blood was the struggle for dominance, its antitheses were international humanitarian ideas. Freemasonry, Christianity brought by the Latins, Marxism or any form of *international* socialism, and "international Jewish capital" opposed and undermined German greatness. All the pieces fell together for Himmler into a monolithic ideology of race and blood and a set of equally absolute, abstract enemies: not human beings, but the agents of evil forces.

Well before his exposure to Nazism, Himmler had expressed a desire to settle in east-central Europe like the medieval Germans. He saw the future of Germany in eastward settlement, as in the romantic past. By the time of his Nazi propaganda work, it became obvious to him that such an eastward movement meant the displacement of the Slavs, who had reversed the process by infiltrating Germany. Slavs thus joined the list of enemies.[13]

During his formative years, Himmler had read casually on the subject of national security agencies, influenced by one book in particular, Colonel Walter Nicolai's *Geheime Maechte*.[14] A comparative study of intelligence operations during World War I, the book attributed Germany's defeat in large part to shortcomings in that realm. Nicolai argued that unlike the consistent approach of the French and Russians, the Germans developed intelligence services against their wartime enemies only sporadically and never in a coordinated way. They left political intelligence in the hands of diplomats, chosen usually for social reasons and guided in action by "social points of view." Lacking initiative, foreign office civil servants "scrupulously followed the line." The independently operating military intelligence lacked guidance from the political leadership, which did not understand its needs or support it. What Germany needed was statesmen with "a clear-sighted policy of force" to pursue national interests and a central, politically directed espionage service to uphold that policy.[15]

Nicolai emphasized that minorities, especially Jews, and internationally connected churches and their leaders represented threats to national security. Given this, it should be the province of the intelligence service to deal with a nation's immigration and racial problems. As for the origins of political action, "the idea of a revolution was not carried from the German East front into the homeland but from the homeland to the front."[16] Here lay the seeds of Himmler's later concept of a Reich Security Corps and the future roles of Sipo and SD. He may never have understood how intelligence and security agencies operated, but his objectives for them were firmly set.

By the time Himmler acquired control of the SS, he already perceived the rudiments of its future missions, including those of the SD. The SS would be a racially pure military order of Teutonic warriors who would cleanse Germany of its internal enemies, guard against enemy penetration from abroad, maintain order at home, and conquer and colonize the East, ensuring the ties between blood and soil. Himmler's ideas, reinforced by those of Darre, soon formed the stringent racial requirements for SS membership and produced the marriage code that subjected all SS fiancées to approval.

If "racist crackpot" aptly describes one aspect of Himmler's character, it would be a mistake to discount his abilities. The tendency to dismiss Himmler too quickly led to the popular belief, at various levels of Party and state, that Himmler was merely a shield, a dupe behind whom Heydrich was free to build a great and powerful empire.[17] Such an explanation hardly accounts for what Himmler achieved without Heydrich.

Himmler was certainly a man to be reckoned with in the milieu of the Third Reich. Felix Kersten, Himmler's masseur and confidant, described him as, on the one hand, "a crass rationalist coldly taking account of human instincts and using them to his own ends . . . yet at the same time a romantic."[18] Himmler could indeed behave with cool rationality, yet as with Hitler, one often wonders whether he was in control of his myths or vice versa. Though he could certainly use the SS mythology with calculated effect, he also believed most of what he said.

Heinrich Himmler indeed had talents. Although he has been described as a clerkish pedant, a plodding worker who is attentive to details can be handy in a small, poor political party, where he can gain a position of strength. More important, Himmler was a skilled organizer and manager, adroit in developing and exploiting contacts.[19] These qualities, along with his racist ideals, gave him a ready-made place in Hitler's hierarchy.

In view of Himmler's considerable skills and many achievements, the other extreme is to overestimate him—as did Willie Frischauer in his image of an "evil genius." In fact, Himmler cultivated such an image. He reveled in the role of manipulator, which he practiced all the more viciously because of feelings of insecurity. He loved to pontificate on the art of manipulation, and undoubtedly greatly exaggerated the degree of preplanning that went into a victory. The art of manipulation as he practiced it made use of strict rules and austere standards stringently enforced, though counterbalanced in many cases by a free rein for subordinates and the lavish awarding of prizes, honors, and titles. In emulation of Hitler, he played his underlings against one another.[20]

Himmler had another characteristic that well suited his role—a conspiratorial mentality. Since he firmly believed in looking behind the scenes for the "wire-pullers," any new development frustrated him until he could "determine" the person or persons who "engineered" it.[21] Such a view of reality predictably affected the operations and organizational structure of the agencies that developed beneath him, particularly Sipo and SD.

Other qualities in Himmler had their effect as well. For instance, among the romantic qualities imbued in young Himmler were sacrifice and undying loyalty. Loyalty became the hallmark of his self-image and the ideal of the SS. For Himmler the only true proof of ultimate loyalty became "the willing execution of orders and the assumption of responsibilities that others find immoral or distasteful."[22] Such a concept of loyalty helps explain the role of Himmler and his ranks in police terrorism and crimes against humanity, for neither he nor most of his Sipo and SD leaders were sadists.

The loyalty that Himmler imparted to the SS determined its future bond with Hitler, who needed absolute loyalty. The potential value of Himmler's influence on the SS must have become apparent to Hitler by the beginning of 1929, for he made him Reichsfuehrer SS, head of the entire SS. Hitler nevertheless manifested ambivalent attitudes toward Himmler. At times he displayed an uneasiness about Himmler's ideology, perhaps because he saw its absolutes as potential restrictions on his own flexibility.[23] The following chapters will describe several occasions when Hitler avoided an expansion of Himmler's power. Hitler saw Himmler's SS as an ideal security force *within* the Movement, but may have foreseen no greater role.

Meanwhile, however, Himmler's appointment in January 1929 came at a crucial time for Nazism. Election results had recently shown that the rural population and the lower middle class offered rich prospects. Appealing to them required shifting emphasis from "socialism" and the street tactics of the SA rowdies to legal tactics, conventional political campaigning, and appeals to traditional German values. Although Rabble-rousing and anti-Semitism still remained for the hard liners, this tactical shift increased Party tension. The restraint, legalism, and electoral politics that bourgeois respectability demanded, and the dealings and compromises with reactionaries, repulsed many among the young radicals and in the SA. The Party thus needed more than ever a police force to ensure adherence to legality and to prevent the sort of incidents that would alienate the middle class or result in bans on the Nazis.

Tensions heightened over the next five years, increasing the need for a Party police force. In the spring of 1930, a crisis occurred when Party radicals came out in support of strikes in Saxony. In the ensuing efforts to impose conformity, Hitler took positions that made an irreparable ideological split obvious to Otto Strasser, who resigned from the Party and began a campaign against Hitler. Shortly thereafter, Pfeffer resigned as Supreme SA Fuehrer because of conflicts over the role of the SA, and in an indirectly related outbreak, the Berlin SA revolted under the leadership of SA Fuehrer East, Walter Stennes. The uprising began as a strike and escalated into a seizure of Party headquarters that could only be brought under control by Hitler's personal attention.[24]

By September 1930, Hitler had assumed the position of Supreme SA Fuehrer, turning to his old cohort and one of the creators of the SA, Ernst Roehm, as the only man who might keep the SA in line. In January 1931, he appointed Roehm chief of staff of the SA with orders to weld it into a centralized military organization. Roehm's efforts to assert discipline sparked immediate opposition, most notably another Stennes-led revolt in Berlin.[25]

In such conflicts and crises, the SS proved itself. In both Berlin revolts, outnumbered SS guards had tried, although unsuccessfully, to defend Party offices. During the second revolt, SS intelligence helped Hitler manipulate the situation. The SS emerged as the obvious police force for maintaining order in the Party.[26] Although the SS had been a subordinate branch of the SA, that subordination came into question when Hitler assumed command of the SA in September 1930. In October Hitler proclaimed the SS as the Party police force and decided to give it independent status, since one of its major missions would be policing the SA. On December 1, Himmler asserted this independence, but Roehm's arrival in January as SA chief of staff disrupted this move. Instead, Himmler became personally subordinate to Roehm, although the SS maintained an autonomous command structure.[27] This compromise undoubtedly grew from the negotiations surrounding Roehm's appointment and the efforts to centralize the Party's paramilitary forces.

The SS had thus emerged as an organization of dual character, both a police service and an elite troop. As a police service it was to maintain security and order, protecting Party leaders and speakers. But most important was the job of policing the Movement—that is, keeping Party and SA personnel from violating Hitler's claim to legality except when he saw fit. In this position, Himmler might be pitted against his nominal chief, Ernst Roehm, head of the SA, and he became free to act more independently than most subordinates. Meanwhile, Himmler and Roehm resumed their close personal relationship, and worked together well. Nevertheless, when the SS reserved the Party police force as its domain, it established a logical claim to much of its future role. Hitler desired an unrestricted police force, under his immediate control and with military capabilities, that in the event of war could keep the morale of the German homeland and Army free of decay. Such a mission was consistent with Himmler's ideas, but it would take him time to convince Hitler that the SS was that desired police force.

Meanwhile, the SD emerged at this point as a predictable product of internal strife and rivalry, and of the Movement's conspiratorial drive for power. The security aspect of the mission that the SS had acquired involved the activities of *Abwehr* and *Gegnerforschung*, counterintelligence, and the investigation of enemy movements. As the SS grew, a specialized branch inevitably appeared to assume these duties.

Photo Essays (cont.)
C. The Consolidation of Police Power, April 1933-April 1934

Right: A press release photo of 12 April 1933, showing Hermann Goering, just named Prussian prime minister.

Below left: Rudolf Diels, Goering's Gestapo chief. U.S. Document Center, Berlin. Below right: A later photo of Arthur Nebe as SS and police lieutenant general and head of the Reich Criminal Police.

Above: NS paramilitary leaders in the vortex of intrigue, 13 August 1933. Far left, symbolically distancing himself from his comrades-in-arms, is Kurt Daluege, who was working closely with Goering and Frick and was soon to be removed from his command of SS-Group East; at center, SA Chief of Staff Roehm and Reichs-fuehrer SS Himmler, still frequently cooperating in the NS takeover of the police; to the right of Himmler is Sepp Dietrich, leader of the new Hitler Staff Guard and an alternative but independent source of SS power in Berlin. Below: Himmler and Heydrich on an inspection tour through Baden and Wuerttemberg, March 1934, typical of the many tours during which Himmler established and entrenched himself in the states outside Prussia. Notice the SD patch on Heydrich's sleeve.

Above: SS Major General Heydrich in Bavarian Political Police head-quarters in Munich in early 1934 as Himmler's deputy commander of the political police of the *Laender* "outside Prussia." Below: Goering appoints Himmler inspector of the Prussian Gestapo, April 1934.

D. The Selling of the Police State: Propaganda and Personalities, 1933-1936

Left: A seal posted by the Bavarian Political Police announces "Business closed by the police for price gouging" and "Proprietor in protective custody in Dachau." Now the enemies of the *Volk* would be handled properly. Who could object?

Below: "Papa" Eiche (center, smiling) conducts Dr. Robert Ley (second from left) and other dignitaries on a tour of Dachau, February 1936. At this time Himmler opened Dachau as part of a grand tour for all Party leaders, obviously to quell concerns about the camps and to demonstrate that the enemies of the Reich were subject to proper NS discipline.

Propaganda photos taken at Dachau in May and June 1933 to show that its inmates were happy, healthy, well fed, and properly exercised, but required to earn their keep at such heavy, honest labor as road work. Such pictures accompanied articles to refute stories about the camp.

Above: The Gestapo Museum, Berlin, was established to educate the public on the Red Menace. Photo ca. 1934. Below: A collection of seized communist hand guns in the museum.

Above: "Thus intellectual Communists conceal their weapons. A seized revolver concealed in a book as it was found in the library of a Communist." Below: "From a Communist arms craftsman. A weapon camouflaged as a walking stick with which Communists move about inoffensively as strollers at a demonstration."

Right: A display of "fully armed Red Front fighters ready for revolution" in the Gestapo Museum.

Below left: Werner Best, Heydrich's lieutenant for Gestapo and SD organization, legal problems, and Abwehr-police, and the key salesman of the police state.

Below right: Heinrich "Gestapo" Mueller, Heydrich's lieutenant for combatting the enemies of the state and the Movement. Both from U.S. Document Center, Berlin.

2

The Roots of the SD

Although no documentary records of Nazi intelligence agencies predating 1930 have surfaced, ad hoc Party and SA intelligence organizations did exist as far back as the early twenties.[1] A few years later, the Reich Propaganda Leadership under Gregor Strasser and Himmler were using their apparatus to assemble material on political enemies and individual Party members, and Himmler used the SS as a source of similar intelligence. Early Reich-level intelligence made no use of specialists, however, and most operations were purely local, such as several Gau intelligence services that existed at least as early as 1930.[2] Like much else in the Movement, such operations were totally subject to local politics, and from Himmler's perspective, hopelessly distorted and unreliable.

Others obviously shared Himmler's concern, for by 1930-31 both the Reich Propaganda Office, now under Goebbels, and the SA had formed centralized intelligence agencies before the SS. Beyond gathering intelligence about the enemy, they felt a growing need for counterintelligence and countersabotage. The recent electoral victories had produced a bandwagon effect for the Movement, and the influx of personnel eroded the reliability and controllability of membership, improving the chances for spies and agents provocateur. Success had bred a security problem.

When Otto Strasser resigned from the Party, Hitler saw him as an enemy—a police spy and provocateur. Strasser's subsequent anti-Party campaign confirmed this belief, and since Strasser had voiced many of the SA's discontents, his later alliance with Walter Stennes led to the widely held belief that the Party was extensively infiltrated.[3] The activities of Strasser and Stennes, and of turncoat Nazis appearing on Communist platforms, soon created a spy scare.[4]

Such a scare was hardly unfounded. When the Party rose to political eminence, the Communists intensified their interest in the Nazis. They tried to infiltrate the Party and used Nazi defectors for propaganda advantages. To combat this threat, the SA produced the first truly central intelligence agency of the Movement. In the fall of 1930, shortly before

Roehm's return, a former captain, Herbert Riester, had established a local operation that reported to the regional SA staff in Munich. By the winter of 1930-31, perhaps as a result of Roehm's organizational reforms, it had grown into a central intelligence and counterintelligence branch of the Supreme SA Staff known as the Ic division, the German military staff designation for intelligence.[5]

Through a network of SA observers, Riester assembled reports on the activities of enemy movements and on the mood and political attitudes of civil servants and police and military personnel. Unfortunately for Riester, his very success in penetrating state agencies, especially the military, led to his downfall. In February 1931, a police raid on his home uncovered the scope of his activities and resulted in a charge of high treason.[6] The compromise of Riester's activities led to a temporary hiatus for the SA Ic service. Under the pretext of economy measures, Roehm dissolved his Ic office, dispersed the compromised personnel, and assigned the gathering of information reports to an auxiliary staff under his adjutant.[7]

Of course, Roehm's people had no intention of doing without an intelligence branch or of leaving one undeveloped, but before they could properly reestablish the SA Ic, Goebbels's Reich Propaganda Headquarters (RPL) gave birth to an organization that would offer itself as the Party Intelligence Service. During 1930-31, the Reich Propaganda Headquarters had already created propaganda staff positions at all levels of the Party and developed a system of monthly reports from the lower levels (*Bezirke* through *Gau*) to the RPL.[8] There is no indication that Goebbels took any personal interest in an intelligence service, but his deputy, one H. Franke, who had replaced Himmler at Munich headquarters, apparently felt the same needs for intelligence as Strasser and Himmler before him. By May 1931, the significance of intelligence work became so obvious that the RPL called for the creation of a *Nachrichtendienst* (ND) to parallel the propaganda staff structure down through the Party organization. In June or July, Arthur Schumann, Gau propaganda leader in Saxony, was summoned to Munich to take over ND work. In his office there, variously titled Division of Subdivision ND, Schumann labored under serious difficulties, for he had to assert his authority over a field structure being built from below and staffed by the appointees of regional Party officials, and he had to deal with the Party infighting directed against Goebbels and himself.[9]

Meanwhile, within two months after Roehm dissolved the Ic staff position following Reister's compromise, he had completely reorganized his own staff, and a new Ic office emerged, directly responsible to him. Under its chief, Count Karl Leon Du Moulin-Eckart zu Vertoldsheim, the new SA counterespionage office began producing thorough reports on such matters as the espionage organization of the Red Front.[10]

Despite its potential efficiency, Du Moulin's Ic attracted notoriety. In November 1931, the *Muenchener Post* published a list of victims the Nazis allegedly intended to murder. The list, supposedly signed by Du Moulin himself, proved to be a hoax. The forger confessed to being an agent of Du Moulin who was playing a bizarre double game to destroy the credibility of the Social Democratic press and its sources by planting and exposing such forgeries. The police ascertained the facts, and the subsequent trial totally comprised Du Moulin.[11]

Meanwhile, in revenge the *Post* exposed the whole network of Nazi intelligence agencies, ridiculing the organizations of Schumann and Du Moulin. It gave special attention to the SS intelligence service, labeling it the most secret agency, slated to become an NS Cheka if the Nazis seized power. The *Post* identified the real brains behind this organization as an ex–naval lieutenant Heydrich.[12]

The exposé of Heydrich's operation was premature. The SS intelligence service hardly existed as an organization in the fall of 1931; it certainly had no priority among the various intelligence agencies, nor any guaranteed role in the future Reich. Nevertheless, the socialist press had picked up the special hint of eliteness and destiny that characterized the SS and its organizations. Ironically, the propagation of that aura by friend and foe alike would help the SS and SD assume their future roles.

During 1930-31, Himmler felt even greater pressures than those that induced Franke and Roehm to form their agencies. After his initial 1926 reading spree on police and intelligence agencies, his interest had lagged until the spring of 1930, when he read *Spionagezentrale Bruessel*, lent to him by none other than Hitler. Undoubtedly, as the spy mania mounted, the two discussed espionage. Perhaps Hitler encouraged Himmler to develop his counterespionage efforts, or perhaps Himmler simply expressed the intention of doing so. In either case, their feeling that this novelistic, spy chase story offered "much to learn" indicates their primitive conceptions of counterespionage.[13]

Hitler, Roehm, and Himmler also took specific action that reaffirmed the central role of the SS in security work. Ongoing concern for the security of Party leaders led in February 1931 to the formation of another SS personal bodyguard. As director of this new Security Service, Himmler coordinated security wherever Hitler appeared.[14] The continued personal contact with the Fuehrer ensured that Hitler associated Himmler's SS with intelligence about the intentions of all enemies.

If Himmler's memory was reliable, he felt a need for fulltime specialists to handle such intelligence functions as early as 1929-30, and he began assigning special Ic men in each SS *Sturm* to gather and forward intelligence. Fearing that the parochialism of local units threatened such work, he experimented with posts at higher levels in the organizational structure. Although Himmler recalled establishing a centralized system as early as 1930, the first surviving document of such dates from May 1931. By that time, he had set up an Ic section on his staff, but not until June 9 did he order an SS-wide duplication of the Ic staff structure at the divisional and regimental levels.[15]

As Himmler's staff chief, Prince Josias Waldeck-Pyrmont headed the Ic section, responsible for collecting the reports of the Ic men in the field. Without any consideration of suitability or special knowledge, Himmler decided that divisional and regional adjutants would also head their Ic divisions. Nevertheless, he realized that he needed a suitably trained officer on his own staff to distill the field reports into coherent intelligence. Having heard of the ex-naval "intelligence" officer who was offering his service to the Movement, he appointed Reinhard Heydrich after a brief interview.

Reinhard Heydrich Takes Command

Heydrich's was a character at least as complex and enigmatic as Himmler's. A short study of his background reveals the evolution of a personality consistent with both the image of a cold, calculating, evil genius and a very real man of many weaknesses.[16]

Reinhard Tristan Eugen Heydrich was born in 1904, the son of the securely established head of a music conservatory in Halle. His sharply contrasting parents may have contributed to his contradictory personality, for witnesses describe his father as an easy-going, self-made man, and his mother as the arrogant, harsh daughter of a court tutor. As a child, Heydrich apparently identified more with his mother's strength and consistency. He developed her arrogant, biting manners, yet simultaneously demanded love and recognition. From an early age, he was extremely competitive, pushing himself in a variety of sports.

As he grew older, a gnawing sense of being unwanted manifested itself in increasing aggressiveness and demands for love and attention. Toward "social inferiors" he was described as being cruel or disdainful, yet in his love for romance and music he displayed tenderness and sentimentality. One strikingly consistent characteristic emerged, however—extreme self-doubt. Self-doubts are inevitably exaggerated by the trauma of adolescence, a stage in Heydrich's life that coincided with the trauma of the German experience. The politically conservative Heydrich family had imbued its children with middle-class values, including respect for the authority of the state and loyalty to the nation, but the young Heydrich also acquired a special attitude toward Jews.

The hard times that befell the family fortunes paralleled the fate of the German nation, and the juxtaposition of personal and national loss produced a marked transition from nationalistic conservatism to reaction against threatening forces of change, specifically the "Red menace." For the young Heydrich, such evolutions in political attitudes mixed with a powerful patriotism fired by the romantic nationalism of the war. In the environment in which he matured, the emphasis on national traitors, the vigilante of *Feme* murders, and the bloody suppression of Communist revolts became almost an accepted way of life. He joined the Free Corps movement and *voelkisch* organizations, but nothing indicates any direct, brutalizing experience. In tune with the mood of his time, his nationalism became mixed with an ostentatious anti-Semitism. Perhaps in this display Heydrich sought to free himself of his alleged "Jewish stigma."

Throughout the Third Reich and down to the present, rumors have persisted that Heydrich was of Jewish ancestry. Of course, his ancestry is irrelevant, but the "stigma" was not. Reinhard's father, the subject of the rumors, often bore the epithet of "Isidor Suess"; the father's stepfather had in fact been named Suess, but there was no Jewish ancestry, although no one knows when young Reinhard learned that truth. Playmates often cruelly teased and badgered him because of his "Jewishness," and as a child he created fables about his father's past to convince his friends that he really was a "pure German." Genealogical uncertainty may have been a major source of Heydrich's self-doubts and growing sense of persecution, driving him to act out anti-Semitism to prove himself. After the war, while his father's convictions led him to the National Voelkisch Party, other family members, perhaps including young Heydrich, kept themselves informed about Hitler's new movement.[17]

Although it would not do to overstate his intelligence, Heydrich's career proves that he possessed a certain sharpness or cleverness. Nevertheless, he often behaved impetuously and frequently bluffed or bullied his way through problems, and although certainly diligent, he was not personally thorough. He had a phenomenal memory for details and used it to impress people, yet later he would profess to avoid the distraction of details. This was a man who often acted impulsively and instinctively, in contrast to the more cautious, procrastinating Himmler. Rash action got Heydrich into more than one difficulty, however, and, as Hitler lamented, contributed to his death.[18]

It was apparently his brashness that led to the end of Heydrich's first chosen career—that of a Navy officer—and set his future in line with that of the Nazi Movement. In 1922 he won an appointment as a naval cadet, and by the end of 1928 had achieved the final rank of lieutenant. During his nine-year naval career, Heydrich established a secure and respectable position for himself, although he did not gain the social acceptance of his fellow officers. He developed no close relationships with his peers, and he came to feel that everyone was against him, for the "Jewish stigma" had followed him into the Navy. Several incidents, some related to the supposed stigma, led many of his fellows to assume that he lacked officer qualities. Then came an incident in which he allegedly "compromised" a young woman of prominent and powerful family. By all modern standards, the relationship was innocent enough, and Heydrich refused to marry her because he was already engaged, to the woman who would become his wife. In a court of honor, his firm, "arrogant" refusal to bend under pressure led to the end of his naval career.[19]

A few months short of eligibility for a pension, denied the essential prestige of his uniform and humiliated before his family, Heydrich emerged a crushed and desperate man. Despondent, he fished about for a position suitable to his status. At this point he turned to the National Socialist Movement, a resurrection of adolescent associations, which his fiancée, a follower of Hitler, convinced him was his best alternative. On June 1, 1931, he joined the Party, writing to a friend of the family, Baron Karl von Eberstein, an SA major then prominent in the Party, requesting a "major leadership position."[20]

According to his wife, Heydrich had no prior ideological or political commitments; his nationalism was traditional, and he had even made fun of the Nazis. Perhaps he had done so, but right-wing nationalistic, anti-Republican sentiments pervaded in the military and social circles that Heydrich frequented,[21] despite the military's technically nonpartisan political posture. Whatever attitudes he might have publicly expressed, his lifetime experience had made him susceptible to the Nazi Weltanschauung and to the image of elitism. Like many other men encountered in this study, Heydrich was well prepared for the Movement and needed it, along with the SS and the organization he himself would build. In his later public statements, he led in developing the more extreme forms of the Weltanschauung. In private, according to his wife, he expressed cynicism about Nazi beliefs, especially Himmlerian ideas. Since arrogant disdain for what other Nazis believed would not be uncommon among his SD men, cynical comments hardly meant a rejection of the basic NS Weltanschauung. Such comments represented instead a typically individualistic and selective commitment to certain specific aspects while rejecting others.

When Heydrich's letter of application, which had passed through Roehm's office, arrived on Himmler's desk, the ex-naval officer became a candidate for the Ic position. When Himmler saw in his photograph the "Aryan" prototype, Heydrich's stock rose still more, but Himmler procrastinated. As if to set the pattern for their future relations, Heydrich settled the issue. He went straight to Himmler and engineered an interview.[22]

The story of this meeting unfortunately derives from secondhand sources. Himmler allegedly asked about experience in counterintelligence, and Heydrich bluffed his way through. Trying to present the image of a decisive commander, Himmler told Heydrich that he needed an Ic man and gave him twenty minutes to draft the proper orders and job description for the position. Heydrich easily set down the requirements in military format and jargon, and he got the job.[23]

On August 10, 1931, the newly commissioned SS Lieutenant Heydrich was ordered to assume the direction of the Ic Division of Himmler's staff.[24] As soon as he arrived in Munich, he found his raison d'etre, making himself indispensable. On August 26, the new Ic officer addressed an assembly of SS commanders in the Brown House, Party headquarters. Based upon the sort of reports the spy mania had inevitably fostered, and playing to a mood anyone could sense, Heydrich painted a picture of the Movement as being thoroughly infiltrated by police and enemy spies and agents. They leaked information embarrassing to the Movement and created incidents and unrest in the ranks. He claimed that his knowledge was backed by solid research, and he cautioned the commanders to be on guard against traitors.[25]

From this time onward, Heydrich built his authority upon an ability to paint two pictures convincingly. He depicted first the Movement, then the national community, as surrounded and penetrated by enemies, successfully camouflaging themselves as loyalists. By wooing the unwitting to their own purposes, they could hamstring even the greatest of forces in all history. It was necessary not only to confront the obvious enemy and destroy him in open combat, but also to ferret out and eliminate the camouflaged villain and identify and reeducate his thoughtless accomplices. Such a campaign obviously required an extraordinary and unhindered counterespionage strike force, and Heydrich capped these images by depicting himself as the master of the necessary mysteries.

Growing Amid Competitors

Shortly thereafter, on September 4, SS Order No. 43 outlined the formation of the new intelligence service. The work would be done openly by Ic staff personnel to be named at the divisional level by at least October

1, and at the regimental level later.[26] Henceforth, rather than adjutants, specialists would fill the Ic position.

~~Every effort was made to avoid the impression that SS men would~~ be spying on each other. Specifically, Ic work was to be entirely legal: no meddling in state organizations. Obviously, the very nature of counterespionage made such precepts impossible to observe, for by definition the camouflaged enemy was everywhere, including the SS and state offices. But such restrictive orders were necessary for the outward appearance of comradeship that Nazis had to maintain, and they typified Nazi legality. The working personnel could not be allowed to create problems that might result in compromise or charges of treason—the fate Riester's Ic had recently met. Of course, such directives could be violated on orders from above.

Meanwhile, Heydrich worked alone as the sole member of Himmler's Ic staff at Munich, his empire consisting of half an office in the Brown House. He had no control over the other Ic personnel on the field staffs, for their reports came to him through Prince Waldeck.[27] In other words, Heydrich did not yet head an intelligence service; he was merely a staff officer.

According to his wife, he complained as early as November 1931 of the counterproductive competition between NS intelligence agencies and wanted them absorbed into the SS.[28] But for the time being, he had his hands full with his own mission and needed all the help he could get from Schumann and Du Moulin. Although he undoubtedly had conflicts, and petty jealousies strained his relations with his rivals, much of what has been seen as his calculated maneuvers against them probably grew spontaneously from the confusion and lack of coordination in the Movement.

When friction occurred, Heydrich's organization may have been a major offender, but the evidence allows only for vague impressions. For instance, on November 26, 1931, the Reichsleitung issued a joint letter signed by Roehm, Himmler, and Franke, Goebbels's deputy, stating that each of their intelligence services would cooperate in a spirit of camaraderie, and report friction to the proper offices so it could be alleviated.[29] Although the directive denied that the three duplicated each other's missions, they obviously did so. Throughout the history of the SD there are documents of this nature, always issued in times of friction with other organizations. Sometimes Himmler and Heydrich merely subscribed to such statements as outward forms of propriety; more often, however, they desired to pull together with rivals toward common goals. Most often, both motives prevailed.

In any case, Party Leadership by November 1931 had recognized each of the three agencies as a Party intelligence service. As the largest

and most significant branches, the SA Ic and the Gau NDs under Schumann's office seemed to have developed a symbiotic relationship, holding many personnel in common.[30] The alignment had undoubtedly
grown from the crisis developing around Gregor Strasser, whose shifting
stance and increased administrative power had pitted him against elements like Goebbels, Goering, and Roehm's SA.[31] In a temporary Goeb-
bels-Roehm alliance, Himmler must have stood as an ambivalent
subordinate; unfortunately the shifts in his relationship with Strasser
remain uncharted. Beyond this consideration, the SS Ic, as the smallest
component, was the least essential to joint work, and as a newcomer to
the Movement, Heydrich may have found close cooperation difficult or
uncomfortable.

In any event, while his competitors grew apace, Heydrich merely
inched forward. Although this may have bothered him, he had com-
pensations. By the end of 1931 he had married, been promoted to SS
major, and replaced Waldeck as exclusively responsible for Ic, as well
as acquiring a two-room apartment, separate from the Brown House, as
an office for himself and two or three assistants. Although Himmler
sought finances from the Party treasurer, Heydrich had no budget.
Himmler met expenses with special appropriations, and Heydrich recruited his helpers from unemployed volunteers.[32]

The Bavarian police knew of Heydrich's office as an Ic branch of
Himmler's staff; however, it went by the innocuous title of Information
and Press Desk. As a Reichstag deputy, Himmler was legally entitled
to a press service, which gave the small Ic legal immunity and a cover
of propriety. Compared with Du Moulin's service, quite clearly labeled
Counterespionage, Heydrich's tiny office appeared to be a more or less
inoffensive branch of the "Nazi Intelligence Service." The police viewed
the various NS agencies as parts of a whole under the command of Du
Moulin, and interpreted all information they received in that context.[33]
They had evidence, however, that should have altered their view of the
SS Ic.

In the winter of 1932, the police in Oldenburg, a small state on the
North Sea coast, stumbled on an SS spy net that had penetrated a fortress
garrison. They captured Franz Nawroth of the garrison, who revealed
the identity of Herbert Weichardt, who in turn admitted that he collected
reports from agents like Nawroth and forwarded them to a Herr Kobelinski in Brunswick (Braunschweig), a small inland state. Although
the police identified both Nawroth and Weichert as SS men, they con-
fined their interrogation to questions about the "Nazi Intelligence Service." Ironically, catching this little SS Ic cell at military espionage merely
served to heighten Du Moulin's bad reputation; the police made nothing
of the SS Ic service.[34] Why the police remained indifferent to the SS Ic

relates closely to the problem of how Heydrich's SD went on to edge out its competitors. Aronson has suggested that Heydrich threw the police off his own scent by deflecting their attention to Du Moulin's people.

At some undetermined time, Heydrich acquired agents with whom he had direct contact. Tradition has it that one was an agent of the Bavarian police who had penetrated the Movement. Heydrich unmasked him and forced him to become a double agent in his service, feeding false information to the police and facilitating Nazi penetration into Bavarian police ranks.[35] Aronson places the date of this coup around November 1931, basing his argument on the fact that from that time on, little information exists in the police file on Heydrich's Ic work.[36]

Circumstantial evidence supports this view. In February 1932, the Bavarian police were in possession of Himmler's September 1931 order creating his Ic and delimiting its mission. They noted especially the injunctions for legality, but most significant was their belief that Himmler had entrusted this intelligence service to none other than Du Moulin.[37] Even if such interpretations were the work of Heydrich's agent, Du Moulin might in fact have approved such a decoy. Since the police already knew his own organization, he might have allowed its use as a screen for the SS Ic.

But even if Heydrich was running a double agent, that hardly explains the failures of the police. One double agent could not have completely paralyzed the police intelligence office in Munich, which controlled more than one agent and which had clearly directed a number of highly successful feelers into branches of the NS Movement that it considered dangerous. A single agent in the Bavarian police could not have misled the Intelligence Assembly Office in Berlin, where he would have had no direct contacts. The police undoubtedly failed to concentrate on Heydrich's office because, compared with the SA threat, it still appeared insignificant, and because Himmler—and perhaps Heydrich— had been so insistent on maintaining the appearance of legality. Heydrich's service did not triumph by sabotaging the opposition and outmaneuvering the police. Rather, it won because of opportune political developments inside the Movement, and because at this crucial time it remained relatively harmless, too small to draw much negative attention from the police.

Roehm's SA and Du Moulin's service discredited themselves. Since the summer of 1931, the Social Democratic press had had a field day at Roehm's expense, for they had acquired some of his personal letters revealing his homosexuality. The press freely associated the entire SA command structure with this stigma.[38] Scandalized, some elements in the Party resolved to eliminate the source and assembled assassins from the fringes of the Movement to murder Roehm and others. Although one of the would-be assassins defected to Du Moulin, who uncovered the plot and saved the intended victims, the whole circus became a public spectacle during 1932.[39]

The ultimate blow soon befell Du Moulin. The increasing attention drawn to the SA and to his office led to a series of police raids in the spring, exposing the subversive activities and plans of the SA and its Ic service, which had concentrated its penetration on the police, public transportation, and communications, obviously important targets for any power seizure.[40] Despite Du Moulin's rapid success, this exposure destroyed his organization. On April 1, Roehm quietly transferred Du Moulin to Berlin, and in the following weeks the federal government banned all NS paramilitary organizations. Although the SA would re-emerge in June, after the ban was lifted, and although it would continue to keep an Ic slot on its staffs,[41] the SA Ic was too discredited as a central intelligence agency of the Movement to regain its former hegemony. More important, given Roehm's position in the Movement, many other leaders preferred any alternative to his dominance of Party intelligence.

Since many of the bureaucrats of the Party organization saw Roehm as a threat, those who had Hitler's ear capitalized on every SA embarrassment. By the same token, the worse the SA looked, the better the SS appeared to some of those close to Hitler. The ambitious Martin Bormann passed such observations on to Rudolf Hess, Hitler's personal secretary and a contender for second position in the Party. The SS thus emerged as a badly needed source of security and order within the Party, and Heydrich's agency assumed a concomitantly dominant position. Bormann's and Hess's backing would prove crucial to the advancement of the SD. Nevertheless, it would oversimplify the complex relationships to describe the SD as an anti-SA arm of the Movement. According to Heydrich's wife, Roehm, as head of both SA and SS, also funded the early SD, especially after his own Ic collapsed. The Himmler-Roehm relationship remained warm, and Roehm became godfather to the Heydrichs' son.[42]

Even if the SA Ic ceased to be a major competitor for Heydrich, there still remained Schumann's service. By this time, Schumann had managed to erect an impressive-looking ND. By at least mid 1932, his office had acquired the title of Main Division III of the Reich Propaganda Headquarters (RPL), with ND leaders present in most Gau down to at least the *Kreis* level. His office issued regular mimeographed reports, "Information on the Enemy," seemingly thorough, detailed analyses of opposition forces. A February report on the "System" (the establishment) contained stolen police studies, including reports on the Communist Party. A July report dealt with "Propaganda Work of the Jews against

the NSDAP," and an August study covered the right-wing Tannen-
bergbund.[43]

It is difficult to evaluate the quality of this work or of the organization
itself. Regardless of quality, Schumann's ND reports may not have
pleased Hitler and other users. The *Muenchener Post* exposé pictured
Schumann as pedantic and inept, deluging NS leaders with voluminous
reports. Although the reports were no more voluminous and detailed
than good intelligence studies should be, the opinion of the Socialist
press may have been close to a fundamental reality. According to some
who worked with Hitler on intelligence, Werner Best for instance, Hitler
was unimpressed by detailed, thorough reports and preferred intuition.[44]

Schumann's ND may also have become a victim of the sharp rivalry
between Goebbels and Gregor Strasser during the latter part of 1932.
For whatever reason, Schumann's service suffered in some way, for
surviving records on the ND during the fall of 1932 are rare, and by the
time it reappeared in the documents of 1933, it had been split in two.
Schumann then headed a branch of Alfred Rosenberg's Foreign Political
Office, focusing primarily on foreign intelligence; the rest of the Party
ND remained active only at Gau and lower levels, no longer a central
intelligence agency of the Movement.[45]

Schumann's ND probably lost in the competition primarily because
it was not high among Goebbels's priorities, and it suffered the same
problem as the SA Ic. They both lacked real central control over their
field structure, the quality of which depended on the local functionaries.
Throughout 1932, for instance, Schumann continued to complain that
some of the Gau failed to make their monthly reports. Furthermore,
local Party leaders undoubtedly censored both the ND and the Ic.

First Strasser, then the circle around Hess desired more control over
the Party from above, through the Party machinery, putting them in
conflict with independent and powerful local Party leaders. Any intelligence service dependent upon reports forwarded through local leaders
offered few advantages to Party leadership. What the leadership needed
was a centralized intelligence service with a field net independent of
local Party powers, able to inform against them if necessary. Although
Hitler generally stood above such struggles, Hess and Party Treasurer
Franz Xavier Schwarz had the authority to grant the title of Party intelligence agency and to provide finances. Unlike Roehm and Goebbels,
Himmler did not rival or threaten Hess, so when Himmler supplied the
necessary service, Hess would accept it. Nothing better explains why
the SD prevailed.[46]

Although the field of domestic political intelligence lay open to Heydrich, there were other entrants to contest the way. Furthermore, his

newly important service might well have become the target of police exposure but for the change of political atmosphere during the summer of 1932. The political police had ceased to harass the Nazis and even sought their cooperation against the left, a shift that was extremely well-timed for the future of the SD.

Meanwhile, Heydrich and those in his service ceased being merely staff officers. The lack of control revealed by the Weichardt incident, the collapse of Du Moulin's service, and the disastrous ban on the SA and SS apparently goaded Himmler into forming a highly centralized, autonomous intelligence service and giving Heydrich direct command at all levels. During the ban, Heydrich's office in Munich dropped its "Ic" designation and hid its connection with the SS. His office fell back on the old, safe camouflage of Reichstag Representative Himmler's Press and Information Service (PI). At the same time, Heydrich acquired central command over a true intelligence service. After the lifting of the ban in June 1932, the Sicherheitsdienst-SS—the SD—emerged, with Heydrich as its head.[47] The service that would win Hess's support had come into being.

Heydrich devoted the rest of 1932 to the recruiting of SD personnel and the establishment of an intelligence network that was to spread over the entire Reich. The most important region in this growing SD network was centered on the Reich capital, Berlin. In SS-Group East, thirty-two-year-old SS Captain Hans Kobelinski, Heydrich's highest-ranking Ic officer, had been serving on the staff under Kurt Daluege since July. There Kobelinski created the new SD-Group East, which became official on September 15.[48]

The creation of SD-Group East under Kobelinski was undoubtedly a Munich-based effort to extend influence into the domain of the independent SS General Daluege, who since his role in the suppression of the Stennes putsch had rivaled Himmler in Hitler's confidence. Nevertheless, nothing indicates that Kobelinski and Daluege had anything less than smooth relations until well into 1933. By then a rift had developed between Heydrich and Daluege that complicated things.

While Heydrich built the SD, Himmler turned his attention to the police of Germany. He intended for the SS to play a special police role after the Nazis seized power. Even before 1933, he apparently had plans to fuse his SS with the police of the future Reich to create a suitable institution for guaranteeing order and security: a state protection corps (Staatsschutzkorps). SS members were to imbue the police with suitable discipline, attitudes, and values and to provide the necessary "racial stock" for a corps of men attuned to the needs of the Volk and their state.[49]

Before the power seizure, Heydrich had no preordained role in this

SS police mission. Although members of Sipo and SD often stated in later years that Heydrich fathered the whole idea of controlling the police through SS and SD penetration, Aronson, Heydrich's most scholarly biographer, considers this unlikely. Indeed, subsequent events indicate that Heydrich developed an appreciation for Himmler's scheme only gradually.[50] Even so, he undoubtedly played a significant role in its refinement and application.

Other than SD traditions, no significant evidence supports an argument that either Himmler or Heydrich preconceived the role that the SD would play vis-à-vis the personnel of the political police—the later Gestapo. Nevertheless, Himmler did choose Heydrich as head of the political police agencies that soon fell under his command, probably more because of the working relationship between the two than for any other reason. Heydrich's position as head of both political police and SD eventually tied the two together more securely and inevitably than any preconceived blueprint.

In January 1933, when Hitler became chancellor, neither the SS nor the SD guaranteed Himmler or Heydrich his future power, as the two organizations were relatively weak and poorly developed. Their eventual victory was difficult, for it was won from rivals with similar objectives who were initially more powerful, and it met with resistance among the police forces whose attitudes and values shaped the course of events as much as any other factor.

3

The Weimar Police

The detectives who became an element of Sipo and SD were but one part of the larger German police establishment, which requires a brief description to clarify the process of its absorption. Since Germany was a federation of states with decentralized police forces, each state, or *Land*, had its own police establishment, as did many municipalities, and the Weimar constitution left most police authority to the states. Consequently, aside from small special forces, no true Reich police force existed before the Nazis. The Reich Minister of the Interior had relatively little police authority, not even command over a Reich bureau for the investigation of crimes, nor a Reich border patrol.[1]

To counterbalance decentralization, the Reich government did have some leverage. It defrayed part of each state's police budget with an annual subsidy, which served as a direct lever for Reich pressure. This subsidy justified federal legislation that required some degree of organizational uniformity among the state forces, in a attempt to keep them free of partisan politics. Consequently, the Reich Minister of the Interior could count on more than the goodwill of the states in implementing his guidelines; however, even the threat of withdrawing the subsidy had its limitations.

The decentralization of the German police resulted primarily from traditional state and regional particularism that blocked centralization or coordination. State governments, generally suspicious of the federal government, jealously guarded their police powers. The Allies, having their own suspicions that the Germans would use a centrally commanded, militarized police to circumvent restrictions on the German Army, imposed decentralizing restrictions on Germany's police. The matter was of concern also to the bitterly divided parties of left and right, each fearing that the other would capitalize on a centralization of police power.

Nevertheless, German law enforcement was not chaotic, for sheer necessity produced voluntary cooperation. Although the Reich Ministry of Interior had little police authority, it did at least maintain offices for coordinating the exchange of information. Furthermore, the problem of coordination was not as great as those faced in the contemporary United States, for instance. Among the seventeen states having separate police forces, a single large state, Prussia, had authority over two-thirds of the territory of the Republic and approximately sixty percent of all police. With the exception of Bavaria's, no other state force was equal in size to the metropolitan force of either contemporary New York City or Chicago.[2]

Each state police force had a complex structure, however, producing further decentralization. The bulk of the uniformed police in Prussia, called Schutzpolizei or Schupo, found their counterpart in most other states and free cities under the same or a similar name, like State Police (Landespolizei) or Order Police (Ordnungspolizei). Under normal conditions, units of these police assigned to major urban centers came under the command of state-appointed civilian officials, usually called police presidents or police directors. In addition to the Landespolizei, some states, like Bavaria, had a separate state municipal police force. Assigned to major cities to do the more usual police work, such forces came under state-appointed commanders rather than the city government that commanded regular municipal police. For the countryside and rural communities, the state provided a Gendarmerie, or Landjaegerei. Scattered over rural areas, they fell under the authority of regional administrators, subject to regulation and supervision by central state offices.

Thus, even as a collective force, the centrally administered, uniformed police of a state had a decentralized command. In matters of training, personnel policy, equipment, and the like, these police came directly under central authority—the state ministry of interior or a comparable agency—but command fell to state authorities with regional and local jurisdictions. Although these authorities were in many respects subordinate to the state ministers, thus creating an indirect central command, the realities of politics could disrupt that control significantly.[3]

At the heart of the state police establishments lay paramilitary strike forces, organized and trained along military lines, housed in barracks, and instantly deployable in full unit strength. They existed to maintain internal order and security as the army or a national guard might in other countries.[4]

The Versailles Treaty restricted the size of all these police forces. Article 162 limited increases in state and local police forces beyond their 1913 strength by tying such increases to population changes. The Interallied Military Commission set more precise details, originally decreeing a maximum of 92,000 men, but gradually raising it to 157,000. Of this total, the maximum was 105,000 for state police, of whom a limit of 35,000 could be housed in barracks. German authorities kept state forces near the allotted maximums, while the municipal police fell below them.[5]

By no means did these limitations restrict Germany to a small police establishment. The final limit set by the Interallied Commission was a ratio of approximately one policeman to every four hundred inhabitants. Berlin had the largest local police force: seventeen thousand policemen in the late twenties, or a ratio of roughly one to every 240 inhabitants. A significant change from the prewar ratio of 1:324, it reflected the increased tension in that urban center. Overall, the increased police force was probably justified by the lack of military forces to support them, which becomes apparent from the figure for 1935, when the Army absorbed the armed police and the ratio changed to 1:536.[6]

These ratios become more meaningful when compared to those of other countries. In the United States during the 1920s, the national ratio of police to inhabitants changed from 1:1,000 to 1:800. Of course, any direct comparison is invalid because of the significant differences in population density, internal order, and the ready availability of the U.S. National Guard as a supplemental force. For a more meaningful comparison, France in the twenties had a ratio of roughly 1:500, but France also had a much larger army to support its police. In the more law enforcement–conscious United States of today, the ratio of police to population is 1:550, despite the same considerations of population problems, internal order, and National Guard availability. In France in the late 1960s, the ratio was the same as Weimar Germany's 1:400. As for the urban figures of the 1920s, Berlin's ratio of 1:240 compared strikingly with Chicago's 1:500 and Washington, D.C.'s 1:350. However, today an American city with over a half million population might have a more comparable ratio of 1:250.[7]

Of more relevance to this study are the German plainclothes detectives of the twenties, especially the political police. Except for a few in the municipal forces, the criminal and the political police were plainclothes detective branches of the state police. As such, the criminal police in most states had support and were well organized and coordinated. There was no Reich criminal police, however, not even an investigative bureau nor an official structure for coordinating interstate crime fighting. The political police occupied an even weaker position. Political investigative offices existed in most states, but with perhaps the exception of Bavaria, there were no centralized state political police forces. Despite their reasonably efficient service, they represented small, peripheral units compared with the forces maintained by many modern states.

In the historical development of the political and criminal police, Germany had not assumed the lead. As a matter of fact, the German police derived largely from foreign models, especially French units. Certainly, the political police did not have as deeply rooted a tradition in Germany as in many other European states.[8] In the old Reich, the criminal police had been limited to the municipal forces, low in efficiency, especially against mobile criminals and organized crime. In 1897, *Land* representatives met in Berlin to increase coordination among the states and free cities for identifying criminals, but controversy over methods hindered fully satisfactory solutions until 1912. Then the war frustrated plans for a Reich information center on crime.

Since these problems continued in the Weimar Republic, the Reich government had sought to pass legislation creating a Reich Criminal Police Office. The heightened rate of crime in the postwar years, topped off by the assassination of prominent political leaders like Walter Rathenau, provided special impetus. In 1922, the Reichstag passed a law to create a criminal police office under the Reich Ministry of Interior to combat interstate crime and to provide for coordination among the state police. Particularism prevailed, however, and with Prussia and Bavaria in the lead, several states blocked implementation. The Reich Ministry of Finance also created obstacles. Since the Reich government could not effectively press its case, it had to emasculate its Law for the Protection of the Reich and abandon the Reich Criminal Police Office.[9]

In compliance with the move to establish a Reich Criminal Police Office, however, the states did at least rationalize their own criminal police forces. In 1921, Saxony went the furthest by bringing all municipal criminal police into its state police system, and by 1925 all states had state criminal police forces coordinated by a central office. In the case of Prussia, this office, opened in the summer of 1925, came under the Police Presidium of Berlin. It coordinated the work of similarly constituted detective offices responsible for the provinces or districts.[10]

Meanwhile the state criminal police offices set about collectively to solve problems of Reich-wide coordination in their own way. In the summer of 1925, a police conference at Karlsruhe created a German Criminal Police Commission of police technicians who made recommendations to state governments, an informal but fairly efficient form of cooperation. Intelligence centers, laboratories and technical facilities in the various states for combating specialized aspects of crime became responsible for interstate coordination in their specialties. For instance, Dresden became the central office for missing persons and for identifying unknown bodies, while Munich assumed the specialty of "Gypsy excesses." The extensive Berlin office became a veritable Reich criminal police office because of the wide range of offenses it coordinated: forgery, pickpocketing, bank and train robberies, white slavery and pornography, and a central fingerprint file.[11] Criminal police work in Germany thus became more coordinated than any other sort, but largely because joint effort was essential to its success. The coordination remained a purely voluntary effort between the states, however, with no equivalent of the U.S. Federal Bureau of Investigation.

In the case of the political police, the Germans did even less to pioneer in their development. In this area, even Prussia lagged well behind Austria, not to mention Russia and France.[12] Although there had been an Office for Political Affairs in the Berlin Police Presidency since 1850, the advent of a significant political police came only with Bismarck's Reich, when, after 1878, his war on socialism produced an independent political police office. Nevertheless, the political police office in Berlin at no time exceeded two hundred civil servants, because of the low incidence of political crime in Imperial Germany.[13]

According to most accounts, the Revolution of 1918 brought a brief interruption in the "tradition" of political police in Germany—such an institution of oppression being incompatible with a democratic government. In fact, any real disruption resulted mostly from temporary disorganization, and the climate of violence and conspiracy then called even more political police into being. All factions sought to create or preserve the means to know their enemies. Political police offices were maintained or quickly reestablished in several police presidencies and state interior ministries. As tension subsided, however, unremitting public suspicion forced this particular branch to justify its very existence, unlike other sectors of police.[14] The publications that sought to gain the mere acceptance of a political police clearly reveal that there was no strong German tradition for a secret police, with its network of spies and informers.

Nevertheless, political crime most persistently demanded the attention of the Reich government, which continually groped for ways to centralize or coordinate its control. From the Spartacists and the Kapp Putsch to the Munich Putsch of 1923, revolution and civil war posed real threats, and the Reich needed its own defenses, including centralized political intelligence. In this respect, a lack of consensus in political attitudes exaggerated the stubborn coolness of the states toward Reich interference in police affairs. Conservative parties, which dominated states like Bavaria, perceived the Social Democrats (SPD) as veritably Red and distrusted the federal government, even when the SPD was not involved. SPD leaders, more firmly in control in states like Prussia, not only distrusted the right but opposed increased Reich control and, therefore, more conservative influence over their political police. Such concerns lay behind the sabotage of efforts to create a Reich Criminal Police Office.

Until the spring of 1920, the Reich government depended largely on the Prussian State Commissioner for Public Order to inform it of hostile political intentions. The Commissioner's office sought to coordinate with political intelligence agencies in the other states, but neither the Reich nor the other state governments did much to facilitate teamwork through this Prussian agency until the Kapp Putsch increased anxieties. When it became obvious that the Reich Criminal Police Office would not materialize soon, the federal legislature sought to fill the gap with the creation of a Reich Commissioner for the Supervision of Public Order, naming as commissioner a Major Kuenzer, former commander of the Baden Gendarmerie.[15]

The Reich commissioner, commanding nothing more than a central political information-gathering office, depended totally on the cooperation of the state political intelligence agencies. Nevertheless, he facilitated improvement in each state through joint effort. Until 1923, meanwhile, efforts continued toward the creation of the Reich Criminal Police Office, which would have incorporated the commissioner's functions as well as combating treason, espionage, and sabotage. But by the spring of 1923, the Reich Ministry of Interior had to abandon this campaign. The Reich commissioner remained the extent of Reich coordination until the renewed political turmoil after 1928.[16]

During the intervening years, most states and free cities developed political police agencies as part of the state police systems. Except in Bremen, with its fusion of separate branches of the uniformed and detective forces, these political police formed a branch of the plainclothes administrative and detective police. As such, they belonged to the decentralized state criminal police that prevailed everywhere except in centralized Saxony.

Inevitably, the largest and most important of these forces was that in Prussia. In the police administrative offices for every province and district after 1928, Division I, Political Police, served as the link between the government and the working political police offices. The Division I in the police presidium of each provincial capital and in Berlin (originally IA) matched an office under the Prussian Ministry of Interior, but the real working political police offices were branches of the State Criminal Police, designated Division IAd (Aussendienst). These police performed the investigative functions and compiled the reports used by Division I. Division IAd under each State Criminal Police Post, located in major cities, served the provinces, while a central Division IAd existed in the State Criminal Police Office of the Police Presidium in Berlin. The field posts reported regularly to the Berlin Division I which served as a political information office for Prussia, providing technical services and advisors for the entire state, although it had no command authority. Above it, even the Political Subdivision of the Ministry of Interior could impart directives to the local political police only through the police presidents and regional administrators—it had no direct command authority.[17]

In contrast, Bavaria came the closest to having a centralized political police. There, Division VI of the Munich Police Directorate, by working closely with the Ministry of the Interior, short-circuited many of the regular government channels and became a veritable state political police office. Although it had no real central administrative authority, it coordinated a centralized political intelligence system for reporting to state and Reich authorities, coordinated counterespionage work throughout the state, and, unlike its Prussian counterpart, had the executive authority to order searches and arrests.[18]

The tumultuous Weimar period had thus produced political police forces more numerous and pervasive than those of the quiescent imperial era. Albert Grzesinski, twice police president of Berlin, estimated that his city alone had a force of three hundred. The rest of the state establishments scaled down in size to that of tiny Schaumburg-Lippe, where two detectives doubled for both criminal and political work. Since political and criminal investigation overlapped so greatly, often involving the same support personnel, the size of the political police establishment in Germany prior to NS reforms cannot be determined. Nevertheless, a 1935 police report estimated that as of January 1933, approximately 2,500 of a total of 10,000 detectives did political work, with an annual budget of 10,860,000 RM.[19]

After 1928 this loosely coordinated system of decentralized state political police forces again became embroiled in political turmoil. Given their general agreement that a real threat came from the Communist Party of Germany, which had recently returned to more active tactics, German officials agreed to strengthen cooperation. On July 1, 1929, they replaced the old office of the Reich commissioner with an Intelligence Assembly Office (Nachrichtensammelstelle) in the Reich Ministry of the Interior. This new office sought to tighten and rationalize the various internal intelligence reporting systems.[20]

Meanwhile, for those who could see the problem objectively, the Nazis also began to pose a significant threat to the Republic, and the efforts of both the right and the left to subvert the military and the police had achieved alarming proportions. Carl Severing, then Prussian interior minister, proceeded to beef up the appropriate section of the Prussian State Criminal Police Office for dealing with such activities. In conjunction with the Reich ministers of the military and the interior, he converted it into a de facto Reich central office to collect information and coordinate the prosecution of offenders. This special office, designated I_4, was overwhelmed from the beginning. Because of manpower problems, it began functioning in January 1932 with a staff of only nine, and as late as the fall of 1932 it still had difficulties in coordinating with other state offices.[21]

Despite its efficiency and its capacity to deal with the paramilitary forces of either left or right in an open confrontation, the police were ill-equipped to save the Republic from the forces that in the end overwhelmed it. They were unprepared even to defend themselves against subversion.

4

Plans, Preparations, Penetrations: 1931-1932

At the same time that the NS intelligence agencies were forming, preliminary NS maneuvers for police power took place with little concern for the embryonic SD. For his part, Himmler clearly planned a link between SS and police, and every component of the SS therefore involved itself in efforts toward that end. The SD was no exception, but its work contributed only incidentally to the initial penetration of the police. Furthermore, although Himmler and his SS entered early into the NS contest for police power, they faced powerful competition.

Since 1928, both the KPD (Communist Party) and the Nazis had increased their militant activities and thereby their confrontation with the police. Simultaneously, both movements had intensified their efforts to infiltrate and subvert the police. After their 1930 electoral victories, the Nazis smelled success and began to make more concrete plans for their Third Reich—plans that included the police.[1]

Unlike the Marxist-Leninist analysis of the police as an instrument of the capitalists—with its imperative to replace them with a people's militia—National Socialist guidelines in this area were lacking. The general conception of the NS revolution was nothing more concrete than a seizure of power that would employ the instruments of state to serve properly the interests of the racial community. It remained unclear whether this meant completely sweeping away the old police establishments and replacing them with something new, or merely taking them over from above and purging them. As usual, Hitler failed to provide his lieutenants with any definite, limited line of action. His pronouncements contained only a vague mixture of Machiavellian attitudes about the exercises of the state's police powers and an authoritarian-racist view of police responsibilities toward citizens.[2] Without limiting guidelines, Hitler's lieutenants went off in many directions.

Among Nazi leaders, one major question affected attitudes and strategy: Did the road to power lie through a putsch or through legal action?

The more activist or putsch-inclined groups (like the SA) contained radical and uncontrollable elements who often showed little respect or sympathy for the police. Given their many street confrontations, SA-men
often thought of themselves as locked in a state of combat with the police.
Since the police represented an obstacle to revolutionary victory, SA
leaders remained ambivalent about whether the police should be swept
away completely or whether most of them could join in brotherhood
with the Movement. In general, the SA inclined toward replacing them
with a version of the people's militia. The SA approach thus mixed
wooing trained policemen into their ranks, on the one hand, and, on the
other, subversion designed to weaken the police for the eventual coup.[3]

In contrast to hostility against the police, those who followed Hitler's
path of legal power seizure shaped the "official" position on the police:
gaining control of them from above, then remaking the police into the
appropriate instrument of the NS state. Some purging, reorganization,
reorientation, and reeducation would follow, but how much remained
unclear. As Dietrich Orlow has observed, their intended means and the
extent to which they would "partify" institutions like the police would
determine decisively the relative success of those men who competed
for the role of Hitler's agent. Those who had the most ambitious plans
for imposing NS values on society and those who had the best-developed
organizations for executing those plans would be the winners.[4]

One contender for control of the police in the forthcoming Reich,
Wilhelm Frick, headed the Party Legal Division and definitely belonged
to the legal power seizure school. As an Old Fighter and a ranking
administrator in the Munich police, Frick had had a role in the 1923
putsch and was slated to become Police President of Munich. From that
time on, in Hitler's mind, Frick had a claim to control of the police.[5]

Frick also directed the first major experiment in the Nazi absorption
of police power. Following the 1930 electoral gains in the *Land* Thuringia,
Hitler engineered Frick's appointment as *Land* minister of the interior.
From this ministry he controlled the state police and prepared to carry
out a purging and appointment policy designed to clean out the "Red
revolutionaries" and to "National-Socialize" the police and other civil
service posts. In the context of the time, he provided a shocking example
of Nazi extremism, and the Reich Ministry of the Interior could only
slightly moderate his efforts in Thuringia. Hitler described Frick's progress as a sound experiment in the tactics that would accompany victory.[6]

In approving this experiment, Hitler indicated his predilection for
the legal acquisition of police power from above and a nazification of
the existing police forces. Clearly the police, like the Army, had indispensable skills and organization, not to be destroyed but absorbed. He

saw in Frick the man for the job, a thorough, loyal National Socialist, skilled in law and civil service machinery.[7] For several years, Frick remained a likely agent for the nazification of the police.

Frick planned simply to convert the state and municipal forces into a centralized system under reliable Nazi command, purged of questionable elements. He would give the resultant police force a properly authoritarian concept of mission, in tune with the values of the new nation; however, he wanted it to remain a "professional" force, with much of what that word implies. Its "partification" should not involve extreme measures. Components of the Movement could propagate NS values among policemen, but the Movement would not command the police; the NS State and bureaucrats like Frick would run the police as a proper instrument of the state.[8]

One example of these notions was published by an NS police group in Hamburg in October 1932. Carefully phrased to maintain legality and avoid conflict with civil service principles, it claimed a Nazi policeman would suffer no conflict of interest. His professional responsibilities would always come before Party obligations. As a matter of fact, the publication professed opposition to partisan political influences in the police (that is, the SPD Marxists), and sought a police that represented and served all the people objectively. Although the statement was obviously made for effect, it was no less sincere in its convictions.[9]

This line of attack had the merit of appealing to more respectable Party members and civil servants, in and out of the Movement. Unfortunately for Frick, the plan was neither an ambitious "partification," comparatively speaking, nor did its supporters constitute an organization Frick could mobilize. Instead he sought to woo an existing, non-NS, state organization—the police and the administration above it.

Regional leaders of the Party, especially the powerful Gauleiter (Party district leaders), constituted another element in the struggle for police power. In their own regions, they fostered penetration of the police and made direct appointments to police commands whenever the Party participated in local and *Land* government coalitions prior to the final NS takeover. Few of these men had either coherent plans for "partification" or any special organization for accomplishing it. Regardless of their attitudes toward the police and how they visualized a future police force, local police power would be part of their base of personal power, and that determined the roles they played. Although they would ardently impose NS values, their ambitions were inseparable from personal power, and their organizational force was largely local.

The NS organization strong enough to fully "partify" the police was the SA. But its primary focus on the military and its ambivalence about the police as an institution stood in the way. Nevertheless, whenever an opportunity arose, its leaders would assume police offices and Storm Troopers would gleefully exercise police power. The most dedicated of all competitors, however, was Heinrich Himmler, with big plans for an SS dominated police force for inner security. Seen from the outside, his SS seemed a logical heir to police power in a Third Reich; consequently, some Nazi-inclined policemen and police organizations sought contact with him as insurance against the future.[10]

The SS in fact recruited most effectively among the organizations of former policemen. Because not all retired policemen parlayed their retirement benefits into a secure position, and some had been discharged or had resigned because of incompatibility with the institution, there were many disgruntled ex-policemen.[11] From them the SS acquired a trained cadre without violating the laws against active policemen holding membership in NS organizations. In July 1931, Himmler got an especially intriguing invitation to tap these resources. One Pauls, writing in the name of the Local Group Gross-Essen of the Former Prussian Policemen, told how members of his organization, dissatisfied with the Weimar system, were willing to serve as policemen in the Third Reich. He estimated that forty thousand former policemen could be brought together in that way, but most significantly he asked whether the SS would be the police of the Third Reich, and if his group would be able to join the SS. Himmler quickly reacted to Paul's letter, immediately traveling to the Ruhr and Berlin to establish contacts.[12]

Perhaps it was on this trip to Berlin that Himmler met Paul Scharfe, who soon became Himmler's staff expert on police affairs. Born in 1876 in Danzig, the son of a school principal, he pursued proper channels through gymnasium and War School to become a lieutenant in the Army by 1897. After six years in rank, in 1903 he married and retired into the reserves in order to take up a police career. After a short interruption for active duty on the Polish front in 1914-15, he returned to police service, and from 1921 to 1931 served as major and finally lieutenant colonel in the Prussian Schupo. During 1931, as he approached retirement age, he began to display pro-Nazi sentiments, forming clandestine NS cells in the Berlin Schupo. Immediately upon retirement, he turned up in Munich as an SS lieutenant on Himmler's staff, joining the Party shortly thereafter.[13]

On October 27 he assumed direction of Division Ig of Himmler's staff, the old Security Service which was now redesignated Police Affairs. Apparently these developments related to growing SS interest in the police, for Scharfe's office now had a double mission: on the one hand, the Party police function of protecting leaders and, on the other, providing insights into the professional police. Although nothing indicates that Ig played any direct role in infiltrating the police or recruiting them

into the SS, it screened at least some police candidates for SS membership. Regular recruitment continued through the normal channels of the
SS.[14]

For intelligence work in the police, Scharfe's office shared responsibilities with Heydrich's Ic, and the parallel growth of these two organizations indicates the very limited mission reserved for the SD in its
initial stages. Well after he had established the Ic, Himmler created Ig
to fill a role vis-à-vis the police that he did not associate with the future
SD. Until 1933 the organizational history of the Ic and Ig was similar,
and until that same year Heydrich and Scharfe advanced in rank at the
same pace. On July 19, 1932, when Heydrich became head of the newly
named SD, Scharfe also emerged as head of the equally new Police
Division (*Abteilung*) of Himmler's SS Office (*Amt*). Not until June 1933
did Scharfe become chief of the SS Court and abandon the field of police
affairs to Heydrich and Kurt Daluege. Thus he may have originally been
the contender for SS police command, raising further questions about
any alleged future police role for the SD. Even if it is argued that the
political police represented a logical exception preserved for the SD, the
evidence does not support this. Although Heydrich may have had an
agent in the Munich political police, other SS contacts with the political
police were rarely affiliated with his SD until later. Available information
contradicts the conventional thinking that from the beginning Heydrich
was to be the political police chief.[15]

Throughout 1931-32, Scharfe's office advised Himmler on how to
appeal to policemen, and they apparently played a decisive role in the
development of his propaganda line. For instance, under Ig guidance,
Himmler sought to dispel rumors that NS leaders would fire younger
policemen, replacing them with SA- and SS-men. Instead, he assured
them that in the Third Reich the police would have increased esteem
and respect and that NS leaders would support them more decisively.[16]

The impact of this NS propaganda and of their subversive efforts
against the police has yet to be documented. More clear is the extent to
which the majority of these policemen became effective components of
the NS police state during the following years. The question of what, if
any, shifts in ideological orientation this required among these policemen warrants serious study.

Until recently, students of the Weimar police generally agreed that
they dutifully served the Republic to the end. Scholars also agreed,
however, that powerful authoritarian traditions and the problems facing
the police had prevented a successful introduction of liberal democratic
principles into the police ethos.[17] They should thus have been less resistant to the right-wing arguments and more resistent to those of a
government that would "democratize" them. Their loyalty was not so

much to the democratic constitutional Republic as to the mission of "law and order," which included defending the state against lawless forces. More recent studies emphasize a severe problem in police attitudes.[18] Generalizations about such attitudes are difficult because "the police" were not homogeneous. Nevertheless, server hostility toward the Reds was almost unanimous, while attitudes toward the Nazis covered the complete range from hostility through ambivalence to sympathy and support. Although policemen may have begun with a general disdain for the Nazis, two factors made some of them increasingly less hostile, even amenable, to growing Nazi power: their preoccupation with the threat of Communism and, after 1929, the growing strength of the forces of the conservative counterrevolution. The two worked well together to fan police dissatisfaction with the Weimar system and to heighten distrust of anyone who stood left of a conservative center. These two factors more than Nazi efforts probably best explain the availability of the German police for their later NS role.

For instance, statesmen who clearly perceived the NS threat and political specialists among those detectives who would support them ran into a wall of frustration. Given Hitler's "legal" tactics, they could not easily depict the Nazis as a subversive threat unless they could show that the Nazis plotted a putsch. Since the political policemen who studied them often failed to analyze their threat in any other terms, the Nazis appeared to many to be less subversive than the Communists. With the creation of I_4 in the Berlin Police Presidium to combat subversion in the police and military, most army and police officials treated it as a counter primarily to the Communist threat, despite Prussian Interior Minister Severing's efforts to have reports on right-wing subversion forwarded to it also. The majority of politicians, military officers, and police preoccupied themselves with the Red menace. Even before July 1932, their reports of "right-radical" subversive activities were infrequent compared with reports of Communist efforts: from January of that year, only 7, contrasted with 491. Their efforts to prosecute these offenses were equally disproportionate and revealed a stepped-up countereffort only against the KPD.[19]

Ambivalence about the NS threat characterized the gradual shift to the right in the police, and after Papen's Prussian coup in July 1932, the implications of that shift became especially obvious to career-conscious policemen who wanted to ensure their jobs and advancement. Federal Chancellor Franz von Papen achieved a major goal of the political right when he removed the Social Democrats from power in Prussia and brought the *Land* and its police under his authority. Using the worsening political violence as his pretext, he charged that the Prussian government had failed to maintain law and order, and he appointed Reich commissioners to run the *Land* government. What followed was a complete purge of Prussian officials, especially police officials with SPD appointments. Thereby, the SPD was branded as an organization to be viewed with suspicion by those responsible for national security.[20]

Papen's coup capped the trend to the right in Weimar politics and opened the police to NS penetration. The new mood created by the coup lifted the shadow of subversion from the Nazis and proclaimed them allies of the police in the fight against Communism. All over Germany, laws against police membership in the NSDAP were dissolved or undermined, and in Prussia punishments for Nazi membership were corrected retroactively. I_4 simply ceased to record reports of "right radical" subversion, if indeed any came in. Most significant, the political police began to cooperate at least unofficially with Nazi intelligence agencies against the KPD and the SPD, who now came under official suspicion. Specifically, in the Berlin political police office, Dr. Heinrich Schnitzler, the official assigned the new task of observing the SPD, established contact with the Nachrichtendienst of the SA and initiated a close cooperation that carried over into Goering's Gestapo. Although he did this on his own initiative, his actions conformed to the new mood.[21]

While this "subversion" of the police transpired, the society they would guard, the law and order they would maintain, deteriorated despite their valiant efforts. Between 1930 and 1933, the four-way struggle among the Red Front, the Reichsbanner of the SPD, the Stahlhelm of the nationalist right, and the SA brought Germany to the verge of open civil war. Several thousand times a year, the police had to intervene in political combat in the streets and at rallies. The master of this "paramilitary politics" was Hitler, who campaigned on the promise of law and order while orchestrating disorder. Rather than test the solidity of the Army and police in an open civil war, key military and political leaders turned to an alliance with Hitler to win his SA and the Stahlhelm for the forces of order.[22]

By January 1933, the way had been well paved for an NS takeover of all branches of the police. Since legally constituted government officials never called upon the police to block the Nazis, there was no ultimate test of police attitudes. Although some policemen still resisted passively, and although many still looked askance at the Nazis, they had little initiative for any serious opposition. To have displayed any would have been professional suicide and an assault on the "legitimate" state they were sworn to defend. In the end, they found it easiest to cooperate against their common enemies, the Reds.

5

Prussian Beginnings

When Hitler became chancellor on January 30, 1933, Franz von Papen, his vice chancellor and the man who had largely engineered the new government, intended to restrict the powers of the Nazi leader and his Movement. Papen and the other nationalist leaders with whom Hitler had ostensibly agreed to share power hoped to control Hitler and use him for their purposes. He seemed in check because, at the Reich level, the Nazis held only two ministerial seats, Wilhelm Frick's less-than-powerful Reich Ministry of the Interior and Hermann Goering's position of minister without portfolio. Hitler's access to the presidential powers of Paul von Hindenburg lay through von Papen, who had the old man's ear. Although Nazi power at the state and local levels varied from little to fairly extensive, even at their strongest they were usually hedged in by coalition arrangements.

Against these checks the NS takeover was a poorly disciplined and loosely coordinated process, in some ways as "spontaneous" as the Nazis claimed. Around Hitler, competitive followers struggled for power in every sphere of German life, and police authority became an early and bitterly contested battleground. During the first months of 1933, various Nazis established control over police agencies at every level all over the Reich. Each federal state was a different story, but the most decisive early developments occurred in the two largest, Prussia and Bavaria.

In Prussia, the largest single police force came quickly under Nazi command. Here too, Papen had hoped to limit Nazi power, for as part of his deal with Hitler, he resumed control of the Prussian government as Reich commissioner. In this arrangement, however, the key post of provisional minister of the interior went to Hermann Goering, giving him extensive authority over the Prussian police. Goering and the other Nazi leaders quickly showed themselves beyond Papen's control.[1] Goering was to play the role of a unique version of the regional Party leader. The extent of his "region," the *Land* of Prussia, combined with his growing Reich-level offices made him extraordinary. His intentions of imposing NS values were ambitious, but lacking any real NS organizational power base, he had to search for a base in the form of allies.[2]

The real contest for the Prussian police developed not between the Nazis and those who would block their way, but within the Movement itself. Goering and the SA became the first major contenders, but other elements joined in—Frick trying to assert himself as Reich minister of the interior and Himmler adding what began as a weak fourth. The various contenders did not fully anticipate this power struggle, however, for the first two months (February and March) were a honeymoon period for the "revolutionaries," joined in an enthusiastic struggle to nazify Germany and defeat their mutual enemies. At first, they also shared a common sense of emergency, believing a Communist counterstroke to be imminent. As long as this threat remained real in their minds, their common goals eclipsed their personal power rivalries. Only in light of their ideological bonds is it possible to understand the enigma of Nazi rivals alternately sharing and vying for power, a paradox that extended throughout the history of the Third Reich.

During February and March, Goering initiated several crucial aspects of the future Nazi police state.[3] Some students of these developments argue that he did not anticipate a radically totalitarian Third Reich, rather a relatively more conventional authoritarian dictatorship that would eliminate all divisive opposition. The state would have unlimited police powers and would resort to terror for striking down its enemies, but would not necessarily force itself into the lives of most good Germans. The eventual relationship between the leaders and their people would be harmonious rather than based on terrorism. Above all, Goering had no desire to see Himmler's elite guard or any other NS organization penetrate and control his police. Consequently, despite his rhetoric, police measures in Prussia were more conventionally authoritarian than revolutionary.[4] In terms of police state ambitions, although Goering knew no limits that prevented his trying to please Hitler, he had less imagination than Himmler.

Nevertheless, Goering established two major precedents for the future SS and police. First, he created an unfettered police force for maintaining law and order and for protecting the community from its "antisocial elements." Second, he established an independent political police for ferreting out political enemies, both open and clandestine. As he put it, "For the consolidation of power the first prerequisite was to create along new lines that instrument which at all times and in all nations is always the inner political instrument of power, namely, the police."[5]

To provide this instrument with new directions of inner political power, he ensured that its leaders would make it perform according to the standards of the national Movement—that is, free from concern for constitutional limitations and due process. The Prussian administration thus underwent its second purge in a year's time, completing the job begun by Papen. In the police offices of the Ministry of Interior and in the Berlin Police Presidium, the thoroughness of the Papen purges had left little to be done but to transfer the most significant positions to even more trustworthy NS sympathizers and to the few Party members with appropriate credentials. Outside Berlin, all twelve provincial governors (*Oberpraesidenten*) were replaced, mostly by Nazi Gauleiter and locally powerful Old Fighters. Among those more directly involved in the command of the police, the positions of thirty-one of the thirty-four district governors (*Regierungspraesidenten*), all of the police chiefs (*Polizeipraesidenten*), and a majority of the mayors and county prefects (*Landraete*) fell to Nazis.[6] Local SA and SS commanders usually got the police offices.

It is misleading to describe what happened as "Goering's purges," as though he were directing changes from the center. Usually the decisions reflected the realities of power in the Movement, with haste, individual initiative, and the spirit of Nazi comradeship often determining appointments.[7] Consequently, most officeholders were caught in webs of complex interpersonal relationships. The resultant feudalization of the Prussian field administration repeated itself across the Reich. Left to its own devices, such an administration was anything but an efficient machine for directing "the inner political instrument of power." The spontaneous Nazi terrorism may have seemed efficient, but it made subtle or routine police actions more difficult. The initial power seizure hardly promoted either the efficient police power desired by Goering or the eventual totalitarian police state.

From the upper levels, as seen by Frick and Goering, the chaotic police power structures had to be coordinated and streamlined. This would have to be done, however, at the expense of local Party, SA, and SS leaders who directly controlled the Nazis' mass base of power. Such a direct confrontation of the problem would have been suicidal for either Frick or Goering, who had little influence over either the local leaders or the NS masses. Only Hitler had their ears (or hearts), but he needed their "spontaneous" action and support to entrench his power. Consequently, Frick or Goering could succeed only through skillful maneuver and gradual reorganization of the machinery they would control.

Goering's maneuvers were indeed masterful. In the spirit of the coalition and of administrative propriety, he assigned the Police Division (*Abteilung II*) of the Ministry of Interior to Dr. Ludwig Grauert, a politically unaffiliated nationalist with connections to industry. To offset Grauert's establishment image, he created a commissioner for special duty (*Kommissare z.b.V.*), naming the commander of SS Group East, Kurt

Daluege. Although the special commissioner was supposed to have limited authority (merely to oversee the work of the ministers and to coordinate between the administration and the Movement) in reality Daluege became Goering's major executive in police affairs [8]

The choice of Daluege was crucial for the subsequent power struggle. As the independently powerful SS leader of eastern Prussia, he had won Hitler's personal esteem. His Berlin SS had worked against the SA rebellions, earning the SS its reputation for stability, loyalty, and obedience. Entrenched in the Reich capital, he established important connections with national Party leaders and other potential allies. As his appointment showed, he had rapport with Goering, and after Hitler moved into the Chancellery, Daluege's connections extended to others who had left Himmler behind in Munich.

In appointing Daluege as his personal lieutenant in the Prussian police, Goering won a man who could coordinate Party and police, a man who commanded the SS in eastern Prussia but represented none of the disadvantages of alliance with Himmler. Since Himmler had no legal influence over Daluege's growing police responsibilities, which were not SS appointments, Daluege could be a powerful ally in Goering's struggle with the SA, Himmler, and other troublesome elements of the Party.

To develop the police state as he saw it, Goering had to reverse former liberal trends toward protecting the citizen from the police powers of the state while tolerating open, extreme opposition to the state. Between early February and early March, his orders, in conjunction with Reich-wide developments, struck down significant constitutional guarantees and freed the police from many procedural limitations. With this came perversion of the concept of "protective custody" into a major device of police power.

Legitimate protective custody for the protection of the individual had long been standard in Germany. Like many of the state's powers, however, during World War I it was considerably stretched to justify detaining suspects under the rubric of national security. The beleaguered Republic permitted similar police custody, but with proper due process and a 24-hour limit before a hearing by a court. By 1933, however, the growing reaction had set the stage for Hindenburg's February 4 Decree for the Protection of the German People, which made possible preventive police custody for up to three months in cases involving suspicion of planned criminal activities. Despite provision for appeal to a judge, the Nazis now had legal means for harassing political enemies.[9]

After the Reichstag fire of February 28, Hindenburg consented to the more extreme Ordinance for the Protection of the People and the State, suspending the basic rights of the constitution and imposing capi-

tal punishment for a wide range of offenses against public order. Goering's order for the execution of this ordinance freed the police from
further administrative limitations on their authority. It made them responsible for regulating reductions in freedom of the press, personal
freedom, the rights of assembly and privacy, and for monitoring private
communications through the mails, telegraph, and telephone. The ordinance also facilitated the further development of "protective custody"
arrests. Henceforth, police arrest powers no longer depended on the
authority of the public prosecutor nor were they limited to punishable
offenses. The police could combat "subversive activities" through preventive custody, by arresting any suspected "subversive elements." The
right of court appeal was generally denied.[10] The Nazis now had legal
means for destroying their political enemies.

No matter how powerful the police had become nor how willing
they were to do the bidding of their Nazi commanders, the events of
the Nazi revolution threatened to leave them behind. By March, the SA
seemed ready to take over their function. On February 22, in anticipation
of a showdown with the Communists, Goering had ordered that police
auxiliaries (*Hilfspolizei*) be drawn from units of the SA, the SS, and their
allied paramilitary forces, the Stahlhelm and the German Nationalist
Kampfring. They were to supplement the police, still weak by Nazi
standards. The SA and SS soon appeared all over Germany as auxiliary
police, and, in the explosion of activity following the Reichstag fire,
threatened to become uncontrolled police forces, often more locally autonomous than responsive to Roehm or Himmler.

Goering's maneuver had backfired. He originally intended for the
auxiliaries to be called only for emergencies, to be limited in number by
the police authorities, and to operate under police command, subject to
the summons and dismissal of police officials. These restrictions might
have harnessed the growing rowdiness of the SA. As a matter of fact,
Roehm apparently feared such a loss of control and cautioned his commanders against weakening their units through loss of strength to the
auxiliary police.[11]

Thus the auxiliary police became an SA challenge to Goering's police
authority. They freely violated his intended limitations and by April
outnumbered the regular police severalfold. Entire units of Storm Troopers went into action while the police officers supposedly commanding
them had to stand back and watch. Worse yet, both the SA and SS
assumed their own arrest authority, rounding up thousands and herding
them into abandoned factories, warehouses, and basements, where they
initiated the most sensational horrors of the concentration camps. Party
leaders like Goering had initially needed and called for SA and SS involvement and the creation of their camps to handle the vast numbers

of "enemies." However, the open, lawless brutality that resulted and the clear challenge to authority soon created intolerable disruptions of their revolution from above.[12]

The Birth of the Gestapo

Amid this internal competition and uncoordinated power seizure, Goering had proceeded with his second major police achievement, the creation of an independent political police. They became for him not only a sharp instrument for striking down the enemy, but also a legitimate force that belied the need for extraordinary police powers demanded by the SA and SS. In this respect, the Gestapo was born, not as a revolutionary component of the totalitarian police state, but as Goering's personal organization of more conventional state power[13] and as a manifestation of fear of the left. When the new political police officers became separate and independent from conventional police agencies and gained more freedom of action, it was to defend the society and preserve the order favored by those who did not treasure the individual rights of liberalism. This agency posed a threat to conservative interests only after SS–police-state tendencies prevailed.

The man who reorganized Goering's political police and became the first head of the Gestapo was a thirty-two-year-old civil servant from the Ministry of Interior. Rudolf Diels had entered administrative service in 1921 while pursuing a typical preparatory education in law and economics for higher civil service ranks. Before this, he had experienced the war on the western front, then joined the fight against Communism in the Free Corps. Despite his conservative, nationalist inclinations, he did well under the SPD-dominated Prussian administration, ultimately moving into the work he believed Germany so badly needed. In 1931 he became a government counselor in the Political Police Section of the Police Division of the Ministry of the Interior, assuming responsibility for combating the Communist movement.[14]

Diels was never a party man—as a matter of fact, the Nazi Party denied him membership until 1937. Nevertheless, his desire to save Germany from the left led him to play political roles. He provided reports that encouraged Papen to proceed with his seizure of the Prussian government from the SPD in July 1932. Thereafter, antisubversive police work focused entirely on the left, and as political police officers began working with the Nazis, Diels established his own contacts. He became a contributing member of the SA, a type of affiliated membership for financial supporters who could not or would not join or who might not be granted membership. Such affiliations with either the SA or the SS were safe for civil servants for whom full membership might be illegal or professionally damaging.

Diehls also developed a personal liaison with Goering and evidently with Daluege. The relationship apparently began when Diels in his official capacity had to work with Goering as president of the Reichstag. Their common concern with the Red menace drew them together initially, and later Diels allegedly provided Goering with information useful against Party rivals.[15] When Goering took over the ministry, he extended Diels's authority in the Political Group (Abteilung I) of the Police Division under Grauert in the Ministry of Interior. Diels immediately cooperated with Goering and Daluege on personnel decisions, and, more important, he soon received the task of building a newly organized political police force directly subordinate to Goering. Diels's lack of political standing made him Goering's client, independent of the SA and SS. Equally important, as an established civil servant, Diels knew the ropes and had contacts throughout the administration. He could keep the machinery running while simultaneously reorganizing it and cleaning out unreliable elements, for he best knew who could be trusted.[16]

Diels began work in early February 1933 and during subsequent weeks expanded beyond the Ministry of the Interior. He absorbed the former Section IA of the Berlin Police Office, the coordinating center for the political police in Prussia. The State Criminal Police Posts were ordered to forward through the regional governors reports of political significance, and his Berlin office had the power to make direct inquiries of any local or state police authority.[17] To go beyond mere intelligence gathering, however, a true political police force had to order and conduct searches and arrests or perform "executive" functions, as the German police called them. A prerequisite was to establish direct control over the political police officers in the field, who were still under the command of regional officials.

Meanwhile, although in reality Diels worked directly under Goering and Daluege, the process of separating his political police from the authority of other administrative offices took time. "Secret" police must be physically removed from the prying of regular bureaucrats who could interfere. Toward this end, Diels got new quarters for his offices. The first such move came on March 8 when his Special Section for Combating Bolshevism, the key office of his new force, got separate rooms in the Horst Wessel House (formerly the Karl Liebknecht House), recently seized from the KPD. The physical separation process was completed in mid-April, when Diels's entire political police organization took up residence at 8 Prinz-Albrecht Strasse, soon to become notorious as Gestapo headquarters. The new building was conveniently near the offices Goering had just assumed as prime minister of Prussia.[18] Following the electoral victory of March, Hitler had removed Papen as a check on NS power in Prussia, so Goering now reigned free, responsible directly to Hitler.

By this time, Diels's office already had its own executive section under Police Counselor Arthur Nebe. Nebe had entered the Berlin detective force in 1920 and made a prominent career for himself. Like Diels a conservative nationalist, he became more comfortable during the shift to the right in the 1930s, but he went further than Diels, entering the Nazi Movement as it rose in prestige in 1931. Nebe became a contact man inside the Criminal Police for one of the many early Nazi intelligence branches, perhaps Daluege's personal Nachrichtendienst in Berlin, for in June he became a contributing member of the SS. A month later, he joined the Party and in November, the SA. In early 1932, Nebe and like-minded detectives formed the NS Civil Service Society of the Berlin Police, and he simultaneously became liaison man for Daluege. He was obviously Daluege's man, probably placed in the political police to keep an eye on Diels.[19]

Nebe represented the cutting edge of a small but significant NS presence in Diels's early political police. Although Goering called for a thorough purge of the political police throughout Prussia as an alleged SPD instrument, and although he boasted to his last days of having purged this office most thoroughly, in reality he relied heavily on Diels's judgment. As a result, relatively few significant changes were made in political police personnel, at least in the Berlin offices. Much shuffling of personnel and the gradual influx of new people initially brought few Nazi gains. Most of the men came from Diels's old office and the IA or were drawn from the Ministry of the Interior and the detective force, all administrative or police civil servants. The small core of new Party enlistees among the professional detectives also belonged mostly to Diels's personal circle[20] and generated little trust in established NS ranks.

After Diels had gathered the proper personnel and von Papen had lost his last vestige of control in Prussia, the Gestapo could emerge officially. On April 26, legislation establishing a Secret State Police Office created the Gestapo and gave it the legal powers it had already assumed.[21] The name Gestapo, which has become a label for uncontrolled or terroristic police, was born innocently enough. The official title of Secret—or perhaps more accurately, Privy—State Police (Geheime Staatspolzei), had been fairly traditional in the German states and was a logical choice. According to Diels, the first abbreviated form, GeStapa (Geheime Staats-Polizei-Amt), was an invention of postal officials. Goering had rejected GPA because the initials sounded too much like the Russian GPU.[22]

Officially, the Gestapo Office at 8 Prinz-Albrecht Strasse achieved the standing of a state police authority, assuming the former political police duties of the State Criminal Police under the police president of Berlin. Beyond this, it gained executive powers, meaning arrest authority. The political police who had formerly worked in the field under local police authority were reorganized into Gestapo regional offices (Staatspolizeistelle). Although these regional offices remained part of the regular state police, in political police affairs they took their orders through Gestapo channels. Most important, Goering removed the Gestapo from normal channels within the administration and placed it directly under himself as Prussian minister of the interior.

Officially, the reasons given for these actions were "the interests of uniform higher direction of the political police." Toward that end, he proclaimed that: "In order to secure the effective combating of all of those efforts directed against the stability and security of the state, the state government had decided to fashion more tightly than before the organization of the political police and to create the necessary prerequisites for a quick and successful work."[23]

One should not dismiss these phrases as mere Machiavellian camouflage for the first deliberate step toward the eventual totalitarian police state. They simply expressed the general concern for creating adequate means to defend Germany against its "internal enemies." Goering had hardly cut through all the red tape developed to protect citizens against arbitrary police actions. Appeal against Gestapo measures was still possible through the administrative courts, although with diminished effectiveness amid the atmosphere of cooperation generated at most levels by the fear of bolshevism.

A significant hindrance to centralized control of the political police action resided in the Gestapo regional offices formed during the spring and summer. Although a direct command authority now existed between the Berlin central political police office and these regional offices, they remained organs of the regional police authorities as well. These authorities—the highly independent Party and SA leaders—interfered considerably with efficient, centralized command. In places like Altona, Kassel, Koenigsberg, Potsdam, and Stettin, local SA and SS leaders, as police presidents, took direct command of their Gestapo regional offices. Even in other locations with offices headed by Nazis with appropriate civil service qualifications, such men often responded more readily to local power than to Berlin. Any Gestapo leaders actually chosen for their qualifications, regardless of Party affiliations, existed tenuously in the tug-of-war between local power and Berlin. To complicate matters further, Himmler intruded tentatively into Prussia. At Frankfurt and Aachen, the Gestapo leaders joined the SS. In Breslau, the local SA leader and police president, Edmund Heines, relied on Detective Inspector Dr.

Emanuel Schaefer to head the Gestapo office. But his deputy, Government Counselor and SS Lieutenant Guenther Patschowski, was an SD member, making another key point for Himmler's penetration.[24] Obviously, real power relations in the early Gestapo field structure were extremely complex, sometimes to the detriment of central authority. Nevertheless, when the Gestapo or the Auxiliaries struck, their victims, who never knew the source of the arrest order, experienced only an "efficient" NS police terror machine.

During the first three months, meanwhile, Diels played a role that must be understood in terms of efforts to increase "legitimate" police power and authority, while limiting the excesses of those revolutionary elements threatening the professional police. Unfortunately for Diels, given existing conditions, these were not compatible goals, as the SA excesses of March soon revealed.

Diels's bond with the Nazis stemmed from a common cause against the Communists. That common cause was his only hope for building Nazi dependence upon and trust in his police. For years, political policemen had based their existence and advancement on exposing and combating the Communist threat. Accustomed to selling their case to more resistant liberals and Socialists, men like Diels continued to present agitating evidence to the new Nazi bosses, who hardly needed it. Goering seemed to thrive on every piece of evidence for a Communist uprising, and both he and Diels eagerly sought a pretext for a decisive move against their enemies. Diels and his men joined in the campaign to heighten public fear and justify action. They staged sensational raids, but if they went so far as to plant forged evidence, as alleged, they never released that evidence to the press, for nothing could live up to Goering's exaggerated press releases. Then came the Reichstag fire. Regardless of who started it, police and Nazi alike seized upon it as the long-awaited pretext for open war on the KPD, whom they accused of initiating an uprising for which the fire was the alleged signal. Although such agitation helped Diels build the extraordinary political agencies he desired, it was probably unnecessary, for that goal was a foregone conclusion. Instead, he probably exaggerated the chances of independent SA action from below that threatened him and his legitimate police. He claimed to have realized this danger after the Reichstag fire, and to have reversed this tactic, playing down Communist threats to security thereafter.[25]

In the ensuing roundup of Communists and other enemies, Diels worked closely with Special Commissioner Daluege, who provided some modicum of coordination between police and Party. Their victims could be arrested at three different levels of action. Those taken by the police through more traditional arrest channels came immediately under Ministry of Justice jurisdiction, where due process might result in their release. Since these subjects had to be charged with a specific crime, few political enemies came under this process. Those arrested under the evolving concept of protective custody encountered increasing durations of confinement without recourse. At least twenty-five thousand fell into this protective custody category for varying periods during March and April. At the third level of "arrest" action, the independent SA and SS spirited away the victims, often without official record and with no hope or protection under the law. Daluege and Diels naturally wanted to concentrate all political arrests under their control, while extending their own independence as arresting authorities. Consequently, they tried to operate their own concentration camps with more reliable auxiliary police personnel. Such maneuvers produced a multiple tug-of-war over the evolving concentration camps. Diels and Daluege asserted Gestapo interests, the Ministry of Justice and more legalistic elements in the Ministry of Interior insisted on their jurisdiction, while the SA maintained its own autonomy. The SS, which in Prussia spread well beyond Daluege's control, complicated matters as a fourth autonomous holder of prisoners in concentration camps and bunkers. Since they needed the SA and SS camps for the indefinite future, both the Reich and the Prussian interior ministries provided financial support, and Diels's Gestapo sent its arrestees to the camps and maintained liaison officers in them. Adding to the frictions, Diels and Daluege did not always work together well.[26]

In all of this, Goering, Daluege, and Diels cannot be understood as bloodthirsty sadists playing a preconceived role in building a terroristic police state. They firmly believed they were locked in a life-and-death struggle requiring action against enemies on whom they had projected the worst imaginable characteristics. Finally free to move against a foe who supposedly had always enjoyed the upper hand, they considered terror a justifiable weapon—in fact, the only adequate weapon against such evil. Their struggle required cunning to combat the sort of "underhanded methods" that the enemy employed. They could not see themselves as destructively inhumane, nor were they totally indifferent to the possibility, regardless of their tough rhetoric. Although selective murder was the order of the day, it would take years to dull their conscious restraints to the point where they could give orders for mass murder. As a head of state, Goering had to carefully marshal human resources, not squander them. Not only did he seek to win over the unaligned, he even spoke of the need to reeducate as many misguided Germans as he could possibly salvage.[27]

At this point, Goering's actions offer another example of how he combined combating the enemy with his own empire building. To control its enemies, the authoritarian state must be able to monitor secretly all public and private communication. Toward this end, he officially established a special facility, ostensibly as part of his Air Ministry, that absorbed and expanded on the Cipher and Monitoring Office of the Ministry of Defense. His so-called Investigation Office (Forschungsamt) was primarily concerned with military and foreign intelligence, monitoring radio communications outside Germany, and intercepting telephone and telegraph messages between foreign agencies in Germany and their outside connections. It compiled regular reports rivaling those of the Foreign Ministry, another competitor in intelligence work. Although Diels may have been instrumental in its development and operations, the major functions of the Investigation Office were not internal police spying. Nevertheless, it worked closely with the Gestapo. While Diels's office monitored the mails with post office cooperation, the Investigation Office facilitated internal telephone tapping for police purposes.[28]

Since the Investigation Office existed in a maze of official entanglements—financed by the Reich, administered as part of the Prussian government, but answerable only to Goering in his various Reich and Prussian offices—its establishment, ostensibly under his Air Ministry, became decisive in future power plays. In the ministry, it was free from the prying of the police and bureaucrats, and, therefore, from the later SS-police system under Himmler. It became one more competing/cooperating agency with which Sipo and SD had to deal. Goering may not necessarily have contrived all of these complexities, however, for financing and allotments of personnel came from wherever they could be gotten, and the Reich Air Ministry was a much more appropriate location than his state offices in Prussia for international and military intelligence operations. The Air Ministry location also facilitated cooperation with the military Abwehr, which will be described later.

Although the Investigation Office did not grow from his fear of rivals, throughout 1933 Goering had reasons for concern in that area. By April, more than SA lawlessness threatened his control of the police, for the early ambiguous relations between the SS and the Gestapo also produced their share of problems. At that moment, however, Daluege still commanded the local SS around Berlin, and his desires to command the police in his own right apparently outweighed his loyalty to Himmler, a situation that usually, but not always, worked to Goering's advantage—at least as long as he could offer Daluege the most in the form of the Prussian police. In May, he made Daluege's police authority official, naming him to replace Grauert as head of the Police Division of the ministry.

The extent of Himmler's influence inside Daluege's fief is impossible to calculate, but Himmler was not about to let Daluege and his divisions simply slip away. Heydrich's SD group in Berlin had become enmeshed in the local power struggle; the local SD leader, Hans Kobelinski, maintained close relations with Daluege's camp. To convert the Berlin SD into a sharper wedge for penetration, Heydrich later replaced Kobelinski for, among other reasons, suspicion of conspiring with Diels.[29] Mean while, Daluege had carefully built his own independent intelligence ser vice in his section of the Ministry of Interior—modestly titled Special Division Daluege.[30] During these early months, tension developed be tween Daluege and Heydrich. Since January, Heydrich, subordinate in rank to Daluege, had been assigned to Himmler's staff for special mis sions. For an indefinite period before the power seizure, Berlin had been his center of operations, where he served as one of Himmler's repre sentatives. While he built his own SD base in the capital, he cooperated with Daluege in intelligence operations. Regardless of any early collab oration, however, by the first days of March Daluege had cut Heydrich off. After trying unsuccessfully to get through Daluege's "protective screen" of receptionists for a personal meeting, Heydrich returned to Munich on March 5, bitter over the rebuff.[31]

Meanwhile, Daluege's command of the local SS created a relation ship between Gestapo and SS upon which Himmler and Heydrich later capitalized. During the early months, while trying to form his yet un official Gestapo and assume executive authority for it, Diels had trouble dealing with leaders in the Party and the SA, especially those entrenched in police offices. Most viewed civil servants and policemen like Diels with contempt, and they ignored or impeded his executive and inves tigative efforts. For executive field work, Diels needed men who carried some weight with the Nazis, thus Nebe's appointment as head of the executive section. In any case, by summer the problem led Diels to turn to Daluege's SS for men who had influence among Nazis to do Diels's executive work.

This growing bond between SS and Gestapo was part of an increas ing tendency among Nazis to identify the SS with political police work. On April 21, Grauert, as Goering's head of the Police Division in the ministry, issued a decree designed to help bring SA and SS excesses into line. Most important, this decree divided the Auxiliary Police into two categories: regular police work fell to SA auxiliaries, while the SS aux iliaries were to work with the political police.[32]

By June, this relationship became more specific when Himmler, as Reichsfuehrer SS, was made Prussian ministerial commission for aux iliary police personnel of the Gestapo Office.[33] Henceforth, not only Daluege's SS but also Himmler's established a foothold in the Gestapo. However, this gets ahead of the narrative. By mid-1933, Himmler had done much on his own to enhance the association of the SS with political police work.

6

IIimmler in Bavaria

After Heydrich left Berlin for Munich on March 5, 1933, events soon presented Himmler with opportunities more exploitable than those in Berlin. Bavarian developments had lagged approximately one month behind those in Prussia; ironically, the home of the Movement was among the last German states the Nazis "coordinated." Prime Minister Heinrich Held and his Bavarian Peoples' Party retained enough strength to shape any coalition government as long as Hitler's Reich government refrained from intervention. Since Bavaria, with its strong traditions of suspicious independence from Berlin, represented a touchy situation, any seizure based on power from Berlin might well backfire. The Nazis preferred to let developments in Bavaria "take their own course"—or so it had to appear—so that Papen and Hindenburg would not be forced to defend Held's independence.[1]

Both Roehm and Himmler had had to remain behind in Bavaria, with no place in the Reich coalition. Along with the local *Gauleiter*, they waited impatiently for an active role in seizing power. Since at least mid-February, the political police in Bavaria had been tapping rumors of a pending SA coup,[2] and on March 9, it happened. While the SA and SS seized key government buildings, Roehm, Himmler, and Gauleiter Adolf Wagner presented Held with an ultimatum for the appointment of Franz Ritter von Epp as general state commissar. Held's protests to Berlin fell on deaf ears, Epp became Reich commissioner, and Nazi control began in Bavaria. Under Epp, Gauleiter Wagner became provisional minister of the interior, and he, as highest police authority, made Himmler his provisional police chief over the Munich Metropolitan Police (Polizei-direktion Muenchen), while Roehm became a state commissioner for special duties. How and why Wagner allotted these posts in this manner remains unexplained.

Himmler and Roehm got minimal offices considering the key role they played in this local power seizure. Roehm's vague position was especially minor in view of his prospects during the previous weeks, when he had allegedly proposed himself as either a general commis-

sioner for public security for the entire Reich or, at least, a Reich commissioner for all non-Prussian states. As such, he would have consolidated control over all the police forces of the states and the Party (SA
and SS).[3] If such an ambitious bid was in fact rebuffed, it revealed the
strength of Roehm's opposition. Undoubtedly Hitler had second
thoughts about putting such control in Roehm's hands and may have
welcomed the need to placate conservative allies as an excuse.

At this point Himmler may have pinned his aspirations on Roehm's
dreams, for their cooperation and division of labor in Bavarian police
work during the following months indicates a harmonious working alliance. Why Himmler got his initial police position remains a key unan-
swered question. Apparently Party leaders identified him with police
and security work. In all probability, Wagner saw in the relatively insignificant Himmler a controllable subordinate through whom he could
direct key police forces. Himmler, however, may also have been a Trojan
horse in Roehm's scheme. In the same vein, Hitler may have encouraged
such appointments as sops that would keep his two potentially troublesome paramilitary leaders on the shelf in Bavaria.

The Bavarian Political Police

More than "a minor appointment," or the "degrading job of Munich
police chief," Himmler's new office was a necessary first step from which
to build state police power, for the Munich police chief held a key position. Although Bavaria supposedly had a decentralized command over
its police, in fact the Munich Metropolitan Police worked directly with
the Ministry of Interior, bypassing normal channels, and served in many
respects as a central police authority for Bavaria, especially for political
police affairs. The Political Division, Department VI of the Munich Metropolitan Police, coordinated political police work for the entire state.[4]

Munich Department VI and the comparable department in the Nuremberg Metropolitan Police served as intelligence centers for South and
North Bavaria, respectively, compiling regional reports from the political
situation reports forwarded from the provincial and county political police. Munich in turn assumed the role of the central state office by as-
sembling a consolidated state report and forwarding it to state offices
and the Reich intelligence center in Berlin. For counterespionage work,
the Munich office coordinated with the military and Reich Railway authorities, and could order arrests for political offenses anywhere in the
state. Thus, when Himmler also became provisional police chief for Nu-
remberg-Fuerth on March 26, 1933, he apparently had approval to con-

solidate still further the central control of police work against the "enemies" of the Reich and the NS Movement.[5]

The conversion from a de facto to a de jure Bavarian Political Police, with almost unlimited, independent executive authority and a closely related system of SS concentration camps, came rapidly. Himmler's acquisition of such rank power can be understood only in terms of the period of the revolutionary honeymoon, and the fact that Wagner saw him as an ally rather than a rival. When Himmler took over his new office, he sent Heydrich in as head of Political Department VI. Heydrich may not have fully appreciated his slated mission, however, for according to his wife, he disdained the political police, saw this assignment as temporary, and preferred to build the future Reich through the SS. Accordingly, he moved his SD headquarters and his family to Berlin, and initially performed his Bavarian police duties as a commuting commander.[6] Either Heydrich did not foresee the significance of the Bavarian position as the stepping-stone to Himmler's control of the German police, or he did not understand how carefully such steps had to be taken.

Meanwhile, however, Himmler could not extend his control over all the Bavarian police. He and his SS remained subordinate to Roehm, with whom he cooperated closely. Apparently, Himmler's authority remained limited to the political police as part of prior arrangements, while the SA generally infiltrated the regular police. The seizure of local police authority by SA leaders followed the pattern set in the rest of the Reich, as did the appearance of SA-dominated auxiliary police. Roehm established a system of special commissioners to coordinate the police with the new NS ministers and with the organizations of the Movement. These commissioners called forth auxiliary police from the SA, SS, and Stahlhelm, who proceeded to their predictable excesses.[7]

During mid-March, the heads of all elements of the Movement worked together reasonably well in trying to maintain some semblance of order and to regularize police authority. On March 27, Wagner issued another decree clarifying the new relationships and setting some limits on auxiliaries. Most significant, he proclaimed a division of labor between SA and SS that soon repeated itself across Germany. He created two branches of auxiliary police: the Political Auxiliary Police and the Auxiliary Security Police (Sicherheitshilfspolizei). He named Himmler, as Reichsfuehrer SS, leader of the Political Auxiliary Police with power to appoint regional and local commissioners (*Beauftragten*) of the SS to exercise command over the political auxiliaries. Roehm had a similar position in commanding the Auxiliary Security Police—the nonpolitical forces.[8]

Through these appointments Wagner sought to limit the auxiliary police as to who and how many could serve. The decree also emphasized that auxiliaries were a temporary expediency for the emergency situation, financed by limited funds that the administration could withdraw. Furthermore, the appointment of heads of auxiliary police *within* the administrative chain of command brought their auxiliaries under administrative control, or at least so the new NS ministers tried to make it appear. In reality, Roehm and Himmler, as heads of NS organizations, had their own independent power and authority, derived from their direct subordination to Hitler, producing a confusing web of interlocking NS and state chains of command and authority.

Roehm knew how to use real power; however, in the long run he failed to exploit his fully. He suffered from the true rebel's distaste for administrative structures, bureaucratic red tape, and due process, withdrawing from bureaucratic entanglements for fear of contamination, thereby reducing his effectiveness. In contrast, Himmler gradually developed the plan to mesh his SS thoroughly with the existing police and administrative machinery. Although he shared Roehm's distaste for bureaucrats and their milieu, he reveled in his own versions of their game. He freely involved himself and his SS in the establishment. As Aronson has argued: "From this point of view, Himmler was more 'revolutionary' than Roehm. Himmler was apparently prepared to work within the existing state machinery, but only in order to adapt it, in the course of time, to his own ideas."[9]

Although Himmler's methods in building the Bavarian Political Police revealed a rapidly evolving distinction between his plans and techniques and those of his competitors, the SA and the Prussian Gestapo, in some respects he merely expanded the Bavarian pattern of an efficient, centralized political police. On March 15, Minister of the Interior Wagner named him his political section chief (*Referent*) within the ministry. Wagner subordinated all the political police of Bavaria to Himmler, and the Bavarian Political Police (BPP) now became an official reality. As direct subordinate to the Minister of Interior,[10] Himmler theoretically had central command over the state's political police.

When, however, the March 27 order on the auxiliary police supplemented Himmler's appointments, the first real indications of his new course emerged. The Political Auxiliary Police not only gave Himmler a considerably enlarged force for executive actions, they were also SS-men whom he commanded as Reichsfuehrer SS. Himmler's direct command over SS men, serving as auxiliaries of the state, confused normal lines of authority. Whenever a local police official sought to restrict the auxiliaries, the SS could ignore him, claiming authority directly from the ministry through Himmler. When challenged by his government superior, Wagner or Epp, Himmler could find recourse to his authority as Reichsfuehrer. Here lay the significance of any government position to which he was appointed in his capacity as Reichsfuehrer SS.

On April 1, long before such relations became apparent to him, Wagner made "the Reichsfuehrer SS, Heinrich Himmler," the political police commander of Bavaria. Apparently Wagner saw such appointments for Roehm and Himmler as the only hope of controlling the "wild police" actions of the SA and SS, respectively. The continued inclusion of Himmler's SS title in his assignments to state offices inevitably solidified the association of SS and political police. In most respects, the enactment of April 1 also completed the process of establishing a centralized political police. Himmler's office as commander directly within the Ministry of the Interior removed the Bavarian Political Police from the local entanglements of the Munich Metropolitan jurisdiction. In addition, Wagner gave Himmler command over all remaining local political police in Bavaria (such as those in metropolitan forces or the political section chiefs attached to offices of the regional and local administration). Not only did the Auxiliary Political Police remain under his authority, but now he could overcome their inherent limitations. Only extraordinary circumstances justified the SS auxiliaries, and budgetary realities prohibited their free use. Himmler's new office found two ways around these limitations: He could order local uniformed or regular police to perform executive missions for his political police, providing a reservoir of manpower for large arrest actions, and, more important, he could draw SS personnel to his political police legitimately. There they could continue their double role of SS and policemen, but with legality and a greater degree of permanence.[11]

The April 1 enactment placed one more significant tool in the hands of the commander of the BPP: concentration camps—those already existing and those yet to be created. In contrast to the chaotic status of the autonomous, "wild" SA and SS camps in Prussia, the Bavarian camps technically came under the authority of the state administration through Himmler as their commander. The intention was to bring them under proper administrative control, but that goal soon paled in light of the advantages Himmler derived from official sanctioning of his camps. He got state funding for his camps and therefore for his SS guards, and they got a facade of propriety and legality. A side benefit was that his system of partially covering expenses through camp labor appealed to local leaders, whose dependence on Reich supplemental financing increased the threat of Reich controls by bureaucrats in the Reich Ministries of Finance and the Interior. Above all, this system created the triangle of SS, political police, and concentration camps bound together with interlocking personnel under one commander, the Reichsfuehrer SS, Himmler.[12]

For the time being, SS command in the police extended only to the political branch. Shortly after becoming commander of the BPP, Himmler relinquished his positions as police chief in Munich and Nuremberg. In

April, the Munich post fell immediately into SA hands. In Nuremberg Himmler managed to keep an SS man in office only until September. These developments impeded slightly the SS monopoly over political police affairs, for SA auxiliaries dominated NS work with the Nuremberg Political Police until spring 1934.[13] Despite such temporary obstacles, however, Heydrich successfully conducted the more immediate task of SS penetration of the political police.

Dachau and Opposition

In direct proportion to Himmler's growing power and prominence, opposition to his system developed, first locally and then nationally. For instance, his acquisition of command over concentration camps, which grew out of opposition to excessive arrests, in turn produced stronger and ever-widening opposition. The process began with the wave of arrests following the coup of March 9, 1933, which had filled the prisons and jails of Bavaria to overflowing. By April 1 they would hold five thousand internees. Consequently, Himmler announced to the press on March 21 that an abandoned munitions plant near Dachau had been converted into a facility for holding the overflow of political internees. When the Landespolizei officer whom he had put in charge objected to the inadequacy of these facilities and questioned the legality of the arrests, Himmler took over as head of the political auxiliaries (SS), who would henceforth provide the staff and guards, displacing the usual police personnel.[14]

To deflect the civil service protests about lack of due process, Interior Minister Wagner self-righteously dismissed any need for excessive concern over the internees, reminding his fellow ministers that when Party members had been subject to such mass arrests, "they shut them up in any empty ruin and did not worry if they suffered the inclemency of the weather."[15] He then recommended establishing special facilities, separate from the standard prisons under Ministry of Justice authority. After the April 1 announcement of Himmler's authority over the camps, Dachau evolved as Himmler's solution to the problem, increasingly free from the control of regular state authorities. Like every other component of his SS–police state system, the Dachau model grew quickly as a product of a vague NS ideological consensus adapted to rapidly evolving functional pressures by Himmler, always ready to insert his SS as the appropriate vehicle.

With Wagner's April 1 order making Himmler commander of the BPP and all concentration camps, Himmler achieved an unrivaled police power. He controlled not only the police but also penal facilities normally under the Ministry of Justice. Since he was a devout Nazi, in contrast to his Prussian competitor, Rudolf Diels, his NS comrades trusted him to handle their enemies "properly." Completing the picture, he had Roehm's support in curbing local SA competition of the sort encountered elsewhere.[16]

Not all Nazis trusted Himmler's propriety, however. Many already worried about growing excesses. In April, Hans Frank, the provisional minister of justice, had expressed concern about excessive and ill-founded protective custody arrests, and he succeeded in getting Epp and the other ministers to pressure Wagner for reform.[17] This, however, merely encouraged Himmler to ensure an SS-controlled system of camps, free of administrative interference.

Nevertheless, Frank intended to prove that no matter how far things had already gone, Himmler's organization could not literally get away with murder. He made his point on June 1 by charging Dachau Camp Commandant Hilmar Waeckerle and his staff with aiding and abetting murder. Under Himmler's orders, Waeckerle had issued camp regulations providing for the execution of internees "who made trouble." From the SS takeover in mid-April to late May, at least eleven men had either been shot "while fleeing or attacking guards," or had "committed suicide." All were Jews and/or KPD officials except for one alleged spy within the NSDAP. These were early cases of "special handling," although it is unclear where the decision for execution had originated. Four cases were so flagrant that the prosecutor's office pressed charges against Waeckerle and his staff, and Frank felt compelled to bring the problem to his fellow minister. Responding to the attack in a typically "constructive" manner, Himmler dismissed Waeckerle, but the independence of the camp administration remained untouched.[18]

For new commandant, Himmler chose Theodor Eicke. This forty-one-year-old had suffered the usual ups and downs of postwar employment. Along the way, he became a dedicated Nazi and entered the SS in 1930. Unemployed by 1932, he became a freebooter available for special assignments. An effective leader by SS standards, he rose rapidly to become head of the SS in the Palatinate. There he had a confrontation with Gauleiter Buerckel, who took revenge by committing him to a psychiatric clinic in March 1933. Finally released at Himmler's behest for the job at Dachau, Eicke would serve loyally the man who gave him a prestigious position.[19]

He whipped Dachau into shape, usually controlling excesses that might threaten its independent existence under Himmler. This he did by eventually welding together his own disciplined command of SS concentration camp guards, the Death's-Head Formations. Although terroristic brutality remained the guiding principle behind the camps, the object was to control this brutality—to use it with calculation for official reasons rather than personal, sadistic ends. Understandably, many outside Himmler's circle did not appreciate such a fine distinction; the camps therefore continued to provide bases for assaults on his position by conservative Nazis in the state administration.

The knowledge that Heydrich never had authority over Dachau or any other camp is necessary to understand these struggles. Throughout the history of Sipo and SD, the political police (later Gestapo) and concentration camps remained separate entities under Himmler. Their creation as individual institutions left Heydrich with no say in the matter. Eicke outranked him, also enjoying direct access to the Reichsfuehrer.[20] As the official most directly responsible for the protective custody system, however, it was Heydrich who made the arrests and determined who was committed. To maintain control over the ultimate fate of internees, as early as April he had established a Political Department to provide liaison with Dachau. As the local organ of the BPP, it decided questions of release and retention.[21]

The opposition developing against Himmler's system and his emerging counterarguments and tactics would shape significantly the future of Sipo and SD. The rapid growth of Himmler's power in Bavaria, based on a centralized, independent political police with almost uncontested protective custody arrest powers and on an SS-controlled concentration camp, was essentially revolutionary. His success is understandable only in the context of the three-sided power struggle among (1) offices of the state resisting the Nazi revolution, (2) Nazis who entrenched themselves in state offices and based their power on traditional state authority, and (3) the irregular "revolutionaries" who threatened normal state structures. In this struggle, Himmler played all sides against the middle and triumphed through "subtly revolutionary" tactics, using the argument that extraordinary measures were needed to deal with the extraordinary threats to society.

From the beginning, the Nazi leaders of Bavaria began to take sides. A conservative wing dominated state offices with the support of Reichsstatthalter Epp. Its key movers included Ludwig Siebert, unfortunately not a well-established Party man but a high-ranking professional civil servant, and the jurist Hans Frank. True to their professions, they perceived the Third Reich as an authoritarian state in which the Nazis ruled through administrative and legal channels. They relied on Epp's authority as Hitler's personally appointed governor of Bavaria.[22]

Ranged against the "conservatives" were the more "radical" *Gauleiter* and SA. Although many in their ranks had seized official positions or had become commissioners, they nevertheless wanted a real revolution to sweep away the old order. They tended to behave as a law unto themselves. Countering Epp's personal authority, the *Gauleiter* and Roehm were also Hitler's personal appointees and they refused to recognize Epp's claim to higher authority.[23]

As both *Gauleiter* and Minister of the Interior, Wagner held a more ambivalent position. He inclined toward radical changes in the system and was largely responsible for Himmler's early gains. However, since his ministry was his own personal empire, as soon as others threatened his supremacy he showed more concern for the proper machinery of state authority.[24] As Wagner's ostensible subordinate, Himmler could play one of several trumps. He could alternately employ the authority of the state and of the revolution, and as an ultimate ploy he too could claim final recourse to Hitler, either through Roehm or directly. Although Wagner had originally accepted Roehm's SA police commissioners and auxiliaries, he had immediately moved to limit their power over his police, relying on Himmler as a useful tool in the process. When, however, the conservatives had begun to attack SA excesses in March, Wagner had weakly defended the SA actions as necessary. It was in this context that Frank had first succeeded in bringing pressure through Epp and the Council of Ministers to make Wagner exercise more control.[25]

Unfortunately, as minister of justice in Bavaria, Frank held a poor position for limiting police power. The Bavarian system did not duplicate the procedures of most other states for administrative appeal against political police orders (*Verfuegungen*). Administrative courts were especially powerless in this respect.[26] Furthermore, Frank, thoroughly imbued with the NS spirit, had himself reduced the judicial proceedings still necessary in the early stages of the protective custody system. By April, he had lost or relinquished all control over protective custody cases that were handled directly by the BPP. Consequently, Frank's subsequent assault on Camp Commandant Waeckerle had required recourse to the Weimar Constitution, a very inappropriate tool for Nazis to use against their comrades.[27]

Even before that, however, the protective custody arrest process had reached a state of near-anarchy. Every NS organization or official who thought it possible to get away with it arrested enemies of the Movement and personal enemies as well. Nazis even used the threat on each other. The constant lawlessness produced continued pressure on Wagner from the Council of Ministers, giving him the encouragement he needed to try to curb the SA and keep the BPP under his control.[28] On May 17 and 22 he issued two orders for the regulation of protective custody. Limiting its use to significant suspects only, he required bimonthly reports to his office on the status of all internees. Most significant, he limited protective custody powers to police authorities, with Himmler, the political police commander, as the ultimate arbiter. To top it off, he

repealed an order of March 20, now embarrassing, in which he had
encouraged the SA commissioners to make unlimited use of protective
custody powers.[29] He thus set the official chain of authority for protective
custody in Bavaria as Reichstatthalter Epp, Minister of Interior Wagner,
Commander of the BPP Himmler, his chief Heydrich, and regional and
local police officials. Wagner effectively shielded Himmler's police from
Epp, while believing he was bringing the system under his control.

The conservatives under Epp used as their slogan Hitler's proclamation that "the Revolution is over." Revolutionary measures should
cease and the authority of the state be restored. The conservatives as-
saulted the position of the SA and SS with the argument that since the
emergency had passed, the extraordinary organs of the Movement, excessively expensive, could withdraw from action and police work be
returned to properly trained personnel.[30]

Against this attack Roehm proved ineffective. For the sake of his
own authority, he had to exercise control over his men, curbing them
to some extent. He also believed that the SA should be the force of
movement in the new order, standing outside the administration as its
gadfly, its opposition. As such, however, the SA would be denied a
forceful role as true policemen or administrators. Roehm was thus defenseless against the financial arguments. As early as May, the powers
and the number of auxiliary police were reduced, and their eventual
termination became inevitable. Roehm's bases for legitimate action
shrank.[31]

In contrast, Himmler entrenched himself and key SS men like Heydrich as legitimate police officials, using traditional police justifications
for attacking the problem of finances. In May, while the auxiliaries were
being reduced, Himmler approached the Reich government for increases
in supplementary funds for police purposes. He pleaded for his over-
worked civil servants, putting in seven-day weeks of fourteen to sixteen
hours a day. He warned of the threat of a growing army of spies and
traitors in the service of foreign powers that feared renewed vigor in
Germany, and, of course, he warned of the ever-present Red Menace.
Such threats were guaranteed to worry conservatives, be they Nazis or
their allies.[32]

Consequently, although Siebert, at a July meeting of the Council of
Ministers, moved to replace Himmler with "an experienced administrative jurist,"[33] outside his own circle he found little sympathy in the
Movement for such a reactionary change. As long as Himmler retained
the necessary staff of police experts and jurists, got them to work diligently for the new order, and succeeded by Nazi standards in defeating
the enemy, his position remained secure. He won the support of police
professionals by appealing to them and he satisfied the Movement by

revolutionizing the old system and creating the necessary free, strong forces needed by the NS state.

In the continuing debate over police authority, Himmler argued for a tactic that foreboded his "silent revolution" and revealed his emerging concept of a state protection corps (*Staatsschutzkorps*). The SA and the SS (still allied in his mind) would infiltrate and gradually take over the state. To remove them from their present positions would reverse the process and dangerously weaken the revolution. He and Roehm insisted that the police and administration were by no means reliable National Socialists. Since Catholics, reactionaries, and camouflaged liberals and Marxists still occupied the bureaucracy, the replacement process had to continue.[34]

Despite Himmler's gains, he could not overcome all legal limitations to the increasingly extraordinary police powers that he exercised, and Frank would remain an indefatigable advocate of those limitations. Unfortunately, given the mood of the times and the values of the Movement, he occupied a weak position against Himmler. As a police chief, Himmler could tap the full potential of "reasons of state" and arguments for "national security." The defense of the nation against its enemies remained paramount. As long as he painted the threats in sufficiently disturbing colors, any criticism of the police, the state's instrument of internal defense, could be a threat to the prestige of the state and to national security, deserving to be called treasonous.[35]

The ordinary person who dared criticize openly faced charges of treason and protective custody. The higher official found his own arguments sounding strangely unpatriotic and his standing in the Movement weakened. When one successfully portrayed the victims of the police and the internees in the camps as Communists, traitors, and dangerous antisocial elements best removed from society, they became unworthy of the sympathy or concern of good citizens. The cloak of national security enveloped the political police, their activities, and the concentration camps. Such definitions of national security and treason kept the press in line, making it impossible to mount a public campaign against the police or the camps. Since the press dared publish only what the police released, Himmler, Heydrich, and amenable policemen had ready-made machinery for propagandizing the attitudes they wanted to sell. Show trials "exposed" the hidden enemy and played upon public attitudes and fears. The SS definition of "the enemy," and its desire for freedom to fight them, were implanted in the public consciousness.

In the fight against the Catholic Church, a good example is the case of the three priests—Muhler, Thaler, and Sollacher—who had expressed concern over Dachau. In late November, following an investigation, they admitted "spreading" such "atrocity stories" and were arrested.

Searches of their quarters turned up the inevitable "extensive Marxist literature" and other circumstantial evidence associating them with Communism, all of which was duly publicized. The Church could not defend them against their admitted offense of undermining state authority. Despite the fact that the literature included only what an educated anti-Communist priest would read, Heydrich could not be forced to retract the "facts" he had publicized.[36] He successfully painted a picture of a Communist-infiltrated priesthood and the need for a police proven capable of fighting such a menace.

Such developments combined with the constant erosion of the Weimar system of checks and balances to undermine Frank's bases for action, and by the end of the year he stood completely stalemated. Himmler's system became less vulnerable even to charges of outright murder in the concentration camps, as in the cases of Handschuch, Frantz, and Katz, who were tortured and beaten to death at Dachau in the fall of 1933. Frank's officials investigated and determined the real causes of death. But having no desire to destroy the system being built, merely wanting to bring it under proper control, Frank simply presented the cases to the Ministerial Council, where concern had grown to the point of determination to bring the BPP under control.[37] Yet, Himmler could cool Frank's ardor with relative ease and ensure Wagner's support before the council, simply by arguing that the investigations threatened the prestige of the NS state and should be terminated for reasons of state. This was not enough for the Council of Ministers, however, who must have realized that illegality constituted the real threat to the prestige of the state, and perhaps also that no one was safe if this course continued unabated. At their December 9 meeting, they ordered Frank and Wagner to continue proceedings and to use the uniformed police against the camps if necessary.

Himmler turned to Roehm for support, and together they responded that, since Dachau was a camp for political prisoners, the affair was a political issue and had to be settled by political authorities, not judicial. They then played their trump, referring the matter to Hitler, where the proceedings ended. With this precedent, other proceedings against camp guards had to be dropped. Both Frank and Wagner had to accept the fact that for disciplining the SS as either camp guards or as auxiliary political police, Himmler had sole authority. For such Nazis as these, this would not be an entirely unpalatable pill, for, unlike the SA, the SS did have a reputation for propriety and discipline. Its excesses were not as much illegal as they were extralegal "necessities."

In addition to revealing the tactics that Himmler, Heydrich, and their SS and policemen were evolving, these developments shaped still more definitively the future of Sipo and SD. The obstructionism of Frank and

Sievert and the weak support from Wagner must have reinforced Himmler and Heydrich's hatred of jurists, bureaucrats, and Nazis with a parochial perspective. Such groups all lacked a clear understanding of the problems and had to be replaced by men who could be won over to the SS viewpoint and who, in turn, would be succeeded by a fully indoctrinated younger generation of SS men. Ironically, the opposition forged more firmly in each man's mind the broad outlines of the state protection corps.

Meanwhile, Himmler had succeeded in building a local combination of SS, political police, and concentration camps that had a usefully ambiguous image. For the more conservative elements, the SS had a distasteful air of evil to be shunned, yet its radicalism and "virile" brutality had an appeal. Readily available to do whatever was necessary, including what respectable citizens avoided doing, the SS offered the totalitarian efficiency that many believed essential to defeat the enemy. Yet in contrast to the SA, it appeared less offensive, less crudely radical, and increasingly capable of tapping more respectable types for service. On another level, the SS represented an alternative to the SA that was, nevertheless, thoroughly NS. Although Himmler worked well with Roehm against the conservatives, his SS and police had also worked well against the SA. Their efficiency made SA illegality unnecessary. In place of blatant SA illegality, the SS represented cleverly packaged extralegality. This image proved invaluable in the pending struggle for control of a Reich-wide political police system.

7

The Vortex of Intrigue

By the time Diels's Gestapo and Himmler's BPP had emerged, moves to create a centralized Reich police force were well under way, with Reich Minister of the Interior Wilhelm Frick taking the lead. In his newly acquired role, Frick had attempted to assert his authority even before the imposition of the *Reichsstatthalter* had given local Nazis control over the police of the various states. He became a natural rallying point for those who shared his objectives—the creation of a Reich police force purged of the enemy and obedient to a central command under the Fuehrer, but at the same time a professional force not extensively "par-tified."[1]

Unfortunately for Frick and those who supported him, they had neither the ruthless determination nor the means to accomplish their goals. They usually avoided the open confrontations necessary to bring Goering or Himmler into line. To be successful, such confrontations had to elicit clear definitions of the limits to which the Nazi Weltanschauung could be carried in violation of law and tradition, and experience showed that Hitler accepted such limitations only under great pressure from the powerful institutions of German society, specifically finance, industry, and the military. In trying to orchestrate a coalition of pressure, the Frick faction moved too cautiously. For their part, the conservative Nazis and non-Nazis who might have supported Frick were less aware than they should have been of the need to set clear limits. Their own reactionary, nationalistic, imperialistic aspirations blinded them to the full extent of the threat. They were also ambivalent about Frick as an ally.[2]

Perhaps the major obstacle to Frick's success in the struggle for police power, though, lay in the scope of his objectives, for the police were merely a part of his overall plan to centralize an administrative structure for the entire Reich and to refurbish the civil service for a leadership role. In this, he not only sought to block all revolutionary elements of the Movement who would replace the state, but he also ran afoul of all the particularist elements of the bureaucracy who had no desire to be centralized under his leadership. The overwhelming scope of his plan often held his attention at levels above the more specific problems of building a police state—the step-by-step process in which the Goering-Diels-Daleuge and Himmler-Heydrich combinations involved themselves. Frick thus had to find and rely on allies who could concentrate on the police.

As a further weakness in vying for Hitler's support, Frick lacked the necessary radicalism. He purged the Reich civil service only minimally, and appealed to the conservative bureaucracy by proclaiming it an indispensable pillar of the Reich. In his view, turning the bureaucrats into an efficient instrument of an authoritarian dictatorship did not require extensive "partification." Of course, Frick would have the Party Leadership set political policy, but the Party itself should be merely the machinery for propaganda to imbue the nation with the new spirit. It would not penetrate and interfere with the machinery of state for the execution of policy. In contrast, Hitler thoroughly distrusted bureaucrats. For him, the revolution required a total change of attitudes and values on the part of the men who operated the machinery of state.

Frick's inability to consider tactics that violated his sense of propriety handicapped him against less conservative opponents whom he could not force into line without Hitler's support. However, Frick's plans for centralizing the police offered Hitler no extensively new base of power but would mean a decision against Goering, Himmler, Roehm, the *Gauleiter*, and innumerable lesser holders of police power. Given this, Hitler would not back Frick and instead procrastinated. Meanwhile, however, Frick appeared to have the lead. In the backlash against uncontrolled and violent power seizure, pressures to regularize the state led in April to the Law to Restore a Professional Civil Service and subsequent legislation and decrees that gave apparent force to reform under the Reich Ministry of the Interior. For the first two years, Frick maneuvered with considerable hope of success.[3]

Despite his relatively conservative bent, Frick avidly pursued development of a police state. For instance, in April and May he provided Reich supplements for the auxiliary police and the concentration camps of the federal states. Although this increased his leverage to control them, it also assured their availability for NS terror.[4] In his drive for a Reich central police, his legislative and administrative changes—even those meant to check Himmler—nurtured the police state, for they also deliberately undermined concepts of the inalienable rights of the individual, as well as constitutional checks and balances on the power of the state.

On May 11, Frick made his first overt move by announcing his intention to centralize the Schupo. On the following day, as a first step he approached Goering, who, being responsible for the largest state force, would be indispensable. Goering had already done much toward creating a reliable state police, including a more centralized political police. He knew of plans for Reich centralization, saw the need for it, and supported the idea.[5] He might cooperate if it were to his advantage, but the more immediate need to tighten control in Prussia took precedence. For instance, through connections with the Prussian ministries, Frick knew that Goering and Diels were working toward the independence of the Gestapo. He therefore told Goering he wanted a unified Reich political police, asking him to take no action until he could make appropriate proposals.[6]

As a result of subsequent conflicts between Frick and Goering, the latter is always depicted as uncooperatively frustrating Frick's every move. Indeed, throughout 1933 he and Frick constantly sought to outflank one another; however, their relationship was not limited to competition. Nothing indicates that Goering reacted defensively to Frick's initial proposal. Instead, he played his cards shrewdly, always holding out and working toward an advantageous compromise. Soon Daluege and Diels became directly involved in Frick's planning and negotiations. Rather than trying to hinder this liaison, Goering probably commissioned it. As a matter of fact, Diels would later complain that Goering waited until as late as November to make the Gestapo independent.[7] If he delayed because of Frick's request, that response would indicate that Frick's plans for Reich centralization did not seriously threaten Goering at this time—that Goering in fact hoped to capitalize on them.

Before the end of May, Frick presented concrete proposals for Reich centralization, concentrating for the moment on the criminal and political police. He proposed merely a vague "arrangement between the Reich and the states" that would preserve the police sovereignty of the states. Goering's Prussian State Criminal Police Office and Prussian Gestapo Office were to be the Reich coordinating agencies, while Frick cautiously broached an eventual, yet-to-be-defined Reich authority over these offices. Furthermore, Frick promised to settle all matters with Goering before approaching the states other than Prussia. Although the details of Frick's proposal threatened potential loss of police power to Frick, there must have been positive aspects from Goering's point of view. Not only was the proposal in line with his desires for a strong, efficient police, but it also offered the possibility of bargaining for the best possible deal for himself. Toward such an end, his position was strong, for his Gestapo had inherited and continued to exercise all of the Reich-wide coordination activities of the various former Berlin political police offices. He ordered his staff to do everything to accelerate and facilitate negotiations. As late as July, when Frick spoke before a conference of *Reichs-*

statthalter advocating a Reich police central command, Goering apparently did not oppose and may even have supported him.[8]

From May on, Daluege and, to some extent, Diels spent progressively more time with Frick's staff, planning police centralization. In this way, Daluege established a closer relationship with the Frick circle, where he gradually emerged as the prime candidate for command of a Reich police.[9] Daluege could thus parlay already extensive police power into much higher stakes as he moved into a position to side with whoever might win. Meanwhile Goering continued to entrench and extend Daluege's police powers in Prussia. Undoubtedly, the success of the revolution at this stage and the more imminent threat of the SA remained Goering's prime concerns. For both Frick and Goering, Daluege's reputation as the powerful SS leader who hindered SA excesses made him a valuable ally. They also hoped to capitalize on his independence from Himmler.

Neither Frick nor Goering had any reason to suspect the full extent of Himmler's police aspirations, for, according to Werner Best, he carefully restricted his long-range planning to an intimate circle that excluded Daluege.[10] Consequently, as long as Frick stuck to his promise not to contact other states until matters had been settled with Goering, plans for a Reich police force developed in circles that did not include the future chief, Himmler.

At this crucial time, Daluege's power was a product of the very uncontrollability of the SA and SS units that Goering wanted him to tame. Control of funds for the SA and SS or their auxiliary police was the major leverage that Party and state officials had against these organizations. Party Treasurer Schwarz had worked hard before 1933 to secure such control over all Party finances, and in the early part of 1933 state and Reich administrations could set some limitations on auxiliary police through financing; however, the freewheeling nature of the power seizure threatened to undermine such controls. Many local Party and organization leaders supplemented their finances through special collections from individuals, businesses, and other organizations. The contributors obviously had mixed motives. Some simply payed protection money, or insurance against the future; others contributed to the defense of law and order and the reconstruction of the Reich. Contributions during the early months also came from industrialists worried about the threat of Communist sabotage.[11]

Recourse to financing in the form of special collections gave a freer hand to the uncontrolled and extremist elements of the Movement, but they hit some firms much harder than others—often to the point of overtaxing them. To counter such threats to conservative supporters,

Rudolf Hess, Hitler's deputy in the Party, created the Adolf Hitler Fund. This centralized the collection of all "special funds" and reensured control over the purse strings of Party organizations and local leaders. For the industrialists, regular contribution to a single fund was a budgetable expense that they paid more willingly to the responsible heads of Party and state. They paid for the sort of law and order they wanted—at least the Nazis stressed that theme in the patriotic appeals that they made for the funds. In return, the industrialists expected the Nazis to control the mass base upon which modern society rests. The means were less significant than the ends of preserving profit and property. Any qualms the businessmen had were suppressed by their fear of the left and the SA.[12]

Under Daluege, SS Group East had gathered its share of special contributions. Some surviving correspondence to and from his office in June 1933 casts light not only on his power and position at this time and on the significance of fusing SS with state police offices, but also on the involvement of leading businessmen in the establishment of the police state.[13] In early May and again in June, Count Karl Schimmelmann, Daluege's adjutant, contacted among others Dr. Ernst Poensgen, a Duesseldorf industrialist on the boards of numerous Ruhr industries. He asked Poensgen to arrange for contributions for the SS Auxiliary Police.[14] Such money would also finance the SS concentration camps around Berlin.

Poensgen responded that the newly created Hitler Fund now served that purpose and that Daluege should turn to Hess. Schimmelmann persisted, however. He called for a public service donation "in the interest of peace and order and a stabilization of the bases upon which the reconstruction could be begun." Law and order was in question in no less than the Reich capital. The adjutant also argued that this special request exceeded the purview of the Hitler Fund and the organizations it covered. Coming from the "Chief of SS Group East and the Prussian Police," Daluege's requests transcended the limitations of either the Party or local concerns.[15]

With the Hitler Fund as insurance, Poensgen felt confident enough to draw the line. On June 21 he appealed to Grauert to end Schimmelmann's persistent requests and told Schimmelmann that Daluege would have to be satisfied with the Hitler Fund.[16] Although they asked few questions about means, at this stage such industrial magnates preferred to deal with the more traditional and trustworthy bureaucrats and Party heads, expecting them to control their tools of police power. Their more direct contact and support for Himmler's SS and police developed later, when that agency became the proper machinery of state.

This episode illustrates four important points. It paints a general picture of powerful vested interests who did not overly concern themselves with the moral and political implications of how the state exercised its authority, as long as it represented and preserved national strength and their apparent interests. Although the pressures of the moment and lack of viable alternatives made their behavior understandable, a powerful element of society had thus failed to demand control of the police forces. Second, the episode reinforces the argument that a union of the SS and the police stood above Party lines of control. Third, it shows the extent to which Daluege operated independently. Finally, the Hitler Fund stands out as a means for the conservative establishment and many Nazi leaders to tame the NS revolution, especially to bring the SA into line. Concern about the SA was mutual for Goering and Frick, eventually drawing them into alliance with other like-minded elements. Until it finally brought Roehm down, this alliance included such unlikely bedfellows that it barely held together, especially the Goering-Frick-Himmler triangle that would soon emerge.

The SA threat was part of the so-called Second Revolution Movement: radical elements frustrated by the limits of the power seizure. Not only did the SA leaders dream of replacing the Army and the police, but they and others had their eyes on big business, heavy industry, and financial capital. Among small businessmen, workers, and peasants, many elements had subscribed to the Party rhetoric against monopolistic capitalism, and they wanted that part of the revolution fulfilled. They failed to appreciate how essential the "capitalist establishment" was to Hitler's position and to their own nationalistic aspirations. Not only did this movement threaten establishment conservatives and Nazis like Goering and Frick, but its anarchic independence also undermined the authority of the Reich Leadership of the Party, notably Hess, Ley, and Schwarz. Even many *Gauleiter* felt threatened, and some began turning to the Reich Leadership for support against SA and SS interference in political affairs.[17]

Meanwhile, the forces of decentralization in the Party had grown so great that Hitler made a move to strengthen the anti–Second Revolution forces. On April 21, he appointed Rudolf Hess deputy fuehrer. In typical fashion, Hitler made the new office prestigious and powerful, but not decisively so. Hess's full authority over the Party organization remained indirect, and his relationship to the other Reich leaders and the Gauleiter remained unclearly defined. Although Hess's appointment merely maintained the balance of indecision, it did enhance the anti-Roehm elements. Hess and his ally, Franz Schwarz, Reich treasurer of the Party, used the Hitler Fund to tighten the purse strings and to bring the SA more under

Central Party and *Gauleiter* authority. They and the conservatives in business who made jobs available to unemployed Brown Shirts did much to take the edge off the Second Revolution.[18]

In the same way that the Second Revolution threatened the Party Organization, it jeopardized Frick's power base in the existing machinery of state. The SA directly threatened him through their assaults on the bureaucracy, their seizure of the police, and their excesses that disrupted law, order, and proper administrative procedures. Because the SA had no regard for his legalistic methods, Frick and his conservative allies remained largely impotent against them. For instance, in late April Frick persuaded the cabinet to approve a law establishing disciplinary machinery for SA and SS members. Unfortunately, although Hitler would become increasingly concerned about reactions to the April and May violence, boycotts against Jews that backfired, pressure on the churches, and threats to business, he would not give such a law real teeth.[19] He left Frick to his own, largely inadequate devices.

Nevertheless, a growing pressure eventually forced Hitler's hand. Big business and the military would remain dissatisfied until they felt more secure about the SA. Von Neurath, the foreign minister, gave Frick ammunition by promising the French, concerned over SA and SS paramilitary forces, that the auxiliary police would be reduced as soon as possible. Given the delicate situation at the Geneva disarmament talks, this argument carried weight. On May 12, Frick announced that the auxiliary police would be dissolved in a few months, and he soon had Hitler's support in encouraging the *Reichsstatthalter* to follow suit.[20]

The Prussian Imbroglio

While opposition coalesced at the Reich level, Goering moved against the SA in Prussia. Their flagrant lawlessness, especially their unofficial concentration camps and torture chambers, openly challenged his authority. As April and May wore on and he refashioned his police, he could no longer ignore such affronts. He reacted by moving to close the illegal camps all over Prussia and ordering the auxiliary police to behave more circumspectly.[21] According to Diels, however, Goering acted so reluctantly that Diels virtually forced the issue. He claimed that he had his police break into SA and SS bunkers and camps and expose their gross inhumanity. Armed with such shocking evidence, the story went, he then moved Hitler to order a housecleaning, even to the point of giving Diels army artillery to break up the SS camp at Papenburg in April.[22]

Diels undoubtedly ended some excesses of the Brown revolution;

however, his version obscures the subtleties involved, especially his ambivalent relations with both the SA and SS. Christoph Graf's study of the early Gestapo emphasized the mixed nature of the relationships. Gestapo, SA, and SS worked together well to terrorize and destroy the KPD, SPD, and other enemies. For every exchange of complaints among them, there was an expression of appreciation for successful cooperation. For each "curbing of excesses," there was a matching case of Gestapo complicity in NS crimes and extralegal actions.[23] In building the police state machinery he thought necessary, Diels facilitated or excused many NS excesses, whether he approved or not.

Meanwhile, Goering was not just dragging his heels; he played a cautious game, using his influence in the SA to play factions against each other, for he had enjoyed good rapport with various Berlin units since the days of Stennes.[24] Goering's main concern was that if he moved too rapidly, he would show his hand. Instead, in May he merely issued a decree excluding policemen from membership in either SA or SS. He used as his pretext Frick's decree making the SA and SS self-disciplining organs of the Movement, which would subject policemen who were members of SA or SS to divided loyalties.[25] How long or how seriously Goering enforced this exclusion or when it lapsed remains undocumented. Apparently it was only a gesture.

The carefulness of Goering's game is apparent in his orders of April 21 and June 7, dividing the auxiliary police into SA teams, on the one hand, to support regular police, and SS teams, on the other, to back up the Gestapo. By making Roehm and Himmler special commissioners for each of their branches of the auxiliary police,[26] he invited the supreme leaders of these organizations to discipline their own men. Although relatively ineffective with Roehm's SA, this gesture must have appealed to Himmler's sense of order and may have led eventually to the Goering-Himmler alliance.

Diels's claim to have brought "the SS" into line is hard to square with his relationship with Daluege. Early in April, he and Daluege coordinated the conversion of Sonnenberg into a state camp guarded by Police Major Wecke's special police group.[27] Despite his "success" against the SS camp at Papenburg, Diels claimed he could not crack the SS bunker, Columbia House, in Berlin.[28] Undoubtedly, he skirted that thorny problem because it lay directly under Daluege's nose, unlike Papenburg, which was in western Prussia, outside Daluege's SS domain. Wedded as Diels was to Daluege's SS, the Columbia House was part of his modus vivendi with them.

Goering still hoped to tame and live with the radicals, while Diels continued his own convoluted maneuvers. In late June, Diels notified Daluege of his desire to recruit Gestapo executive personnel exclusively from the SS. He would use their weight in the Party to win respect for his police, while gaining control over the SS-men through proper training and the civil service command structure. With such SS-men in the police, the less controllable auxiliary police would become superfluous.[29] Diels obviously believed that by relying on the proper sort of SS-men, the regular police could survive in the new order without sacrificing their professional identity and integrity. In September, when Daluege became lieutenant general of the state police and commander of the police in Prussia, Diels's plan seemed secure, for here was an SS commander whom the Party respected and who would preserve the traditional police force. When Himmler made Diels an honorary SS lieutenant colonel in the same month,[30] it seemed that the SS had at last officially endorsed him as head of the Gestapo and accepted its own role as a support force.

In fact, things seemed to fall into line faster than Diels had hoped. On August 2, Goering dissolved the auxiliary police in Prussia with a note of finality.[31] To end the illegal camps, in late September he decreed a system of state-controlled installations under his own director. In addition to two prisons, there were to be four camps: Papenburg (Osnabrueck), Sonnenberg (Frankfurt a/O.), Lichtenburg (Merseburg), and Brandenburg, all to be staffed by regular Prussian Schupo rather than SA and SS auxiliaries. The transfer of internees to these locations began in October, so the other camps could be dissolved by the end of the year. Review of all protective custody cases would eliminate all but the "serious threats to security." As early as July, fewer than fifteen thousand such cases remained in all of Prussia, which compared favorably with the total of over four thousand cases in either of the much smaller states of Bavaria and Saxony.[32]

Roehm also cooperated, for he clearly needed to bring his SA under control. He ordered the end of SA involvement in auxiliary police and on October 7 created the SA Feldjaeger Corps, his last effort to arrive at a workable compromise with Goering. The Feldjaeger, a relatively small elite force, was to police the SA. Ordered to work closely with the Gestapo, who controlled their finances and helped select their personnel, their job was to arrest for the police SA-men suspected of crimes. To eliminate clashes between the police and SA, the police were to avoid arresting and disciplining SA-men, except to prevent a crime in progress.[33]

According to Diels, once the major points of friction had been settled, he reached an understanding with Roehm and Karl Ernst, head of the Berlin SA. They shared his concern about the growing threat of Himmler and about their need for allies. At first they wanted to draw Diels into the SA; then, as an afterthought, Roehm supposedly advised Diels to take the SS uniform to fool Himmler. How much of Diels's version can be accepted is debatable; however, Diels obviously played all ends against the middle.[34]

Diels had reason to be pleased with himself, for he now commanded a Gestapo that operated throughout Prussia and served as a Reich co-ordinating office for all countersubversive work in Germany. Where police forces were inadequate, he could use SS men in great numbers. Undoubtedly, his offices had accomplished many of the inroads against the KPD and other "enemy" organizations, but where they might have been inadequate, spontaneous SA terrorism had completed the job. Diels probably had some justification for his boast that the Communists and other enemies of the Reich had been brought to heel, and that "through their union with suitable National Socialists the [police] authorities had earned the trust of the national Movement, especially the SA and the SS."[35]

Although Diels would make this boast in September, by November his neatly arranged order lay in shambles. The SA refused to be tamed, and the emerging coalition against them came apart. Throughout the Reich, SA-men still behaved as a law unto themselves. The SA assumed it had police authority and exercised that power on whim, creating numerous embarrassing incidents for the regime, including the harassment of representatives of foreign governments. In the very same week that Roehm had established the Feldjaeger, Frick had instructed the police authorities to crack down on SA excesses. In the non-Prussian states, he admonished them to rein in the auxiliaries, and Goering ordered that Frick's directives be applied firmly to Prussia.[36] Consequently, any efforts at Roehm's level to smooth over tensions were undoubtedly lost on the SA ranks, whose freedom was being curbed.

Meanwhile, tension between Goering and SA leaders grew into an irreparable breach. According to Hans Gisevius, a conservative plant in the Gestapo, Goering at this time was planning a grand spectacle in tune with his decadent lifestyle. SA leaders protested to Hitler against this unsocialistic pomp, and Roehm ordered his SA leaders not to participate. To avoid embarrassment, Goering sent formal invitations to Roehm and Himmler to be honored guests. Although this ensured SA participation, the local leader, Karl Ernst, turned the grand parade into a casual walk-by, obviously snubbing Goering. Goering's position was clearly unten-able unless he took decisive action, and he now relished thoughts of revenge.[37]

Unfortunately for Goering at this moment of insecurity, Frick made new proposals for centralizing the police. He now wanted the political police of every state directly responsible to his Reich Ministry of the Interior, although they would remain nominal police forces of the states.

Toward this end, he drafted a law and, in line with their previous understanding, submitted it for Goering's consideration.[38]

Goering's reactions to this proposal and his subsequent moves have been interpreted as deviously defensive efforts to checkmate Frick and preserve his own police powers.[39] Although Goering hardly stood above such behavior, there is room for another interpretation, since initially he reacted ambivalently to the proposal, not yet overly defensive about Frick's plans. True, Goering had hastened to see Hitler about police centralization, and he let Frick know that the Fuehrer had doubts about centralizing the Schupo. It is not clear, however, that he tried to give Frick the impression that Hitler opposed a plan to centralize the political police. Instead, Goering responded to the proposal in a cooperative tone. Nevertheless, he said in effect that Frick's plan was unnecessary—out of tune with developments. Goering claimed he intended to dissolve the Gestapo and reintegrate political police work into the ordinary police machinery. To facilitate this, he would make Diels a vice president in the Police Presidium of Berlin to coordinate all detective work, the intelligence service, and political observation.[40]

If Goering were to dissolve the extraordinary political police, one of the conservatives' main concerns would vanish, derailing Frick's drive to assert his command over them. In this light, Goering may well have considered "breaking up" the Gestapo. As for Diels, Goering by this time had come to distrust him, perhaps to the point of removing him from command of a political police executive force and returning him to a more harmless position in the Police Presidium.[41]

The basis for Goering's growing distrust of Diels lay in the rats' nest of intrigue that the Gestapo Office had become. Diels and Gisevius have painted pictures of the early Gestapo as rife with confusion, internal strife, and conspiracy. Within his own office, Diels encountered a variety of opponents aligned with the factions vying for police power. Caught up in a struggle in which opponents were eliminated in any way possible, even a devout Nazi like Nebe supposedly avoided front entrances, crept around the back corridors of the building, and carried a cocked pistol for his own protection.[42]

Since the summer, when Diels had turned to Daluege for SS recruits for his "executive" force, the SS had poured into his service. Most of them came from the lower ranks, below any conscious involvement in struggles between Daluege and Himmler; however, coming from Daluege's command, they, like Nebe who led them, represented a powerful and growing faction. They had begun their Gestapo affiliation through the SS Auxiliary Police, some being drawn rapidly into the Gestapo proper. Then, with the dissolution of the auxiliaries, they became the SS-Kommando Gestapo, officially designated as civil service employees in the Gestapo as of October 1. To facilitate this process, Daluege had ordered the bending of employment criteria.[43]

Although the vast majority of SS-men were the lowest-ranking functionaries in the Gestapo, by drawing them in in his effort to ensure his survival with the Nazis, Diels had laid the foundation for the SS-police state. Even if many of the SS had originally been Daluege's men, they became levers for Himmler. Since April at least, when Himmler became special commissioner for the Gestapo's SS Auxiliary Police, he had stationed his own liaison man in the Gestapo Office—SS Lieutenant Walter Sohst, who remained until Himmler took over. Himmler and Heydrich also managed to insert a number of others into the Gestapo who could use their positions to manipulate the Gestapo's SS contingent.[44] In a coup de grace on the very same day that the SS Kommando was taken into police service, Himmler relieved Daluege of his command over SS Group East and made him a member of his staff for special duty (z.b.V.). Ostensibly, this move followed the pattern of allowing SS men in the police to devote themselves fulltime to their work; however, Daluege, who seems to have been taken completely by surprise, knew how seriously this undermined his power base in the SS.[45] Himmler was clearly taking over the Prussian SS, and with it the Gestapo contingent.

In contrast to growing SS influence, a few in the Gestapo sympathized with the SA, some joining in the mistaken belief that the future of the police lay there. An even more significant element, best labeled conservatives, wanted a return to normalcy after the Left had been broken. Many old policemen fitted this category, and the conservative elements in the Party and their allies in government reinforced them with carefully placed assignments. One such was Gisevius, who had been sent into the Gestapo by Goering's State Secretary, Grauert, to keep an eye on Diels, and who took his job seriously.

Diels had miscalculated the complexity of his opposition, believing them united in support of Himmler, for their combined effort did indeed undermine his stock with Goering. In their common opposition to Diels, Gisevius and Nebe drew together in the Gestapo, and, according to Gisevius, Nebe then won Daluege to their way of thinking. Gisevius had had a distaste for Diels since school days, and Nebe had gotten along poorly with his boss from the beginning. Both men were ambitious, and a hostile Diels blocked their way. Ironically, Nebe decided Diels was a crypto-Communist, tolerating the excesses of the Brown rabble to discredit the Revolution and undermine law and order, and catering to the "National-Bolshevist" wing of the Movement. With such arguments, Nebe bent Daluege's receptive ear.[46]

Regardless of whether he believed Nebe's version, Daluege moved against Diels. A special SS squad raided Diels's home in October 1933, and when Diels arrested the SS-men, Daluege turned to Goering to get them released. To justify his actions, Daluege painted the case against Diels very black, and since other powerful forces such as Hess-Bormann and *Gauleiter* Koch were after the hide of this "reactionary traitor," Goering became concerned enough to put a check on Diels's power, especially when he saw Diels's files on himself and other Party leaders.[47]

According to Diels, Goering ordered his arrest, and teams of SS and Schupo men secured Gestapo headquarters against him, but Diels heard of these developments in time to flee to safety in Czechoslovakia for a brief time. Neither the alleged arrest order nor the exact dates can be verified, however. Diels, extremely nervous—indeed paranoid—amidst this intrigue, may have cracked on hearing rumors and fled unnecessarily. Goering may merely have "kicked him upstairs." His removal seems to date around mid-November, and the duration of his flight seems much shorter than he indicated.[48]

As Diels's successor, Goering appointed an Old Fighter, Paul Hinkler. Although this appointment is usually analyzed in terms of Goering's calculations, Hinkler in fact was Daluege's man, further evidence that Diels's dismissal was more Daluege's maneuver than Himmler's first major thrust. Although an old-timer, Hinkler had little prestige in the Movement, and no credit where it really counted. He had once been a Gauleiter, but in 1931 Hitler had removed him. A corrupt and inept intriguer, he blamed his fate on Gregor Strasser, but Frick apparently played a direct role as well. For a while Hinkler had worked in the Lie Defense Post (Lugenabwehrstelle) of Goebbel's Propaganda Office, where he was liaison with the Intelligence Service of Arthur Schumann, who, by the fall of 1933, was directing an intelligence service for Arthur Rosenberg's Foreign Political Office. However, this significant list of friends and enemies takes second place to Hinkler's ties to Daluege. They were intimate friends (*Duzbruder*), and Hinkler repeatedly turned to Daluege to secure positions in the Movement for him.[49] When Daluege proposed the inept Hinkler as Diels's replacement, he revealed poor judgement in his choice of allies, even if he had wanted a weak and pliable Gestapo leader.

Whatever action Goering may have taken against Diels, in less than a week he anxiously sought his return. Hinkler had quickly proved a complete failure, and something like chaos ensued. Hitler, who still held Hinkler in low regard, was disturbed and apparently favored Diels. According to Diels, Goering had Koerner trace him down by phone and tell him that both Goering and Hitler wanted his return. Goering in fact became so desperate that he personally telephoned to lodged his plea: "Herr Diels, I beg you pressingly to come back. I want to get rid of the *Dumkopf* Hinkler today. I have prepared a decree, which gives you independence. I want what you want. I want to have order. When can you be here?"[50]

There were other reasons for Goering's anxiety besides Hinkler's ineptitude and the pressure from Hitler; the decree (*Verordnung*) he mentioned to Diels lay at the heart of the matter. Goering, outmaneuvered from several sides, must have learned that Roehm was to join him on the Reich Cabinet as a minister without portfolio. In NS rivalry, a return to the proximity of the Fuehrer threatened Goering's position. This was thus no time to tamper with the Gestapo, which on the contrary had to be more powerful and reliable than before. Indeed, upon his return, Diels launched a renewed cleanup against SA illegalities, in which Goering called for a show of close cooperation with Himmler's SS, their common ally against the SA. Diels complied and the Gestapo began cooperating more closely even with Heydrich's SD.[51] To set the stage, Himmler had already promoted Diels to SS colonel on November 24, about the time Goering began trying for Diels's return.[52]

Yet another development favored Diels's recall: Frick's maneuvers, which aggravated Goering's insecurity. Abandoning his proposed law to centralize the political police, by mid-November Frick moved into a more dynamic phase of his plans to set his Reich Ministry of the Interior over state governments. Throughout 1933, Goering had successfully blocked this tack, but the general idea was central to NS principles, and he must have known he could not hold out forever.[53] He had to bargain for the best possible deal, and he had a need for conservative support against Roehm, which helps explain his apparently cooperative responses to Frick's earlier proposals. Goering had to maneuver carefully, keeping the Gestapo in good order. Hinkler's bungling and a return of the Gestapo to the regular police could cost Goering everything when Frick increased the authority of his ministry. The "November decree" resolved that crisis by letting Goering hold the Gestapo as his high trump until the hottest series of bargainings.

In fact, what Goering had issued was the Law over the Secret State Police of November 30, which removed the Gestapo from the control of Goering's Prussian Ministry of the Interior and directly subordinated it to the prime minister of Prussia—again, Goering. This sleight of hand would frustrate Frick's efforts to control the Gestapo through an interior ministry chain of command, while allowing Goering to be otherwise cooperative with Frick. When Frick later acquired the Prussian Ministry of Interior, the Gestapo remained outside his jurisdiction. Goering made himself chief of the Gestapo and created for Diels the joint position of inspector of the Gestapo and head of the Gestapo Office.[54] Diels thus became an independent central state authority, comparatively free from interference by the rest of the administration. With enhanced authority vis-à-vis the Gestapo field posts and local police officials, he could order the latter to use their regular police to support the Gestapo. Although unable to end Nebe's strong position in the Gestapo, he at least eased Gisevius out.[55]

Although the long-range effect of the Gestapo Law of November was to keep the Gestapo out of Frick's hands, Goering had aimed primarily at creating a more freewheeling police and strengthening Diels against opposition, while at the same time increasing his own personal control. As soon as he realized that the case against Diels had been largely manufactured, he anxiously reset the balance. He removed the Gestapo from the Ministry of Interior not just to frustrate Frick, but also to free it from the red tape of bureaucracy and the interference of conservatives like Grauert who backed Gisevius.[56] As part of this move, rather than leaving Diels below Daluege, who had plotted for his dismissal, Goering set Diels beside Daluege and directly below himself. Finally, trusting no one, Goering reserved for himself all appointments of key civil servants and heads of field posts,[57] thus denying both Diels and Daluege the freedom to insert their followers in decisive positions.

Ending any authority over the Gestapo that Daluege might have exercised may well have pleased Goering as well as Diels, for at any moment Daluege might cast his lot with Frick or Himmler. Although he played ally with Himmler, Goering had new reasons to be nervous about the Reichsfuehrer's growing strength. Himmler had begun to emerge as a strong claimant to command over any centralized political police force. Even before that development, however, further growth by the SD was to signal an increase in his power.

8

The SD Emergent

Between its official emergence in the summer of 1932 and the fall of 1933, the SD became dominant among Party intelligence agencies. The impetus for this rapid rise seems related to the fall of Gregor Strasser and the subsequent realignment of factions within the Movement. Throughout the summer of 1932, Strasser's star had been in the ascendant. As Reich Organization Leader, he had reorganized the Party, consolidating more power in his hands than Hitler had ever allowed any one man, and he had determined the Party's strategy. In September, however, urged on by more activist elements like Goebbels and the SA, Hitler abandoned Strasser's strategy for a more militant stance. In December, the dissillusioned Strasser resigned his Party post.[1]

Strasser's resignation came during the crucial round of negotiations that would eventually lead to Hitler's chancellorship. Previously, he had been a key contact with General Kurt von Schleicher, who was maneuvering to form a government including Nazis. Although Strasser did not want to split the Party, his opponents, primarily Goering and Goebbels, undermined Hitler's confidence with rumors to that effect, giving Hitler the explanation he needed for Strasser's resignation: Since Strasser no longer stood obediently at his side, he must be an enemy. This explanation rapidly became the official position on Strasser, who was read out of the Party.[2] Despite rumors that Himmler had "betrayed" his former boss and comrade to ingratiate himself with Hitler,[3] we may never know whether he played such a role.

Regardless, the Strasser affair must have intensified Himmler's drive to secure the Movement and the future Reich from enemies. Since September, the uncontrolled, often rebellious actions of SA units had compelled Hitler to change his tactics, and this sort of undisciplined initiative always disturbed Himmler. Furthermore, Strasser's removal and the disruption of his more rationalized Party structure fed internal rivalries. Himmler's desire to build a machine obediently responsive to the will of his myth, Hitler, included the creation of an extended security service to strengthen the SS for its police role within the Movement. The new

SD thus acquired greater priority. Similar concerns apparently prompted Hess to see Himmler's SS as useful against the uncontrolled elements. This would also account for his interest in the SD, his support for its early development, and his apparent backing for its monopoly in Party intelligence.[4] Hess's support would be crucial to both the growth of the SD and to Himmler's political police power.

The power seizure immediately eroded the SD's new-found priority, however, for Heydrich had to pursue the double track of building the SD and assuming control over the Bavarian political police. The SD might have been useful for work that could not be trusted to the professional, non-Nazi police, but the professional police were indispensable for the internal security of the Reich, and the SD inevitably took second place. After January 30, 1933, the SD immediately slipped into that status, for neither the SA nor the SS had any official role in the new coalition Reich government. Only individual local SA and SS leaders got police positions of importance. Hundreds of others searching for jobs worked their way into the police from below. Only in March, with his appointment in Bavaria, had Himmler joined the power seizure and begun to coordinate the infiltration process.

The small size of the SD meant that few members had the credentials or positions to make significant contributions to infiltration. The regular SS men played the key roles, and even if the SD had been intended for dominance in the political police, any effort to force SS members of those police into the SD would have been premature and incautious. Consequently, for several months Himmler and Heydrich preoccupied themselves with police affairs. Without a clear mission, the SD had a year of uneasy transition. Its members felt pressure to assert for themselves a key place in the security of Party and state, but they lacked Heydrich's full attention or guidance.

By January 1933, Himmler knew he had in Heydrich a man of ability who shared at least the rudiments of his dream of the SS and police. He could not leave such a man doing paperwork when he needed agents for action and negotiation, so on January 27 he made SS Colonel Heydrich (who was already at work in Berlin) an officer for special duties (*Fuehrer z.b.V.*) on his staff. What followed, among other events, was Heydrich's previously described service as Himmler's agent in Berlin. The allegation that Heydrich and Daleuge collaborated during this period to set the Reichstag fire has recently gained some acceptance. Although it cannot be totally dismissed, the current version rests entirely on rumors originating in hostile SA circles and other questionable sources. Until more substantial evidence surfaces, it cannot be given credence.[5] Instead, Heydrich's primary mission in Berlin was probably to pave the way for an anticipated move of SS headquarters, including SD Central.

Another area of excessive speculation is the fact that Himmler's order separated Heydrich "as Staff Fuehrer of the SD from the Staff of the Reichsfuehrer SS" and assigned him "as SS Colonel z.b.V. to the Staff of the Reichsfuehrer SS" with the powers of an Office Chief (*Amtschef*).[6] One recent study converted this change of title into Heydrich's resignation from the SD, which he then cut adrift because it could not serve his advancement in taking over the police.[7] In fact, at no time did Heydrich cease acting as head of the SD, for the order did not remove him from the SD. It changed his title but named no replacement. During January and February, he continued to forward reports from Berlin as staff fuehrer of the SD, and SD Central followed him to Berlin, where most of its staff would remain for several months after he returned to Munich. During this period Hans Kobelinski, head of SD Group East, assumed an undefined role in directing SD work. This ad hoc arrangement was, of course, untenable during such eventful times. Consequently, when Heydrich returned to Munich in early March, he called Paul Leffler, now SD leader in Brunswick, to become staff leader (*Stabsleiter*) in Berlin. Leffler did not assume Heydrich's title, *Stabsfuehrer*, and, if his memory is accurate, Heydrich approved his replacement in Brunswick, indicating Heydrich's continued command. Kobelinski still played an undefined role in central management,[8] while Heydrich remained in charge of the SD through Leffler and Kobelinski.

During the spring of Heydrich's reduced involvement, the SD had a series of clashes with powerful leaders of Party and state. Innumerable clashes at lower levels must also have occurred, only to be hushed up, but at least two offended parties brought their conflicts into the open. The first occurred in Hamburg, where the activities of the local SD leader led to charges of conspiracy against Gauleiter Karl Kaufmann. In May, Kaufman became aware of the activities of Ferdinand Funke, head of SD Group Hamburg. As Kaufmann understood it, Funke had assigned two of his men, including a non-Party member and Russian émigré, to spy on Kaufmann and to assemble material against him and fellow Party leaders. When confronted, Funke denied the charges and hastened to Berlin to consult Heydrich, breaking a promise to remain available to Kaufmann. Kaufmann then claimed to have uncovered a whole nest of Russian emigrés in SD service against him and had Funke arrested by the Berlin police on charges of embezzlement. What happened next, according to Kaufmann's sources, was that Heydrich personally gained Funke's release "against the will of" Goering.[9]

On June 1, Kaufmann queried the Berlin SD Central about Funke. Kobelinski denied that either he or the Munich Office had given orders about spying to Funke, and that they would ever do such a thing. By this time, he said, Funke had been severely disciplined and relieved of his post.[10] With evidence that Kobelinski was lying, on June 22 Kaufmann sent a formal protest to the Reich Party Leadership. He charged that not only had Funke gone unpunished, but also that the Hamburg police had monitored calls from him warning his people to join him in Prussia, bringing their materials. Of course, all had been arrested with the incriminating evidence. Furthermore, Kaufmann charged, Heydrich had set Funke up in Munich in a camouflaged office to continue his operations against the *Gau* Hamburg leadership. The new contact man in Hamburg, a certain Bartholomae, had also been arrested. In a sweeping conclusion, Kaufmann charged that assembled evidence indicated that Otto Telschow, Gauleiter Hanover-East, Hinrich Lohse, Gauleiter Schleswig-Holstein, Alfred Rosenberg, and Goering were also targets of this spy net, and that SA leaders were involved with the SD. He contended that evidence from all over the Reich supported his charges and demanded that such operations be ended, thereby denying the SD its cover of official Party support.[11]

Should they be uncovered, relevant SD records may cast a different light on the affair, as indicated by the second open attack on the SD— a more dangerous crisis in Brunswick.[12] Before his transfer in March, the local SD district leader, Paul Leffler, had become involved in internal rivalries in Brunswick, where an Old Fighter who had monopolized local power came into conflict with one who had not. Building from his position as minister of interior and education since 1931, Dietrich Klagges had become prime minister in 1933. By controlling local election lists, he restricted the power of a major rival, Ernst Zoerner. Allied to Klagges was SS officer Friedrich Alpers, who first commanded the auxiliary police and then won a ministry in Klagges's government. Alpers's rise marked the displacement of Zoerner, who left Brunswick during the summer.

Since Zoerner and his circle had ties with Leffler, the local SD developed sources inclined against Klagges and Alpers. Imbued with the SD concern over behavior that discredited the Movement and the regime, Leffler became alarmed over the excesses of Alpers's auxiliaries. His coworkers were SS-men hostile to Alpers and Klagges's appointee, SS-General Friedrich Jeckeln, head of all state police. In a further twist, Leffler learned that Hess supported Zoerner against Klagges and Alpers. When Leffler moved to Berlin Central in March, he left local SD affairs in the hands of Gerhard Klare, charged with reporting on the Klagges-Alpers politics and on local reactions. He left Klare with a high sense of intrigue, and Klare carelessly expanded the net of agents nosing into the Klagges regime. Further disturbed by the charged atmosphere thus generated, Leffler, now running the SD central office in Berlin, wrote a report in April stating that if the Klagges reign were not broken, there would be dire consequences, perhaps a local coup by military and conservative circles.[13]

The crisis broke in june or July, when Klagges and Jeckeln got wind of the affair. The most damning evidence came from SD associate Wilhelm Bonewald, who charged that Klare had orders to compile evidence to overthrow Klagges, Alpers, and Jeckeln. He quoted Klare as having stated that Heydrich was directly involved, out of a desire to break Jeckeln's control of the state police. He even implicated Himmler. Jeckeln reacted by taking Klare and some associates into "protective custody," and after an "investigation" he charged them with conspiracy and requested that Himmler discipline them. Himmler immediately expelled them from the SS.[14] In August, Klagges brought charges in state court against Herbert Selle, the non-NS chief of uniformed police and an ally of Zoerner. Leffler was called to testify, and the trial escalated into charges against Leffler in the High Party Court, as Klagges sought to expose and break the SD.

The evidence assembled from the SD for the subsequent trial undermined the sensational charges. Of course, the evidence may have been engineered, and NS judicial procedures generate little confidence, especially since the High Party Court was under Walter Buch, increasingly an admirer of Himmler and—in this case at least—aligned with the Hess faction. The SD records indicated that neither Heydrich nor Himmler had paid much attention to Leffler's Brunswick activities prior to Selle's trial. Himmler's first inquiries into the affair followed his expulsion of Klare. Leffler's version made it all sound like a routine and proper procedure that had simply gotten out of hand. His April report had reached Himmler, but the Reichsfuehrer's marginalia indicated that he considered it of questionable accuracy and had not forwarded it to the Reich Leadership. Finally, the prime witness, Bonewald, had been functioning as a double agent, perhaps inducing Klare to exaggerate. Klare's earliest testimonies had been taken after a beating, and he later denied the most incriminating parts.[15]

The various contradictions leave the affair open to interpretation. Leffler had clearly carried out the SD mission of reporting on all affairs of Party and state that could harm the Movement. From the SD and Reich Leadership perspective, this was proper, but from Klagges's it was sinister. The SD mission thus lay at the heart of the crisis, but beyond that, it may have been nothing more than the work of uncontrolled local operatives; however, Hess's interest in the Klagges-Zoerner rivalry and the untestable allegations that Heydrich wanted to break Jeckeln's police power leave open the possibility of a conspiracy. That suspicion is reinforced by Hess's growing appreciation for the SD and by the decision of Buch's court exonerating the SD, with only a slap on the wrist for the lower-ranking participants most directly involved.[16]

By the summer of 1900, the SD had obviously come under attack from powerful quarters, and a dark cloud of suspicion had descended upon it. For several months, its survival remained in question. Undoubtedly, Himmler ordered Heydrich to keep a tighter rein on his business, and toward this end he resumed full supervision of SD work, especially of personnel matters as early as July, and by August had assumed the title of chief of the SD.[17] Apparently at this point, Heydrich also returned SD headquarters to Munich.

The return to Munich related directly to another conflict, for during the summer of 1933 tensions between the Himmler-Heydrich combination and the Goering-Daluege interests also erupted. The traditionally cited March date for Goering's order to arrest Heydrich is questionable. Only in the summer did the full extent of Daluege's double game and the exposé of SD spying come into the open. When Himmler received complaints in mid-July about Daluege's previously mentioned fund raising, several industrial directors were so disturbed they wanted to meet with Himmler. An SD report from Berlin roused suspicions that Daluege used such funds for his own organization rather than the SD, for which they were ostensibly raised.[18] By autumn the breaches with Goering, several *Gauleiter*, and local NS governments had come to a head. Klagges had filed charges in the highest Party court accusing the SD of conspiring to overthrow NS governments. The attack had become so severe that rumors spread that the SD would be dissolved.[19]

Under attack, Himmler must have turned to the Reich Party Leadership for support, and at Party headquarters he apparently found it. Martin Bormann, Hess's staff leader, who considered the SS a desirable foil for uncontrolled elements, had shared his opinion with Hess. With Hess, Buch, Ley, and Schwarz, concern over the Second Revolution was mounting. Undoubtedly, they had received from Himmler useful material gathered by the SD, and they appreciated the need for intelligence not censored by local leaders. Such local autonomy thwarted the central Party Leadership who were best situated to defuse the SD crisis.[20]

The move to save the SD appears to have been well coordinated. In the autumn, Himmler announced a delimitation of its mission: Henceforth, it would probe into Party affairs only on the specific orders of Hess, the deputy of the Fuehrer, or the competent political leader for the branch in question. All subsequent reports were to be factual and free of personal interpretations. The slate was wiped clean by using the NS leadership principle to give the SD a new veneer of propriety, and by giving Party leaders a minimal guarantee against renewed spying.

With these changes, Buch's court could minimize the Brunswick affair, reducing it to the level of a misunderstanding.[21]

Up to a point Hitler shared Hess's concerns, so it must have been easy to persuade him to preserve the SD officially and thereby terminate the attacks. If Hitler did in fact prefer settlements preserving the balance of power, such an action was perfect. On October 17, he allegedly announced that the SD would remain. Thereafter, Hess's office responded to all rumblings about SD dissolution by reminding the *Gauleiter* of the Fuehrer's decision.[22]

The decision to preserve the SD meant more than a maintaining of the balance of power, however, for it elevated the SD at the expense of Party rivals. In November, Hess announced that the SD would absorb the ND of the Foreign Political Office.[23] Apparently Hess had parlayed several problems into a solution that saved the SD. The head of this ND was none other then Arthur Schumann, the competitor encountered previously in Goebbel's ND. In 1933, his service had transferred from Propaganda Command to the new Foreign Political Office, where it became Main Division I, responsible for intelligence. The Foreign Political Office was a new creation, a sop for Alfred Rosenberg, whose desire to become Reich foreign minister had been frustrated. The office's erratic work created problems for the Foreign Office, for Goebbels, and for Joachin von Ribbentrop, Hitler's foreign political advisor. Rosenberg had been one of the reported targets of SD spying, which activity may have helped the SD justify absorption of Schumann's rival service.[24]

Having secured the survival of the SD, Himmler on November 9 made it the fifth Office (*Amt*) of the SS, elevating both the SD and Heydrich, who acquired the appropriate rank of SS major general.[25] The troubled period of transition ended with the year. The SD had survived the relative neglect of Heydrich's preoccupation with the police, it had survived a concerted attack by powerful Party leaders, and it clearly had the support of powerful allies in the Reich Party Leadership. As Himmler and Heydrich expanded their political police influence, SD contacts and influence grew accordingly. The political police provided a coattail to ride upon.

9

Toward Command of a Reich Political Police

Himmler's claim to command a centralized political police drew strength from more than just his success in Bavaria. From the beginning, he had nursed the SS image as the proper security force of the Reich. Perhaps with the intention of playing on Hitler's phobias, or perhaps just to proclaim a success, in March he released to newspapers reports about plots he had uncovered to assassinate Hitler, enhancing the image of his SS-SD-BPP team. If he intended to remind Hitler how he had always relied on the SS for personal protection, there was no need to do so. Hitler had already repeated that pattern when on March 17 he called on SS Major General ("Sepp") Dietrich to form a new SS guard for the Reich Chancellery, eventually christened Leibstandarte SS Adolf Hitler.[1] This development significantly enhanced Himmler's influence on political security over the entire Reich.

Originally, Hitler's choice of Dietrich had little to do with Himmler's influence, for Dietrich resembled Daluege in many ways: a highly independent SS man, long associated with Hitler's personal security. He was Hitler's rather than Himmler's man. Although Dietrich and his Leibstandarte remained largely independent until the late thirties,[2] Himmler tolerated men like him and Daluege for several reasons. Given their connections, he had no real choice, and by patiently enmeshing them in the bureaucratic machinery of the SS, he exploited their connections and tightened his own control over the instruments and power bases they established.

Meanwhile, Dietrich's newly formed staff guard created a model upon which Himmler could capitalize immediately. Along with the Special Prussian State Police Group to which it was attached, it performed a variety of assignments in the Reich capital. Goering appreciated its value, and it soon became the SS Special Detachment Berlin (Sonderkommando Berlin z.b.V.). Quickly turning into one of the more trustworthy auxiliary police units, it probably had much to do with the SS becoming the sole source of political police auxiliaries under Goering and Diels. In this way, Dietrich's Sonderkommando *Berlin* provided Himmler with an alternative to Daluege for influence in the SS contingent of the Gestapo.[3] Each was available to some degree, and when one was too independent, the other might be more cooperative. Even beyond Prussia, Himmler capitalized on the pattern set by the Sonderkommando Berlin. In the following months, similar SS *Sonderkommando* and political alarm squads (*politische Bereitschaften*) appeared elsewhere as political police auxiliaries, and, as in Prussia, often established connections with the political police that survived the dissolution of other auxiliaries.[4] In so doing, they augmented Himmler's thrusts beyond Bavaria.

By the fall of 1933, those thrusts began to produce results, as the political police of the other states fell under Himmler's command like a line of dominoes. First came Hamburg, Luebeck, Mecklenburg-Schwerin; then, in December, Anhalt, Baden, Bremen, Hessia, Thuringia, and Wuerttemberg; and in January 1934, Brunswick, Oldenburg and Saxony completed the line. Only Goering's Prussia and its tiny enclaves, Lippe and Schaumburg-Lippe, remained.[5]

Historians have several explanations for Himmler's success. Some contend he must have had Frick's support as part of the alliance against Roehm, although Frick denied this and had good reason to oppose Himmler's expansion.[6] Some have also presumed that Himmler had Hitler's backing in these developments.[7] Although Himmler clearly tried to give the impression of Hitler's support while negotiating for command in some of the states, he achieved it on his own without the active support of either Frick or Hitler.[8] His victories resulted from a long campaign that won him the cautious and vacillating consent of those directly below Hitler—like Hess—who had reason to support a centralization of authority at the expense of the independent elements of the Revolution. Since each of the appointments involved only a small detective branch in a single little state, they hardly required the Fuehrer's attention, nor would they have attracted anyone else's until their cumulative effect appeared. Whatever support Himmler got from above came only as he proved he could succeed.

From the beginning Himmler could count on the widely held presumption that the SS would play a police role in the Third Reich. For example, when the Brunswick government planned to consolidate its police organization in June 1933, the minister of the interior, Dietrich Klagges, wrote Himmler that he had heard of Reichsleitung guidelines on the takeover and reorganization of the police that apparently gave some preference to the SS. He asked if the intentions of his government in this area were appropriate.[9]

Since there are no copies of, or other references to, these alleged guidelines, since SA Brigadier General Sauke was the intended appointee of the Brunswick faction, and since the position went to Munich-based SS leader Friedrich Jeckeln after Klagges consulted with Himmler, Klagges may have been creating a pretext to avoid Sauke. Such a pretext had the advantage of credibility, and Himmler would obviously have cooperated, but this incident proves nothing about support for Himmler's acquisitions. In no other state for which records survive is there any indication that Himmler had a voice in police command appointments before autumn 1933. In some cases he undoubtedly had an input but, as in Brunswick, even the appointment of a locally favored SS man guaranteed no direct influence for Himmler. For instance, Jeckeln was more Klagges's man than Himmler's.

Regardless, Himmler exploited this and every other opportunity. As early as May he began touring SS units all over Germany, established or strengthened personal contacts with local political leaders, and cultivated bonds between the SS and the political police. Although he progressed unevenly, he carefully nurtured his gains, apparently avoiding premature bids so as not to alert the opposition. Then, in the fall, he gathered the small states quickly.

The First Fruits

In Hamburg, his first coup, many clues explain Himmler's success, all based on three factors: the SS image, its ability to attract useful members, and Himmler's personal diplomacy.

By early March, through a combination of local NS pressure and Frick's authority as Reich Minister, the Nazis broke SPD influence in the Hamburg police command, and on March 5, SA Colonel Alfred Richter became Reich commissioner of the police. The takeover began immediately with the appointment of former Police Lieutenant Colonel Ernst Simon as commander of the uniformed police. Both Richter and Simon were former Hamburg policemen, Simon being the most recently relieved, due to his notorious NS cell building during 1932. Knowing the Hamburg force intimately, they led the purge, eventually removing approximately one hundred.[10]

In a similar manner, the political police fell to local Nazis and NS policemen. The Hamburg State Police, as they were called, were a division of the detective force, or Kriminalpolizei. On the morning of March 6, Richter began their coordination, turning command over to Anatol Milewski-Schroeden, who had run the information service of the local *Gau* (Ermittlungsdienst der Gauleitung Hamburg der NSDAP). The Hamburg State Police had consisted of fifty-six officials and a twelve-

man search-and-arrest team (Fahndungskommando), few of whom required purging. Having no real experience in such work, Schroeden
relied heavily on Detective Peter Kraus, who took over the search team
and began rounding up KPD members. Kraus, a pro-NS policeman, and
his men now had complete freedom of action and unleashed a pent-up
energy that earned them an evil reputation among Communists and
Socialists.[11]

As in Prussia, local Nazis and trusted professional policemen ran
things, and Himmler had no ready-made entrée. Only a few qualified
officials were SS men. On March 15, one of the first acts of the NS-
dominated Senate created an auxiliary police that began functioning
within a week with the usual ratio of SA, SS, and Stahlhelm.[12] In the
explosive atmosphere of March and April, the situation got out of hand.
The SA took the initiative, and policemen and auxiliary teams got free
rein, resulting, as elsewhere, in competition among factions and a lack
of coordination. Perhaps Himmler capitalized on such conditions by
offering SS reliability and the Bavarian model as the solution to Hamburg's problems.

From the Nazi perspective, the problem was an establishment inadequate to destroy the KPD and other "enemies." The Hamburg State
Police could conduct the defensive police practices of the Republic, but
an NS revolution demanded openly offensive action, at least in terms
of numbers arrested. As head of the State Police, Milewski-Schroeden
lacked experience, and he drew constant criticism from Party and state
circles. As a result, on May 15 Police Captain Walter Abraham took his
place, becoming head of an enlarged, reorganized State Police, removed
from the regular detective force and set directly under Police Senator
Richter, the political head of the Hamburg police.[13]

Long before this administratively more proper solution, on March
24 the chief of the uniformed police, Simon, created his own Kommando
z.b.V. Originally consisting of thirty-six police officials under Police Lieutenant Frank Kosa, it soon included auxiliaries, the most notorious of
whom were SA-men. Although this team made raids and arrests for the
State Police, its subordination to Simon created problems of control, and
its methods led to a number of embarrassing incidents for NS state
officials. At first, leaders like Reichsstatthalter Kaufmann praised the
commando for its "efficiency," but as incidents mounted, they began to
feel the need for better controls. SA-men went directly to the commando
with denunciations, and given only strained conspiratorial theories and
circumstantial evidence, Kosa acted without much coordination with the
State Police. Since such denunciations often involved state officials, considerable conflict ensued. Furthermore, the commando's reckless action
resulted in legal suits and provided anti-NS propaganda about sadistic

interrogation methods. Himmler's people could build convincing arguments for the need to bring such excesses under control.[14]

The concentration camps posed other problems. During March and April, 1,315 official arrests filled detention facilities to overflowing. A wing of the correctional institution at Fuhlsbuettel set aside for political internees soon housed 478. This expensive arrangement allowed the internees to sit around indulging in political discourse, which NS circles criticized as coddling enemies while the state financed their political intrigues. Given general agreement that political internees should earn their keep, in April Hamburg officials built their first concentration camp at Wittmoor in a peat processing plant. But since this small operation never housed more than 140 internees, the problem remained unresolved. With both of these facilities entirely under regular police and penal authorities, a reasonable degree of propriety reigned, with only incidental brutality until late summer.[15]

By the time that considerable dissatisfaction over political police work and the handling of political prisoners had developed, Himmler had a number of allies in Hamburg to present his case. His road to power would be neither smooth nor straight, however, for his forces remained uncoordinated and occasionally too obvious in their approach. The SD constituted the major problems in this respect.

According to Heydrich's wife, one of Heydrich's men in the Hamburg area, Karl Oberg, had sought the command of the State Police, but could not get along with Gauleiter Kaufmann. If Kaufmann had distrusted Oberg and the local SD, his suspicions were confirmed when in May he uncovered Funke's spy ring.[16] Kaufmann's fury made the SD counterproductive for Himmler's immediate purposes in Hamburg. To offset the SD blunder, Himmler could capitalize on his personal relationship with Kaufmann, for they had been close friends (*Duzbruder*) since 1927. Kaufmann apparently felt some obligation to Himmler, who had helped him in conflicts with von Pfeffer and Goebbels,[17] and probably did not consider the SD actions as treachery by Himmler. The incident could be attributed to uncontrolled locals, and Himmler undoubtedly hastened to reassure Kaufmann.

Himmler made several trips to Hamburg, not just to soothe Kaufmann but to further his influence. In so doing, he established allies who must have looked upon him as a beneficial contact and upon his SS as offering solutions to local political police problems. One such ally seems to have been the head of the Senate, Buergermeister Carl Vincent Krogmann. Although in March 1933 he had not yet joined the Party, Krogmann got his high post through his involvement in the Keppler circle. Himmler, who courted Keppler's business contacts, had put in a word for Krogmann with the reluctant Hitler.[18] Another ally, Dr. Hans Nieland, had become police president on March 14. According to Nieland, during the summer Himmler had personally drawn him into the SS with the rank of major. If so, the appointment remained a secret, for Himmler did not process any papers until after his appointment in Hamburg, when he fulfilled his promise retroactively and rapidly promoted Nieland to colonel. Nieland represented an early pro-Himmler influence at the head of the police, and later, as senator for finance, he would insure financial support for the local SS.[19]

By October, with such a power base, Himmler was well entrenched, as two new appointments clearly revealed. On October 7, Nieland, who had been called to the Senate in May, turned his police officer over to SA Colonel Wilhelm Boltz. Not an ordinary SA man, Boltz commanded the Hamburg SA Marine Squadron and stood on good terms with Himmler and Heydrich.[20]

The most significant of these October appointments, however, was SS Major Bruno Streckenbach. Although his background in business hardly gave him any special credentials, he won the favor of Kaufmann, who later noted that Streckenbach's "special suitability and talents" recommended him for a "leading post in the Hamburg police." On October 5, he became government counselor (*Regierungsrat*), and on October 20 he replaced Abraham as head of the Hamburg State Police.[21] Streckenbach's appointment may have marked Himmler's direct acquisition of the Hamburg political police as early as October. Himmler officially became commander only on November 24, but such delays in formalizing realities were typical. Regardless, clear influence began with Streckenbach's appointment, for that SS-man was no Daluege, and he allegedly traveled promptly to Munich to study the Bavarian system under Heydrich.[22]

In gaining Kaufmann's support, Himmler should have had little trouble convincing his old friend of continued loyalty and, most significant, Himmler could argue that a position of local state authority would enable him to control the local SS and SD more tightly. To wrap things up, he made Kaufmann an honorary SS general (*Oberfuehrer*), and Kaufmann's personal associate in the *Gau* Leadership, Senator Georg Ahrens, an SS colonel in the SD. The availability of suitable local SS men whom Kaufmann trusted gave Kaufmann a sense of sharing control with Himmler: a local man, Streckenbach, a known element, would actually run the Hamburg State Police, and in so doing would also keep the local SD in line. Toward that end, Streckenbach, like Ahrens, became a member of the Hamburg SD, facilitating its return to smooth operations in that city.[23]

In Streckenbach's efforts to copy Himmler's model of the system that combined SS with political police and concentration camps, he had two major problems: the concentration camps under the penal office, and the Kommando z.b.V. under the chief of uniformed police.

Previous developments had laid the foundations for an incomplete victory over the camps. Under increased pressure to see that political prisoners were handled "more properly," and impressed by the SS camps at Dachau and Boergermoor in Westphalia, Kaufmann had called on the Twenty-Eighth SS-Standarte to guard the facilities at Fuhlsbuettel and turn it into a concentration camp. To strengthen the regime and retain state control, he put the guard and the camp under the penal authority, whose provisional head, Max Lahts, would guarantee a severe regime.[24] SS Lieutenant Dusenschoen, head of the SS guard, carried out Lahts's orders for a stringent new regime, and his men immediately displayed the most infamous traits of SS camp guards. The commandant under the penal office was a mere figurehead; Dusenschoen actually ran things. Fuhlsbuettel rapidly became publicly notorious, generating concern at all levels. Guards made free use of their rifles to enforce petty rules, and sadistic torture was so common that many inmates sought escape in suicide.[25]

Once again, uncontrolled local SS behavior created a situation that inadvertently played into Himmler's hands. Effective December 1, to bring it under control, the camp guard was placed under the authority of Streckenbach's State Police. The transfer was incomplete, however, because the Fuhlsbuettel facilities themselves remained under the control of the penal office, which successfully argued that the Dachau system could not be made to work in this environment. Thus the SS-police-camp system remained incomplete in Hamburg. However, Himmler skirted the issue the following summer after he took over the Prussian camps. Fuhlsbuettel returned to regular police control, and his police sent their political internees to Prussian camps.[26]

Streckenbach was able to resolve the other problem, the Kommando z.b.V. more completely. The logic of centralized and uniform control was overwhelming, and the bad reputation of the commando led to its dissolution on Streckenbach's recommendation. He absorbed twenty-eight members into the State Police, and returned the remainder to the uniformed police.[27]

Meanwhile, the neighboring city of Luebeck and state of Mecklenburg had become Himmler's next prizes, although his official appointments as commander of their political police forces actually preceded formal accession in Hamburg. The process has yet to be elaborated, but it seems to have been similar. For instance, although the *Reichsstatthalter* for both governments, Friedrich Hildebrandt, was not on close terms with Himmler, he became an honorary SS brigadier general.[28]

In Mecklenburg, where the Nazis had participated in the government since July 1932, they and their allies had quickly created a political section in the State Criminal Police Office (*Schwerin*). Here the Streck-enbach role as trusted insider was played by Ludwig Oldach, a forty five-year-old, high civil servant with twenty-six years' service in justice and finance for both state and federal agencies. As an Old Fighter, he had become *Kreisleiter* and NS member of the State Assembly. Himmler's appointment undoubtedly included an understanding that Oldach would become head of the Mecklenburg Political Police, which he did on November 15, 1933. He had become a candidate for SS membership in September, and was officially admitted as a lieutenant on November 1.[29] How he moved into this relationship with Himmler remains unclear; however, the availability of this insider certainly facilitated Himmler's appointment, since Oldach, a known quantity with Hildebrandt and other locals, would be doing the real work in Mecklenburg.

The rapid succession of announcements from Luebeck, Mecklenburg, and Hamburg produced a snowball effect in the remaining Hansa lands. Meanwhile, Himmler had been at work in the local power struggles, aligning himself effectively so that when the time came, he would have allies. In Bremen, they stood at the very top. Frick had appointed Dr. Richard Markert as Reich commissioner for Bremen, and on March 8 Markert established the usual auxiliary police and named as chief of police (*Polizeipraesident*) the local businessman Theodor Laue, an SA major. In these moves Markert also had the support of the local *Gauleiter* and later *Reichsstatthalter*, Carl Roever. Laue was their man, for he had conflicts with the more radical elements of the local SA.[30]

Bremen already had an adequate political police, now directly under the authority of Laue. In June, this Central Police Post (*Z-Stelle*), as it was called, was rechristened the Secret State Police. Under the uninterrupted leadership of Police Captain Heinrich Kruse, the political policemen worked well for the new NS regime. Typically, most of them had been political conservatives and nationalists, and some inclined toward Nazism.[31] Although none of these political policemen became official members of the Party before 1933, NS and SS penetration had begun as early as 1931. For instance, police Lieutenant Erwin Schulz, a member of the intelligence section of the political police, was a crypto-Nazi, working conspiratorially for SA Leader Paul Wegener (later *Kreisleiter*) and the SS.[32]

Meanwhile, developments in Bremen paralleled those in the rest of the Reich, and the excesses and tensions of 1933 had their local effect. Both the professional police and local Party leaders like Roever and Markert felt the pressure of Party radicalism, especially in the SA. After a visit in May, Himmler had developed contacts in Bremen, and a crisis that occurred in October benefited him. As a result of Laue's breach with the local SA general, Roehm expelled him from the SA without a hearing. If he did not already belong to Himmler's camp, this drew Laue in, for Himmler became Laue's champion, initially working for his reinstatement in the SA, with whom Himmler still tried to maintain close working relations.[33]

By the end of November, Laue and Markert, still supported by Frick, had clearly allied with Himmler. On November 28, Laue notified the Senate of Himmler's appointments in the other Hansa states and stated that Burgermeister Markert would discuss the matter with Reichsstatthalter Roever. They clearly capitalized on the bandwagon effect. On December 14, Roever consented, and Markert contacted Himmler, who accepted immediately. On December 22, the Senate learned that Himmler would become commander of the political police of Bremen, effective the next day.[34] Meanwhile, on November 13, Schulz had taken de facto command of the Bremen Secret State Police. In May 1934, this position became official, and he remained to become head of the Gestapo in Bremen, which remained for some time only nominally under Himmler's command.[35]

The appointment in Bremen apparently led to that in Oldenburg, for on January 5 Roever named Himmler commander in both states. Unfortunately, details about the Oldenburg appointment may never be known, because the relevant documents are lost.[36]

Meanwhile, Himmler had been accumulating other appointments, working on the states of the south, where his first fruits appeared in Wuerttemberg. His itinerary of May tours had included Stuttgart, and from that time he wooed the Gauleiter and Reichsstatthalter Wilhelm Murr. There too, after the March elections, SA and SS auxiliary police had gone into action under the Reich commissioner, SA General Dietrich von Jagow. The usual excesses followed, resulting in efforts to normalize police functions while ensuring that they came under proper NS leadership. Toward this end, on April 28, an old NS member, Amtsrichter Dr. Mattheiss, formed the Wuerttemberg Political Police from the former political detectives in the state.[37]

As elsewhere, the SS Auxiliary Police, operating under Special Commissioner SS Colonel Robert Zeller, were attached to the political police, but in a more direct manner than usual, for Zeller became an assistant to Mattheiss. These SS auxiliaries, soon designated political alarm squads (Bereitschaften), survived the later efforts to dissolve the regular auxiliaries. Over a year later, Murr would recall that Himmler had convinced him of the desirability of having commandos for "special actions" for which one could not trust the regular non-NS police. Somewhere along the way, Himmler had also given the impression that Hitler favored such a close SS–political police relationship.[38]

This case illustrates how the *Leibstandarte* model benefited Himmler. Hitler's creation of this special SS unit, and its role in Berlin, facilitated SS work elsewhere and gave Himmler a claim to Hitler's support, proba bly well beyond anything Hitler actually said. Himmler thus had a strong image with amenable local leaders like Murr. As 1933 wore on, Murr encouraged organizational developments in his political police that secured for Himmler "most extensive influence," or at least so Murr later claimed.[39]

In fact, Himmler's early influence remained limited. As a local SS leader, Zeller had closer ties to Murr than to Himmler, and Himmler may have accepted Zeller's independence in order to build bridges with Murr. Murr himself maintained a direct personal interest in the political police until shortly before Himmler assumed the title of commander.[40] For their part, Mattheiss and his supporters in the state ministries developed a resistance to meddling in the political police by either Murr or Himmler. Influence, not control, characterized Himmler's relationship in Wuerttemberg, and it could not have been overly extensive.

Even SS penetration among key political policemen grew gradually, having little significance either before Himmler's appointment or immediately thereafter. For instance, on May 24 Dr. Walter Stahlecker, later Himmler's head of the Wuerttemberg Political Police, was quickly called as deputy leader of the Political Police. He had tenuous NS and SS affiliations, for his actual SS initiation may have resembled that of Nieland in Hamburg, the 1932 date of his membership being set retroactively. Regardless, Stahlecker was as much Murr's man as Himmler's, and he became Murr's trusted agent. In addition to his political police position, he served as the special commissioner of the *Reichsstatthalter* until November 21, when Murr transferred him to Berlin to serve as his representative at the Reich capital.[41]

On December 9, Murr named Himmler commander of the Wuerttemberg Political Police. Subsequently, the press described the appointment as the realization of a fact that had existed organizationally for several months, and proclaimed it as a guarantee that the will of the Fuehrer would be fulfilled uniformly throughout the Reich.[42] Murr apparently made this move entirely on his own, without signs of any opposition. Perhaps everyone saw it largely as an act of NS camaraderie, for Mattheiss remained the actual head of the political police, to the apparent satisfaction of the subsequent opposition to Murr and Himmler. Meanwhile, Murr probably had concrete reasons for turning to Himmler. The expensive auxiliary police and the costs of maintaining their excessive numbers of protective custody internees was bankrupting the state. Since September, the finance minister had made such an issue of the matter that Murr, Minister of Interior Schmid, and State Minister

Morgenthaler had to find a solution. Furthermore, the impending demise of the auxiliary police simultaneously threatened the loss of proper no influence in the police. Consequently, with an eye toward Himmler's successful model next door in Bavaria, Murr decided Himmler could best handle their problem of political police and concentration camps.[43]

Mattheiss remained the local head, undoubtedly to keep Morgenthaler and the other locals happy, but that could not last. Himmler's entrenchment, which took several months, came only after he had taken control of the other state political police, including those of Prussia. Meanwhile, friction developed between Mattheiss and the SS, and he, an SA officer, maintained SA links with the political police. Furthermore, as the rivalry of Morgenthaler and Schmid against Murr increased, the SA courted them as well. Himmler backed the right horse by supporting Murr, who replaced Mattheiss with Stahlecker on May 11, 1934. Stahlecker and Himmler had become well aligned, both being in Berlin while the conspiratorial tensions came to a head. Morgenthaler protested in vain against Mattheiss's dismissal and turned to Frick, where he found support, but all this foundered on Murr's determination. The political police leadership was purged; for instance, a Dr. Roller (deputy leader and a Morgenthaler-Frick candidate for command) was replaced by Dr. Wilhelm Harster, a recent SS recruit. The fact that Mattheiss soon became one of the victims of the Roehm purge indicates the heat of the struggle.[44] It would seem that Himmler's ultimate victory in Wuerttemberg also related to the alignment of Party forces against Roehm.

As in the north, Himmler's appointment in Wuerttemberg precipitated similar announcements in neighboring states. In the adjacent Land of Baden, Reichsstatthalter Robert Wagner fell in line on December 18. Although the details of that victory may never emerge, it seems to fit the general pattern. Karl Pflaumer became state commissioner in Baden on March 9, Minister of the Interior on May 6, and nine days later, at Wagner's request, Himmler drew him into the SS as a colonel. The SD leader for the South West, Werner Best, handled negotiations, guaranteeing Wagner's continued influence in political police affairs, actually run by his friend, Karl Berckmueller.[45]

Meanwhile, Frick's staff had taken notice of Himmler's appointments and generated a report that gave no indication of pressures from above for Himmler's appointments; rather, it implied local initiative. It attributed the appointments to "the effort for the concentration and unification of the political police of the states." Although the Movement had generally supported such developments in the name of law and order, a combination of legalism, regionalism, and local Party leaders had thwarted progress. Nevertheless, it seemed so desirable and inevitable that some state officials took the initiative to effect progress, establishing contact with Frick's ministry;[46] others, like Himmler's allies, preferred some branch of the Movement as the appropriate vehicle.

Essentially, this report to Frick proposed the creation of a "Secret Reich Police" with an appropriate central office, and there seemed to be an air of urgency about it. The chief of the Secret Reich Police was to be the minister of the interior, Frick, while the real management would be the responsibility of a state secretary. Aside from the personnel of the Secret Reich Police Office, the only Reich officials would be the inspectors of the Secret Reich Police, the respective heads of each state political police. Otherwise, the states would continue to maintain and man the state and field offices. Although the proposal sought to capitalize on the initiative already taken by the states, it indicated a desire to head off further faits accomplis. This contradicts the hypothesis that Frick supported Himmler's appointments,[47] although perhaps he offered Himmler the post of state secretary in order to tap into his momentum, and Himmler would have strung him along until it was too late. But this is pure speculation. Instead, according to Gisevius, at about this time Frick sought vainly to forbid further state governments from appointing Himmler.[48] In fact, Frick did make one such belated effort, unfortunately of little significance.

Frick's move came in the states of Lippe and Schaumburg-Lippe, tiny enclaves of Prussia, which partially explains the success. Both states had small police establishments, and relied upon cooperation with Prussia, especially in political police work, to ensure law and order. Nevertheless, the NS takeover brought about the usual concern over "political enemies," producing almost ludicrous results. For instance, by January 1934 Lippe had a staff of fifteen political policemen, almost twenty percent of the state's total police establishment.[49] The relatively slow pace of life in Lippe and its ties with Prussia help explain why SS penetration was retarded. The bond with Prussia led the Lippe government to call upon Prussian Police Captain Otto Hellwig to command its state police. Hellwig soon incorporated the political police under his command,[50] where they remained under professional leadership. Nothing indicates support for Himmler within either the police or state government. The pressure came from the local SS and through the *Reichsstatthalter*, Dr. Alfred Meyer, who held the same position in Schaumburg-Lippe. (The process there remains undocumented, but the pattern was apparently the same as in Lippe.)

For an undetermined period, the local SS commander in Lippe had been pressing State Minister Hans-Joachim Riecke to appoint Himmler; however, Riecke had simply responded that it was "out of the question." Meanwhile, Meyer must have come under similar pressures, perhaps from Himmler, for on December 20, armed with the list of Himmler's appointments and the recent announcement from Baden, he asked Riecke if similar action was not appropriate in Lippe. To this official pressure, Riecke responded that it was now suitable.[51] He may have reversed himself because of other appointments exerted pressure for NS solidarity, and because Meyer may have seemed in favor. However, since both men stood closer to SA circles than SS, neither took action, and they stalled while the remainder of the little states fell in line. Perhaps Riecke also knew about Frick's attitude, for in February, in response to renewed pressure through the local SS commander, he recommended that Meyer refer the matter to Frick. With the support of Frick's Ministry, Riecke and Meyer delayed final action until June 1934, by which time the fall of Prussia had made the whole affair meaningless.[52]

Wrapping Up the Package

Despite these little bars to his progress, Himmler brought the other states into his fold. After Baden, the states of Anhalt, Hessia, Thuringia, and Bremen fell rapidly in line.[53] In the case of Anhalt, the lack of available documents prevents detailed descriptions, but penetration definitely occurred at the top level. There, as a result of early electoral victories, a Nazi, Dr. Alfred Freyberg, had been Prime Minister since April 1932. Himmler drew him into the SS in November 1933 as a lieutenant colonel and *Rangfuehrer* (an honorary position) in the local regiment. Although this may have begun as just another of Himmler's nominal appointments to woo key men, it apparently developed into much more. By April 1934, Freyburg had become a member of the SD, indicating closer involvement in Himmler's plans.[54] The *Reichsstatthalter*, Wilhelm Loeper, was equally amenable, for shortly after Himmler's appointment as commander of the political police, he accepted honorary SS rank as a lieutenant general. Himmler then turned to SS Lieutenant Otto Sens to form the Anhalt Secret State Police as a special division of the State Ministry.[55] From this date, SS dominance ensued.

Unfortunately, lack of surviving documentation prevents reconstruction of SS penetration in Hessia. Local developments did, however, introduce a new character who would become central to the shaping of Sipo and SD. With the NS power seizure in March, Government Counselor Dr. Karl Rudolf Werner Best became special commissioner for the Hessian Police. This twenty-nine-year-old, law-trained civil servant, destined to become second man in Sipo and SD, was at the time only nominally an SS man, recruited in November 1931, allegedly because the SS wanted him to wear its uniform in the Landtag. An insignificant member, he only earned noncommissioned SS rank after he gained police power, which he won purely because of his personal standing among local NS leaders. During the spring, Himmler remained too preoccupied, or for other reasons was unable, to exploit the potential link with Hessia, for, according to Best, he had liaison with him on only a few minor official matters.[56]

As a result of a rift between Gauleiter and Reichsstatthaler Jakob Sprenger and the faction to which Best belonged, around the end of October Sprenger's faction shunted Best out of office.[57] Himmler, by now looking for qualified policemen, drafted Best to begin his more significant career elsewhere. These events provide no insight into how Himmler got Sprenger to accept him as commander of the Hessian Political Police on December 20. Thereafter, his control over them remained nominal until their absorption into Sipo in 1936. Before that, SS penetration occurred only at the lowest levels, mostly employees drawn in from the SS Special Commandos. Only one of these, SS Corporal Friedrich Berges, became a detective employee (*Kriminal-Angestellter*); the rest remained office helpers and drivers. SD penetration began only in June 1935, when Berges and his people entered the SD and formed a post in the Stapo-Darmstadt. As late as February 1936, the head of the Gestapo Office Darmstadt, Dr. Schulze, seems to have been cool toward the SD and apparently remained ignorant of its penetration.[58]

Lack of documentation also obscures the story of Thuringia, but advanced penetration clearly occurred at the upper levels. Since April 1933, the police president of Weimar had been SS Major Dr. Walter Ortlepp, an Old Fighter and jurist who had served with the state prosecutor's office and in state courts. In 1930, when Frick took over the Thuringian police, Ortlepp became his head of the State Criminal Police. In the following year, Ortlepp transferred from the SA to the SS and, as soon as he became police president, jumped to the rank of major. As elsewhere, although Himmler was named commander on December 20, Ortlepp (by now SS lieutenant colonel) actually ran the office as Himmler's deputy, and built the Thuringian Secret State Police Office in Weimar largely from Police Presidium personnel. Again, Himmler's control matured gradually. Ortlepp's deputy, however, was Detective Max Rausch, a recent recruit to the SS and head of an SD post in the Weimar Office.[59] There Heydrich's SD made more open headway.

In January, the remaining states joined Himmler's list, beginning with Oldenburg. The other two, however—Saxony and Brunswick—represented more severe problems, for SS people involved in local politics retarded Himmler's progress. In Saxony, for one, the SD helped overcome the resistance, but did not play the decisive role. Saxony was the seat of the well-established SD Group South East under Lothar Beutel. In the summer of 1933, the local NS regime had built its Secret State

Police Office as an independent central authority under the Saxon ministry of interior. Meanwhile, the SD had won a fairly new Party member who had the proper credentials for a high position in police work. Since 1932 a V-man for the SS Ic, Dr. Herbert Mehlhorn officially joined the SS and SD in March 1933 at the age of thirty. As a doctor of jurisprudence with government experience, he could provide NS influence in the new Saxon Secret Police, so on September 1 he became deputy chief in charge of their administration. At the same time, SS Ic man Horst Boehme also began work with the Secret State Police. The SD link tightened when Mehlhorn became staff officer of SD Regional Office Middle (SD Oberabschnitt Mitte), and Boehme became head of SD District Office Dresden (SD Abschnitt II).[60] Nevertheless, although such SD penetration gave him internal influence, how Himmler got Reichsstatthalter Martin Mutschmann to give in remains unexplained.

A combination of pressure from above and creeping penetration from below apparently weakened the resistance of the Party lord and his independent local SS leader. The Saxon Secret Police were under the command of SS Brigadier General Fritz Schlegel of SS Superior Region *Mitte*. Although he cooperated enough to appoint Mehlhorn on Himmler's recommendation, he made no great concession, for Mehlhorn possessed badly needed administrative expertise and was the protégé of local Party leaders. Furthermore, Schlegel resisted Himmler's dominance and, according to Mehlhorn, preferred to cooperate with Diels in Prussia. To break this resistance, Himmler took direct action. In August, after a breach, Himmler moved against Schlegel for dereliction of duty in command of his SS area. On September 6, he relieved him of his SS command and assigned him *z.b.V.* to SS Group South East. Like Daluege, but with greater severity and humiliation, Schlegel lost his local SS power base.[61] When Reichsstatthalter Mutschmann finally consented to Himmler's appointment in early December, he apparently considered it more of a nominal bow to NS camaraderie than a relegation of real control to Himmler. Although Schlegel subsequently wrote letters pledging eternal loyalty to Himmler as his superior in both state and SS, his hold over the Secret Police remained firm. Himmler's full control was delayed until 1936 when, simultaneous with Schlegel's death, he created Sipo. Meanwhile, Mutschmann continually interfered in the Secret Police. According to Melhorn, he constantly had conflicts with Mutschmann, who finally drove him out of Saxony in mid-1935, threatening to have him arrested.[62]

While the Saxon appointment remains unexplained, the Brunswick appointment reveals a crystallization of support for Himmler, who by early January had abandoned hope for Brunswick, an enclave inside Prussia like the Lippes.[63] In Brunswick, he had an early entree with the appointment of Jeckeln, Munich-based commander of the SS Group South, as head of the Brunswick Political Police. Then the previously described rivalry within his own SS nearly cost him the command. The alleged Heydrich-Jeckeln rivalry, the August exposure of SD intrigues that implicated not only Heydrich and his SD but even Himmler, and Klagges's furious counterattack, all make Himmler's appointment in Brunswick seem amazing.

Apparently he had support from above; for instance, he worked through Reichsstatthalter Loeper, whom he had recently won over in Anhalt. On January 19, Loeper notified Klagges that Himmler had renewed his request that Brunswick fall in line with Anhalt. He noted that Saxony was already completing arrangements, but most significant, he emphasized that the Reich Party Leadership had recommended ("*empfohlen hat*") Himmler's appointment. By this time, the circle around Hess had definitely begun to support Himmler's efforts.[64] They had peacefully settled Klagges's charges and persuaded Hitler to preserve the SD. By entrenching Himmler's police power and pulling together amenable *Gauleiter*, they were building a coalition.

Meanwhile, Himmler had obviously paved the way with Klagges as well, for he soon became one of the honorary SS generals. Since Himmler could blame the SD scandal on overzealous, irresponsible locals, he may have convinced Klagges that he represented no threat, and from at least this time, the two resumed good personal relations.[65] Nevertheless, Klagges made no great concession on January 23 when he made the appointment, for Himmler's command of the political police remained largely titular, a matter of establishing nationwide coordination and preserving the image of NS solidarity. SS General and Police Lieutenant Colonel Jeckeln continued to head the Braunschweig Political Police for several years, and as part of building his bridges, Himmler had entrenched Jeckeln's SS power by making him commander of the local SS superior region, effective August 10, 1933.[66] As elsewhere, establishing tighter control over the Braunschweig Political Police came later.

Although the little states contributed significantly to Himmler's goal of becoming Reich political police chief, their importance should not be overrated. Most were small forces. Furthermore, in the case of many, like Baden, Bremen, Brunswick, Hessia, and Saxony, local NS lords hedged Himmler's powers, for he remained technically their subordinate. Not until after he became Reich police chief in 1936 did such subordination become nominal; he and Heydrich had to build the independent power of the Gestapo slowly and patiently. In these initial penetrations, the SD played a minimal role. A well-placed negotiator, like Best, helped in Baden, as did SD penetration in Saxony. But in most cases of successful SS penetration, the men involved did not enter the

SD until later, in Bremen and Wuerttemberg only in 1934 or 1935. True, Sens (Anhalt) became a local SD leader within a couple of months of Himmler's appointment, and Rausch provided open SD liaison in Thuringia; however, Streckenbach's case may provide the explanation. In Hamburg, the SD had been so discredited with the Gauleiter that only Streckenbach's affiliation with the SD could establish goodwill. The SD benefited more from the process than it contributed to it.

As for how Himmler got the local NS lords to appoint him, nothing indicates direct support from Hitler. Except for Brunswick, in every case where the arguments of Himmler's supporters survive, they mention no outside support. Himmler worked entirely from within or through amenable *Gauleiter* and *Reichsstatthalter*. Only as late as January in Brunswick is Reichsleitung support mentioned, although that may also explain Saxony and Hessia. If Hitler had given his support, Himmler's supporters would have made note of it, for that would have been significant. Furthermore, for Hitler to give decisive support to one faction would have been out of character, especially during this period. True, he increasingly welcomed counters against SA lawlessness, but it strains logic to argue that in late 1933 he saw a political police monopoly for Himmler as a solution. Instead, one must attribute Himmler's success to the desirability and inevitability of police centralization, to the image of Himmler and his SS, to his ability to win the services of men in key police positions or those with the credentials and contacts for such positions, to his personal diplomatic skills, and to the growing tension over the SA, which drove local and national Party leaders to see Himmler as a desirable foil.

An efficient police to combat the enemies of the nation was such an accepted part of NS propaganda that local leaders could not long ignore the logic of a unified political police command. Pressures for such centralization increased precisely because the Nazis claimed to support it. However, local leaders grew ever more hostile toward Frick's efforts at administrative centralization. Since Nazis harbored a deep hatred for bureaucracy even when they commanded it, many opposed Frick for ideological reasons as well as personal power considerations. Given their further distrust of the old police establishment, a centralized political police was a suspicious proposition.

Himmler at least offered a compromise. As agents of the Movement, he and his SS would deal "properly" with enemies. They were often better controlled than the SA, or at least seem to have had that reputation. In the Party's Reich Leadership, Himmler's SS had won this image before the power seizure. Where the local SS was less reliable, Himmler apparently promised to work with amenable *Gauleiter* and *Reichsstatthalter* to turn it into a useful tool if they would give him local police authority. Himmler could point to his Bavarian model as proof that he had the knowhow the local Nazis lacked.[67] As he had done when under fire in Bavaria, Himmler may have hinted of his dream of a state protection corps: a plan to replace police bureaucrats with the NS men of the future. As with Murr in Wuerttemberg, he may have *claimed* Hitler's support; all he need do to reinforce this claim was offer reminders of some of the Fuehrer's speeches about the SS mission. He could also point to the frequent occasions in Bavaria when Hitler's support, alleged or otherwise, had been decisive in blocking efforts to curb him. Successful checks on the SS, like Diels's in Berlin, were camouflaged by the image of Himmler's cooperation and approval—for instance, Diels's honorary SS rank and the extensive SS role in the Gestapo.

To local NS leaders, the mild-mannered Reichsfuehrer hardly seemed as threatening as Roehm and local SA leaders. When he promised personal loyalty, he embodied Reich centralization without threatening the NS locals' power—they could have their "political ideals" and local power too. As Werner Best remembers it, Himmler, the consummate tactician, recognized each *Reichsstatthalter* as his personal superior and promised to fulfill any condition, for at the moment the most important object was to win the titles to buttress his case in Berlin.[68]

Before the spring of 1934, probably during January, Himmler established a Central Office (Zentralbuero) in Munich to coordinate his separate commands. From this office Heydrich increasingly did the real work of coordinating the political police while the more tactful Himmler concentrated on building the power base.[69] Meanwhile, in Berlin, in his last big step, Himmler redoubled his penetration tactics. Here too, the SD played a significant, though not decisive, role, and some of the success hinged upon advanced recruitment into the SD of men with proper credentials for government offices. In 1932, in the Silesian province of Prussia, twenty-nine-year-old Dr. Guenther Patschowski joined the SS, then the SD. After the Nazis came to power, he became a logical recruit for the local Gestapo regional office.[70] Silesia was the domain of SA General Edmund Heines, who as police president of Breslau had made himself head of the Gestapo Regional Office there. Of course, he had turned the actual running of the office over to a qualified man he thought he could trust, Detective Inspector Dr. Emanuel Schaefer. Schaefer's new subordinate, Patschowski, recruited him as an SD "associate" (*Mitarbeiter*, an informal affiliation).[71] Early in 1933 the Silesian Gestapo thus came under the covert influence of Himmler and Heydrich, at a time when Berlin controlled that area minimally. From there they could build another road to Berlin.

By this time, Diels was expanding his facilities for combating sabotage and espionage, a traditional responsibility of the Berlin-based political police as a support for the Abwehr office of the military. Himmler and Heydrich would have known through their liaison man of Diels's plans to create a special division for this work and of his need for a suitable director. According to "Heinrich Orb" (a pseudonym), a traditional source for inside stories of the early Gestapo and SD, Himmler and Heydrich succeeded in placing Patschowski's name on the tongues of the Reichswehr people to whom Diels turned for a suggestion. Allegedly, SS General Udo von Woyrsch, SS Fuehrer South East, used his family connections in the military to boast of Patschowski's exploits as head of the counterespionage division.[72]

Whether these details are accurate or not, Diels drafted Patschowski into the Berlin office in November. When the reorganization created Division IV, Treason and Espionage, new Assistant Commissioner Patschowski was in charge. Through his close work with the Reichswehr, Patschowski could weaken some of Diels's support and pave the way for Himmler. With Nebe as head of Division III, at least two of Diels's four major working divisions at that point lay in the hands of his opposition.[73]

Photo Essays

A. The German Police Besieged: Events and Personalities, 1929-1932

Above: A posed photograph of the Prussian Schutzpolizei in action in the working-class neighborhood of Berlin-Neukoelln during the bloody May Day riots of 1929. Below: Police caught in a fight between the Red Front and Storm Troopers.

Unless otherwise stated, all photos are from the Bundesarchiv, Koblenz.

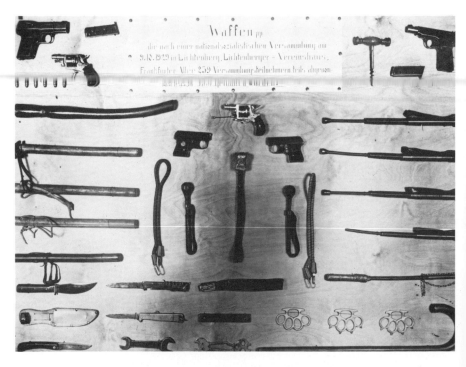

Above: A police display of captured Nazi weapons in 1929, an effort to reveal their threats to law and order and the security of the Republic. It is in marked contrast to the increasing emphasis on the threat from the left. Below: A police raid on NS offices. A Nazi propaganda photograph taken in Berlin during the SA prohibition, 13 April 1932.

The targets of the Papen Putsch (from left in the front rank): The popular commander of the Berlin Schutzpolizei, Police Colonel Magnus Heimannsberg, leader in the police reform movement and model of "the people's police officer," temporarily arrested on 20 July 1932; Berlin Police President Albert Greszinski, Severing's appointee, dismissed on 20 July; and Police Vice-President Dr. Bernhard Weiss, father of the new Prussian political police and modernizer of the detective force while their chief, also temporarily arrested on 20 July 1932. Both Greszinski and "Isidor" Weiss had been major targets of Goebbels' campaigns against "marxist-Jewish domination" of the Prussian police.

B. Spontaneous Terror: The Nazi Seizure of Power
in the Spring of 1933

A press release photograph of the NS party leadership at the time of Hitler's appointment as Reich Chancellor, 30 January 1933. Seated is Wilhelm Frick, new Reich minister of the interior and the only Nazi member of Hitler's cabinet with portfolio. Standing fourth from left is Joseph Goebbels, Reich propaganda leader and *gauleiter* of Berlin. At rear center, between Hitler and Goering, is Ernst Roehm, chief of staff of the SA. Hermann Goering is in trench coat, the only other NS cabinet member, as minister without portfolio. To the right of Goering stand Walter Darre, Himmler's mentor on blood and soil; Heinrich Himmler, still only Reichsfuehrer SS; and Rudolf Hess, party secretary.

Above: The NS Hilfspolizei, SA men acting as Auxiliary Police in Berlin, March 1933. Below: SS men being sworn in as Auxiliary Police.

Above: SA Auxiliary Police arrest Communists in Berlin, 6 March 1933, one day after the national elections. Below: SS Auxiliary Police ready for action in a police raid.

Right: SA guards outside Concentration Camp Oranienberg near Berlin.

Below: A roll call of internees inside Oranienberg.

Above: The police raid a Jewish quarter of Berlin in a search for "Communist leaflets and undesirable aliens," early April 1933. Below: SS guards at "Protective Custody Camp" Dachau near Munich, 24 May 1933.

10

Acquiring the Prussian Power Base

While Himmler's people nibbled away from within, the power struggle at the Reich level matured into a complex web of rivalries. Frick wanted to curb independent powers like Goering and Himmler and to subordinate their police to his ministry. Outside Prussia, Himmler, building his model of the efficient, unrestrained police state, strove to impose it on the Reich. Within Prussia, Goering had to defend his power base from Frick and Himmler and to parlay it into Reich-wide power. What was common to all three was a growing concern over Roehm and the SA. Others shared this concern: the Reich Party Leadership; many local Party leaders and conservatives in the Movement; and the conservative establishment in business, industry, the military, and government, including many professional police and bureaucrats. Since the realization of benefits to be won from the support of others escaped none of the competitors, by the spring of 1934 they all drew hesitantly, and with several reverses, into an uneasy alliance.

In these maneuvers, Goering's tactics are the most difficult to unravel because he was working his way through at least three options: the Second Revolution, represented by the SA; a silent, controlled revolution of the sort Himmler supported; and a conservative end to the revolution represented by Frick. More decisive than any ideological considerations were the threats each course posed for his position, which by now had made the SA option completely unacceptable. Since Goering inclined toward a controlled revolution, having SS support pleased him, but only if he could keep Himmler at arm's length. Goering had a healthy distaste for both Himmler and Heydrich, and if he could have had his way, they would never have moved to Berlin. Frick recalled a conversation from about this time in which Goering had said, "For God's sake, if Himmler takes over the police force in Prussia, he will kill all of us." Both of them shared low opinions of Heydrich because of the exposeés of SD spying against Goering as well as the *Gauleiter*.[1]

Since Goering needed Frick and other conservative allies to avoid too tight an embrace with the SS, he continued his complex game of working with Frick against their common enemies, while increasing the autonomy of his Gestapo as a check against loss of everything to Frick. The two had the common objective of controlling police powers, then being exercised indiscriminately, so by the beginning of 1934 they cooperated in opposing the trends toward police anarchy, limiting extraordinary police powers, and restoring an "appropriate" amount of individual rights and freedom. Although each clearly worked toward an NS police state, had they continued on their course the Third Reich might have remained a more traditional authoritarian dictatorship.

Unfortunately, the road toward the police state was a narrow, slippery slope, down which both men intended to travel. Even NS conservatives like Frick had no intention of limiting the power of the state to do what they considered necessary for "reasons of state."[2] Likewise, Goering dedicated himself to building a strong "inner political instrument of power" in the police. In this respect, he must have had a certain admiration for Himmler's model. He definitely tried to solve his Prussian police problems along the lines of the political police–SS–concentration camp relationship rather that through Frick's more bureaucratically centralized, legalistic approach. In settling on his course, Goering must have looked to Hitler for some clues. What he found was not only a studied indecisiveness about such internal struggles, but also a clear predilection for unlimited instruments of power like Himmler's model. As the buildup of pressure from the SA pushed Goering toward a radical solution, he had to balance his conservative allies against the need for instruments of power. The need prevailed in favor of Himmler's SS–police state. By March, with Frick revealing his limitations and Himmler showing his strengths, Goering settled on a compromise that brought Himmler and Heydrich to the Gestapo Office—the very course of action that before that time he had fought doggedly.

Maneuvering for Position

The year 1934 began with a seemingly united front by Goering and Frick against the abuse of extraordinary police power by both the SA and the SS. However, all first-hand accounts and sources paint a confusing picture of mixed motives and contradictory actions, especially at the Prussian level. Diels maneuvered against the SA and SS, while conservative government officials simultaneously fought not only against the SA and SS but also against Diels. To further complicate matters, Diels played some SS factions against others, while some of his conservative opponents established contacts with SS factions as well as with Frick.

Diels has left us contradictory impressions of his position at the center of this vortex. For instance, he contended that from his return in December until sometime in March, he got Goering to support his fight against NS excesses. From Hitler and Goering he got a Christmas amnesty for most concentration camp internees. On December 8, Goering announced the release of five thousand, giving Diels wide authority to select them. By the end of the year, supposedly only about twenty-eight hundred remained in the legal camps, which Diels claims to have begun dissolving. His version is partially supported by surviving documents and by publicity he arranged in March, boasting of the end of the camp at Brandenburg and the imminent dissolution of Sonnenberg, leaving only two others.[3]

Nevertheless, the claim of dissolving the camps was at best a half-truth. Indeed, old camps like Brandenburg and Sonnenburg could be phased out; they had been makeshift to begin with. More adequate and less easily compromised camps under construction would replace them. Esterwegen, Boergermoor, Neusustrum (the Paperburg complex), and Oberlangen joined the list of state camps. By February the camps already had a capacity of six thousand, with a projected increase of two thousand.[4] Even worse, these official state camps, which only recently had been brought under the command of Schupo officers, were being returned to the care of SS police auxiliaries. The extent of Diels's control over these developments is uncertain, but they conform with his previous suggestions of tightening working relations between the Gestapo and the SS.

In the reorganization of the Gestapo Office following Diels's return, and "executive" section no longer existed under Nebe. Instead, as part of the Gestapo Office, an SS Commando Gestapa under SS Brigadier General Henze had its headquarters at the old Columbia House, which remained an SS way station for Gestapo arrestees.[5] This relationship between the Gestapo and SS Columbia House clearly indicates that Diels at least tolerated its atrocities as part of his working arrangements with the SS.

The explanation for the complex Goering-Diels maneuvers must be that while they campaigned to eliminate SA power in police affairs, they intended their discipline of the SS to prepare it for a dual role as support for the Gestapo and as alternative to the SA. Nothing better explains why they broke up some SS camps, while others, like the Papenburg complex and Columbia House, remained as Gestapo instruments. For instance, in March 1934 Diels and his allies in the Prussian Prosecutor's Office succeeded in disbanding the notorious camp in Stettin run by SS

Major Joachim Hoffmann, also the veritable head of the Gestapo regional office (*Stapostelle Stettin*). They arrested Hoffmann and his cohorts, who had been appointees from Daluege's Berlin SS, and replaced them with professional police. Although the Stettin case was an example of uncontrolled "SS and Gestapo" abuses, while Hoffmann typified the independent local SS leader, Diels struck at the Stettin SS-Gestapo only to establish a reliable centralized political police instrument. Goering and Diels made no effort to break SS control, for their newly appointed police president was ex-police major SS Lieutenant Fritz Herrmann, another of Daluege's people, but one more accustomed to a disciplined working relationship.[6]

Diels's "subtle" tactics of playing all ends against the middle probably backfired. On the one hand, he built on his relationship with Roehm and Ernst and improved Gestapo-SA cooperation. On the other, he transparently sought to assure Daluege and Himmler of his loyal cooperation while trying to engineer actions to curb and control their SS.[7] Eventually, his duplicity may have discredited him even with Goering.

Meanwhile, in January, during Goering's housecleaning in Prussia, Frick also overplayed his hand. First he sent a notice to the state governments decrying the misuse of protective custody, demanding caution and due process, and specifically noting that protective custody was not to be used as a form of punishment. He focused his criticism on the situation in Bavaria,[8] where Himmler's continued, diligent prosecution of Germany's "enemies" gave Frick cause to escalate his attack. To curb protective custody abuse, he called for centralized control of all police under his ministry. He then complicated his relations with Goering when he proposed the Law on the Reconstruction of the Reich, which passed the Reichstag on January 30. On paper this law gave Frick, as Reich minister of the interior, power to exercise the authority that had formerly belonged to the federal states and the *Reichsstatthalter*, and to intervene in state (*Land*) affairs at will. Unfortunately for Frick, Hitler, who actually desired some such increase in central authority, would not back him in any real confrontation with the local NS leaders, who were Hitler's real base of power. Their resistance became especially apparent when on February 19 Frick tried to cement his authority by decreeing his command over the police forces of their states. The move apparently alarmed Goering despite Frick's continued proposal of Goering as chief of Reich Police. Frick thus created a common interest between Goering and Himmler, who had many "allies" in nullifying his maneuver, which was premature from their perspectives. To complete the circle, when allies like Wagner, the Bavarian interior minister, obstructed Frick's centralization, they unwittingly forced him to seek alliance with Goering and

Himmler—police leaders powerful enough to help fulfill his goals when they were ready to cooperate.[9]

If Frick had been Goering's only problem, Goering might have easily prevailed. According to Diels, at this time Goering planned to offer Hitler his Prussian police as a model for a Reich police. However, when confronted with Frick's drive combined with the need both to break SA police powers and to discipline the SS into alliance, Goering required either an alliance with Himmler or Hitler's strong support. As early as December, all concerned had gotten the true measure of Hitler's position on the question of curbing extraordinary police powers. In a discussion with Goering and Diels, who had expounded his plans for the December amnesty, Hitler showed more concern about preserving the new power to eliminate enemies.[10] At this same time, Roehm and Himmler were able to claim Hitler's support against an effort by the Bavarian Council of Ministers to interfere in protective custody matters.[11]

As for Himmler, conditions had ripened for him to move from his lesser position to one of more strength in any arrangement with Goering. First, he had undermined Diels by coalescing the broadening base of opposition against him (ranging from conservatives like Gisevius and Grauert through Nazis like Nebe and Daluege), uniting it with the Berlin SD and his agents in the Gestapo.

The conservative attack on Diels had resumed as soon as he returned to office in December. In January, Grauert gained the recall of Gisevius from provincial exile and established him in a special Interior Ministry office for coordinating the affairs of the Gestapo that still concerned the ministry. He even ordered the provincial authorities to have duplicates of all Gestapo reports, including those of the regional offices, forwarded to this office. Goering, learning of this more than a week later, curtly countermanded Grauert and put him in his place for interfering with "police efficiency." Even so, Grauert circumvented Goering with a bureaucratic sidestep. He continued the camouflage of Gisevius's office as a liaison with Gestpo, took Goering up on a promise to have the Gestapo inform this office routinely of all business, and used Gisevius to sift out incriminating evidence. What they could not get from the Gestapo they allegedly acquired through correspondence intended for the Gestapo but mistakenly sent to the ministry.[12]

At some point in the early months of 1934, Himmler and Heydrich used Sepp Dietrich to establish contact with Gisevius and Nebe, who were still conspiring against Diels from within the Gestapo. At their meeting, according to Gisevius, Dietrich "congratulated us in the names of Reich Leader Himmler and Group Leader Heydrich for so stoutly leading the fight against corruption in the state and the Party. As we all know, he said, Himmler detested the excesses of the SA. Above all, he could no longer put up with the rampant sins of the Gestapo. Would we please set forth in writing . . . all our grievances. Naturally everything would be held in strictest confidence. Himmler wanted to use this material as the basis for a personal appeal to Hitler."[13]

The SS-men may in fact have believed their own posturing, and so greatly did Gisevius and Nebe hate Diels that they joined in the conspiracy, although the advantages they saw are not at all clear. Gisevius and Nebe compiled evidence against the Gestapo, including "instances of extortion, torture and killing" and also what they "knew of the Reichstag fire."[14] What, if any, of this Himmler could have used to win his case with Hitler we may never know, but clearly he gathered material and allies for his assault on the Gestapo. According to Gisevius, Daluege, nervous about the developing alliance and especially fearful of Heydrich, allegedly warned, "You will end by using Beelzebub to drive out the Devil."[15] Regardless of any such reservations, Daluege by this time was also thoroughly involved with Himmler. Undoubtedly, Diels's increased power and independence displeased him, and he saw that Himmler's growing strength demanded better relations with his Reichsfuehrer.

One source of this growing strength was the Berlin SD. By this time Heydrich had returned his energies to building the SD, with the Berlin office more firmly under his control than before. Around the first of the year he designated it the Major Regional Office East (Oberabschnitt Ost) and soon replaced Kobelinski with SS Second Lieutenant Hermann Behrends, and old personal friend and loyal follower. Behrends had followed Heydrich into the SS, the Party, and then the SD when Heydrich needed men he could trust with important posts, such as the Berlin office, where he could not otherwise easily apply direct personal pressure. According to Alfred Naujocks, who claimed to have informed Heydrich, Kobelinski had been dealing with Diels. In any case, they drummed Kobelinski out of the SS.[16]

Behrends's primary duty was to support the assault on the Gestapo. Using the SD agents within that office, he collected and forwarded to Himmler every useful intelligence. According to Orb, they had established a line of communication between Berlin and Munich that was unknown to Diels's Gestapo. Behrends also provided a secure link to— and undoubtedly a watchful check on—Daluege,[17] whom Himmler had carefully removed from all direct SS command. Daluege thus lost the SS power base that had induced Goering to give him police command, and his attempt to topple Diels had backfired, discrediting him with Goering. Given these developments, from February through April Daluege worked increasingly with Himmler against Diels, and by late March he clearly anticipated Diels's ouster.[18] By spring, to sum it up, the SS factions and some of the conservative factions allied with Frick had drawn together loosely in a common front against Diels.

Meanwhile, Goering and Frick drew together once again in their common effort to regulate uncontrolled police power. In February, after the Reich reform, Frick, better situated to clamp down on the abuse of protective custody, decreed procedures severely limiting the authority and extent of such powers. Despite their differences, Goering continued to support him on this issue, and in March he issued for Prussia a regulation to curb protective custody abuses along the lines of Frick's decree. Henceforth, protective custody could be ordered only by the Gestapo Office Berlin; Goering excluded local government (*Kreis*) and regular police officials—often uncontrolled SA- and SS-men. Wrapping it up, Goering made all arrests not initiated by the Gestapo Office subject to his own review within twenty-four hours, and unless he extended them, they were to expire after eight days. Only Goering's and Diels's office retained unlimited protective custody powers in Prussia, and the latter initiated much tighter controls, serving essentially as the review board.[19]

Although Goering by no means submitted to Frick's authority, his obvious cooperation was a great step forward. Together, on March 23, they met with the *Reichsstatthalter* to gain their support and proposed a Reich law modeled after Goering's regulation. In response Reichsstatthalter Fritz Sauckel claimed Thuringia already had a similar law. In Saxony, the Ministry of Interior responded merely by making the Secret State Police Office (nominally under Himmler) the sole authority for issuing and reviewing protective custody orders. In Bavaria, at least, Reichsstatthalter Epp used the occasion to mobilize against Himmler. Reconstituting the coalition of the previous fall, Epp and Frank, the Bavarian minister of justice, pressured Minister of Interior Wagner for restrictions along the lines of Frick's decree. But once again Wagner shielded Himmler from such interference in his ministry, stalemating the attack.[20] As long as Frick had to rely on Goering's tactic of developing the state police, the Gestapo, as a legitimate replacement for NS police excesses, Himmler's comparable state police power grew apace—a point that apparently did not escape Goering.

Meanwhile, Goering hastened to counterbalance Frick's expansion. In March, as part of the continued process of removing the Gestapo from normal government channels, he separated regional offices (*Stapostellen*) from all regular police connections and local government controls and made them "independent authorities of the Gestapo." Now, when Frick moved into the Prussian Ministry of Interior, all components of the

Gestapo would by beyond his reach.[21] Of course, this move also tightened Goering's control over embarrassingly independent regional offices like that at Stettin

Pursuant to tighter controls, Diels also tried to rein in on personnel policies. On March 15, he insisted that rigid civil service criteria be restored and tried to establish a screening process that would give him control. He specifically stated that rank in the SA or SS no longer carried weight in recruitment.[22]

The Fall of Diels

It was too late, however, for Diels to reverse SS penetration of the Gestapo. He soon learned of Goering's liaisons with Himmler and how he himself might lose his office. Perhaps that explains why, a little over a week after he had tried to tighten personnel policies, he reversed himself. In a memo to Goering, he highlighted the services rendered by SS-men, bragged of having rewarded them with status as civil service candidates and police employees, and requested Goering's approval of Daluege's former policy of modifying government requirements to draw SS men into the Gestapo.[23]

All such complicated maneuvers came to a head in April, however, when Frick issued a definitive regulation of protective custody affairs for the entire Reich. At first it seemed that the alliance against SA and SS had prevailed and Himmler's police powers would be controlled, yet Frick's alliance with Goering required a compromise—a compromise that offered Himmler many loopholes.

Frick's prologue to the protective custody regulation ambitiously claimed that the suspension of personal freedom was a temporary emergency measure, to be lifted when the time was right. He thus, by implication, claimed the right to dissolve all extraordinary police powers. Beyond that, however, his decree merely took Goering's Prussian regulation of March and applied it with appropriate changes to each federal state. He limited the offices empowered to order arrests, applied the Prussian limits of duration and provisions for review and due process, and, most important, limited conditions for arrest to avoid the worst abuses of the past. Following the Prussian pattern meant that, as with Diels's office in Prussia, Himmler's political police commands in the other states enjoyed preeminence in protective custody arrests, subject only to the approval of the head of each federal state.[24]

This last clause embodied the compromise, for the heads of federal states, such as Goering, and the *Reichsstatthalter*, not the Reich Minister, had the direct power of approval. In other words, Frick tacitly deferred his claim to Reich central authority. Any real, long-range limitation of Himmler's political police powers would have required similar limitations on Goering. Before that could happen, Frick needed more personal power, especially influence with Hitler. Until then, his only recourse was compromise with Goering and Himmler to curb all others.

The alliance among Frick, Goering and Himmler worked itself out in this way during March and April. With careful checks and balances to preserve what he could, Goering had to share his Prussian state and police authority with Frick, other Reich ministers, and Himmler. Frick would absorb the Prussian Ministry of Interior and the regular police. For all of Germany, Himmler would head the independent political police offices, including the Gestapo, but as the subordinate of the head of each federal state, which in the case of Prussian meant Goering. Beyond their common opposition to an uncontrolled SA, the motives of the three allies are at best problematical, as is Hitler's attitude about these developments. For Frick, whose power remained largely nominal, this arrangement may actually have been a wise move in a well-planned strategy. Its eventual failure for him resulted less from the terms of the compromise than from his inability to follow it up.

The complex union of the Prussian and Reich Ministries of Interior under Frick began in March and was completed by autumn. Meanwhile, Daluege assumed a Reich position as head of the Police Division of the Reich Ministry of Interior, slated to exercise command over all uniformed police in Germany.[25] Frick obviously intended the cooperative Daluege as a brake to Himmler's ambitions, and it might have worked had Frick proven strong enough. Unfortunately, as Himmler came to outweigh Frick, Daluege dealt with the more likely victor.

Although from hindsight Himmler's acquisition of the Gestapo was a decisive defeat for Frick, he hoped to reverse it. Aside from the recent limitations on protective custody, Frick planned to eliminate Himmler's political police when the time was ripe. Gisevus and Nebe drew into his camp, the former holding an improved position from which to gather evidence against Himmler and Heydrich. On May 1, Daluege transferred Nebe to the Berlin Police Praesidium, where he assumed command of the Prussian State Criminal Police Office.[26] He was slated to take command of a Reich detective force, an ideal agency for assuming the work of the political police. This makes more meaningful Frick's April admonition that the emergency situation was only temporary, for with it would also go any justification for the extraordinary political police and all of Himmler's police power.

Regardless of his possible long-range plans, Frick accepted a great risk: acceding Himmler's acquisition of the Gestapo and the political police in the little Lippe states where Frick had blocked him.[27] Apparently Frick had to accept Himmler's personal command over all the political police as essential to curbing the revolution. If he saw this as an interim measure, it seemed a small price.

If these were the reasons for Frick's involvement, those of Goering are less clear, especially since he lost so much in the short run. The long and seemingly endless struggle for police power had worn Goering down; both Diels and Gisevius indicated as much. His position had become increasingly indefensible. From the Nazi point of view, even his ideological position was weak, which must have counted for something with a man who loved his own rhetoric. He never ceased to claim for himself the proper NS role of creating an efficient strike force against their enemies, yet building his own police in opposition to efforts at Reich centralization was too obviously personal aggrandizement. His own fight against more particularistic SA police lords must have impressed the contradiction upon him. The very mechanism of bureaucratic imperialism worked against him as he resisted from his regional base the superior claims of Himmler or Frick to provide an efficient national police.[28]

More specifically, the loss of Diels as a suitable head of the Gestapo weakened Goering's position. The strain had been too great for Diels as well. The American ambassador's daughter, Martha Dodd, who saw him frequently during this time, commented on his obvious symptoms of physical and nervous exhaustion. His condition interfered with Gestapo work, and Goering lost confidence in his stability.[29] Furthermore, if Diels's account is to be believed, Goering in fact had reason to suspect that he would not be as decisive an agent as Goering needed for a pending confrontation with the SA. Not only did his illness weaken the effectiveness of the Gestapo, but he allegedly showed signs of unwillingness to flout the law as freely as necessary.[30] Whether any of this was true or not, Diels's personal conflicts with all of Goering's new allies made him a liability that had to be cut.

In his book, Diels left a contradictory account of his removal. The book constantly shifts from references about his dismissal to tales of how he was trying to resign for reasons of health. He claims to have resisted persistent efforts by Goering, Hess, and Hitler to keep him in office;[31] however, Martha Dodd, who verified many of Diels's memories, gives no indication that he intended to resign.

Several traditionally cited but unelaborated stories tell of some coup by Himmler and Heydrich that so undermined Diels that an unnerved Goering called them to Berlin. In one version the SD exposed and assassination plot against Goering that the Gestapo had failed to detect, and in another Patschowski (Heydrich's plant in the Gestapo) used his key position in counterespionage to cause the fall of Diels.[32] Some or

all of these developments may have motivated Goering to turn the Gestapo over to Himmler, but, regardless, Goering's position in the struggle for police power had become weaker and could soon become
untenable. If a deal at this juncture saved a complete loss, it was a deal
and not a coup forced on him suddenly, for all evidence indicates an
extensive period of negotiation. Heydrich's wife remembers several
weeks of maneuvering while Goering tried to keep Heydrich out of the
Gestapo. Himmler insisted and prevailed on this point: Heydrich would
actually run the Gestapo.[33]

Although Goering had ample reason to distrust and dislike Heydrich, someone like Goering would hardly fear him at this early stage.
His distrust of Heydrich probably grew more from Heydrich's unfortunate personality, in contrast with Himmler's adroit use of scapegoats
in building his own image of reasonableness and pliability, an image
significant to his acquisition of political police commands, ostensibly
under Nazi lords like Goering. In fact, according to one associate,
Himmler actually held Goering in awe and diligently sought good relations, even for many years after the balance of power had shifted.[34]

Himmler's reasons for the alliance seem obvious, yet it clearly required a commitment that must have troubled him. Throughout 1933,
his rise had been as much in alliance with Roehm as against SA unreliability. They had worked together well against conservative opposition
as late as December. Yet the obvious appeals of the SS as a police power
were its greater reliability as an alternative to SA excesses, and this
Himmler openly exploited. Between late 1933 and April 1934, he gradually distanced himself from his old comrade and commander, while
many still numbered him and Roehm—SA and SS—together in the radical NS wing.[35]

In all of this, Hitler's position remains the most clouded. Although
historians have generally attributed Himmler's acquisition of the political
police to support from Hitler—even to an uncharacteristic "order" from
Hitler—Edward Peterson may be correct in not dismissing Diels's version that Hitler and Hess avidly sought to restore Diels to office and to
keep Himmler out of Berlin. Goering and Himmler may have even kept
Hitler in the dark about their negotiations. Deeply involved in the delicate operation of balancing the forces of the Second Revolution against
moderate Nazis and conservatives, Hitler might have viewed an advance
in Himmler's power as disruptive of that balance.[36] It is premature to
argue that in April Hitler deliberately built the SS and police in order to
break the SA. In fact, he had not yet decided that the SA needed breaking.

What emerges clearly from the contradictory sources about the developments and deals that brought Himmler to Berlin is a healthy leaven

to stereotyped images of the Nazi leaders as Machiavellian draftsmen of a blueprint for totalitarianism. Their Third Reich grew less from design than as an awkward assemblage of pragamatic compromises made by bitter rivals on the basis of common, but by no means identical, ideological goals. If there were victors, they were those, like Himmler, who combined opportunism with plans general enough to allow flexibility and only specific enough to indicate a general sense of direction.

On April 20 Goering introduced Himmler to the gentlemen of the Gestapo Office. While Goering retained the title of chief of the Gestapo, Himmler became its deputy chief and inspector, and Heydrich became head of the Gestapo Office. This distribution of titles involved more than a change of command, for the political police forces of Germany became further removed from the control of normal state administration and fell increasingly into the hands of leaders of the NS Movement.[37]

Of course, Goering had always been chief of the Gestapo, but those who really ran the central machinery—his former deputy, Chief State Secretary Grauert, and Diels (the inspector and head of the Gestapo Office)—were products of German civil service traditions. Although they had little respect for liberal concepts of individual rights and the limits of state authority, they did at least respect a traditional order that they saw as "legality" and "proper procedures." Even more basic, they displayed some psychological and intellectual restraints related to a respect for humanity. In contrast, Himmler and Heydrich, who replaced them, would sweep away all liberal and conservative obstacles. Nevertheless, they encountered real external restraints, for April 1934 was only a major turning point in terms of long-range consequences, not immediate changes.

Into their hands fell the extensive Prussian political police, rounding out Himmler's control of such forces all over the Reich. With the Gestapo also came control over the border police stations in Prussian territories. As part of his March reforms, Goering had subordinated them to the Gestapo regional offices. In fact, Himmler had long been drawing the border police into the SS empire, for SS-men also had a monopoly on auxiliary border police work in those states with Reich borders. All border police were destined for inclusion in Sipo and SD as a wing of the Gestapo.[38]

By now the newly acquired Gestapo had grown immensely, although still only a portent of things to come. Before the end of 1933, under Diels, the rapidly growing Gestapo Office already included 122 civil servants and 600 police employees, with a budget of 3,950,000 RM for the Gestapo and 9,850,00 RM for the concentration camps it administered.[39]

Although this was a much needed resource for Himmler's always inadequately funded SS, the Gestapo provided no well of luxurious appointments and easy money. In their desire to build a Gestapo of their own people, Himmler and Heydrich had at least three real constraints. First, for many purposes they needed trained police professionals who could not be replaced by just any SS-man. Second, although they continued to skirt some civil service personnel regulations, Frick and his allies constantly interfered with these tactics. Beyond these limits, they had to consider the power of local Party leaders and debts to Old Fighters in making appointments.[40]

Especially in finances, Himmler and Heydrich found Gestapo resources inadequate for their needs. As a matter of fact, they had more trouble with the Prussian Ministry of Finance than had Diels before them. In particular, funding problems impeded efforts to pump SS-men into the Gestapo as civil service candidates and police employees. For instance, the monthly salary of a police employee (*Krimianlangestellte*) was only 109 RM, basically intended to support young bachelors beginning their careers. This was wholly inadequate for more mature family men like those being brought in from the Movement, and Diels had been able to get supplements to raise their salaries to 160-180 RM. When Heydrich replaced Diels, the source for such supplements temporarily vanished. By juggling, he maintained some supplements, but had to reduce the total by 20 RM per man. Even with Goering's intervention, it took up to a year to settle this one financial problem. As a consequence, according to Heydrich, he could not lure civil service personnel from other agencies or compete with the uniformed police, and the increased demands and extended hours for Gestapo personnel exaggerated such problems. In fact, over the next year the numerical strength of the Gestapo actually declined.[41]

Originally, the terms of the Frick-Goering-Himmler compromise limited Himmler's freedom with the Gestapo, and it took over two years to dissolve those limitations completely. For instance, although Goering headed the Gestapo directly as prime minister, Frick, as both Prussian and Reich minister of the interior, could interfere, at least indirectly, in political police affairs. Furthermore, Goering insisted on being informed of all significant Gestapo business, and since he offered a necessary screen against Frick, Himmler probably wanted him to remain more than a titular head of the Gestapo for the bulk of the year.[42] Heydrich inserted himself only gradually between Goering and the internal affairs of the Gestapo.

On a larger scale, central control of the lower level of the Gestapo regional offices and field posts remained uneven. The ambiguous authority of the regional offices and field posts remained uneven. The ambiguous authority of the regional governors and, for Berlin, the police

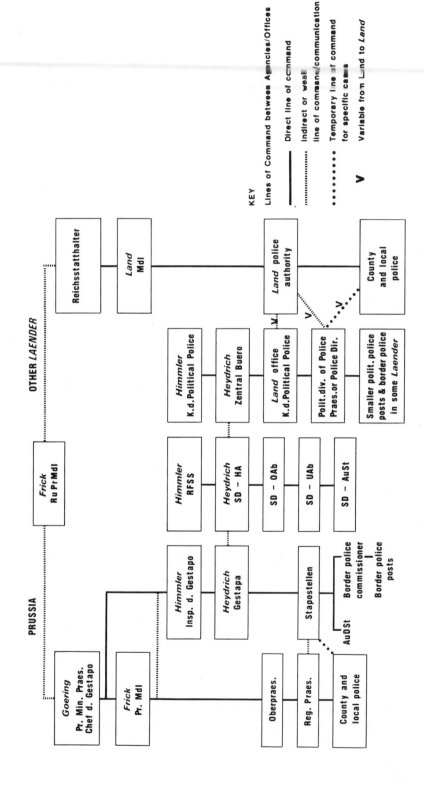

Figure 1. Political Police and SD Command Structure, April 1934-June 1936

president, still provided for outside interference. The governors viewed the regional offices as part of their domains, and played on competition between those regional offices and Gestapo field workers from Berlin. Their success in penetrating Gestapo business depended largely on the character and personal loyalties of the local Gestapo leaders, whose appointments often involved broad political circles.[43] The settlement of these matters occupied the better part of the year.

Despite all the limitations within Prussia, Himmler had achieved a major victory. He rounded out his titles to "Reichsfuehrer SS and Political Police Commander of the States of Anhalt, Baden, Bayern, Braunschweig, Bremen, Hamburg, Hessen, Luebec, Mecklenburg, Oldenburg, Sachsen, Thueringen and Wuerttemberg, and Inspector of the Secret State Police in Prussia"—a compellation to make any feudal lord green with envy. After actually using such a pretentious title, however, he found that things had not gone so far that he could get away with it. Frick turned it into ridicule. Himmler later limited his title to "Political Police Commander of the States and Inspector of the Gestapo in Prussia."[44]

Regardless of how he titled himself, Himmler held Germany's first unified command of political police forces. The direction of each federal state political police force came under Heydrich, who issued orders under Himmler's titles. The facilities of the Gestapo Office in Berlin included the Central Bureau of the Political Police Commander of the States.[45] Although 8 Prinz Albrect Strasse became the first common headquarters, the political police were legally united only under Himmler personally. Financially and organizationally, they remained divided. However, having achieved even these limited victories, Himmler and Heydrich began consolidating and exploiting their power base. Toward this end, the role of their political police powers in the purge of the SA proved decisive. At the same time, the SD developed significantly enough to be ready for a role in the purge.

11

The SD and Conservative Opposition to June 1934

With guaranteed survival and the increased appreciation of the Party Leadership came badly needed funds. When Party Treasurer Schwarz calculated the SD budget in January 1934, he set it at 4,000 RM per month. Shortly thereafter, perhaps in May, he increased it to 20,000 RM. Heydrich had argued for more funds on the basis of increased responsibility for Party intelligence work and the need to reward field service personnel with salaries after their long period of unsalaried sacrifice. He badly needed money to establish the still embryonic SD and to secure personnel who might otherwise turn elsewhere for better pay. Nevertheless the financial problems of the SD remained, for Schwarz failed to produce even the originally budgeted funds on schedule. In May, SD salaries fell in arrears so badly that, according the Heydrich, his men were threatened by their debts.[1] Short funds remained a perennial problem, complicated by an almost exponential increase in Heydrich's demands for further enlargement of the SD budget.

In addition to the budgetary increase, a solitary payment of 68,000 RM was also promised, apparently to cover expenses for the transfer of other Party intelligence organizations into the SD. Such phenomenal increases in funding were tied to the October 1933 order that the SD absorb the ND of the Foreign Political Office. Heydrich had referred to this order in a letter to Schwarz in May, saying that the date of this order "lay so far back that by further delay the danger would appear, and has already partially appeared, that new intelligence services would be formed."[2] Heydrich had good reason to worry about competitors, for since the NS power seizure, Party intelligence agencies had proliferated. The transfer of Schumann's operations to the Foreign Political Office had not terminated intelligence in the Propaganda Command, at least not at the *Gau* level.

For instance, in the *Gau* South-Hannover-Brunswick, local remnants of Schumann's old ND not only survived but also took on a renewed life that easily rivaled the local SD. As soon as the acquisition of power made the destruction of "enemies" a real possibility and the defense of the state a necessity, local Party leaders discovered an interest in intelligence work. In April 1933, the *Gau* Propaganda Command began a crash program to convert its old Main Division III into a proper ND. Within a few months, it was effectively assisting local police in the roundup of Communists and in the persecution of all other "enemies." As a matter of fact, it expected to solve some of its financial problems through rewards the police paid for such services. By June this ND titled itself the Auxiliary Troop (Hilfstruppe) of the Gestapo.[3]

In the nearby state of Lippe in early 1934, State Minister and Gau Inspector Reicke regularly received reports from an ND in *Gau* Westfalia-North and from the Ic of SA Standarte 55. In Gau Cologne-Aachen the police president of Cologne absorbed the *Gau* ND into his political police, where they became Gestapo employees in October.[4] In other words, Heydrich had competition in Party intelligence that also had received support from the political police in *Laender* he did not yet control. Many *Gauleiter*, distrustful of the SD, maintained their own services.

The SD Monopoly

When Heydrich expressed to Schwarz his nervousness about "new intelligence services" being formed, he expected Reich Party Leadership to share his concern. This implies that they had already granted the SD a tacit monopoly over Party intelligence work, perhaps only implied because Hitler had not yet approved, or remaining unannounced because it could not be enforced. By spring 1934, however, Himmler and Heydrich had the means for enforcement and used them fully.

The means came with command over the political police, whose cooperation, or at least tacit consent, had been essential to the operation of rival intelligence agencies, and whose authority could be used to crush such agencies. On May 16, the new bosses ordered that in all cases of high treason and counterespionage the Prussian Gestapo would cease all cooperation with the counterespionage services of the Party Organization, of the NS Organization of Factory Cells, and of the Counterespionage Office of the Labor Front. They were to prosecute any SA actions in such matters. The SD would be recognized in the future as *the sole intelligence organization of the Party.*[5]

This assertion that the SD was the sole intelligence organization of the Party also indicates that prior to Hess's June announcement, the Party Leadership had bestowed a de facto monopoly on the SD. The order to the Gestapo not only enforced this decision before it could be reversed, but also encouraged the Party Leadership in acts of enforcement. The order belongs to the allied effort by Goering, Himmler, and Hess to bring the SA and other elements of the Second Revolution under tighter control. Hess's forthcoming June 1934 announcement about the SD monopoly has often been interpreted as a decision by Hitler to turn to the SS and SD as instruments for controlling the SA. In fact, it seems more complicated than that, and there were good reasons why Himmler and Heydrich were anxious to use their police power to push the claims of the SD.

First, their allies were hardly committed permanently to them and to strengthening their positions. The alliance probably included no agreements about the SD, because Goering remained uneasy about it, and so did Frick. Other components of the alliance against Roehm, like the military and the Foreign Ministry, not only thwarted SA intelligence activity in the realm of foreign affairs (having won Hitler's support toward the end in April), but opposed SS and SD interference as well.[6] By the same token, the military preferred limited dealings with any Party agencies in counterespionage work. Although the military wanted to rely entirely on agencies of the state like the police, especially the Gestapo, manpower needs and the fear of Communist counterstrokes had earlier given the SA a ready pretext for inserting itself into such work. Thus the Gestapo order of May 16 was one big step toward reversing SA involvement and strengthening the bond between military and police. Ironically, such increased military cooperation with Heydrich's Gestapo gave the unwanted SD an entrée into counterespionage. However, that and its involvement in foreign intelligence became serious only after 1934.

As for the interpretation that Hitler had turned to the SD for an instrument against the SA, that remains as suspect as the tradition that he supported Himmler's candidacy to command all the political police. He clearly responded to the pressure from Goering, the Party Leadership, and branches of government to curb the SA, to the obvious benefit of the SS and SD. This pressure probably produced Hitler's consent to an SD monopoly of Party intelligence, but announcements by Hess rather than the Fuehrer, and much foot dragging in execution were more characteristic of Hitler's indecisiveness.

Ultimately Himmler and Heydrich achieved their victory by means of force. With police power, they softened their competition, facilitating the Party Leadership in enforcing "the will of the Fuehrer." On June 9, Hess finally published the order proclaiming the end of all intelligence and counterespionage services of the Party. By mid-July the work of absorbing the internal intelligence apparatus of the Foreign Political Office was to be completed, and beginning in July the *Gauleiter* were to cease funding any other agencies. On July 27, Schwarz issued similar orders. Henceforth the *Gauleiter* were to receive the necessary intelligence from the SD.[7]

Despite the apparent finality of Hess's and Schwarz's orders, the SD victory remained incomplete, and Heydrich and his people had to negotiate and maneuver continually against rivals. To begin with, the order applied only to agencies of the Party, not the state. Neither the Abwehr, the Foreign Office, nor Goering's Forschungsamt came into question. Even the Party agencies of powerful rivals survived, at least in part, and the delimitation of their authority vis-à-vis the SD had to be negotiated carefully. The ND or Ic of the SA would probably have remained untouchable had it not been for the June purge. Even so, it was not dissolved until February 1935.[8]

One powerful rival was Robert Ley, head of the Labor Front (DAF) and key member of the Party Leadership alliance against Roehm. This alliance probably gained his consent to the demise of the Labor Front's Counterespionage Office over to the SD; its dissolution was announced on September 13. Nevertheless, Ley's DAF retained an Information Office that would continue to report on influences affecting the mood of personnel and their recruitment. Although some friction between this office and the SD continued, Himmler confidently asserted that the work of the office should produce no difficulties.[9]

Himmler made this assertion for the sake of appearances, but he was hardly naive enough to trust Ley's good will to carry out his side of the bargain. In typical fashion, Himmler had a reliable SD agent in the DAF to take over the Amt Abwehr, to supervise its liquidation and the creation of the Information Office suitable to SD requirements. His man, SS Lieutenant Felix Schmidt, had been drawn into the SS and SD in March. Schmidt, also an Old Fighter, had well-estalbished roots in Party Leadership and the DAF, ensuring his acceptance by Ley. Although he later drifted from the SD camp, he served adequately for the early years of SD-DAF relations.[10]

Given the official announcement by Hess and the economic strangulation provided by Schwarz, Heydrich used his police to clamp down ever more tightly on any remnants of rivalry and to bring the SA under further pressure. On June 25, he reminded his Gestapo officials of Hess's order, held them responsible for its enforcement, and ordered immediate reports on even the most minor violations.[11] In other respects, too, the acquisition of the Gestapo tremendously boosted the status of the SD as an intelligence agency. It now had access to Gestapo sources and the intelligence-gathering resources of many other state agencies. On May 30, Heydrich ordered all sections of the Gestapo Office to maintain files on all important affairs for the information of the SD.[12]

Continuing Restraints

While the SD developed, Frick's growing concern over the Second Revolution drove him to bring under control all radical elements—especially SA and SS. To limit Himmler, he planned to replace his extraordinary political police with something more traditional. Aware that both Himmler's extraordinary police and the excessive police actions of the SA were possible because the public and powerful elements of German society would tolerate almost anything in the name of law and order, he tried to reduce the public hysteria over "lawlessness" from which this tolerance grew. Both he and Goebbels agreed that the constant reports of enemy theats and police action inflamed rather than assuaged this hysteria. Knowing that the political police fed the media its news, he requested that they severely limit their releases, while Goebbels brought similar pressure to bear on the news media itself. Grudgingly, Heydrich took almost two months to comply.[13]

If Frick could in this way weaken support and justification for extraordinary police powers, he could either reduce the independence of the political police and bring them more tightly under his control, or he could dissolve them. As his April decree on protective custody indicated, he saw something of this sort as the desirable direction, but unfortunately he failed to push for it on every front.

In March, Reich Minister of Justice Franz Guertner and Hans Frank (now Reich justice commissar and minister without portfolio, head of the Party Legal Office, and president of the Academy of German Law) called for an end to the concentration camps and to the entire system that functioned beyond the courts and state penal authorities. Even by the time they coerced Hitler into a meeting of all concerned, including Himmler, Frick had failed to join their cause. Hitler denounced such a move as "premature" in the face of Germany's domestic and foreign problems.[14] Perhaps Frick supported the Himmler-Goering position as part of their alliance against the Second Revolution. Perhaps he still believed he could simply displace his allies and their extraordinary machinery with more professional machinery. Perhaps he knew where Hitler stood.

Even at this stage of their "alliance," Frick wanted to eliminate Himmler from command of the political police, which he could do if he dissolved those extraordinary police after the right conditions had "matured." Of course, this dissolution would require a suitable detective force to replace or absorb those police. Toward this end, in May Frick began the reorganization of the Prussian Criminal Police as an independent, centrally commanded force along the lines of the Gestapo. Simultaneously, his staff studied the problem of expanding the force into a

Reich Criminal Police.[15] Such a Reich agency would be a two-pronged victory, both replacing Himmler's separate political police in each state and creating the sort of centralized police Frick desired

Meanwhile his April decree on protective custody was producing tighter controls. As in the other states, in May collective pressures finally brought Wagner to decree corresponding regulations for Bavaria. He replaced his directives of the previous year with the more restrictive Prussian model.[16] Yet this imposed no really significant limits on the pattern for the police state that Himmler had developed in Bavaria; it even concentrated further extraordinary police power in Himmler's hands. The new decrees eliminated his police competitors such as the SA, leaving only his ostensible state government superiors, whom he had already proven capable of outmaneuvering.

Although eliminating the uncontrollable competition furthered the common Frick-Himmler objective of regulating and centralizing the police, Frick anticipated that that regularization would bring increased stability, which, in turn, would end the need for extraordinary police like Himmler's. Meanwhile, the new regulations provided what was needed: one identifiable authority in each state who bore primary responsibility for all that happened in the way of extraordinary police action. Theoretically, Frick could pressure and control that authority, which was Himmler in every case. Since the regulations also provided for the collection and reporting of complete information on the extraordinary police activities of "these authorities," such information could be used in arguments for the eventual dissolution of Himmler's political police.

Meanwhile, from his position as Reich official responsible for police affairs, Frick could maneuver to weaken Himmler's base of power, using as a weapon the dependence of the *Leander* upon financial support from the Reich. The extraordinary political police had been built on the hysteria of the state of emergency, leading each *Land* to exceed its responsibilities and resources. Frick and the minister of finance maneuvered to reverse these trends by refusing the funds needed to support extraordinary police forces. While at first they directed the attack against the uncontrolled auxiliaries, later they also applied it to Himmler's political police and state-supported concentration camps.[17]

A careful orchestration of his limited authority enabled Frick to mobilize as allies all those state officials opposed to the growth of Himmler's power. For instance, in Wuerttemberg, where Himmler's alliance with Reichsstatthalter Murr had given him titular command of the political police, his real influence was checked by State Minister Morgenthaler and the head of the Political State Police Office, Dr. Mattheiss. But in May, apparently in collaboration with Himmler, Murr removed Mattheiss and sought to replace him with his own man, SS Lieutenant Dr.

Stahlecker, who would work closely with Himmler. Morgenthaler mobilized a counterattack and turned to Frick for support, playing of Frick's claim to have authority over such appointments.[18] The result was a stalemate, with a clear but reversible advantage for Murr and Himmler: Until a definitive settlement, Stahlecker would be acting head of the political police office and Himmler's influence could grow apace. On the other hand, Frick's office had made its own gains by asserting its authority, acquiring allies, and impeding Himmler's progress. With the end of the state of emergency, Frick could hope to be in position to dissolve or absorb Himmler's police.

On the Prussian front, Frick tried to prevent further evolution of the Gestapo toward the Bavarian model. On June 19, as Prussian minister of the interior, he called together the Reich and Prussian ministries, and promised to restore the former relationship between the district governors and the Gestapo field posts. Toward this end, he promised that he and Goering were working on a new decree for the Gestapo.[19] Unfortunately, Goering's staff produced such an innocuous decree that Himmler and Heydrich also gave it their full support. It simply clarified Gestapo responsibilities to the governors without giving them any powers to limit Gestapo action. The governors would retain their responsibility for political problems in parallel with the Gestapo, and the Gestapo posts were to keep them informed through regular reports. The governors could order Gestapo posts in their districts to take political actions, but only so long as their orders were not in conflict with those of the Gestapo Office.[20] Goering was still playing his complex games, for June 1934 was no time to weaken the Gestapo.

Whether he really believed he had Goering's support or not, Frick tried to accumulate allies in Prussia for the future struggle. At his June 19 meeting he courted the governors. Among them, a new appointee for Cologne, Rudolf Diels, more than willingly raised objections to positions taken by Goering and Himmler. Most significant, Frick proclaimed to the governors that the division of police powers in Prussia (that is, between Gestapo and regular police) was justifiable only as a "transitional measure" and must be terminated.[21] Toward that end, Frick needed a cooling-off period after the revolutionary phase, and he greeted the pending July furlough for the SA as just such an opportunity. Frick knew Germany needed a pause and a period of calm for his plans to mature. He had made an open declaration of war on Himmler's extraordinary police machinery and powers, but he needed a period of normalcy to carry out his campaign. Unfortunately, the problem of Roehm and the SA made that impossible.

12

The Roehm Purge

Although conflict between the radical and conservative wings was as old as the Movement itself, Hitler had held them together so well that there had been amazingly few factional splits. However, in the spring of 1934, tensions became so great that Hitler reluctantly approved a decisive purge. The forces of the so-called Second Revolution consisted of those dissatisfied with the extent of the NS revolution. Having broken the power of the left and intimidated the liberals into submission, they also wanted to sweep aside the establishment, especially those allies who had made the initial power seizure possible and whose continued alliance would limit their revolution. Although the ranks of the Second Revolution included a wide range of lower middle class, peasants, and workers organized into the economic affiliates, and at least one-third of the Party leadership at all levels (including some *Gauleiter*), the SA stood foremost in their ranks as the most visibly threatening.[1]

Aligned against the Second Revolution were not only their would-be victims—the leaders of finance, business and industry, the officers corps of the military, the bureaucracy, and conservative political leaders—but also those elements of the Movement like Frick who favored a conservative-traditional dictatorship, or those like Himmler, Goering, or the Reich Party Leadership and certain Gauleiter who favored a controlled revolution. Many of the latter group, although radical in their own right, had based their power on state bureaucratic machinery, so the Second Revolution, especially SA nihilism, threatened them. Although Himmler shared many objectives of the Second Revolution, he was troubled by its lack of discipline, its questionable loyalty to the Fuehrer.

The growing split between Himmler and his old friend Roehm undoubtedly arose from the SS mission—to watch and control those rowdy and undesirable elements that Roehm had failed to control, and that he often inflamed with radical appeals. Nevertheless, the two might have remained allied against the enemies of their revolution; Himmler's acquisition of the police machinery of the state must have driven the wedge between them. Having police authority intensified the tensions between Himmler's authoritarianism and his radicalism, and the forces aligned against the Second Revolution won him as an ally, completing the split between the Party's paramilitary organizations. In the process, Hitler's tactic of pitting the SS and SA chiefs against each other played a decisive role. Nevertheless, since Hitler decided on a radical solution only as late as June, the argument that he made Himmler Roehm's executioner is strained. Until June, Hitler's role remained that of the great arbiter: he meant to maintain distance between his lieutenants, not to split them irrevocably.

The struggle for power during 1933 had brought NS differences to a head and created irreconcilable camps. Once they had formed, they pressed Hitler to his fateful decision. The established social and economic powers of German society felt threatened, and their concern over NS excesses grew. They channeled numerous complaints to Frick and Hitler, and occasionally they pressed court actions. Most significant, however, when Roehm renewed his assault on the military in January and February 1934, he convinced them it was vital to end his threat of displacing them. On another front, the French, still in a position to crush an isolated Germany, applied external pressure to reduce the paramilitary formations. Aggravating the situation, Hitler received constant complaints from all levels of the Party and state leadership, and a growing mood of public discontent over SA excesses became palpable. Until late June, however, this coalition of pressures could not drive him beyond efforts at compromise.

Finally Hitler's paranoid suspiciousness and opportunistic political strategy combined fatally against Roehm. Memories of the Strassers and their links with the early SA revolts, and of von Schleicher's attempt to woo the Strasser wing and the SA were reignited by rumors of their continued machinations, especially after Schleicher's return to Germany. Such rumors usually featured Roehm and other dissident elements, and Roehm's enemies guaranteed that Hitler heard them all. According to Diels, as early as January Hitler had given him direct orders to make thorough reports on the SA, and soon Diels was adding to the rumor mills with stories of Communist infiltration of the SA. At midmonth, in a conference with Goering and Diels, Hitler allegedly referred to the elimination of Schleicher and Strasser. Perhaps it was meant only as Henry II had meant his ill-fated remark about Thomas à Becket, but Goering interpreted it as a death warrant.[2] Regardless, as far as Roehm was concerned, Hitler still pursued compromises until June.

On June 4 he convinced Roehm of the necessity for more subtle approaches to their goals, and they agreed to a rest leave during June for the SA leadership and a furlough during July for SA troops. The tensions heightened, however, on June 17, when von Papen made a speech in Marburg attacking NS excesses and raising the specter of a rightist coalition that could either topple Hitler or destroy his freedom of action. As long as Hindenburg still lived and his succession remained unsettled, the military held a decisive trump card. Around June 21, it apparently played that card, for Blomberg and Hindenburg allegedly threatened Hitler with a military coup if he failed to end the tensions. Hitler then decided to take drastic action. On June 24, Himmler set his machinery in motion.[3]

The roles of Himmler and Heydrich and their organizations in Hitler's decision are the subject of controversy. According to the rumor mills of the Third Reich, the combination, especially Heydrich, initiated a conscious conspiracy to destroy the SA through fabricated evidence of a pending coup. The traditions, reinforced by circumstantial evidence, have been repeated as fact in memoirs and testimonies, and elaborated into sensational histories that require careful examination.[4]

Based largely on the testimonies of involved SS and SD leaders, Wolfgang Sauer assembled a scholarly, convincing account of how belief in a pending SA coup grew largely from grossly exaggerated evidence. Himmler and Heydrich, using SD reports, and Gen. von Reichenau and the Abwehr deluged Hitler and the military with threatening intelligence. When the evidence was insufficient, they even manufactured it. Elaborating on these accounts, Heinz Hoehne described Heydrich as one who had long dreamed of a purge of enemies like Roehm, who worked to win Himmler to his cause by the spring of 1934, and who then did the most to engineer the final event. In contrast, Shlomo Aronson concluded that Heydrich was in no way the central figure in the purge. In fact, although there are indications of Abwehr-SD cooperation against the SA, and although Heydrich clearly coordinated with General von Reichenau (chief of von Blomberg's ministerial office) as the result of a Goering-Himmler-Reichenau alliance, most evidence indicates that the Army, especially von Reichenau, provided most of the incriminating evidence and agitation against Roehm. Heydrich's role appears increasingly that of executor rather than instigator.[5]

Since the documents generated within the police, SS, and SD relevant to June 30 were destroyed on orders, only scraps and vague passing references survive.[6] There are only the memories of witnesses not directly involved or of participants from below the circle accused of fabricating the "SA putsch." They had no firsthand knowledge of the motivations and conscious thoughts of their superiors, other than what they deduced from the passing remarks of men who loved to posture. Goering, a surviving central figure, was uncooperative at Nuremberg, and naturally preferred to shift the blame for "excesses" onto Heydrich.

If Wheeler-Bennett must argue that the stories about the involvement of certain generals "are completely lacking of confirmation and should be treated with great reserve,"[7] the same objective reserve must be applied (although to a lesser extent) to the involvement of the notorious villains of the Third Reich. Although their roles as executioners are beyond doubt, their motives and actions in precipitating the purge require more analysis. A layman's understanding of human psychology suggests several alternatives less sensational than images of Machiavellian geniuses conspiring to destroy their enemies by complete fabrication.

The mental processes of Goering or Reichenau need not concern us here, but rather those of Himmler and Heydrich. For Heydrich, the route from his first position under Himmler in 1931 to June 30, 1934, was shaped by his responsibilities, first as secret service chief and then as de facto head of the political police. A desire to eliminate competitors may or may not have been part of the formula. He learned from the very beginning that uncontrolled, putsch-inclined elements in the Movement or reactionaries who hindered the Fuehrer's goals (as described by Himmler) were as much the proper objects of suspicion as Marxists. He learned that an ability to see enemies behind every bush and to demonstrate the most fantastic liaisons between the most unlikely bedfellows earned an NS secret service chief his laurels. His more cautious, more objective, or less imaginative opponents fell by the wayside. Under such conditions, he may well have lost touch with reality and objectivity.

His responsibilities required winning agents or inserting them into the SA, the Party leadership, the state bureaucracy, and conservative circles. They had to report back with every scrap of suspicious information, every outburst or careless remark of frustrated revolutionaries or worried conservatives. As Heydrich's net grew, the "evidence" inevitably multiplied, increasing his suspicion of a potential coup.[8] As Heydrich presented this evidence from all over the Reich, Himmler, whose own theories of conspiracy had shaped Heydrich's system, must have become equally convinced, especially since the military produced so much corroboration. Although their common desires to eliminate opponents, personal enemies, and troublemakers played a role in their readiness to jump to conclusions, it need not have been a cynically conscious process. In this way Heydrich and his SD offices, Himmler's other lieutenants (like Eicke), and Goering as well drew up their lists of suspects, eventually the execution lists for the purge. Reports of the existence of such enemy lists as early as April are, therefore, consistent; however, the point at which they became "murder lists" is less clear.

Almost all accounts of events leading to June 30 reveal a mutual escalation process that undoubtedly convinced the Goering-Himmler-Reichenau group of the necessity for drastic measures and pressed them to convince Hitler. As the Reichswehr, SS, and police took precautionary measures against the suspected coup, the SA responded to what it saw as suspicious preparations. That, in turn, led to more reports of SA machinations and to more countermeasures. In forwarding such infor mation to Hitler, no one had to resort to deliberate fabrication; they merely communicated their own excitement and fear. Rather than con- sciously deceiving, they exaggerated out of the natural human tendency to convince others as they themselves had been convinced. Of course, they may have consciously fabricated,·but for no other motive than to prove what they "knew" to be true but could not prove properly. Their efforts to seize and assemble proof in the days following June 30 testify to their belief.[9] Even if they suspected that their case was really weak, psychological mechanisms would suppress their doubts, for they had risked everything and exposure could destroy them. Since the forces of the Second Revolution were indeed capable of doing what was sus- pected, they would always be a threat, and there was every reason to nip them in the bud once and for all. In this way the victims of June 30 (most of whom were far less innocent than the other victims of Nazism) fell prey to the very same mechanisms that destroyed all other "enemies" of the Third Reich.

The precedent for the purge lay in the actions against the Marx- ists. The Roehm purge followed as the second logical step in the self- righteous destruction of "enemies" on the grounds of suspicion. That, after all, was the essence of "preventive law enforcement," the phi- losophy of the police state. This process reached its logical conclusion in genocide, the destruction of "enemy races" during time of war.[10] This is the context of the cold-blooded behavior attributed to Heydrich and his agents, including many who later accused him. There is no need to question the many corroborating testimonies of the manner in which Heydrich issued his execution orders or of the ferocity of their execution, directed against enemies on whom the executioners had projected the worst of their own hates and fears.

SS and police—both uniformed and political police—were available all over the Reich for the purge, or "counter-coup." They had material support from the Reichswehr, whose troops stood by in case the SA could not be emasculated. They operated under the direct orders of Hitler at Bad Wiessee, Roehm's vacation headquarters. Heydrich, work- ing in unison with his superiors, Himmler and Goering, directed op- erations from Berlin. All over Germany his SD and police lieutenants followed written and oral directives for specific actions. In a few cases, local initiative or rashness added to the deaths. Most SA leaders involved were arrested, though a few were shot on the spot. The key personnel were then summarily shot, and the less significant eventually released.

In most cases involving those who were not SA-men, Heydrich allegedly gave orders that they be shot for resisting arrest, or that a "suicide" be arranged.[11] Which of these names, if any, Heydrich personally added to the list remains debatable.[12] Undoubtedly he and Himmler consulted with Goering about many "preventive executions," but it is mere speculation to assign specific responsibilities.

For Himmler and Heydrich personally, the purge conveyed some clear message and some invaluable opportunities. If, as argued, they had not intended a fusion between SD and political police all along, they increasingly pursued that line of action after June 30. Himmler had long seen the necessity and the benefits of joint command over SS and police. If Heydrich had missed the value of this before, it now became apparent. Until this point the SD and the political police had been merely complementary organizations united only in his joint command. SD-men in the political police had facilitated his control in some cases, but they had not been indispensable. Most SS members of the political police were not directly under his command as SS-men but merely as policemen. Any police could have been relied upon to make the arrests between June 30 and July 2. When an instant execution was intended, however, SS-men usually got the assignment. Political policemen accompanied them to the place of action to provide the cover of a legal arrest but were not trusted to shoot. The most crucial roundups were assigned to units of the Leibstandarte, to Eicke's concentration camp guards, or to other special SS units, in the pattern of the SS Bereitschaften—for use where the general police could not be employed. The Prussian Gestapo were still considered too close to the general police to be completely reliable.

The reason is clear. One cannot legally order a policeman to go beyond the limits of his authority; that is, he cannot kill except in self-defense of to prevent a dangerous criminal from escaping or committing a serious crime. Heydrich could not rely on policemen to assume the role of executioner. At any moment their sense of propriety might take over and they would insist on due process. Men like Leibstandarte Captain Kurt Gildisch, believing that prompt, decisive action was necessary to prevent an uprising, simply obeyed orders and executed their victims on the spot. They adhered to their oath to obey Hitler and their SS superiors. Their responsibilities did not include questioning SS General Heydrich about the particulars of his orders to shoot someone, at least not during a state of emergency.[13]

June 30 made integration of the police with an obedient SS command an obviously desirable course. In his SD, Heydrich already had subordinates who ranged from those who merely felt a strong sense of obedience—as long as they believed that the fuehrer principle worked for the best—to others who would do any kind of dirty work. For such reasons, in areas where control over the political police had been tenuous, on June 30 he dispatched reliable SD officers as provisional heads of the local Gestapo—for instance, Ernst Mueller in the area of Breslau and Liegnitz. Subsequently Heydrich told Goering that he needed to replace the majority of Gestapo field post leaders as a result of their performance during the purge.[14] Obviously it would be to Heydrich's advantage if the remaining SS-men who were not SD were to be transferred to his command as chief of the SD. They had to become SD members.

The purge tightened Himmler's control over the political police and eliminated some opposition among the rest of the police. A number of those purged were SA police presidents like Heines in Silesia, who had interfered with control of the Gestapo. There, after the purge, SD Police Commissioner Ernst Mueller became head of SD Major Region Southeast, which was then freer to function in the former SA stronghold of Silesia. In the Breslau Gestapo office, he was succeeded by Anton Dunckern, one of the Bavarian police reliables recently drawn into the SD.[15]

The purge also provided a pretext for inserting SD men and other trusted agents into organizations and agencies that they wished to observe. Surveillance of the SA seems in fact to have increased rather than diminished.[16] The SA Ic or ND was finally dissolved in February 1935. Had he remained, Roehm would certainly have preserved this rival of the SD. The purge also induced many to volunteer their services to an SD, now credited with having saved the new Germany from anarchy and rule by undesirable elements. In this way, the contacts of the SD information net grew.

Although the purge clearly strengthened Himmler and Heydrich's control over the political police, it unevenly shaped their positions in the general power struggle. Himmler and his SS had proven, as never before, their "loyalty" to the Fuehrer and reminded him of his dependence on them. As a reward, Himmler and his SS became fully autonomous, free of all ties to the SA. As several scholars have stated, Hitler abandoned the forces of the Second Revolution, with whom he sympathized, because he realized they were impractical and anachronous. He retained, however, their goals of breaking the old order and raising a new one. He understood the techniques of modern revolutions, which function more subversively but produce more pervasive changes. Himmler and the SS-police concept provided a reliable instrument for such a cold, silent revolution, which undermined and replaced the old order slowly, operating below a surface of seeming normality. Within a generation they would pervade society with a whole new world view.[17] The elimination of the SA forced Hitler to rely on the SS to save him from control by the old order. The same developments entrenched the

SD as the information service of the new order. However, although the Party leadership around Hess had groomed Himmler, the SS, and the SD as allies, thereby elevating them considerably, their role in the purge made them independently powerful rivals.

For one thing, the purge affected their public images in conflicting ways. The role of the SS and SD in suppressing undesirable elements enhanced their image with some. As they dominated various legitimate functions in Germany, specifically the police administration, they became avenues for advancement for either families of note or the lower middle class who wanted to rise in the world. Entry into higher social circles thus became easier, and SS contacts with powerful circles of business and finance increased.[18] This newly acquired preeminence, as well as the brutal SS role in the purge, brought the equally negative reactions of fear and distrust. The total image of the SS and its police affiliates can only be understood as a peculiar synthesis, as was also true of the relations between Himmler and his former allies.

When the military, Goering, and the Party Leadership first allied with him, Himmler was a useful junior partner with valuable instruments at his command. Fortunately for him, they did not all see him as the next Roehm, but to prevent that from happening he had to maneuver carefully, maintaining an image of propriety and cooperation. The continued growth and entrenchment of his SS-police system depended on his ability to play the game subtly enough to avoid a united opposition, yet forcefully enough to win. To do this he had to keep his SS and police in line. As for Heydrich, head of the political police and SD, he generally understood the rules and played them well, but at times his ego problems or his impulsiveness created more troubles like those of the previous summer. The same was true of others in the SS.

In general, the military came out of the purge in a state of complacency. Most generals realized the implications of what had happened only in stages and at different rates. At first, a generally cooperative spirit prevailed between the military and the political police, although attitudes toward the SS and SD were ambivalent. Gradually, an opposition to Himmler's system developed, but never decisively enough to break the military from its dependence upon the SS for the "necessary" dirty work of the Third Reich. This dependence emerged when they relied on the SS to execute the SA. It would find its logical conclusions in the *Einsatzgruppen* on the Russian front years later.[19]

As for Goering, he gradually relinquished police power to Himmler, while retaining enough of a foothold to bolster his prestige. Meanwhile, June 30 restored—perhaps increased—his former suspicions of Himmler and especially of Heydrich. From this point on, he played them off against his other opponents in the state and Party. Within the Movement itself, the Party leadership discovered that while the SS had replaced the SA as a threat, they, like Hitler, were dependent on the SS as an instrument for controlling the revolution. There thus emerged a three-sided tension among the SS, the Hess Schwarz leadership, and Robert Ley's machinery, specifically the DAF. In this struggle, the SD spy net would prove a valuable tool for Himmler.[20]

The remaining factor, the conservative bureaucratic leadership, exemplified by Wilhelm Frick and entrenched in the machinery of state, drew a clear lesson from the blood purge. They knew they could not accept the SS—they had to shunt it aside also. With no interruption in the assault they had developed prior to June 30, Frick and his cohorts continued their conservative counterattack against the growing system that combined the SD, police, and concentration camps. In this counterattack, they had hopes for appeal to Hitler. By most accounts, Hitler was shocked and upset by the full scope of the bloodletting, and suffered psychologically from so brutal a split with old friends. Regardless of how much the purge had served his immediate needs, psychologically he must have blamed those who encouraged it, specifically the military and Himmler, on whom he allegedly vented anger when first shown the full death list.[21] Despite his obviously growing dependence on Himmler for police and security services, Hitler had good reason to remain ambivalent about further expansions, even about continuation of Himmler's police power.

13

The Conservative Counterattack

If Frick had not been building his forces before June 30, the experience of the purge would have compelled him to do so. On the first day of the action, when he realized that something was afoot, he rushed to Goering, who was busy coordinating things with Himmler and Heydrich. Goering allegedly dismissed him, telling him not to worry, that things were being taken care of and that he could go home.[1] If Frick had needed it, he now had a clear lesson about his relative standing among supposed allies. They had maneuvered without his knowledge and would conduct their extraordinary police work without his interference.

On Monday, July 2, at the end of the purge, Frick issued a decree—not a product of haste but part of his ongoing campaign, for it had been in preparation for a week before June 30. Even so, the wording and conception of the decree made it a self-defeating choice for a test of strength against Goering and Himmler, especially at that particular moment. In it, Frick attacked the participation of non-police agencies, specifically the SD, in political police work. Disdainfully, he referred to the SD as "the private security service of the Reichsfuehrer SS." He charged that such unsuitable cooperation interfered with routine, endangered secrecy, and made it impossible to discipline or punish those responsible for abuses. He notified all state governments that he strongly desired such cooperation to cease immediately.[2]

Of course, Frick was attacking the uncontrolled exercise of police power by an organization of the Movement, the very abuse he had sought to curb by cooperating with Goering and Himmler. Breaking the SA had eliminated one major component of the problem, but the role of the SS and SD in the purge put their threat in sharper focus. Unfortunately, that role also made their link with the political police at least temporarily unassailable. By flying in the face of a real constellation of power, Frick may well have predetermined his failure.

In one fatal move, he challenged Hitler's recent acknowledgement of the SD, almost as though he sought to shock Hitler into a return to proper procedures of state and to a relegation of Party organs to their proper position vis-à-vis the state. He apparently assumed that most of what had happened was without Hitler's knowledge, and that Hitler would support him if he set things right. Perhaps Frick wished to test the Fuehrer's sincerity about the order Hess claimed he had given on the SD's monopoly, or perhaps he believed recent events would induce Hitler to reverse or to limit his support. It that was the case, for a man who was losing the means to play such a game he chose a poor tactic. From this point on, Frick's formerly close working relationship with Hitler deteriorated.[3] Coming as it did in the heat of the "suppression of the coup," a time when Hitler felt his rule had been narrowly saved, Frick's maneuver must have given Hitler further doubts about one who insisted on due process during "emergencies." This gambit, like many others culminating in futile appeals to the Fuehrer, must have undermined Hitler's respect for Frick. Losers, especially those who made an issue of their losses, did not earn the respect of one who believed in social-Darwinistic processes.

If this move undermined Frick's standing with Hitler, it directly affronted Goering. Always amenable to efforts to counterbalance Himmler, Goering was susceptible to appeals for more proper (that is, more rational and efficient) police procedures. Instead, Frick's tactic openly challenged Goering's power and the "sharp strike force" he wanted to develop. On July 5, he responded decisively and self-confidently. Citing the free hand Hitler had given him and Himmler for the political police work of the preceding days, he claimed that Frick stood in opposition to the Fuehrer's guidelines. Under these conditions, SD cooperation was indispensable; therefore, Goering asked Frick to rescind the decree as far as the political police and the SD were concerned, and informed Frick that he had already instructed Prussian officials that the decree was inoperative for the Gestapo.[4]

In no position to question or test Goering's assertions about Hitler's orders, Frick stood checkmated on the political police. Nevertheless, as Goering's response indicated, in regard to the regular police he could press his case more successfully. For instance, by October, Saxon law once again forbade state policemen to be members of the SD. Throughout 1934 and 1935, a variety of regulations appeared prohibiting SS membership among uniformed police. Some emanated from police authorities, some from the SS itself. Although they were inconsistently enforced, it seemed that Himmler could be excluded from authority over all the regular police.[5] If the political police remained Himmler's only special domain, Frick then had all the more reason to try to terminate their extraordinary status.

Himmler reacted to Frick's attack more adroitly and less sponta-neously than Goering. The response reflected the necessity for him to balance carefully two opposing pressures: the more radical NS pressure to "partify" the police and put police work in hands that would deal properly with the enemies of the nation; and the demand for a return to normal, legal and proper (though "effective" and authoritarian) police institutions. The former demand had helped Himmler win command of all political police; he sought constantly to remind NS circles that he had given these police their proper ideological directions. On May 24, Hey-drich had attempted a visual reminder of this state of affairs by en-couraging Gestapo personnel to wear their NS uniforms to emphasize the identity between Gestapo and NS.[6]

Himmler responded to Frick on July 4. Without reference to Frick's circular letter, he ordered on his own authority that, given the SD's special position as sole security agency of the Party, it was a special "supplement" (Ergaenzung) to those organs that protected the state. However, he promptly and carefully balanced this order with an appeal to those yearning for more normality in police affairs by forbidding fur-ther executive action by the SD and limiting its cooperation with the police to informational support.[7] He thus defused Frick's major argu-ment, simultaneously calming fears of SS power growing out of June 30. After such maneuvers, the purge represented proof of the continued need for extraordinary powers, rather than the threat of an uncontrolled SS. Henceforth Himmler needed only to maintain an image of propriety sufficient to stifle fears that that power would be abused.

On the same day, Himmler made yet another significant move to elaborate his SS–police–concentration camp model. Since May, Eicke had been reorganizing the Prussian camps, so Himmler named him "Inspector of the KL (concentration camps) and Fuehrer of the SS Camp Guard Units [Wachverbaende]." A step toward his goal of creating a centralized concentration camp system for the entire Reich under his command as Reichsfuehrer SS, this maneuver eliminated state control (Goering's, Frick's or any other minister's) over the Prussian camps and made Himmler answerable only to Hitler for their management.[8] He also tried to use his position as commander of the political police in the other states to achieve a similar goal, bringing his Dachau model to the Reich level. Although this tactic had failed, at least temporarily, in Ham-burg,[9] it apparently succeeded in Saxony. Success or failure in the smaller states mattered not, however, for he dissolved their little camps and transferred all internees to the Prussian, Saxon, and Bavarian camps.

The confidence with which Himmler attempted this coup grew from the service the SS rendered on June 30, and there is no indication that he discussed it with Hitler. Goering must not have known of it, or at least he failed to understand its full significance. Himmler obviously attempted it without the knowledge of Frick and other ministers. They knew Eicke had taken over the Prussian camps, but they must have assumed he came under Himmler as inspector of the Gestapo, and, therefore, under state control.[10] Since Himmler concealed his full intentions until August, however, this coup remained unchallenged.

Meanwhile, Goering made the next gambit in coordination with Himmler and Heydrich. It resulted from the "lessons" of June 30 and the troublesome interference of bureaucrats, like Frick's futile attack on the SD-Gestapo relationship. On July 6 Goering issued the decree on the Gestapo that he had promised Frick for the clarification of relations between Gestapo field posts and the regional governors. Now, however, he responded to Frick's previous declaration of war with a double blow, dealing both with the field post problem and with Frick's contention that the status of the Gestapo was provisional. Goering stated that he had intentionally removed the Gestapo from all other police and administrative channels and made it an independent part of the administration directly under him. He had endowed this department with an especially great meaning for the stability (*Bestand*) of the new state, and he intended to stand by that decision. He would administer the Gestapo field posts. As a special authority, the Gestapo would handle all complaints and appeals itself, with himself as the final appeal: "Only if, in important cases, my orders go with the least delay directly to the authorities responsible for executive action, and only if I can receive from them important reports in the same manner, is the work possible in the Gestapo which the situation requires."[11]

Concerning the field posts, Goering reiterated their separateness and independence from the regional governors, and he clarified the division of labor. As partial compromise, the regional governors retained responsibility for political police work, with the Gestapo posts keeping them informed by regular reports and executing their directives unless they contradicted Gestapo orders. Goering, expecting this duplication of responsibilities to increase efficiency rather than cause competitiveness, ordered all authorities to cooperate: "The *sharp instrument* of the Gestapo, which I have created for the new state, has necessitated undoubted rifts in the structure of authority. However, *bureaucratic friction* can be avoided through a sincere cooperation."[12]

On the very next day, before he had full knowledge of what Goering had done, Frick continued on his aggressive tack. First he notified Goering that he intended to resubordinate the Gestapo field posts to the district governors because of the problems resulting from their separation. Then he issued orders to all *Land* governments that provincial and district governors were to forward monthly political situation reports to him. In this order, Frick tried to place on record two significant facts and to create mechanisms for the eventual replacement of the extra-ordinary political police. First, he remarked, as if in passing, that the independent political police resulted from the special circumstances surrounding the power seizure—a reaffirmation of his major attack. Then he argued that their separation from regular administrative channels had cut the rest of the government off from its normal sources of political information, depriving the Reich ministries of knowledge they needed. Frick's order creating the governors' reporting system gave them the pretext for establishing their own political intelligence system independent of the political police.[13]

Goering's response to both acts came two days later, in the form of a letter to Frick. He nullified Frick's intended resubordination of the Gestapo field posts, because his decree of July 6 had settled the problem and, as he had stated in the decree, conditions necessitated the independent political police. He elaborated in a handwritten note appended to his official response: The "Roehm revolt" had clearly proven the necessity of the Gestapo; freed of bureaucratic encumbrances, it existed for the lightning-quick execution of the Fuehrer's measures. Goering then promised Frick to forward a report; after Frick had studied it, they could discuss the matter.[14] Initially, Goering also responded mildly to the creation of a political situation report system in the administration. He welcomed it as a complement to his July 6 decree on the Gestapo and noted that he had already ordered the field posts to give their political situation reports to the governors. He then asked to receive *directly* copies of the governors' reports. Perhaps intentionally, Goering avoided any reference to the "temporary special police" argument that Frick pursued.[15]

If Goering's initial response to Frick's move was as mild and co-operative as this correspondence suggested, he soon changed. Perhaps he began to realize the full significance of Frick's move, or perhaps some of those around him, like Himmler and Heydrich, incited fears of a devious plot. In any case, on July 11 he then drafted several very hot responses to Frick that made some distorted interpretations of Frick's order. Unfortunately, the surviving records do not indicate whether Goering actually dispatched such letters to Frick, but clearly they were defensive and hostile reactions to Frick's latest move.[16] Whether or not it was Himmler and Heydrich who had incited Goering's anger, they certainly fanned the flames later in the month. On July 21, they forwarded a report from the Duesseldorf field post complaining that the local governor was establishing a political system separate from that of the Gestapo. They complained that duplication of effort would hinder their work and asked that the governor be ordered to turn to the relevant Gestapo field post for his reports.[17]

Meanwhile Frick and his allies pressed Goering with numerous accounts of the problems created by an independent political police. Frick complained that the Gestapo Office disobeyed Goering's repeated orders to keep all responsible agencies informed. For instance, Frick still lacked complete knowledge of the fate of many officials after the recent purge. Governors and local police officials generally remained in the dark, and the political police who should be accountable to them were actually conducting investigations into their affairs. Sometimes local Gestapo leaders questioned the authority of governors to give them orders. Frick and his officials, supposedly responsible for law and order, could not function.[18]

This campaign began of July 13 with a letter of complaint from Frick to Goering. He expressed the surprise with which he had received the decree of July 6 and objected to matters of such significance to his ministry being decided without his knowledge or participation. Indeed, Goering had led him to believe that he was going to restore the authority of the governors over the Gestapo field posts. He requested that in the future such misunderstandings be avoided by a closer cooperation with his ministry. Although he insisted that the situation be corrected as soon as possible, he accepted Goering's explanation that it was necessary as a *transitional solution* because of the tense political situation caused by the "Roehm revolt."[19] While trying to stand his ground, Frick apparently hoped to establish a closer relation with Goering and to build an overwhelming case for his cooperation in controlling and eventually eliminating the extraordinary political police. In the following days, Frick continued with this tactic.

On July 16 he issued two orders. In an order to the Prussian governors, he began by asserting that his basic thesis was generally accepted—that is, that the separation of the Gestapo field posts was only a transitional settlement. Then he ordered complete reports on every problem arising between the governors and the Gestapo. He would build his case thoroughly.[20]

In the other order, Frick sought to arouse a broader awareness of the problem of the political police. He ordered lower-level state police authorities, especially the political police to observe more carefully the limits of their authority and, before taking an action, to check its propriety with the highest Reich and state authorities wherever possible. He specifically criticized the political police for losing sight of their proper mission and expanding their activities into more totalitarian controls, such as dissolving societies that were not illegal, or forbidding their meetings, or prohibiting the distribution of church literature of a purely church-related nature. He defined their competence as limited to the observation, discovery, and legal prosecution of political crimes.[21] As if the disappearance of the SA danger would make the growth of the political police a more obvious threat, Frick hoped to generate support against Himmler's controls and to induce from the responsible police officials more self-restraint.

Meanwhile, the even more glaring abuses of the concentration camps won Frick more conservative allies for the counterattack. Even in staunch Nazi circles, the camps generated a growing awareness that the police state threatened them as well. During the summer of 1934, from all over the Reich came challenges to the concentration camps and to the recent excesses of the purge. In Breslau, the public prosecutor had twenty SS men arrested in conjunction with especially wild actions there. In Saxony, the prosecutor collected evidence leading to a state case against twenty-five SA guards from the defunct camp at Hohnstein and against the Saxon Gestapo official who delivered prisoners to them. In Bavaria, Himmler's opponents temporarily reopened the case of the deaths of Franz and Katz at Dachau. Frick assembled evidence that numerous Party members and even Old Fighters had been languishing in the camps before the purge. Belatedly, Frick had joined Hans Frank and Frantz Guertner in their attack on the camps.[22]

From top to bottom, the state bureaucracy aroused itself. Even the Party split over the issue of the camps and extraordinary police action. No one doubted what had happened in the camps in the past, and the rumors of what went on during the purge had spread across the land. In his own speech on the "Roehm revolt" before the Reichstag on July 13, Hitler had elaborated on the SA excesses and on the "wild" camps, including the case of the SS-Gestapo camp at Stettin, for which Hoffmann and other SS-men had been shot during the purge.[23] If these were examples of the uncontrolled behavior of the "enemies" just purged, they would seem to call for a push to abolish the system that allowed them.

Stalemate

In fact, nothing better than a temporary stalemate resulted, lasting into 1935 and followed by the long-range victory of the SS-camp system. Most opposition efforts initiated in 1934 petered out or hung fire until a new wave of counterattacks in 1935. Hitler stood by his earlier decision to preserve the developing machinery of the police state, while at the same time not confronting the conservative opposition with a clear defeat.[24]

Preserving some semblance of a compromise, Hitler and Himmler sought to calm the fears of those who felt threatened. On August 7, after Hindenburg's death and Hitler's assumption of the presidency, they proclaimed a general amnesty for many in protective custody, especially SA-men seized during the purge. Hitler then announced that, since the crisis of June 30 had passed, he wanted Frick's more restrictive protective custody regulations (of April 12 and 26) "to be carefully observed by all authorities." The result was a general, significant reduction of the total number of camp internees.[25]

This development encouraged the conservatives to believe in the viability of their argument that the extraordinary system was a transitional measure, and that given time and continued pressure, the Fuehrer would restore a more normative legal order. Meanwhile, their own efforts to break up the system met with delay and obfuscation by Himmler, repression by more radical NS leaders, and often final defeat when Hitler consented to have a strong legal case quashed. Each time they had to accept one or more of three different arguments as prevailing: First, the enemies of the nation were still strong enough to require a continued state of emergency. Second, any assaults on the system manned by the SS and police would undermine the authority of the NS state, thereby playing into the hands of the enemy. Finally, the system had been brought under proper control, the "wild" stage of the revolution had passed, and further abuses would be so insignificant that the system could handle them properly. The last two arguments contained just enough truth to be convincing in right-wing circles, thereby undermining support for the conservative counterattack.

In fact, the consolidation of the concentration camps and the political police under Himmler eliminated many bases for complaints against the system. Lest this statement be misunderstood, it requires qualification on two significant points. The "improvements" in question in no way prevented the later horrors of the camps; as a matter of fact, in their own insidious way they made them more possible than the previous "wild" system. The "wild" camps caused alarm and provided an irrefutable basis for demands that they be eliminated or controlled. On the other hand, the camps under Himmler, officially and rigidly regulated by a disciplined organization accountable to the head of state, created the impression of responsible state management and made it possible for some to believe that any abuses that remained were merely incidental.

The nature of the improvements also requires closer analysis. First, in regard to the concentration camps, Eicke gave the new Reich-wide system the same regulations and disciplinary code that had cleaned up Dachau in 1933. In all of the "wild" camps, the horrors resulted from woefully inadequate facilities and the lack of regulations for the behavior of guards. Without guidelines for behavior toward internees, conditions conducive to orgies of sadistic vengeance had developed in most camps. Eicke replaced this with a regimen designed to regiment the prisoners and to dehumanize their relations with the guards. To ensure rigid order and obedience from the internees, a system of graded punishment ranged from denial of mail and reduced rations through corporal punishment to execution. For some offenses, such as attacking guards or attempting escape, execution would be immediate. In other cases, it would be ordered by a camp court, with no outside appeal. To dehumanize relations with prisoners, the guards' behavior was regulated to maintain distance and to eliminate human contact. Taught to treat internees "objectively," that is, as objects, the guards could execute discipline obediently and without qualms. This eliminated sadistic excesses that provided the bases for outside attack and undermined discipline. Simultaneously, the guards were constantly indoctrinated with the line that the prisoners were "dangerous enemies of the state" who deserved no pity. Prisoners thus became suitable objects of retribution, preventing questions about the propriety of extreme forms of punishment. Rather than as individuals, the guards as groups administered the punishments at assemblies of the internees, giving it all an air of due process.[26]

Of course, shooting prisoners on the spot or executing them on the orders of a camp court remained illegal where not absolutely necessary, and it could provide the basis for a legal action and an attack on the system. The maintenance of this threat guaranteed a period of relative moderation in the camps that prevailed through 1935 and until 1938-39.

Improvements in the Prussian Gestapo were in much the same vein. Himmler imposed his control over the Gestapo from central office to field post, not only to build his own empire but also to eliminate the abuses that made it vulnerable to criticism and "bureaucratic" interferences. Primarily for this second purpose, Goering supported him. The tightening of the direct authority of the Gestapo Office over the field posts eliminated their irregularities and removed them from the undisciplined authority of local NS leaders. The appointment of SS officers to their command or the absorption of their leaders into the SS not only facilitated SS penetration but also ensured Himmler's and Heydrich's personal control of them. Diels had lacked this institutional authority, which was the basis of Himmler's victory. For that reason, one can assume that Himmler and Heydrich were sincere in issuing the orders to regulate police behavior and to prevent excesses by the Gestapo. Such orders were not a facade, as is usually contended. They were of a more insidious character that must be understood.

As early as June 16, Goering had decreed a complete accounting of all protective custody internees. Heydrich tried to follow suit; however, establishing discipline with the newly acquired Gestapo took time. The freewheeling actions of the purge disrupted the process, and a full accounting of the internees was impossible before August. Heydrich resorted to reminders about the terms of Goering's and Frick's regulations as he strove to eliminate uncontrolled abuses by Gestapo personnel. A typical guideline reminded them that "it is unworthy of a member of the Gestapo Office to insult or to handle internees unnecessarily roughly. In case it is necessary, the arrestee is to be treated with the necessary severity [Strenge], but never with chicanery and unnecessary persecution. I will prosecute severely, with the most rigorous means, offenses against this order."[27]

On October 11, Himmler spoke to all the personnel of the Gestapo Office. The speech provides insight into what he wanted the Gestapo to be. First, he proclaimed June 30 as the heaviest of burdens that could have befallen those who had to shoot down old comrades who had failed and become untrue, indecent, and disobedient. The day had proven that Hitler's state was not yet victorious but that the Gestapo consisted of the most absolutely useful, loyal, and obedient people. He then pointed out that behind the events of June 30 were Jews, Freemasons, and Ultramontanists who had infiltrated the Movement and brought on chaos, hoping that foreign enemies would intervene once again in Germany. Using this as a springboard, Himmler lectured all the detectives on searching for the Jewish enemy who lay behind everything that was subversive and destructive of German society. He made it clear that from here on, the investigators who operated with an understanding of the racial conspiracy behind all crime would be the most successful.[28]

After this insight into basic ideology (an insight that came almost as an aside to his scapegoating), Himmler described the working procedures and the image he desired for his organization. He proclaimed that, as opposed to a bureaucracy, the Gestapo should handle its business with soldierly speed. By "bureaucracy" he did not mean careful efficient work, but just the opposite: red tape and an anonymity that produced irresponsibility. He wanted prompt responses to all queries from other agencies, and, where that was impossible, assurances that the matter was being pursued. When an official completed his responsibility for an assignment, he would personally bring it promptly to the attention of the next official rather than shuffling it through the paper mill.[29]

Such behavior would establish the proper image with the public. The Gestapo was not to appear as a blind, anonymous bureaucracy, especially in cases concerning protective custody. When "the little man among the people" reported something, or when the wife waited in fear to hear of the fate of her husband taken into custody, they were not to receive facsimiles of paperwork sent as a matter of routine. For that reason, Himmler insisted on personally signing orders and reports for which he was responsible, and others would do likewise.

The *Volk* must hold the conviction that the most just authority, which works the most exactly in the new state, is the dreaded Gestapo. The *Volk* must come to the view that, if someone has been seized, he had been seized with right; it must have the view that, in all things that are not to the detriment of the state, the members of the Gestapo are men with human kindness, with human hearts and absolute rightness. We must not forget—beginning from the highest to the last official and employee—that we exist for the *Volk* and not the *Volk* for us.

I also wish that everyone who comes to you will be handled courteously and sociably. I wish that you will use on the phone a courteous and proper tone. I wish further that no man will growl in any way. Please, see yourself as helpers and not as dictators.[30]

These last passages reveal Himmler's contradictory and ironically naive concepts. They compare well with the previous analysis of the camp regulations. Himmler wanted the Gestapo to be dreaded for its efficiency and coldblooded thoroughness in dealing with enemies, yet he wanted the good citizen to know that there was no need to fear that organization. He actually believed that policemen could successfully distinguish between the enemy and the citizen good at heart, that he could eliminate the enemy objectively and behave toward everyone else with, not just propriety, but also humanity. Himmler was convinced that the people could see "enemies" among them seized and crushed and not respond to the police with some hostility grown of fear and distrust. Of course, he was not so naive as to believe that all this could come into being immediately; it would take time for the "poisons of the old order" to wear away. What we see in Himmler was not atypical of Nazis. It was his genuine conviction that totalitarianism could produce a harmonious, egalitarian, and paternalisticly authoritarian society.

Himmler's speech also sought to dispel rumors that he feared could damage harmony and morale in the Gestapo. He cited stories that he and Goering or he and Goebbels were enemies, that Goering and Hess were bloody rivals, that the SS and the military were enemies, that General Fritsch aspired to replace Blomberg or that Heydrich coveted his position, or that Heydrich had been overthrown, even murdered. Of course, Himmler dismissed all of this as seeds of doubt sown by the enemy.[31]

Two facts are significant here. First, it was already common gossip that Heydrich would overthrow Himmler if he could. This, the basis for many of the legends that still surround the Gestapo and SD, might be an accurate description of their later relations, but for these years, it was mostly premature. Heydrich's biographer, Aronson, put this in its proper perspective by emphasizing the debt that Heydrich owed Himmler and the extent to which he was dependent on Himmler for his position at this time.[32]

Second, Himmler's concern about rumors of real rivalries grew from several considerations. He did not want his subordinates to view their milieu conspiratorially. Not only would that be detrimental to morale, it would also encourage them to conspire, creating problems of control. Some might betray him to his enemies, other might seek his favor by being spiteful toward his opponents, generating incidents and more tensions. To prevail, he had to control his organizations and ensure that they acted against his opposition only as he saw fit. Of equal importance, however, the spirit of camaraderie in the Movement had to prevail. By the time Himmler gave this speech in October, the complex web of rivalries had reached the point where he began suffering some setbacks, fueling his need to control his people and maintain an image of propriety.

On August 18, Himmler had revealed his hand and overplayed it. He notified the Prussian Ministries of Finance and Interior that the budgets for the state camps, Papenburg and Lichtenburg (the only two official Prussian camps), were no longer correct. "The responsibility for the camps, which were formerly directly subordinated to me [as Inspector of the Gestapo], will henceforth be assumed by [me] the Reichsfuehrer SS." Furthermore, he had taken over the former jail at Columbia House and the SA camp at Oranienberg. Effective September 1, they would be financed through a new budget line and one lump sum for the administration of all four facilities would be paid to him as Reichsfuehrer SS. The SS personnel for the camps would be paid on a military pay scale. As a result of these changes, the minister of the interior no longer had responsibility for the camps and all requests for funds would go directly to the minister of finance.[33]

Himmler had to reveal his hand in order to establish the budget for the next fiscal year. He had already broached the matter personally with the minister of finance, whom he wanted to deal with Frick. The directive apparently reached the offices of the Interior Ministry without warning. On first reading, everyone was puzzled over Himmler's sleight of hand. Then the passage about the authority of the Prussian minister of the interior made it obvious.[34] Countertactics began.

The finance minister informed Goering through a note. While professing a willingness to cooperate, he made sure Goering appreciated fully that through this move he would also surrender the political affairs of the camps to the Reichsfuehrer SS. He went on to observe that the whole matter seemed inseparable from Goering's plans for the future organization of the Gestapo.[35] Goering was not fully aware of the significance of Himmler's tactic, and his staff also seemed unaware of what Himmler was doing with the camps. Even if the note from the Finance Ministry failed to arouse him fully,[36] a little thrust from Frick might have pushed him into action.

On August 28, however, Frick gave his consent to the general terms of Himmler's proposal, apparently with ulterior motives. Since he had no real control over the economic affairs of the camps, he lost nothing. Instead he hoped that the separation of the budget for the camps from that of the Gestapo would eliminate some of Himmler's freedom, for he used inflated camp funds to expand his police. Meanwhile, he apparently intended to hang Himmler up on technicalities related to his proposal.[37] He probably believed the camps would soon be eliminated anyway. Having retreated from a fight he thought no longer important, Frick sought to tighten other screws and to goad Goering into action against Himmler's Gestapo. In Prussia, Frick's staff had been developing regulations to control the actions of all executive police, hoping to include the Gestapo. Toward this end, they sent a draft of the regulations to Himmler for his comments on how they should be developed. Himmler sought to sidestep this maneuver by responding that because of the independent and extraordinary status of the Gestapo, it should be excluded from such a regulation.[38]

Independent responses similar to this one gave Frick a pretext for taunting Goering about his failure to exercise enough direct control over the Gestapo. On September 27, Frick chided him about correspondence of political significance being answered by the Gestapo Office itself and perhaps not even being seen by Goering.[39] This and the note from the finance minister apparently roused Goering to action. In October, he ordered that his ministry exercise more direct control over Gestapo correspondence, and he assured Frick that he was developing tighter control.[40] Indeed, Goering quickly asserted himself. Although he supported Himmler's effort to keep the Gestapo free of external controls, he sought to preserve his own personal control. He made a move he had been contemplating for at least a month, notifying Himmler that it was time to formalize their relationship with a clear delineation of authority that he intended to decree. As an interesting aside, his message clearly revealed that he suffered from what he called his "work overload," and that his drive was weakening.[41] Even so, Himmler had overplayed his hand and was threatened with some loss of ground. Heydrich had tried to avoid anything that might give Goering offense or create enough concern to produce such a move as this. Toward that end, he had begun to review carefully all correspondence between Gestapo offices and

Goering.[42] Of course, this inevitably led Heydrich to insert himself increasingly between Goering and his "sharp instrument."

The resultant clarification of Himmler's authority that Goering issued on October 15 has been interpreted as a clear but temporary defeat for Himmler. A temporary obstacle it was, but hardly a defeat. Himmler had been summoned to work with Goering's staff on the drafting of the clarification, and at that time he apparently began a concerted but tactful drive for more independence that gradually wore Goering down.[43] By the time he issued the clarification, Goering had lost some of his initial determination. He merely specified the general understanding he thought he had had with Himmler in April, reasserting the subordination of Himmler as inspector and of the Gestapo under his authority. Although he insisted that, except for political situation reports and certain emergency measures, correspondence with other state offices was to go through his offices, he gave Himmler considerable leeway on the basis of the understanding between them. Significantly, Goering retained control of budgetary matters and the appointment, promotion, transfer, and release of all the highest officials. Beyond that, the Gestapo would be run by Himmler under whom, *as inspector of the Gestapo*, the state concentration camps would also be administered.[44] This last point was the closest Himmler came to a defeat. Himmler did not run the camps as Reichsfuehrer SS; instead, Himmler held them as Goering's appointee—a position Goering could modify of terminate if he so chose.[45]

Even the retention of the camps under the Gestapo, and therefore under Goering's authority, was only a temporary setback. Himmler had complete control of them and they certainly remained free of Frick's influence, as before. Goering's bureaucrats were frustrated in their attempts to exercise any influence, because, although Eicke administered the camps under Himmler as inspector of the Gestapo, he was commander of the SS camp guards under Himmler as *Reichsfuehrer* SS. Eicke simply ignored their instructions and requests.[46] Meanwhile, for Himmler, Goering remained a valuable ally because his primary concern continued to be preservation of the "sharp strike" capacity of his Gestapo.

In contrast to whatever reversal these developments may have seemed for Himmler, they actually brought increased freedom of action and an expansion of his official authority. For instance, he apparently convinced Goering that his title as inspector of the Gestapo poorly portrayed his full authority as Goering's deputy. As a result, by the end of the month protective custody arrest orders no longer had to be issued under Goering's direct authority as "Prussian prime minister and chief of the Gestapo," but rather under Himmler's as "Prussian Gestapo deputy chief and inspector."[47] Goering increasingly withdrew from direct responsibility and involvement. He hardly abdicated everything to Himmler at this point, however, for his retreat remained incomplete until 1936. Meanwhile, he would make gestures toward asserting himself and would complain to Himmler about failures to honor the recent guidelines. Nevertheless, Goering's staff was powerless to exercise any control and told him so. Goering lacked the confidence to turn to Hitler to control Himmler, because Himmler's obstructionist tactics were so frustrating.[48]

In the end, Goering gave up and revealed the full extent of his abdication. On November 20, he essentially reversed the previous month's restrictions, made Himmler, as his deputy, solely responsible for the Gestapo, and removed responsibility from his ministry offices. All correspondence henceforth went directly to the Gestapo Office. Goering maintained direct control only of the finances, merely demanding that he be kept fully informed of all other matters of significance. He instructed Himmler that he wanted the Gestapo freed, as far as possible, from executive responsibilities, and that he especially wanted the field posts brought into closer association (*Zusammenhang*) with the governors and the state administration. Despite this general expression of support for some of Frick's arguments, Goering trusted Himmler to work out the details with the ministers involved.[49] In other words, Goering withdrew from the contest between Himmler and Frick, while trying to maintain an appearance of neutrality. Perhaps he was also trying to save face, for the contest must have become too much for him. He had been torn for too long between the contradictory desires for a "proper" order and for a freewheeling police force to defend the new order. After all, the former concern was being pursued most properly by Frick, and he had entrusted the latter to the able hands of Himmler.

By the end of 1934, Frick had thus generally lost ground in his efforts to control Himmler's power in the political police and concentration camps. He could only hinder their growth, limit their finances, and obstruct some of Himmler's infiltrations of SS-men into positions of command. Beyond this his real hope remained a tighter control for himself over all other police. Central to this tactic was the establishment of a Reich criminal police to replace the political police when a state of normality was restored.[50]

14

The Selling of the
Police State

Between 1934 and 1936, the nascent police state evolved into an established system, with Himmler in command. Before he could overcome Hitler's ambivalence about his control of all police and gain appointment from the Fuehrer, Himmler had to reduce opposition to more extensive police power. To do this, he had to "sell" the idea of a permanent police state. In that "sales campaign," the major thrust had to be against the contention that the extraordinary political police and concentration camp system was only a temporary response to a state of emergency. Beyond Himmler's opposition, the targets of the campaign were the rest of the establishment and the NS leadership who could affect the decision. The more general target is less easily defined. It included the judiciary, the civil service, especially the police, the General SS, broad segments of the Movement, and even the general public, for all contributed to the power bases of those struggling over the police.

Himmler's "sales campaign" to win approval of a stronger police is not to be seen as a contemporary public relations campaign, but rather as a fight to convince opponents and to educate key segments of society. It was not a carefully planned and coordinated program, but one that evolved in response to a complex environment. It was such a natural process of argument and counterargument that surviving participants are amazed at the suggestion that there was any campaign to sell the police state.[1] Even so, there can be no denial of the striking contrast between the surviving evidence and the traditional image of a police state grown out of secrecy. Equally striking, the components of the "sales campaign" have long been recognized as the propaganda base of the Nazi regime.

The uses of foreign policy adventures, imperialism, orchestrated fears, and scapegoating as devices for establishing and maintaining totalitarian regimes are established parts of the model for analyzing the Third Reich. Nevertheless, for two reasons this model requires re-examination. First, its specific application to the selling of the police state has yet to be documented in any detail. Second, the general acceptance of the totalitarian model as an explanation for the workings of the NS police state has led to oversimplification in the literature, both popular and scholarly.[2] Unfortunately this has clouded the extent to which the process was intuitively and/or spontaneously generated, rather than cynically calculated. There is a general failure to comprehend the role of mutual escalation among the participants.

Modern radical right revolutionary movements employ both foreign affairs distractions and scapegoating tactics. Specifically, in the National Socialist world view, the Germans, as inherently superior people, were the victims of a conspiracy to prevent their natural hegemony. Other nations and international forces ensnared Germany in external entanglements and undermined her internal strength. This explained all the frustrations of German history, especially the current humiliations. The proper response was a determined defense and an aggressive counter-offensive. From this position, it was easy to move to imperialistic adventure in fulfillment of the natural destiny that one's opponents sought to deny. By implication, aggressive expansion became the only secure defense against the nation's enemies. Such scenarios, built on the themes of national greatness, defense, and security, have proven useful for distracting the economically, socially, and politically frustrated, focusing their attention on "higher" priorities so they can be manipulated. Since elites often believed in such national mythologies, they too became susceptible to manipulation by leaders like Hitler. While Hitler used such appeals to direct Germany toward goals evolving in his own mind, Himmler elaborated on them for the development of the institutions he believed essential to the pursuit of Hitler's goals.

The other side of this coin—scapegoating—developed to its inherent extremes during the Third Reich. Internal conflict in a nation is generally believed to sap its strength for external struggle. Consequently, external or nonnational enemies would seek to encourage, even to generate, internally divisive forces. Within this framework, a xenophobic concern with foreign enemies equates easily with tendencies to distrust the nonconformist. The NS world view, bred from centuries of European intracultural tensions and hostilities, elaborated an international conspiracy theory that linked Germany's external enemies with internal minorities and with a variety of cultural movements. Not only did the Jew stand prominently at the head of the international conspiracy, but Slavs, Gypsies, and blacks played supporting roles. Not only Communism but organizations with international, liberal, or pacifist inclinations, like the Masonic Order or the Esperanto movement, served as the machinery of penetration and discord, as did radical or innovative cultural movements, like the Sex Reform movement, and nontraditional art forms or even new schools of scientific and intellectual thought—Freudian psychology, for instance. Foreign dominated or "Roman" Christianity became suspect for many Nazis, and the most radical rejected even German Protestant Christianity.

Conservative Nazis like Frick and all conservative allies shared this mythology to some extent. The vast majority accepted the foreign affairs scenario as far as justifying some degree of imperialism. Most shared the fears and prejudices upon which scapegoating was based. Consequently, they were open to the selling of the police state as long as it could be tied to the defense of society against such evils.

In 1935, Hitler began an escalation of foreign policy that heightened international and, therefore, internal tensions. The convenient juxtaposition of heightened concern over the external enemy and growing fear of the internal enemy provided the basis for the transition from the nascent police state of 1934 to the more secured one of 1936. The foundations had been laid in 1933 when revolutionary zeal and fear of an imminent Communist coup created an expanded political police and the spontaneous terrorism of SA and SS auxiliaries and concentration camps. The radical menace of the Second Revolution had allowed Himmler to consolidate the initial foundations into the nascent police state by late 1934. Its survival and continued growth depended on new and more sinister internal threats that in turn derived their significance from the heightening international tensions.

Himmler's ability to capitalize best on the juxtaposition of foreign and domestic enemy mythologies lay in his total acceptance of them, combined with both an intuitive and conscious awareness of their political utility. Since the collapse of 1918, he had believed Germany's only hope for the future lay in eastward "settlement." In his early adulthood, the NS world view fortified this belief and fused it with the theories of the internal enemy that provided him with such a coherent explanation of Germany's problems. Subscribing totally to the double myth, he would create the police state or the state protection corps to defend the Reich against its internal enemies, and he would have the SS contribute in every way possible to external adventure and advances. His strength as a rival in the internal power struggle was that he remained dedicated and sincere. He and his lieutenants were able to sell the police state precisely because they were sincere. As their tactics succeeded, an awareness of their utility must have developed. At an early time, Himmler joined the chorus of radicals encouraging Hitler's foreign policy adventures,[3] and as Hitler's posture became increasingly war-prone, Himmler offered the internal security system necessary to prevent a repetition of the "stab in the back." This increased Hitler's willingness to grant Himmler police powers he might otherwise have preferred to distribute among other competing lieutenants.

Following the summer of 1934, Germany's international position had reached another nadir. The abortive Austrian coup of July made Mussolini an enemy, and Hitler's other desired ally, Britain, vacillated between hostility and ambivalence at best. The return of the Saar in January 1935 brought no significant changes in the international climate, but as the first successful restoration of German honor, it whetted appetites. Although Hitler postponed the announcement of rearmament until March, not only the military but also the Party leadership got exciting glimpses of what lay ahead. On January 3, at a conference of *Gau* and Reich Leaders, Hitler revealed rearmament plans and apparently some long-range foreign policy goals.[4] No matter how vaguely stated, they would have fired Himmler's and Heydrich's imaginations, increasing their determination to furnish reliable instruments for the Fuehrer's purposes.

The atmosphere in military, government, and Party circles determined receptivity to Himmler's arguments. A defensive paranoia prevailed, contemplating several years during which Germany would be highly vulnerable to intervention by its enemies. The military had to consider seriously the possibility of a Franco-Italian attack,[5] a fear reinforced in April 1935 by the Stresa Front. To this were added the threats of the Franco-Czech-Soviet pacts in May and the Comintern pronouncement of the Popular Front tactic in August. The "international conspiracy" was obviously mobilizing.

Of course, Hitler and lieutenants like Himmler used these "threats" to manipulate and mobilize Germany as they desired; however, it is a best a half-truth to describe this as a cynical manipulation. The threats did in fact exist, verifying the world view that demanded a new order for Germany. They provided the propaganda base that enabled Hitler to build toward the Rhineland occupation as early as June 1935, and to push it to conclusion by the following March. Of course, that development was, in turn, part of the process of giving Party radicals an outlet for action while driving reluctant conservatives into dangerous international adventures,[6] but it was process that compelled the manipulators as much as the manipulated.

Success in the Rhineland increased both fears and the desire for more. After March 1936, Germany's position improved and, in reality, became secure; however, given a xenophobic world view, one's enemies could be expected to take more decisive action. Popular Front victories and the ratification of the encircling alliances provided the proof that they were mobilizing. Although the Four Year Plan of 1936 to prepare Germany for war reveals aggressive intent, and although the military's contingency plans included offensive as well as defensive actions, this was not simply the behavior of confident aggressors. In the NS view of international struggle for survival, distinctions between offense and defense lost all meaning. By the end of 1936, the growing confidence in Germany also produced an increased anxiety of the sort that is felt as success becomes visible but remains just beyond reach. In this atmosphere of mounting tension during 1935-36, Himmler consolidated his power.

If the external enemy was mobilizing, then surely his internal subversion was on the rise. This assumption went hand in hand with growing frustrations within the Movement about completing the NS victory. Even if the purge had repressed talk about a second revolution, agitation continued for destroying the power bases of internal enemies and for Nazifying the institutions of German society still largely in conservative hands. In this process, Himmler returned to a stance sympathetic to the goals of the Second Revolution, making his SS part of the more radical component. Hitler must have generally concurred, as long as such radicalism did not disrupt his plans and his manipulation of conservative allies.

For the rank and file, frustrations and enthusiasms vented themselves most easily and naturally on the Jews. Beginning in April and May of 1935 and growing through the summer, a wave of "spontaneous" local actions against Jewish property spread across the Reich. As usual, NS leaders increased their power bases by supporting and leading such actions. SS and SD leaders certainly responded to the pressure. The local SS participated often, to the extent of conflict with the local police. Of course Himmler sympathized with the spirit of these actions, but he intended to control his organization as Roehm had not. Consequently, down through the propaganda organs of the SS came official appeals against anti-Semitic excesses.[7]

The responsible state officials were in a comparable position. Most of them, like Frick, though anti-Semitic, were primarily concerned with legality, due process, proper controls, and the necessity of avoiding excesses that might invite economic and international repercussions. During late summer, both Schacht and Frick pressed for government-controlled action to solve the "Jewish problem" and to defuse the pressures for uncontrolled violence. The resultant Nuremberg Laws defined the Jewish enemy and set limitations on his economic and social role. Again, this was a case of the use of ideology and anti-Semitic fervor to manipulate the power base in Germany; however, it was also a case of the agitators being agitated to increasingly radical positions by the very process they employed.[8]

Although the need to attack the "Jewish problem" beckoned Himmler and some of his people, it did not, in its existing, simple form provide all the arguments needed to justify the police state. The real Jew was the target of Nazi frustrations partially because he was so vulnerable: every Nazi tough knew he could handle his local Jews. The Jewish problem did not justify elaborate SS and police institutions. Such institutions instead interfered with those direct, simple solutions the local tough would employ. Nevertheless, new justifications for the police state were needed, for success threatened the old ones. Although dedicated Communists would always be good for periodic roundups and the exposure of new plots, the old hysteria was wearing itself out. The number of camp inmates did not rise after Heydrich took over the Gestapo and Eicke consolidated the camps.[9] Instead, the process of consolidation demanded reductions of internees, and the abatement of the old hysteria provided no justification for anything else.

The new justification required a carefully elaborated scenario portraying an all-pervasive and subtly camouflaged enemy who made necessary an extensive and sophisticated security system to detect, expose, and defeat him. In 1935, Heydrich began openly and publicly to define such "threats" and to propagandize for the means to combat them. The SS press widely disseminated copies of a speech in which he proclaimed that the nature of the NS struggle had changed. The power seizure had not ended it. The enemies of the nation, though denied control over the government, maintained their threat to Germandom. The obvious and basic enemies remained: the Jews and their instruments, the Freemasons, and the politically active priesthood, most notably the Jesuits, who misused the Church. They could either be driven legally from Germany or kept under control. Of course, their international ties would remain an ever-present threat against which Germany would have to steel itself. Such open enemies remained to be dealt with forcefully. But now they were joined by the camouflaged enemy—those who worked secretly from within, trying to destroy the union between the leadership and the people, those who strove to prevent the erection of the NS ideology. These enemies would try to seize and hold key posts in the state and the Movement. They would use bureaucratic red tape to impede the Nazi mission. Like the Devil, who quoted scripture, they would adopt NS jargon for arguments to confuse and misdirect the new order.[10]

To be able to identify the enemy was the goal. State apparatus like the police could not manage alone, for they could only strike against the overtly illegal enemy. As the enemy had adapted himself to the new struggle, so must the methods of combating him be changed. Revolution had changed to evolution, and power seizure had to change to a campaign for ideological and spiritual conversion. For this, the SS was most suitable.[11]

Although he redefined the threat, at this point Heydrich did little more than assert the necessity of a close and continued link between SS and police, and of the maintenance of eternal vigilance against the undefeated enemy. Essentially, his message was intended primarily for SS consumption, demanding of them the more disciplined and controlled behavior needed to combat subtle enemies, but maintaining the radical edge by exhorting them to cold and inhuman treatment of the enemy: SS-men had to set the example and excel in everything they did.

Nevertheless, this pep talk precipitated the campaign to sell the police state, or, more accurately, it established a new plateau in SS-police propaganda. In the following months, Heydrich and his lieutenants elaborated on the theme of the subtle hidden enemy in a broadly based propaganda campaign that will be detailed in subsequent chapters. By April 1936, as the internal struggle for police power moved to its climax, Heydrich reached the logical conclusions of the argument in another article, given broader exposure. Since the enemy sought to insinuate himself into Party and state, there were four consequences for those who bore the struggle against him: (1) The political police must certainly have contact with the state administration, but they must be independent of its control, because the enemy might succeed in penetrating that administrative apparatus. Those involved in maintaining national security must consist of the smallest, most impenetrable circle. (2) The men for this job had to be special. Beyond technical, administrative, and detective training, they had to be imbued with the ideology in order to know the real enemy and to deal with him as would a combat corps. That was why the political police should be SS, as so many of them were. (3) The political police had to work closely with the SD. (4) The SD, as part of the SS and the ideological intelligence agency of the Party, was best prepared to identify the enemy. The police mission was tactical and executive; the SD mission, intelligence gathering and investigative. Together, they provided the strategic basis for the leadership of the movement and, therefore, of the state. The personal authority of Himmler and Heydrich guaranteed this necessary link between political police and SD.[12] Obviously, it had to be preserved and expanded.

For such a small organization, the SD was amazingly well equipped to contribute to this "sales campaign." It had a staff of academic, administrative, and law-trained ideologues with access to popular and professional outlets and to professional colleagues who could be recruited to the cause. For a while it even had what was tantamount to its own newspaper, *Das Schwarze Korps,* the SS newspaper begun under Himmler's commission in March 1935. The editor in chief was Gunter d'Alquen, a Hitler Youth Leader since 1925, NS press member since 1930, SS man since 1931, political editor for the *Voelkischer Beobachter* since 1932, and member of the SD since September 1933.[13] For several years the SD worked through d'Alquen's paper, and through his conducts and others in the Party Press and Propaganda Ministry, other major media were available to push their line. The legal and administrative bureaucracy could be reached through professional organs and through SD-held seats on the Academy for German Law and in the universities.

Nevertheless, such a "campaign" developed more spontaneously than consciously, as a product of minds sharing common convictions and reinforcing one another in a tense environment. The link between the SD and the intellectuals, the judiciary, and the press was a natural rather than a contrived conveyor belt. According to participants d'Alquen and Best, there was no true propaganda campaign. Public relations specialists were nonexistent, there was no clear sense of direction, and those like Best, who presented arguments, argued from personal conviction.[14] Nevertheless, he did orchestrate the Gestapo and SD contributions. But supporting arguments also came from quarters not suspect as Himmler-Heydrich propagandists. Many respectable voices, growing out of the old call for law and order, spoke with conviction of the camouflaged enemy; they responded to the mounting tensions in international affairs and "popular" agitation at home, and were susceptible to Heydrich's appeals. In publications from 1935-36, the voices of moderation were almost nonexistent. It must have been devastating to the morale of those who would have put brakes on Himmler. They must have felt a mixture of fear over being identified with the camouflaged enemy and guilt that they might be weakening the order at its moment of crisis.[15]

In fighting this battle, Himmler's extremist zeal must have worked against him to some extent, however, leaving some hope that he might be curbed. Under pressure from disturbed conservative elements, Hitler had occasionally to rein him in. Regardless of the image of Himmler's SS, it was hardly monolithically controlled, as the Austrian debacle had recently shown. His SD was a constant target of Party leader complaints. Himmler himself sought to push the battle against enemies beyond the limits that Hitler considered necessary at that time. The struggle against the churches is a case in point. Himmler was ranked among the radicals in his attitude toward the churches, especially the Catholic church, which his SS journalists attacked in Das Schwarze Korps. He used his police powers to limit them in every way possible and to force them into the most narrowly defined role of permissible action. Yet Christianity had deep roots in German society, and NS leadership had constant reminders of the need to move cautiously. As elsewhere, the machinery for making policy on religion became a hopeless mire of competing and contradictory influences. Likewise, Himmler's police would find themselves sometimes protecting the church and its property and on other occasions breaking up church functions and arresting individual priests [16]

On religious as well as racial issues, Himmler and his instruments offered Hitler a sharp force for movement along lines he personally favored, but a force that if given too much rein could create dangerous situations.[17] Such considerations must have counterbalanced Himmler's appeal in Hitler's mind during 1935-36, and must have given some leverage, no matter how small, to those who sought to block or limit him. Himmler's radical attitudes about the militay are a case in point, but in this most decisive arena, he managed to maintain his balance long enough to capitalize on and orchestrate the combination of international and domestic tensions of 1935-36.

15

The Military Factor, 1934-1936

Although the military had emerged from the Roehm purge with some complacency and with renewed confidence, tensions soon developed with the SS, and Himmler's attitudes certainly contributed to the problem. Basically, he shared the belief of the Second Revolution that, as a reactionary body, much of the professional officer corps had to be swept away before the new order could be complete. Beyond that, as the agent primarily responsible for security, he knew that the generals' loyalty to the Fuehrer was qualified.

As a counter to the military, Himmler was to build both the SS police system and the Waffen-SS (the Armed SS, the SS military units of World War II) that would threaten to replace the Army. However, until rearmament was announced in March 1935, the miscellaneous armed SS units were no more than a sensitive issue between the military and SS. The *Leibstandarte*, the Political Purpose Squads, the Death's-Head formations (Eicke's camp guards), and efforts of local SS units to be armed as Border Protection forces were minor irritants.[1] The later rivalries between the military and the Waffen SS do not adequately explain early conflicts.

Whatever the reason, in 1934 and 1935 severe tensions developed between the Army and the SS, but especially the Gestapo and SD. In the latter case, this conflict has, among other causes, been attributed to Himmler and Heydrich's desire to have a monopoly in all matters of security and intelligence, including the military sphere, especially its Abwehr agency.[2] Although they eventually pursued total victory over military intelligence, the SD was far from ready to assume such a monopoly in 1934. The early tensions had less grandiose bases for conflict.

Conflict with the Abwehr

Tensions between the military and SS certainly mounted after the Roehm purge, but as an inevitable result of the general mood of conspiracy.

Some of the military resented the murder of those generals who fell victim and disdained, in an elitist manner, all Nazi riffraff. The SS, in turn, were contemptuous of the military. This mutual hostility produced frequent clashes, ranging from fist fights to intrigues, but such tensions would have developed regardless of Himmler's ambitions. Aggravating the discord, elements among Himmler's conservative enemies did everything possible to turn the military against the SS and political police. From the Ministries of Interior and Justice, men like Gisevius and Dohnanyi channeled material to the generals to convince them of their error in continuing to cohabit with the Nazis.[3] Thus they played the role of camouflaged enemy, spreading the devisive rumors that Himmler had fulminated against in his October talk with Gestapo officials.

On the other side, Himmler and his people responded as they had done to the evidence against Roehm. As a result, military and SS repeated the mutual escalation process of the previous spring, but this time against each other. By the end of the year, Himmler had convinced himself of the imminence of a military coup, and his people assembled evidence to support this fear. They especially focused their suspicions on the military Abwehr and General Fritsch, chief of Army Command.[4]

Suspicion of the Abwehr, or of many of its chief officers, stemmed from a longstanding conflict. The Abwehr was a department of the Ministry of War, staffed extensively by military personnel. A unified service for all branches, its responsibilities included liaison with the Foreign Ministry, espionage in foreign countries, sabotage, and counterespionage related to the military and defense establishment.[5] The military thus had an interservice agency for handling all operations relevant to military security and intelligence. Unfortunately, this domain was not clearly enough defined to be free of encroachment.

In two areas Abwehr and police responsibilities were inextricable. The first was espionage and sabotage cases, which the police handled as crimes against the state and against property. Since no clear line separated political crimes that concerned the military from those that did not, the military Abwehr had always worked closely with the political sections of the criminal investigation police involved in such cases, the so-called "Abwehr-police" or counterespionage police. The two had to share information, and in matters primarily concerning the military, the police had to be willing to accept Abwehr decisions about when to take action. The second problem grew from the Defense Ministry's lack of a militarized police establishment like that of some other European states. Since the Abwehr had neither the authority nor the means for searches and arrests in the civil sector, they had to rely on the civil police—even in cases that were clearly military-defense matters. Consequently, in the last year of the Weimar Republic, when responsibility for coordinating work on political crimes and subversive activities was concentrated in the Criminal Police Office under the Berlin president, that office established close contacts with the Abwehr. In May of 1933, when Goering's new Gestapo Office assumed those responsibilities, the close contacts carried over.[6]

If relations between the police and the Abwehr had been relatively smooth in the Weimar period, it was because the police had known their place. Not only had they felt subordinate to the military, but the political police were also too few in number to be overly aggressive in their work. Nor were the police at that time impelled by a conspiratorial world view that created a crisis atmosphere, driving them to intrude into every area out of fear that the traditional guardians lacked the proper ideological awareness to do their job. That was a new mood beginning under Goering's enlarged Gestapo and growing under Himmler and Heydrich. Long before the latter two arrived, the problem of divisions of labor had become triangular with the creation of Goering's Investigation Office for monitoring communications. Bureaucratic competition had begun.

In fact, the rivalries were more complicated than that, for foreign intelligence added yet another dimension to the intelligence-espionage field. In this domain, the Foreign Ministry traditionally considered itself solely responsible for political, as opposed to military, intelligence. Again, the impossibility of any clear delineation meant potential competition and friction that the Nazi advent greatly exaggerated. Not only did the Gestapo and the SD insist that the link between internal and external enemies required their involvement overseas, but a range of other Nazi organizations inserted themselves as well. First Rosenberg's Foreign Political Office, then the Foreign Countries Organization of the Party (Auslands-Organisation der NSDAP, the "Gau" for Party members in foreign countries), and the Ribbentrop Office under Hess became involved in what was only the beginning of a scramble for the intelligence empire.[7] The rapid growth of espionage and counterespionage work immediately after the NS takeover produced serious conflicts.

To handle the expanding Gestapo Abwehr-police work, Diels had transferred Guenther Patschowski from the Breslau Gestapo post in November 1933. He headed the newly enlarged Division IV (Abwehrpolizei), which bore primary responsibility for a centralized direction of Abwehr-police work in Prussia, and, therefore, for liaison with the military Abwehr. If Orb's version that the military nominated Patschowski is true, it complements other evidence that they sincerely tried to minimize problems between the organizations. If he is also correct that Himmler and Heydrich rigged this nomination, they may have been as concerned about the ideological reliability of those in charge as they were with their assault on the Gestapo. Orb contended that Patschowski helped undermine Diels, but he gave no details.[8]

A complete explanation of Gestapo-Abwehr relations must be based on an inevitable bureaucratic competition exacerbated by ideological distrust. Himmler's and Heydrich's aspirations were an added factor that only became significant in later years. Beyond that, many subtleties complicate the analysis. Competition and hostility between organizations is usually limited by the necessity of getting important jobs done and maintaining a semblance of propriety.[9] For instance, from his advent in office, Patschowski's official directives accepted the Reichswehr's traditional Abwehr role and exhorted his subordinates to "a comradely cooperation . . . in the interest of national defense." Although he always sought to preserve the Gestapo's monopoly on executive action, SA involvement caused more concern than Abwehr intrusion; as with the auxiliary police, the increased Abwehr workload had led to the use of SA men as auxiliary Abwehr field agents.[10]

Comparatively, Patschowski must have been able to maintain tolerable relations with the Abwehr, for he held his own. Elsewhere, the Gestapo lost ground and suffered humiliation. For instance, Legations Counselor Karl von Buelow-Schwanten of the Foreign Ministry was able to use an incident to convince Goering that Gestapo involvement in foreign intelligence had been disastrous and harmful to the Reich, and had to be terminated. On January 16, 1934, when Diels went to inform Buelow of Goering's consent, Buelow not only gloated but rubbed Diel's nose in a description of the poor quality of his intelligence reports and the inferior value of Gestapo agents. Diels could only concede.[11]

Goering may well have felt some pressure from above. For instance, since foreign reactions were most important to Hitler, he intervened on several occasions in favor of the traditional institutions and against those of the Movement. Both the military and the Foreign Ministry had Hitler's support in their efforts to curb SA and SS foreign activities in the spring of 1934.[12] Furthermore, as part of his frequent guarantees to the military, in October 1933 Hitler had issued a "Cabinet Order" delegating to the military sole competence for control of espionage and sabotage against Germany's military strength, including related industries and government agencies.[13] Of course, NS leaders did not necessarily take him at his word, and such an order was only meaningful if one had the means to enforce it. The means were the political police, and although they would do away with other rivals to the Abwehr, they never completely terminated their own or SD efforts. For instance, under Diels the Prussian Gestapo violated the Goering-Buelow agreement by maintaining foreign agents, though apparently not as part of any official network. After his arrival, Heydrich tried to establish control over such agents, specifically in the United States, allowing only a special, limited Gestapo contact with them. He thus moved toward conformity with Abwehr and

Foreign Office desires. He also respected Abwehr desires to work only with the police by removing the SD from the distribution list of Gestapo-Abwehr paperwork.[14]

Heydrich apparently tried to maintain better relations, but other pressures intervened. The bloodletting of June 30 exaggerated tensions between the Abwehr and the Gestapo and SD. One of the victims, Major General Ferdinand von Bredow, had headed the military Abwehr prior to 1932. Bredow's death allegedly alienated both Major Hans Oster of the Abwehr (whose role in the conservative resistance is well known) and Navy Captain Conrad Patzig, who had served under Bredow and now headed the Abwehr. Patzig bacame an outspoken opponent of the regime, but especially of radical SS influence. Both men moved into the conservative alliance against Himmler, but this group remained too torn by its own ambitions and jealousies to be effective. For instance, Patzig is said to have sought cooperation with Buelow, but the latter, equally concerned about military rivalry, apparently thought he had the Gestapo under control.[15]

Patzig's hostility may have helped the Ministry of Interior maintain yet another hold on Gestapo affairs, for, according to Gisevius, for some time Blomberg and Frick supervised military-Abwehr-Gestapo cooperation through their respective ministries, and Himmler only gradually persuaded Blomberg that direct dealings with him as commander of the Political Police were more efficient. Unfortunately, Gisevius, always inaccurate and vague about temporal relationships, also failed to define the administrative mechanics of this liaison. According to Orb, it involved the so-called Sonderbuero Stein, a civil office in a hybrid position under the chief of the Heereswaffenamt. Vague in its origins, this office allegedly became the Special Action Post (Sonderdienststelle z.b.V.) in the building of the Police Presidency Berlin.[16] Also according to Orb, it was permeated with SD spies, and became a source of further distrust by the Abwehr when the SD absorbed it after Himmler took over the Gestapo.[17] The Koehler-Orb versions of these stories are so vague and confusing that either they must be fabrications or they were intended to obscure something important.

By October 1934, after Heydrich reorganized the Gestapo Office, he designated Patschowski's Abwehramt as main Division III. Despite Patschowski's alleged role in SD penetration of the Gestapo, this branch contained relatively few SD people, with him and his deputy the only ones of significant rank. Personnel changes remained insignificant during Heydrich's first year, with no increase in SD representation. Except at the lower ranks, experts with counterespionage-police training staffed it entirely. Within the Gestapo Office this Abwehr Branch was an "inner sanctum," with its offices sealed off from the rest of the building and guarded. Heydrich worked intimately with Patschowski, displaying special interest in this area. It had four major subdivisions: III 1 and 2 dealt with high treason and counterespionage cases stemming from Eastern and Western countries respectively; III 3 worked on all politically meaningful foreign intelligence of a non-Abwehr nature; III 4 was a support facility for records, technical support, and training.[18]

Toward a Modus Vivendi

November of 1934 seems to have been an important month in Abwehr-Gestapo relations. To begin with a seemingly small point, four new police officials transferred into the Gestapo from the Police Presidency Berlin and several others from the Berlin Schupo. Perhaps this relates to the dissolution of Sonderbuero Stein; it certainly seems related to more direct Abwehr-Gestapo liaison. Among the transfers, Detective Inspector Ernst Henschel assumed leadership of a newly created section first called Special Assignments (Sonderauftrage), then III *z.b.V.* for Evaluation (Auswertung). Detective Inspector Fritz Bolle took over Desk III 1A for Poland and Danzig, which may be significant in light of contemporary developments to be explained here. Schupo Captains Kurt Pomme and Willy Suchanek became Heydrich's adjutants, and, according to Orb, Pomme maintained liaison with the Abwehr. As professional policemen from outside the Gestapo, these men seemed untainted by SD membership. Thus Pomme in particular may have helped build Abwehr trust. According to Orb, Abwehr leaders developed hostility toward Patschowski as they realized he was an old SD plant. Pomme, as a long-serving liaison between the police and the Movement, could minimize friction.[19]

With Pomme's arrival, the mounting SS-military tensions of the fall of 1934 and the alleged increase in Patzig's hostility was balanced by an improvement in Gestapo-Abwehr working relations, at least from the Gestapo perspective. Patschowski persuaded the Abwehr to let him simplify their procedures in such a way that Gestapo control grew, over observation as well as executive action.[20] This was possibly the first sign of Patzig's ultimate fall.

On December 31, Patzig was transferred from the Abwehr to a ship's command, a clear victory for Himmler and Heydrich, who had constantly complained to Blomberg about him. According to some sources, Heydrich actually engineered his removal, but more likely it resulted from a combination of circumstances and Blomberg's general desire to work well with the Nazis. He found a good pretext in Patzig's aerial reconnaissance over Poland. The maintenance of the new German-Polish agreement, especially at this juncture, greatly concerned Hitler, and Patzig's activities could have sabotaged it. When Blomberg discovered the operation, he ordered Patzig's removal.[21] Many military men strongly opposed Hitler's policy on Poland, giving good reason to believe they would sabotage it. Behind this incident lay other reasons to suspect the Abwehr. One month after the Polish agreement, they had had the bad taste to expose dramatically the Polish spy ring of Captain von Sosnowski, which had been in operation since 1932. Given this history and the mounting tensions with the SS, Blomberg removed Patzig as a gesture of goodwill and replaced him with Navy Captain Wilhelm Canaris.[22]

Canaris's appointment is commonly described as "a blow to the influence of the SS at court" because of the tradition that Canaris was such a capable member of the resistance and a check upon the Gestapo and SD. Such views also presume a check to Himmler's and Heydrich's design to take over the Abwehr.[23] Canaris's ambivalent role in the resistance has been treated elsewhere.[24] It had certainly not begun in 1935. That Himmler and Heydrich could have been so naive as to believe that the Abwehr would be turned over to them at this point strains credulity. Not only were they overextended in digesting what they already had, but the political realities of the military's power and Hitler's promises to the generals stood in the way. Instead, Canaris's appointment was the best that the SS leaders could hope for,[25] guaranteeing smooth personal relations and politically acceptable Abwehr leadership.

The forty-seven-year-old Canaris, a professional sailor since 1905, had been active in right wing and anti-Communist actions following the war, including the Kapp Putsch. As a man who cultivated an air of mystery, he was generally associated with a number of intrigues, including the escape of the murderers of Karl Liebknecht and Rosa Luxemburg. Having no love for the Republic, he displayed enthusiasm for the new regime and was generally considered pro-Nazi.[26] He cultivated social relations with Nazi leaders, apparently to a greater extent than most of his fellow officers. When Canaris was training officer on Heydrich's ship, the two had established a friendly relationship, one of the few Heydrich had with fellow officers. Although this relationship lapsed during the intervening years, they resumed and intensified it in 1935. The Heydrich and Canaris families became neighbors upon Canaris's arrival in Berlin, and they spent much time together. Although this friendship may have been based partially on expediency, third parties' descriptions of Canaris's fear and distrust of Heydrich must be balanced against this intimacy. Canaris also knew Himmler prior to 1935 and carefully cultivated that contact before he became head of Abwehr.[27]

Despite these relationships, Himmler and Heydrich could have played no real role in the choice of Canaris. Apparently, Patzig nominated his own successor. Knowing the problems were beyond his scope, he hoped that Canaris could preserve some control for an indefinite period. Although Admiral Raeder was reluctant to support the nomination, Canaris was simply the only suitable choice for the admiral, determined to maintain the Abwehr as a naval enclave in the ministry.[28]

The transition consumed the latter part of 1934, while Canaris learned the job he would assume officially on January 1. His primary problem was to establish a modus vivendi with Heydrich, who had been pushing for a more equal relationship with the Abwehr. The Sosnowski affair had apparently given him pretexts to press for access to Abwehr files for information essential to Gestapo and SD work. This was only a fair balance for the requirement that the Gestapo turn over all relevant material to the Abwehr, and that they serve obediently in Abwehr searches and seizures. Patzig had doggedly resisted a fair exchange, probably to the point of legitimizing the claim that he endangered national security by his territoriality.[29]

Both Canaris and his superiors felt great pressure to establish mutually satisfactory arrangements with Himmler and Heydrich, both for the sake of their missions and for political harmony. At this point, SS-military tensions reached a crisis. Goering, Himmler, and Heydrich had launched a campaign of accusations directed especially at Fritsch, whom they accused of planning a putsch for January. Hitler intervened and, at the highest levels, both sides made concerted efforts to ease the pressure. On January 3, 1935, at a joint meeting of officers and Party leaders, Hitler proclaimed his absolute faith in the Army. He specifically asserted that his trust was so strong that he would refuse to see any evidence presented against the generals by Party members. This impressed Himmler with the necessity of getting himself and his organizations back in line. On January 13, Blomberg had Himmler speak to a meeting of senior Army officers to explain the role of the SS and to air the growing suspicions so they could be put to rest. At about the same time, the Gestapo published a report, "The Poisoning of the Relationship between the Bearer of the Arms of the Nation and the Bearer of the Ideology in the State and the Party," which also aired suspicions and put great emphasis on the responsibility of "enemies" for developing the tension.[30]

Although such efforts prevented an open rupture, SS-military tension continued. Nevertheless, Abwehr-Gestapo cooperation grew from these efforts, undermining Ministry of the Interior control, and marking a major victory in Himmler's move for police power. Part of the cause of this victory lies with anti-Himmler elements like Gisevius, who overplayed his hand at this moment, enabling Himmler to shift blame for the tensions to third parties with personal ambitions. Someone in the

Abwehr command told Heydrich about Gisevius's approaches to the military, and at the same time Blomberg decided to establish direct working relations with the Gestapo, cutting out the Ministry of Interior as intermediary authority.[31]

The basis for the new Abwehr-Gestapo cooperation grew from a three-hour conference between Canaris and Heydrich on the afternoon of January 17. Also present were Major Rudolf Bamler, head of the counterespionage section of Abwehr (commonly believed to be even more pro-Nazi then Canaris); Werner Best, who had recently come to Berlin to begin his career as Heydrich's deputy and lieutenant for Abwehr relations; Patschowski of the Gestapo's counterespionage police; and SS Major Heinz Jost, who represented the SD.[32]

The outcome was a ten-point program for solving their conflicts, including a division of labor between Abwehr and Gestapo, and a recognition of a legitimate role for the SD. Since the division of labor assigned five missions to the Abwehr and five to the Gestapo, it would seem to be the origin of the term "the Ten Commandments," a label applied generically to this and subsequent charters of cooperation.[33]

As Werner Best observed, they easily defined their separate spheres of responsibility, but the problem lay (1) in the inevitable overlap of these spheres, (2) in Heydrich's drive to build a comprehensive base for his own service, thereby expanding that overlap, and (3) in the military desire to do as much of the work as it could without Gestapo involvement. Officially, the Abwehr had responsibility for military espionage and counterespionage, for control and observation of military installations, for defense of the Reichswehr and related concerns, for all cases involving national defense, and for the regulation of Gestapo executive police support in such work. The Gestapo's responsibility included combating political crime, controlling the border police and their intelligence service, doing countersabotage police work and related intelligence inside Reich borders and in support of Abwehr, handling cases of industrial sabotage and espionage and related intelligence, and monitoring communications in cooperation with the Abwehr and Goering's Investigation Office.[34]

Cooperation Bears Fruit

In a significant achievement of this accord, the SD won official recognition for involvement in Abwehr work, a contact the military had tried to minimize in the past. The accord acknowledged its competence in industrial espionage and gathering intelligence around the borders but did not include intelligence work in foreign countries, probably because

SD work there was too insignificant to attract attention. Nevertheless, such recognition of the SD enhanced its monopoly among Party services, for it further guaranteed the exclusion of the Labor Front Information Service from Abwehr work. Establishment of liaison between SD and Abwehr field posts further expanded SD contacts. In this respect, the SD and Gestapo would play a key role in the selection of counter-espionage workers in the various industries. By November, the Abwehr had accepted the legitimacy of the SD to the point that officers of Abwehr, political police, and SD, down to the level of field post commanders, got together in Gestapo headquarters to become fully acquainted with each others' organizations and operations and to enhance cooperation.[35]

For Himmler, the major coup came when Blomberg agreed to support the expansion of Himmler's police empire in the interest of national security. Heydrich and Canaris drafted a message for Blomberg to forward to the Prussian Ministries of Finance and Interior requesting expanded budgetary support for Gestapo-Abwehr work and for the Gestapo-controlled border police. This required the bureaucracy to release the brake it had applied to Gestapo growth. The request included salaried positions for Gestapo officials to work directly in the military Abwehr, initiating an exchange of personnel comparable to that between the Gestapo and the Investigation Office. In addition to establishing direct relations between the military Abwehr and the Gestapo, Blomberg also urged Frick to proceed quickly with the creation of a "unified organization of the police counterespionage services in the Reich."[36] Thus began support by Blomberg for Himmler's SS-police system based on arguments for national security.

In July, Blomberg wrote Hitler making further recommendations advantageous to Himmler. He complained that the division of the political police into little state forces severely hampered their Abwehr police work, and he recommended a unified Reich political police. Although he did not exclude unification under Frick, he implied a preference for a separate force under Himmler. First he attributed full credit to Himmler for the success being achieved under the existing organization; then he argued for an autonomous Reich political police separate from other administrative authority. His justifications were the need for selectivity, secrecy, and efficiency—by then familiar arguments for an extraordinary political police force. Sufficiently impressed, Hitler arranged a meeting at Obersalzberg to discuss the matter with Blomberg, but unfortunately no minutes have survived.[37] Regardless, Blomberg intervened at a crucial moment, undoubtedly significant to Himmler's final victory.

Other fruits of cooperation redounded to the benefit of all three organizations—Abwehr, Gestapo, and SD. Although their relationship remained basically competitive, sincere efforts at cooperation from top to bottom resulted in the rapid construction of the counterespionage system desired by all parties. Of course, each leader continued to seek advantages for himself and his organization, but they were generally cautious about taking them at the expense of each other. They made every effort to ensure close cooperation at the operational level and apparently achieved it, despite the problems of overlapping jurisdictions.[38]

For the Gestapo, a number of major advantages accrued. Not only did Abwehr police numbers increase as a result of military support for their budget requests, but Himmler increased his powers as de facto Reich chief of political police before this position became official. For instance, as early as April 1936, the Reich Tariff Administration (Reichszollverwaltung) extended cooperation to all of his political police, expanding his effective control over border affairs. Meanwhile, the Gestapo enhanced its freedom to operate in affairs concerning the Foreign Ministry. During 1935-36, given Wehrmacht support and the weight of its national security arguments, the Gestapo gained more leeway for direct relations with foreign police and for the maintenance of agents in foreign countries. In return, it limited and controlled these agents both for improved operations and to avoid incidents that could undermine that freedom. Of course, incidents continued, such as kidnapping Germans in foreign countries for arrest in Germany; however, it is usually impossible to assign responsibility for such infringements.[39] In any case, this increased freedom and the enlarged base of power that came with it indicate that the understanding between the military Abwehr and the Gestapo and SD weakened the Foreign Ministry's resistance.

To preserve its cooperative relationship with the Abwehr, the Gestapo did what it could to minimize the problems of overlapping jurisdictions without surrendering any of its intelligence base. In May 1935, for instance, Patschowski reorganized his Division III, limiting its work entirely to counterespionage-police affairs. As a result, the old Subdivision III 3 for "Elaboration of All Politically Relevant Foreign Intelligence" became a special commission for general defensive and preventive measures, alien and minority affairs, and border patrol. Of course, the Gestapo did not cease its foreign intelligence work, but merely removed it from Abwehr Division III and concentrated it in Division II. Such a transfer of responsibilities would smooth relations by minimizing the conflicting interests of those Gestapo personnel in Division III who worked with the Abwehr. It would also enhance the legitimacy of Gestapo intrusion into Abwehr and Foreign Ministry domains by making more obvious the relation between the Gestapo's foreign intelligence and its fight against internal enemies (the responsibility of Division II).[40]

Despite improved relations, Abwehr resentment continued against Patschowski. Consequently, Heydrich relieved him of his counter-espionage-police responsibilities in the summer or early autumn of 1935. Temporarily exiled to a field post in Breslau, he directed intelligence operations against Poland. Effective January 1, 1936, Best expanded his responsibilities to include direction of Division III; his talents in dealing with the Abwehr had proven valuable. According to Best, his new responsibilities were to be transitory, a gesture of conciliation to the Abwehr, but he developed such a close and cooperative relationship with Canaris that the assignment lasted until his separation from Sipo and SD five years later.[41]

Best gives the impression that for the next five years, military-Abwehr-Gestapo relations generally involved close cooperation, marred only by occasional outbursts of competition and recrimination. Usually the two organizations worked together well, despite extensive duplication of effort. They exchanged information and cooperated like different branches of the same organization. Occasionally, however, an individual member of one branch, driven by professional ambition, resentment, or some other motive, became competitive and failed to keep his opposite number informed. This caused wasteful duplication and left holes in the total intelligence picture that could otherwise have been filled. Once afoot, such competitiveness could become contagious. Best and Canaris had to devote much of their time and energy (to the detriment of other work) ironing out such wrinkles.[42]

Sometimes these attacks on competitiveness required detailed additions to their so-called Ten Commandments. One drawn up in December 1936, apparently marking a high point in the Best-Canaris relationship, nevertheless reveals typical sources of conflict. First, they reiterated their basic division of labor. Military espionage and counterespionage belonged to the Abwehr, and the Gestapo should forward all relevant information it received and provide assistance upon request. The counterespionage police of the Gestapo conducted searches and made arrests in cases of espionage and sabotage inside the Reich, and the Abwehr similarly was to forward all relevant information it had. The police were to keep the Abwehr fully informed in such cases and were to refrain from action until the Abwehr had fully exploited the intelligence value of observing a suspect and his contacts. Military personnel could be present during interrogations that would be conducted by the police. The two organizations were not to employ the same confidential agents; instead, each branch was to surrender any agents who seemed more useful to the other.[43]

Best's descriptions reinforce the general impression emerging from many other documents and incidents. The officials at the top sincerely sought to maintain an efficient cooperation for the sake of their important missions, to avoid the dangerous impression of internal divisiveness, and to ensure discipline and control within their own departments. To defeat competitors, each had to control his own forces, for competition gotten out of hand could be self-defeating. Subordinates, sensing tension, exaggerated it, perhaps to prove themselves and please their bosses. Then the leaders were driven simultaneously to capitalize on spontaneous competition that brought benefits and to cooperate with their competitors in honest efforts to control and minimize the resultant friction.

None of the divisions of labor cited so far prohibited Gestapo foreign intelligence outside the military sphere. Rather than reducing such activity, the reorganization and tighter controls related to these ageements apparently enhanced it. Nevertheless, the surviving files of the relevant sections of Division II indicate that in 1935 Gestapo foreign intelligence remained relatively meager and crude, relying on occasional informants and newspaper clippings until as late as 1937-38. Gestapo personnel devoted special attention to the western border states and to Austria, Czechoslovakia, and Poland. The border police and their contacts did much of the work, especially with the police of the neighboring states. In conformity with the division of labor, the Gestapo focused most of this work on foreign support for "enemies" inside the Reich. By 1938-39, such extensive lists of supporting enemies had been developed that they were easily converted to very thorough arrest or elimination lists. This was, however, a logical product of domestic political police work and should not be extrapolated into advanced work for the conquest and domination of neighboring states. Comparatively speaking, during these early years, Gestapo foreign operations generally conformed to the police practices of other European states. They focused on their defensive police mission and patterned their methods after those of rival intelligence services operating out of Poland and Czechoslavakia through their border police. At least, this was the way the Gestapo saw it.[44]

In much of its work, the Gestapo exploited extensively its natural relations with the police of other countries; their mutual preoccupation with the Communist threat provided an excellent common ground for cooperation. The Gestapo also exploited the minority problems of these countries, reaping benefits by offering a little cooperative support from their side. As a case in point, Best and Heinrich Mueller went to Belgrade in April 1936 to induce Yugoslavian police cooperation based on fears of Communism and problems with Croatians. In return, of course, they allowed neighboring police as little insight as possible into the Gestapo itself.[45]

Along with all the cooperation between Abwehr and Gestapo and its advantages came yet another victory that eventually strained these good relations to the breaking point. As both sides encouraged their personnel to cooperate completely, the Gestapo and SD gained access to military installations and briefings on aspects of military security, thus acquiring a basis for penetration and surveillance that would have taken years to develop otherwise. Although the Gestapo and SD generally preferred to handle the delicate matter of suspected military officers in open cooperation with military authorities, they proceeded clandestinely when they encountered reserved and suspicious responses. For instance, by the end of 1936, the Gestapo and SD had written directives on the observation of Wehrmacht members in which Heinrich Mueller revealed the philosophy of "preventive law enforcement." When they suspected a punishable offense, they would proceed through proper channels, which required military cooperation. When no concretely punishable offense was involved and the military was likely to respond with legalistic resistance, "the Gestapo must stand outside the law, without detriment to the activities of the military legal authorities, and carry out the observation of military personnel." For the sake of harmony, Gestapo officials intended to clear with military officials, at least as far as possible, even this extralegal infringement on the sanctity of the officer corps. Especially sensitive cases, however, such as Himmler's focus on General Fritsch, required complete secrecy. Nevertheless, during the 1935-36 era of relative harmony between Abwehr and Gestapo-SD, most work on such cases stood in abeyance.[46]

Of course, this avenue for surveillance served the military as well, giving Abwehr people a similar access to Gestapo-SD, and later Sipo and SD circles in which they established amenable contacts. Since Himmler could not claim that his own SS was immune to the "camouflaged enemy," the Abwehr-Gestapo cooperation also provided for some survellance of the nascent Waffen SS units (SS-Verfugungstruppen), even after Hitler had withdrawn the right of Army inspection of these units. Perhaps Himmler welcomed this Abwehr, Gestapo, and SD surveillance of Dietrich's SS-Bodyguard "Adolf Hitler," which was not yet under his tight control.[47]

Since the Gestapo and SD usually failed at subtlety and delicacy, surveillance of the military remained a point of tension, disrupting the relative harmony of 1935-36 relations with the Abwehr and leading to further SS-military confrontations. For instance, as early as April and May 1935, the Army discovered listening devices in its telephones. Of course, they may have predated the understanding, but since SS microphones were also discovered in Abwehr offices, Blomberg and Fritsch had the bases for complaints to Hitler, whom they pressed to make occasional reaffirmations of military immunity.[48] Repeated incidents raise the questions of how seriously lieutenants like Himmler took such orders and how well they controlled the competitive behavior of subordinates.

Happenings such as these must have given Canaris second thoughts, making him amenable to the approaches of the conservative opposition to Himmler. By late 1936, when Heydrich began to probe openly into the former liaison between the German military and the Red Army, Canaris became less cooperative. The 1937-38 trials of German military officers that grew out of Heydrich's investigations, followed by the Blomberg-Fritsch purge, would press Canaris into that complex and contradictory role that has credited him with membership in the resistance.[49] By then, however, it was too late to crack the firm foundations of the police state. In playing their political games and placing primary emphasis on the building of traditional measures for national greatness, key military leaders had cast their weight with the arguments for a police state, no matter how ambivalent they felt about the SS. This left the conservative opposition to Himmler to its own limited devices, without the support of key military leaders who could have made it decisive.

16

Persistent Opposition

The period between January and June 1935 saw much legalistic sparring as various elements of the conservative opposition made exploratory probes at the evolving SS-police system. Himmler's people responded by developing rationalizations for the nascent police state and using them to parry the thrusts and to establish a broader base of support for the expansion of their powers. The subsequent display of relative strengths and weaknesses determined the strategy of both sides during the decisive period that followed, from June 1935 to June 1936.

On January 10, Frick initiated 1935 with another effort to prod Goering into asserting himself, apparently without effect. The occasion was a minor matter concerning a veterans' organization that refused to expel its Jewish members. Openly playing the role of *Hitler's* chief of political police, Himmler had gone directly to the Fuehrer with the problem of this organization, whose behavior, he alleged, was a public affront to the Movement. He displayed an overzealousness that Hitler was not ready to unleash at this time, and since his query came during the November period of mounting SS-military tensions, the timing may have been especially poor. Hitler gave him a cool response, rejecting his suggestions and telling him to let time solve such problems.[1]

Perhaps this rebuff encouraged Frick to challenge Himmler's de facto position and to goad Goering into reinserting himself and Frick between Himmler and Hitler. All hope of curbing Himmler hinged on minimizing his direct appeals to the Fuehrer and maximizing his subordination to the legal state authorities. Frick reminded Goering of this and emphasized the necessity of their being the intermediaries in such communications, especially since the case in point involved a Reich ministry— the military.[2] If Frick also sought to shore up the ground he was losing as intermediary in the Abwehr-police relationship, he certainly chose a poor argument to employ on Goering, who had consistently shown that to cut red tape he favored the elimination of all intermediaries in police action.

At the end of the month, Frick directed his search for support into

Himmler's second most important bastion, Bavaria. Hoping to stir
Reichsstatthalter Epp and Interior Minister Wagner into action, he contended that the number of protective custody internees in Bavaria was
excessive, several hundred more than in all other states combined, including Prussia. He ordered that Goering's Prussian system of accounting be applied and that Wagner assume direct responsibility instead of
deferring to the Bavarian Political Police.[3]

Neither Goering nor the Bavarian officials seem to have responded
officially to either probe, but Wagner apparently referred the Bavarian
affair to Himmler. In the ensuing debate, Himmler argued that Dachau,
which accounted for so many of the internees in Bavaria, was more than
a Bavarian camp. In the evolving Reich-wide system, it served as a
terminal base for the more serious cases. Using such arguments on February 20, Himmler took Frick's decree directly to the Fuehrer to thwart
the pressure to release internees *he* deemed dangerous. He got Hitler's
concurrence,[4] and in so doing not only parried Frick's thrust but also
reinforced his de facto position as *Hitler's* chief of political police, for it
was he—not Wagner or Epp—who had channeled the decision over
Frick's head.

Not only was Hitler's decision another legitimizing step for Himmler's uncontrolled reach, but Frick had also conceded important points.
The preface to his order about protective custody in Bavaria agreed that
the "recently observed increasing Communist activity" required sharper
measures and that recidivists in protective custody should be held for
considerably longer durations. Thus he accepted both the basis for continued emergency police power and the argument that, as enemies of
society, repeated offenders had no rights.[5] Common elements of conservative and NS ideology had tied Frick's hands for effectively resisting
Himmler's drive.

Nevertheless, even such self-limiting efforts at opposition encouraged others, throwing up numerous, sometimes serious, obstacles to
Himmler's progress. For instance, throughout the spring and summer,
Epp tried to assert more control over the Bavarian police to curb the
anti-Church crusade in which Himmler and Heydrich were especially
active. In May, Hjalmar Schacht, Reich Minister of Economic Affairs,
protested to Hitler about persecutions of clergy and Jews and about the
uncontrolled Gestapo. Yet these opponents also made concessions such
as Frick had made about defense against the nation's enemies,[6] and
Himmler's people began exploiting them.

Since 1933, a special Criminal Law Commission had been devising
a new criminal code as part of a truly NS body of law for the new order.
This effort represented the thinking of NS jurists like Hans Frank, who
had sometimes blocked, sometimes abetted Himmler in Bavaria. The

commission wanted to create a criminal code based on *voelkisch* principles, freeing the new order from the fetters of liberal constitutionalism
and the inalienable rights of the individual, so the state could take "the
necessary" steps to preserve law and order and build a great nation. As
typical NS jurists steeped in conservative-authoritarian traditions, they
desperately sought a compromise. They expected the police to operate
within the limits of due process, controlled by proper state authority;
yet, simultaneously, they wanted the police to be free enough to strike
effectively at the enemies of society. Early in 1935, Dr. Drews, President
of the Prussian Supreme Administrative Court, proclaimed that the
forthcoming laws would make Germany a constitutional state (*Rechtsstaat*) in the sense that men would be bound by the law, and that, therefore, there would be a legal delimitation of police competence. But
there would have to be exceptions so the police could take action
without legal basis in matters concerning the maintenance and existence
of the state.[7]

Drews's speech was significant because his court heard all appeals
against police action. This advocate of delimited police power fully acknowledged the necessity of allowing the police to go beyond the law
in defense of the state. Thus his thesis had two edges: it applied legal
limits to both the Fuehrer and his police arm, but for the immediate
future, Himmler could use such views about raison d'etat to entrench
his power. In the long run, both he and Hitler would block the final
promulgation of any body of law that limited their power.[8]

Taking their cue from Frick's concessions in his January decree and
building on arguments like Drews's, Himmler and his people directed
their "sales campaign" at Guertner and the conservative bureaucrats of
his ministry. To parry the many legal actions and demands for closer
administrative control that police excesses had provoked, Himmler appealed to concerns over renewed Communist efforts. On March 28, he
sent the minister of justice a long memorandum on the "Communist
movement." Since the "camouflaged enemy" argument was unsuitable
against bureaucrats who were its prime target, he expanded to its fullest
potential their shared concern over the threat from the left. Himmler
began from the secure basis of the NS attack on "liberal-individualistic"
political theory. The NS critique, with which the conservative jurists
agreed, argued that this liberal theory placed the rights of the individual
above the interests of the community; it created a system of legal loopholes through which defense attorneys could guarantee extraordinarily
mild judgments against their criminal clients. The effect was to tie the
hands of the police in preventing crime or exposing the criminal. Himmler then linked this concern to the "Communist threat" by noting how
KPD pamphlets had often instructed the proletariat on how to guarantee

its rights before the law. The forces of Marxism and bolshevism obviously used the "liberal-individualistic" philosophy to undermine the state.[9]

Against the rights of the citizen to respect and due process (which he skirted rather than denied), Himmler raised the concept of a state of emergency in which even the most liberal legal system recognized the preeminence of the survival of society and the state. Then he fused the threat to national survival, represented by Communism, with the threat represented by conventional criminals. Toward this end, he made liberal use of the recent "crisis," the "Roehm putsch," and Hitler's and Guertner's justifications for that action. Those who rise up against society must be struck down commensurate with the damage they intended to do. Himmler concluded that the NS system would always respect the rights of the good citizen, but the criminal element, in removing themselves from the community of citizens by attacking it, naturally forfeited their rights as citizens. He cited the emergency decrees and legislation of 1933 to show that the NS state had left liberal political concepts behind, de facto if not yet de jure. He appealed to the conservative-reactionary desires for a return to the traditional Prussian legal definition of the police mission as that necessary to maintain law and order.[10]

He tried to excuse police excesses by referring to other modern states that used force to extract confessions. Not only did he cite the Stalinist police state, but he also took special pleasure in public statements by American policemen on the necessity for getting confessions to guarantee convictions and to further investigations. He either quoted or misquoted a Major Sylvester of the International Association of Chiefs of Police and a Captain Willemse, former head of the New York homicide squad. From Willemse he allegedly had a frank advocacy of the "third degree" and the use of any trick to get a confession. Even naked force was justified against hardened criminals. Otherwise, the police would be guilty of turning loose on society a criminal who would continue to rob and murder.[11]

To cap his argument, Himmler emphasized how the KPD, ostensibly destroyed in 1933, had completely resurrected itself, perhaps more pervasive and efficient than before. It was indestructible, because it operated with impunity from all neighboring states, supported by the Comintern and the Soviet Union. He depicted an indefinite state of siege for which the police had to be free to act as necessary. Although third degree interrogations were necessary to break the secretive underground system, he had ordered his political police not to use force. Nevertheless, he asked that these special circumstances be taken into consideration, and threatened that if his police were not allowed to crack the KPD with forceful interrogation, the resulting overload of police work might bring about their collapse, leaving the Reich defenseless.[12]

Although such arguments typified Himmler's thinking, the style of the memorandum was not his. Heavily laced with the proper sort of legal references and judicial theory that carried weight with jurists and bureaucrats, it was the handiwork of the law trained civil servants of the Gestapo and the SD jurists whom Heydrich cultivated. First among them was Werner Best, recently arrived in Berlin as Heydrich's deputy at the Gestapo Office. His main Division I dealt with administrative and legal problems, where he served as a buffer between Himmler and Heydrich and the bureaucrats they despised. The perfect man for the obstacles that confronted Himmler and Heydrich in 1935, Best assisted ideally until they moved into a more radical phase in 1938-39. Among NS jurists, he was a radical, expressing views that, compared with those of the conservatives and reactionaries, seemed very suitable to his superiors. Yet he spoke the language of the lawyers and could woo them on their own terms. Once the police system that he visualized had been achieved, however, the limits of his service became apparent to Himmler and Heydrich, always suspicious of lawyers.[13]

Both the eyewitness Gisevius and the scholar Aronson have described how Best dealt with the opposition. Not only could he employ the language of law and bureaucracy, but in his zeal for the achievement of a "cleansed and revitalized" new order, he could also stretch his arguments to cover a world of sins. However, given the combination of legalism and NS values that few dared contest, he must have been formidable indeed. Unlike his bosses, he had the social and professional credentials to gain entry into the civil service establishment, and, more important, the personality and character that engendered cooperative working relationships in the traditional system. He functioned as though he accepted at face value Himmler's expressed desire for a true peoples' police and was really offended by police and SS excesses. Since he shared the conviction that they could be corrected from within through training and indoctrination rather than through external controls, he could have been sincere in promising that reforms were possible if the opposition withdrew their complaints. As Gisevius put it, "It was his business to placate aroused bourgeois consciences." But while Gisevius may have understood Best's role, the calculated cynicism he attributed to Best does not ring true. Best is better understood as one who sincerely believed in his arguments. This explains why "his name was actually included by some credulous persons in lists they drew up of the potential Opposition."[14] Only status as sincere believers explains why he, others like Ohlendorf, and cases like Nebe (who actually was in the "Opposition") served the new order zealously and became involved in its crimes.

Although Best claims that he intended merely to clarify the evolving status of the Gestapo, in his zeal he became a very effective "salesman" for the forthcoming SS-police state. Not only did he publish a number of supporting articles, but he also disseminated other professional publications "with suitable relevance to the education" of the political police. The articles he distributed preached lines similar to Himmler's March memorandum to Guertner, thus encouraging not only the SS elements, but specifically the more traditional, professional police, to serve in the evolving system with the zeal of pioneers in a revolutionary reformulation of German society and national strength. Their roles were to be, simultaneously, defenders and shapers of the new order.[15]

Limitations of the Attack

The combination of legalism, NS idealism, and images of ominous threats to the nation frustrated the conservative opposition during the spring of 1935. Finding every thrust successfully parried, they finally refocused their attack. They assembled every scrap of evidence of past abuses by the SS and political police and in concentration camps, and presented it to all potential allies and to NS leaders who might be goaded into curbing Himmler—either out of some sense of order or out of fear for themselves. The conservatives encouraged legal and administrative appeals against the excesses to bolster their case and to mobilize the machinery of the state for controlling the police before it was too late.[16]

In short, they attacked along two lines: legal action for damages to the victims or their survivors, and criminal prosecution of police officials and camp personnel for mishandling, manslaughter, or murder of internees. In the first category, individual citizens had to initiate the actions. Officials of the ministries of justice and interior encouraged such actions to cite as evidence in their arguments for more stringent regulation of the police and camps. Criminal prosecution could be initiated whenever they learned of an offense and could investigate it thoroughly.[17]

Unfortunately, most of these actions stemmed from the early years of spontaneous terror or the Roehm purge. Given the termination of SA freedom, the tightening of Himmler's control over SS spontaneity, Heydrich's increased control over the political police, and Eicke's consolidation and regulation of the concentration camps, prosecutable incidents decreased significantly,[18] and those that took place were more easily concealed. Already apparent by the spring of 1935, these marked "improvements" coincided with the mounting conservative attack and therefore defused it.

Although some of the cases of pre-1935 abuse could be won, bringing moderate punishment of the offenders, especially SA men, such cases were usually quashed. The defenders of the police system minimized the seriousness of the cases through arguments about the criminal or antisocial behavior of the victim and his un-German character, making sympathy a questionable quality. Even where such arguments were impossible and the excesses could not be excused, the cases had little value against Himmler's system because most of them had occurred before he had established his control. Since his control was eliminating such offenses, continued publicity besmirching the system could be labeled counterproductive. Hitler and other Nazi leaders, even those worried about Himmler's power, responded in favor of a system they believed necessary for defense and reacted against conservative tactics that would limit their own power as well. Given this alignment, Hitler in effect protected Himmler against interference by ignoring conservative appeals for support.[19]

In March and April, Frick made his last significant efforts on this tack. Frustration over his ineffectiveness in controlling Himmler drove him to two futile and self-defeating gestures. The occasion for the first was one of many requests for corrective measures forwarded by his office to Himmler. Probably in hopes of Party support, and capitalizing on strained SS-Gestapo and Party relations, he chose the case of a Party District Leader (*Kreisleiter*) whom the Gestapo had arrested for expressing concern over conditions in the camp at Papenburg. According to Gisevius, in marginalia on the official note Frick threatened Himmler with criminal proceedings if such illegal arrests continued. Of course, the threat was bluff and bluster, because Frick dared not order Daluege to execute an arrest,[20] nor would he risk the likely violent consequences of such an act without Hitler's support. Before it ever got that far, Hitler would quash the proceedings and Frick would again be humiliated.

He immediately followed with a second appeal directly to Hitler, one even less well chosen. The case was that of a lawyer representing Dr. Erich Klausener's wife, who was suing her insurance company to collect for his death. The lawyer, who had attempted to prove that Klausener's death on June 30 was not a suicide but was SS and Gestapo work, had been arrested for slander. Digging into the purge touched a very sore point with Hitler; Frick's conclusion that such incidents merited more stringent Reich regulation of protective custody procedures won no support from him.[21] Frustrated, Frick turned again to Goering. By themselves, Frick's ministerial decrees were ineffective, but when Goering supported them with similar decrees to the Prussian Gestapo, Frick had more success in making his authority felt in the other states, even Bavaria. He thus turned to Goering to issue a model decree for Prussia, but it must have exceeded what Goering considered appropriate, infringing upon the "sharp striking force" of his Gestapo. Preferring to continue his retreat from the struggle, Goering submitted the proposal to the Ministerial Council as a law and invited Himmler to attend, leaving the final settlement to a Frick-Himmler confrontation.[22]

Before the meeting, held in late April or early May, Himmler had sufficient time for mustering support to smother Frick's new-found energy. According to Gisevius, he used Frick's threatening note and the appeal in the Klausener case to turn Party support against Frick. Himmler took both memoranda to a meeting of the Party Reich Leaders, who rebuked Frick for improper relations between Party leaders, thereby undermining his hopes at the Ministerial Council. Himmler completed the destruction at the council meeting by associating the whole attack with Gisevius's personal ambitions and demanding the removal of this source of disharmony. Consequently, Frick's proposed law died, and Gisevius was quietly transferred to Nebe's Criminal Police Office.[23]

Meanwhile, another appeal against a Gestapo order brought an even more decisive defeat to the conservatives. On May 2, the Prussian Supreme Administrative Court of Appeal in Berlin denied the right to contest Gestapo confiscation, arrest, and custody orders (*Polizeiverfuegungen*) in administrative courts. The only channel of appeal was, as Goering had contended, through Gestapo offices to Goering. The court based its decision upon the argument that the November 1933 law had established the Gestapo as a special police, and appeal against this category of administrative agency was expressly excluded from the Prussian Police Administrative Law of 1931. Since the 1931 law was written before the establishment of the Gestapo and therefore did not assign it to either category—ordinary or special police—the burden of deciding the Gestapo's position fell upon the court. The court, which really had little choice considering both its traditions and the logic of the argument, interpreted the Gestapo as a special police authority. Under other conditions, however, the court might have ruled that some Gestapo actions were beyond its authority and therefore subject to review. At least Werner Best was concerned enough to say that in light of the trial, the immunity of the Gestapo from court review had to be ensured by a new law. The court apparently reached a decision it thought "most proper" for this particular case.[24] So far the Gestapo remained beyond the courts because the judiciary did not feel either compelled to exert restraint or capable of doing so.

In determining how much censure is due German jurists for their acceptance of the growing police state, one must consider that they had never occupied a very strong position in shaping law through the courts, for the tradition of judicial review was weakly established in Germany. The court was unaccustomed to making radical decisions. By the same token, court actions of the Weimar period that had gone against open-ended police action to protect "public security and order" had been a target of the law-and-order campaign.[25] Drews's January speech on legal reform had expressed the court's mood: ultimately the state and public order came before individual rights.

In the face of all these defeats, Guertner remained undaunted. On May 14, he forwarded from his ministry a memorandum that, according to Gisevius, was composed by officials to goad Frick to action. Along with the memorandum they forwarded Himmler's letter of March 28 on the "Communist movement." Guertner, clearly unimpressed by the Red scare tactic, knew the Communist movement could be checked but not destroyed. Perhaps such sophisticated conservatives were more cynical in the use of the Red scare tactic than the Nazis. In any case, Guertner argued that (1) the use of corporal punishment was disruptive rather than desirable in penal institutions, (2) officials who practiced brutality should be prosecuted to the full extent of the law, and (3) by Himmler's own admission, forceful interrogation had already proved ineffective in crushing the KPD. He concluded that Frick should decree a uniform regulation for the camps to replace Eicke's, forbidding all forceful in-terrogations, and that both ministries should prosecute and punish offenders.[26] Though frustrated, the conservatives were poised for a more concentrated line of attack.

Even if their thrusts of the spring of 1935 had been successfully parried, they had produced results—unfortunately, results that ulti-mately strengthened Himmler and ironically moved Germany closer to the SS-police state. Largely through conservative efforts, until 1938 ap-parent propriety and control prevailed in Gestapo and concentration camp procedures.[27] For instance, one of the 1935 incidents on which Guertner based his efforts was the shooting of two inmates at the Co-lumbia House in March and April. Under investigation, the guards claimed they had followed regulations that mandated shooting prisoners who resisted, meaning Eicke's orders. If the maintenance of discipline were not reason enough for Himmler, the pretext that such incidents gave his enemies induced him to reduce further the autonomy of his police and camp personnel to exercise terror. He forbade officials and guards to touch prisoners without permission. All requests for corporal punishment or forceful interrogation had to be cleared by him, Eicke, or Heydrich. Punishment was to be public and under the supervision of a commandant, who had to account to him for violations.[28]

Unfortunately, Himmler's every concession to propriety weakened his opponents' case. For the sake of appearances, they had to respond in kind or risk turning Hitler against them. For example, when the camps or the police had a reasonable claim that shooting a prisoner was to prevent his escape or for self-defense, the Public Prosecutor's Offices either had to drop charges or be accused of undermining public confidence in the regime. Even so, unless careful camouflage could be arranged, their close surveillance negated Eicke's provisions for camp executions, which were clearly illegal. Consequently, as early as April, Eicke carefully redefined his orders, issuing a secret order "to the effect that these severe penal regulations are not really used," merely published to intimidate inmates.[29]

Although Guertner remained undaunted and continued to encourage Frick's resistance, both men had to concede important points and fall back on alternative strategies. Their earlier attacks on NS police excesses having helped to concentrate political police power in Himmler's hands, they now sought either to eliminate or control him by concentrating all police authority in their hands. Since all involved accepted the desirability of concentrated police power, the argument now was about who should control that power and define its proper limits.

Building toward Himmler's Offensive

The continuing struggle at the ministerial level affected the evolution of the Gestapo below, which, like the camps, became more controlled and regulated. This process involved a dichotomy. The SS recruits and professional policemen, resorting to spontaneous acts of repressive terror, had to be disciplined so the political police system would be less vulnerable to demands for restored ministerial control. At the same time, this heterogeneous police force had to be welded together into an obedient instrument for repression to be employed as Himmler and his Fuehrer saw fit. Ironically, responses to the opposition shaped the Gestapo as much as ideology or design.

With the January 1935 transfer of Werner Best to Berlin as Heydrich's deputy in the Gestapo Office, the last major personality in the shaping of the early Gestapo had arrived. He brought with him organizational and administrative talents that had served well in the development of the SD. His personality and abilities were well suited for building good relations with the Abwehr and for countering conservative attacks. Since, in addition to being Heydrich's deputy, he headed Main Division I for administrative and legal affairs, and later Main Division III, Abwehr Police, he was in position for his strong personality to shape the Gestapo significantly.

Best immediately organized his new main division and repeatedly shuffled its personnel.[30] His extensive attention to organizational structure and detail helped tighten control of the Gestapo and strengthen it as a force in the internal power struggle. For instance, tighter control required rationalizing the jurisdictional patchwork quilt caused by the geographic division of the German police. The several little states, often incontiguous, and the numerous enclaves that they produced had long been obstacles to efficient police work. During 1935 and early 1936, while Frick's broader Reich reform remained stalemated, Heydrich and Best ironed out a few smaller complications that undoubtedly won points for Himmler and his forces as being the most capable of managing a unified German police command. In 1935, on March 11 and April 1, respectively, they incorporated the political police of the little states of Lippe and Schaumburg-Lippe into the Prussian Gestapo, making them outposts (*Aussendienststellen*) of the Field Post Bielefeld of District Minden. With this as a precedent, Heydrich and Best turned to the Ministry of Interior for support in the subordination of the Gestapo field post in the Prussian territory of Sigmaringen to political police of the surrounding state of Wuerttemberg.[31] Such successful streamlining may have been useful wedges for cracking resistance to Himmler's appointment as chief of German Police.

Simplified and rational organizational relationships were rigorously pursued by the leaders from Himmler down. Too much has been made of how they allegedly employed to their advantage the tangle of administrative jurisdictions. They hardly enjoyed this maze. Either they had inherited most of it from the past, or it had grown during more recent evolutions in the power struggle that had prevented rational development and required piecemeal accretions. Occassional, tempting opportunities did induce Himmler or Heyrich to use deliberately their many jurisdictional complexities as a smokescreen. However, generally they sought to clarify and simplify internal relationships for the sake of efficiency. A continuous stream of directives to assist the bewildered members of lower offices in directing their work through proper channels and to avoid time-consuming side tracks testify to the scope of the confusion cause by the union of separate state political police forces, with their different forms of administrative accountability.[32] This confusion would take years to overcome and required the acquisition of extraordinary authority by Himmler.

Within the Prussian Gestapo itself, they rationalized regional jurisdictions in order to tighten control over field personnel who, by virtue of their distance from Berlin, displayed both independence and susceptibility to local NS lords. Their continued revolutionary indiscretions and police excesses strengthened opposition arguments. Tightening control began shortly after Heydrich took over the Gestapo Office in May 1934. After the distractions of the summer of 1934, he resumed the effort and continued it into 1935. When several of the growing number of field posts were consolidated under the local supervision of one such post, the locally responsible Gestapo official was more capable of exercising direct control than the Gestapo Office in Berlin, especially if he were well chosen. This arrangement preceded the system of superior field posts (*Staatspolizeileitstellen*) that would emerge after the creation of Sipo.

Logically, the first field posts in this regional grouping were those of the province of East Prussia, separated from the rest of Germany by Poland. There, in May 1934, the posts of Allenstein, Elbing, and Tilsit were subordinated to the one at Koenigsberg. Their geographic location gave these posts their importance, yet physical separation from the rest of the Gestapo made control more difficult. Complicating matters, the powerful *Gauleiter* and provincial governor, Erich Koch, who considered the local Gestapo his tool, was unfriendly to the SD.[33]

Suspicion that these regional groupings were designed to neutralize the most troublesome Gestapo field posts is reaffirmed by the order of their development. After Koenigsberg, in July and August, the province of Silesia, recently won from SA dominance, was similarly subordinated to the key post at Breslau. In September, Pomerania, the site of Hoffmann's excesses, was put under the supervision of the Stettin post. Then, in the spring of 1935, following the creation of a new Gestapo jurisdiction in the Saar, the Saarbruecken post received responsibility for that at Trier. Here was a special set of problems requiring rationalization. Saar-Pfalz-Trier, crucial to Gestapo work due to its location on the French-Luxembourg border, included several police jurisdictions: Bavarian, Prussian, and the newly created Reich police for the Saar. It was also the domain of the troublesome Gauleiter Josef Buerckel, whom Best had been at such pains to cultivate.[34]

Best also tightened other mechanisms for control by the Berlin Office—for instance, over the agents employed by the Gestapo. The poor quality of foreign agents had embarrassed Diels and cost his Gestapo a role in foreign intelligence. Domestic agents must also have been a problem, even under Heydrich, but, strangely, little was done by Berlin to exercise control over the agents of the field posts until Best established a centralized reporting and card file system for identifying unreliable agents and informants.[35] The lateness of such a move indicates a high degree of amateurishness during the early years, even among the professional police branch of Himmler's system.

Equally troublesome was persistent, cruel, and high-handed behavior. Himmler's admonitions against such behavior during his October speech expressed the naive ideal he pursued—and unrestrained but well-behaved police. However, he and his lieutenants were neither unaware of nor indifferent to resultant excesses and the problems they caused. The Gestapo needed constant reminders that certain potential "enemies" required careful treatment, especially foreign citizens whose abuse could have international repercussions. Even the treatment of the "little man" among the numerous protective custody arrestees required certain basic precautions and considerations, because the image of propriety and humane treatment were often inseparable. Gestapo members had to be reminded to refer the infirm to hospital detention facilities rather than to the camp regimen, where their subsequent death might require an investigation, or where they might cause discipline and sanitation problems. To combat spontaneous lawlessness in the Gestapo and to preserve propriety, the central office sent constant reminders to field posts to comply with Frick's timetables for due process and review of protective custody cases.[36] These procedures are in marked contrast to Himmler's tactics of ignoring Frick's complaints or coldly excusing Gestapo excesses.

By the same token, Himmler and Heydrich learned that too free-wheeling a police force disrupted authority and discipline within society in general. For instance, too quick a response to student complaints against teachers as politically unsuitable led to unfounded arrests that were "injurious to the respect and authority of the teaching staff." Overzealous political policemen had to be ordered to coordinate action through appropriate officials for education.[37]

The tendency of Gestapo officials to respond to pressure from Party organizations bent on their own objectives caused Gestapo involvement in disruptive and embarrassing actions. Toward this end, Himmler's expanding net of liaison personnel and agencies in the Party organizations regulated Gestapo reponsiveness without ordering Gestapo officials to ignore Party calls for police action. Regulated responsiveness was essential, for an unresponsive police would increase Party hostility, resurrect demands for Party organizations to exercise police powers, and undermine Himmler's appeal as a police leader who guaranteed proper ideological guidance for the police. For instance, Robert Ley's German Workers' Front (DAF), the DAF Information Office, now under SD influence, was sufficiently reliable to screen DAF requests for Gestapo action in economic problems. Both Ley and Best ordered their respective field posts to deal with each other primarily through the DAF Information Office. Once again, the SD served a key function in defusing a tense situation, for the three-way Party struggle among Hess, the SS, and Ley remained acute.[38]

As one side effect of "selling" the Gestapo, Best had to educate his police officials about the press as a tool of public relations. He not only guided them toward behavior conducive to a better public image, but he also instructed them on how to cultivate that image. Typically, their press releases on police actions had been a dry report of the action taken and its legal bases. Best reminded them that the purpose of press releases was "to convince the public of . . . the necessity of the Gestapo regulations." The threat to public security had to be emphasized to win the support of the reader disinterested in legal technicalities.[39]

Overall, such efforts produced a Gestapo sufficiently controlled to be safe from demands for ministerial control, yet efficient enough against "enemies" to satisfy NS demands for security. Such a balance must have pleased Hitler, but hardly moved him to bestow greatly expanded power on Himmler. Instead, the opposition continued for several months more with some hope of reversing his expansion.

17

A Conservative Victory?

Until Himmler's triumph in June 1936, the conservative opposition continued its fight on two major fronts. It sought to curb the Gestapo within Prussia, and it tried to establish Reich central control over all police, including the political police. On the first front, the opposition achieved a fleeting victory in the fall of 1935. On the second, there was a near success, then stalemate.

Despite the curbing of uncontrolled radicals in 1934, the struggle still had more complexity than one between two polarized camps—the conservative opposition versus Himmler's group. It might be described as occurring along a continuum. At one end lay the conservative allies who sought to limit the Nazis and build their own power base. Among their leaders, the one most directly involved in police matters was Franz Guertner, Reich and Prussian minister of justice. Below him, in his and Frick's ministries and in other state bureaucracies, were a rank of professional civil servants hoping to thwart Himmler's growth. Most were too sophisticated to be overwhelmed by NS propaganda. Their mixed motives ranged from honorable to self-serving, but in every case they were bound to the Nazis by mutual objectives and mutual enemies. To fight the Nazis openly was dangerous on two counts: A strike that was not decisive was the same as committing suicide, yet to strike too decisively might threaten mutual objectives and give victory to mutual enemies.

As Reich and Prussian minister of the interior, Frick lay near the center of the continuum, the object of contending appeals from both extremes. On the one hand, a NS conservative with much in common with the professional civil servants, Frick would build a system of centralized, authoritarian government, basically acceptable to conservatives. On the other hand, as a dedicated Nazi, a thoroughgoing anti-Semite loyal to his Fuehrer, he felt the considerable weight of arguments from Himmler's camp, based solidly on the NS world view, and once Hitler indicated support for any of Himmler's positions or actions, Frick's resistance crumbled.

In fact, much of what has been, and will be, attributed here to Frick may well have been the work of officials around him. An older man obviously tiring of the long fight, from day to day he would act decisively or recklessly when frustrated and bitter. At another time, he would be indecisive or lethargic. As an experienced Old Fighter, he knew the significance of his declining status with Hitler and worried self-defeatingly about interpersonal Party politics. Although he sought to play the game at all levels, as his position declined he became less willing to involve directly his legal and administrative experts, whose arguments might have prevailed in an occasional high-level confrontation. Instead he chose to attend such meetings alone. Some witnesses indicate that he lost interest in the details of important policy formulation, and was therefore incapable of arguing decisively.[1]

A gradation of Nazis stood between Guertner and Himmler on the continuum, clouding the sharpness of anti-Himmler arguments. They ranged from Hans Frank, for instance, to Werner Best, clearly within Himmler's camp. As jurists they phrased their arguments more appealingly than Himmler or Heydrich, and, in fact, their positions were more conservative. They weakened Frick's determination to resist Himmler's expansion and undoubtedly served in arranging compromises between Frick and Himmler. Goering belongs on the continuum between Frick and Himmler also, as a vehicle for compromises rather than a member of Himmler's extreme wing.

Above all of this sat Hitler, traditionally described as manipulating such divisions cynically in a divide-and-conquer process, or as slowly and calculatingly building toward his secret goal of a totalitarian police state. Although these were indeed the effects of his role, most evidence indicates that his behavior in this struggle was less calculated and more a mixture of disinterest, fumbling intuition, and an aversion to making decisions, the result being gradual accumulations of power to the most persistent, flexible, and opportunistic competitors, especially if they offered Hitler the power he wanted at a time when he could seize it. In fact, Hitler's decisions affecting this struggle were frequently inconsistent. If success lay through personal appeal to Hitler, Goering and Himmler held most trumps, but Hitler had made no final decisions. As late as 1935, Goebbels allegedly told Diels that Hitler had reservations about the operation of the Gestapo under Heydrich.[2]

Outside this continuum were other potential allies, power bases, and alternative channels of appeal to the Fuehrer. From all appearances, Himmler's people made an effort to "sell" the Gestapo to these potential allies. Regardless of sharp splits among the officers, von Blomberg's support shifted the weight of the military, that bastion of conservative strength, toward Himmler. The role of the barons of finance and industry in this struggle has never been explored beyond their contributions to the SS. They divided themselves into conservative wings behind Schacht, and more pliable and opportunistic wings supporting Goering and Himmlor. Finally, the Party power structure, split at the top between Hess-Schwarz and Ley and ranging down through the *Gauleiter* to local leaders, held numerous government offices with police powers and responsibilities. These Party leaders with their overlapping interests in the state may have been a decisive factor at least in Frick's defeat—if not in Himmler's victory—because Frick threatened their independence.

For Frick, the Reich centralization of the police under his ministry was merely one major aspect of an intended Reich reform that overextended his capacities. He wished to consolidate in one rationalized and centralized bureaucracy all the machinery of governing and policy making, with his ministry as the keystone. Since 1933 Frick had made periodic moves toward police centralization, only to let the matter drop time and again. Goering's tricks with the Gestapo had frustrated his earliest moves to consolidate the political police, and, although he continued to pursue a centralization of all criminal police as a counter to the Gestapo, every obstacle he encountered encumbered his progress unduly. Each time he found a particular thrust frustrated (by Goering's retention of the Gestapo, for example), he marked time for several months, then added it to his growing list of frustrations, creating one massive problem to be solved in toto. Such a spirit certainly permeated a memorandum compiled in June 1935 by Daluege's staff in the ministry.[3]

The memorandum was a position paper on all the problems produced by the different types and concepts of "police" and by the multitude of ministries and state and local jurisdictions to which they were responsible. The authors further complicated their problem by including "special police" who fell under other ministries, such as river and harbor patrols, railroad police, conservation officials and game wardens, air raid wardens, and border and tariff officials. Within this mass of conflicting and overlapping jurisdictions, the problem of the political police, complex enough in itself, became totally submerged and seemingly minor. Only a complete reorganization of the entire governmental structure could solve these problems, an impossible task even in the most totalitarian of states, especially if the Fuehrer did not devote himself to it as a high priority.

If indeed Frick had encumbered the solution of the political police problem with total Reich reform, there is little wonder that he failed to outmaneuver Himmler. He had failed to focus enough energy on either a direct assault on the political police or a clever encirclement—that is, the creation of a suitable replacement, a Reich Criminal Police. If he and his ministry had approached the police problem as a single package, hoping to dilute the intense controversy over the political police, they would have had a viable tactic only if police centralization could have been disentangled from the insoluble issues of Reich reform.

When he finally did make a move focused specifically on the detective police, Frick may have precipitated Himmler's ultimate victory. In late spring 1935, Frick suddenly tried to make Hitler choose between himself and Himmler as the responsible authority for the political police. This maneuver grew from a complex tug of war over accountability for the Reich Security Service (Reichssicherheitsdienst, or RSD), a police detective bodyguard formed for the close protection of the Fuehrer and other key leaders—an organization similar to the American president's Secret Service.[4]

As if to pressure Hitler, Frick complained that he could not assume responsibility for the RSD in his police division of the ministry unless he had complete authority over all involved officials, their service, capabilities, and cooperation with other criminal police. He argued for the unification of all detective police, both political and criminal, directly under his ministry. He buttressed the case with several examples of the domestic and foreign repercussions of political police actions over which he had no control. Unfortunately, his arguments flew in the face of Hitler's desire for personal involvement in the selection of all RSD personnel and for direct command over them through his personal staff. Frick concluded with a child-like demand that Hitler choose between him and Himmler to have Reich-wide responsibility for the political police, solving jurisdictional problems once and for all.[5] Predictably, Hitler procrastinated.

Meanwhile, Frick's staff continued its work on the unification of all police under a central Reich authority. As early as March, they had drafted a law for police administration that would give Frick extensive powers for regulating all police organizations in the Reich. Frick, knowing he was powerless to push through and enforce such legislation, sought support from Hitler.[6] He must have received some encouragement, for by June he was informing representatives of the various states that the uniformed police would be taken over by the Reich on April 1, 1936. Through the entire summer, however, open discussion of centralization remained limited to the uniformed police, leaving the most sensitive issue of the criminal and political police in abeyance. As a matter of fact, as late as August, the criminal police were specifically excluded from centralization.[7]

By this time von Blomberg had gone directly to Hitler to urge centralization of an autonomous political police. Although he had worded his note in such a way as to strengthen Himmler's case, the position he took in person before Hitler is not known.[8] Subsequent documents indicate that Hitler remained ambivalent about the place of the political police in the Reich chain of command, but he apparently consented to Blomberg's appeal for unification. For instance, at some subsequent time, Frick met with Hitler and apparently left with the understanding that the Gestapo would be incorporated under his ministry. By October he was so confident of victory that he not only ordered plans for their absorption but apparently anticipated that the SS and SD could be shunted aside to mere auxiliary police roles.[9]

What Hitler actually told Frick remains unclear, but during the summer of 1935 things became ripe for mobilizing support against Himmler's growing power. The *Gauleiter* renewed pressure against the spy net of the SD, a bugbear for many of them, and friction returned to SD-Party relations in 1935. Throughout the year, *Gau* and Reich leaders, who resented the penetration of SD agents into their domains, fought back with every means available, frustrating specific aspects of SD work and conducting a grumbling campaign in general that aroused further fear and resentment of SD activities.

One basis for such hostility clearly lay in the SA under the new staff chief, Viktor Lutze. Although he had turned against Roehm, the severity of SS repression had shocked him, and he resented it. Frustrated in his efforts to expose the SS role in the events of June 30,[10] he sought to build what machinery he could within the emasculated SA to oppose the SS. One of his creations was a counter to the SD. At some time prior to April 1935, Lutze charged SA General Kurt Kuehme with the formation of an intelligence organization that, although ostensibly focused primarily on the SA, would delve into political developments in general. Lutze approached Hitler and got his support for an intelligence operation to serve the SA as the SD did for the SS and the Party.[11]

Hitler's consent is another measure of how far he remained from the details of constructing the police state. Although he was disrupting Himmler's effort to eliminate competitive agencies, he may simply have seen this as nothing more than a sop to the SA. On the other hand, if he was deliberately counterbalancing Himmler's growing organization, he did so without clear understanding of the division of labor evolving below him. In any case, armed with Hitler's consent, on May 6 Lutze turned to Schwarz with a request for funds. Schwarz's immediate reaction indicated no special concern, and only at the end of the month did he bring the matter to Hess's attention. Hess immediately went to Hitler for a clarification. Hitler then denied or rescinded his approval, and Hess forbade the establishment as a contradiction of the approved monopoly of the SD.[12]

Throughout the summer, it seems, Hitler vacillated. Indecisive about how much to give Himmler and how much of a balance to retain against him, Hitler was certain only of the necessity for internal order and the desirability of extensive police power. Perhaps such a mood encouraged him to nod approval whenever Frick outlined plans for centralizing all police. In any case, Frick's people continued to formulate legislation for a Reich police, with the target date of April 1, 1936. During the autumn they drummed up support in the Reich and Prussian ministries, and by November they were preparing drafts for submission. They planned for all the regular uniformed and detective police in Germany to become Reich civil servants under Frick's ministry. For local direction, the district officials of the states would continue their former function as local police authorities, but under Reich ministry control.[13] Himmler would have to become an obedient civil servant or be shunted aside.

As justification for this proposed police reform, Frick's supporters played on the mounting tension over international affairs and on the belief in the necessity of a Reich police for national defense and security. Plans to create a centralized criminal investigation office added another appeal. They offered the recent success in creating a Reich police force for the Saar as proof of feasibility and as a measure of what was needed. Finally, to combat the general lethargy in Reich reform, they argued that the urgency of police reform demanded action before the completion of a total reform.[14]

With the centralization of all police under Frick's ministry, the Reich chief of police would have been Kurt Daluege as head of the Police Division (Abteilung III). Daluege would have the image of NS reliability to make him acceptable to the Party, thus countering Himmler's appeal; he had fewer enemies in the Movement than Himmler. Consequently, Frick's people had no choice but to continue backing him as their alternative, despite growing suspicions of his ambitions[15] and his increasing subordination to Himmler. They could hope that a Frick victory would win him back. Although he undoubtedly still played a double game, Daluege was increasingly in a position to weaken Frick's work for centralizing the police to the exclusion of Himmler.

By this time, however, the tide had shifted again, in Himmler's favor. Both of Lutze's efforts had been frustrated by a combination of political police action from below and Bormann's support from above. Bormann also cooled the Party leaders' attacks on the SD. When Kuehme continued efforts to build an SA intelligence agency, including clandestine fund raising, Heydrich had his agents arrested and registered a protest with Hess, who, along with Schwarz, took official action to end SA intelligence operation. Although Lutze may have maintained some clandestine operations, any hope of creating a rival to the SD had vanished, given Party financial control and official pressure, and the executive action of Heydrich's police.[16]

Bormann's work within Party headquarters culminated in February 1936 when he issued for Hess an unusually blunt order to the Party to "abandon all distrust of the SD and to support it wholeheartedly in the performance of its tasks. He announced that Hess would receive all SD reports of Party difficulties without embellishment and interpretation, and the proper state prosecutor would be notified of punishable offenses. Henceforth, there should be no cause for friction between SD and Party; any future problems were to be reported to Hess for settlement with Himmler.[17] Bormann and Hess supported the SD because, in their struggles with Ley and the *Gauleiter*, they needed reliable sources of information and checks against corruption in the Movement. With his team of SD and police, Heydrich zealously watched and purged the DAF.[18] Throughout the summer and into the winter, many who had Hitler's ear thus supported one or more aspects of Himmler's growing system. Consequently, at the same time that he may have been encouraging Frick, Hitler was also amenable to Himmler's proposals. Himmler used his direct access to Hitler to outmaneuver Lutze, Frick, and other opponents.[19] Consequently in October, at the same time that Frick was anticipating the absorption of the Gestapo, Himmler had confidence enough to notify his *Land* police offices that he anticipated the creation of a Reich political police with its own autonomous budget.[20]

Hitler had made decisions in Himmler's favor without Frick understanding their full implications. However, Frick should have gotten the message clearly when Hitler finally acted on the Reich Security Service (RSD). On October 21, he notified Frick that although the RSD would always be directly subordinate to the chief of the Reich Chancellery, Dr. Lammers, and commanded directly by Hitler, Hess, and Bormann, Himmler would have formal responsibility for the RSD and the personal security of key leaders. Frick's ministry would merely handle administrative and budgetary affairs.[21] From this Frick must have realized the weakness of his position vis-à-vis Himmler and the danger of pressing Hitler to choose between them.

Meanwhile, Himmler checkmated Frick's proposed legislation. On November 1, in response to a number of attacks on his SS–police–concentration camp system, he again went directly to Hitler and won his support.[22] On these particular complaints and in a number of subsequent cases, Hitler showed continued and decisive support for Himmler's system, and from all appearances he must also have instructed Frick to include Himmler's opinions in any plans for centralizing the police. The matter would now hang fire until spring, when Frick's people began ironing out the details with Heydrich's staff.

Before this stage was reached, however, the conservative opposition had achieved an apparent victory. That success and its subsequent deterioration involved the struggle to limit the power of the Gestapo inside Prussia.

Victory and Defeat on the Prussian Front

If Himmler indeed suffered a setback, it apparently resulted from another case of overplaying his hand. Unfortunately, the evidence for reconstructing these developments is spotty. In the previously mentioned memorandum in which Frick demanded that Hitler choose between him and Himmler, Frick made an allusion to a Gestapo law that Himmler had proposed for Prussia. According to Frick, Himmler's draft asserted that Himmler would determine the tasks of the Gestapo.[23] Since both the final form of the law, issued in February 1936, and a draft discussed by the Prussian ministerial council on June 27, 1935, both reserved determination of Gestapo business to Goering in understanding with Frick, considerable changes must have been made in Himmler's draft between the time of Frick's memorandum (May or early June) and the council meeting.[24]

If Frick accurately interpreted Himmler's draft of the law, then Himmler had certainly bid for greater personal power and independence from Goering. Under the previous laws, Goering, *as chief of the Gestapo,* determined its tasks. If Himmler hoped to assume Goering's old authority, the final Gestapo Law issued in February was indeed a victory for Frick and a setback for him. By the same token, Goering's apparent support for Frick in this new law becomes more understandable. Frick could have goaded Goering into reasserting limitations over Himmler and into sharing this limiting authority with Frick and the regional governors, as checks to Himmler's growing independence, for Goering would not abdicate his last vestige of control over the Gestapo.

In the background of this development, both Goering and Himmler had been under considerable pressure to reform and clarify regulations governing the Gestapo, especially in regard to its relations with regional and local government and also with respect to the concentration camps. They apparently preferred to procrastinate, using their power to set precedents and to create fait accompli. The decision of the Prussian Supreme Administrative Court of May 2, 1935, may have forced the issue, however. Although it recognized the Gestapo as a special police, not subject to the regular procedures for review by administrative courts, it did not absolutely exclude the possibility of court intervention in Gestapo actions. Thus Werner Best had emphasized the necessity of a new law to guarantee the Gestapo immunity from review.[25]

The draft legislation drawn up in Best's office probably included a clause on court review like that in the final law. In addition to Himmler's new claim to power, it probably sought also to guarantee the continued independence of the Gestapo field posts from the regional governors. This, however, was a point of ambivalence for Goering, who did want close cooperation between the Gestapo and the state administration. It might be surmised that Himmler also sought to increase the independence of his concentration camps from state control. Consequently by the end of June 1935, whatever Himmler's supporters may have tried to gain was checkmated or reversed in most cases. At the June 27 meeting of the Prussian Ministerial Council, the draft law, which contained basically the final form of the law, in no way resembled Frick's description of Himmler's proposal. Both the law and the minutes of the meeting require analysis.

In one respect, the law represented an advance of Gestapo power, but in other respects it checked Himmler's independence. All previous laws and the controversial sections of the ordinance of March 8, 1934, were abrogated and replaced by this one law, which reaffirmed the subordination of the Gestapo Office to Goering as prime minister of Prussia; however, its independence from Minister of Interior Frick became less secure than before. Although Goering would still decide what business in particular fell to the Gestapo, henceforth he would do so "in understanding with" (*im Einvernehmen mit*) Frick. Although this was typical of promises easily ignored, it also had teeth. Both Goering and Frick would now issue executive orders pursuant to this law. Indeed, the ordinance for the execution of this law, finally issued on February 10, 1936, was in fact signed by Frick as well as Goering.[26] This gave Frick veto power.

The local Gestapo offices (*Staatspolizeistellen*) were specifically resubordinated to the regional governors (*Rezierungspraesidenten*). The de jure independence of the Gestapo from Frick's ministry seemed considerably weakened. To prevent Himmler and Heydrich from relying on their personnel in the Gestapo field structure and the Gestapo office to ignore and sabotage this piece of legislation, Frick as well as Goering would henceforth supervise the appointment and dismissal of Gestapo civil servants through the usual state civil service procedures. Goering had apparently consented to act in understanding with Frick to curb Himmler.[27]

Despite the fact that Best and his legal experts had been working on the law for at least a year, the only real advance in Gestapo power was the codification of Gestapo immunity from court review of its orders. Frick and Guertner lost in their drive for judicial and administrative review of Gestapo actions because they were opposing the entire, arbitrary concept of the fuehrer principle. As a Nazi, Frick had to acquiesce, for court review was part of the "liberal" system of checks and balances. The NS system demanded that the courts operate in harmony with the executive and not serve as opponents to its power. This concession by Frick is another indication of a possible compromise between him and Goering. By submitting to this clause, Frick made it easier for Goering to support other clauses for increased control of the Gestapo without feeling that he had dulled his sharp instrument.

Some misconceptions about this law and the ordinance for its execution require explanation. The worst error is the contention that this law made the Gestapo a Reich-wide political police force. In his summation at Nuremberg, a Soviet prosecutor said this law had made the Gestapo Office *the central office for all of the political police of the Reich.* This error has been picked up and repeated by academic and popular historians, some of whom have even cited the February 10, 1936, law as their authority.[28] The contention is totally fallacious, for it was a purely Prussian law. Although the Gestapo office physically contained Himmler's "Central Bureau" for commanding the political police of the other states, this bureau existed only under Himmler's personal authority as commander of these police in each state. It had no official place in the Gestapo Office, and the Prussian Gestapo law of 1936 left this unchanged. Unfortunately, later Gestapo training materials contributed to the confusion. When interpreting the law of 1936, they often added to Section 3 that the Gestapo Office had the authority to "decree regulations for the entire Reich." This interpretation was rendered later, however, after the developments of July 1936. Other official publications also twisted or reversed the significance of the law. Since they sought as usual to maintain outwardly the image of propriety within the NS government, they usually hailed the law as a codification of the Gestapo's development up to that point, thereby obscuring the law's possible significance as a potential check on Himmler.[29]

Another source of misinformation has been Section 2 (4) of the Executive Ordinance, which read, "The Secret Police Office administers the state concentration camps." This is traditionally viewed as an aspect of Heydrich's struggle to build his personal power within the SS system in rivalry with Himmler. Heydrich allegedly engineered this clause to have the camps directly subordinate to himself rather than under Himmler through the SS chain of command. Because of subsequent sabotage of this clause by Himmler's actual operating procedures, the Gestapo Office exercised control only to the extent that it assigned internees to camps of its choice and ensured that they were treated commensurate with their "offenses." A standard interpretation states that Himmler carefully maintained personal control of the camps to keep Heydrich from gaining too much power.[30]

Control of the concentration camps may well have been one aspect of a developing Himmler-Heydrich rivalry, but the popularity of this version has further obscured the real significance of Frick's potential victory in the February law. If Frick and Goering had kept the camps under control of the Gestapo, while continuing to extend their own control over it, they would have won a most significant victory over Himmler's emerging system. Himmler's success resulted from his ability to keep the camps independent de facto of state supervision. In this context, Heydrich should have been supporting rather than opposing the removal of the camps from the Gestapo, a state agency.

Best's testimony at Nuremberg is the prime source that this clause of the ordinance represented a power play by Heydrich. In fact, energy was generated in the Gestapo Office to regain control over the camps, but that came after the June 1936 reorganization of the police nullified this clause of the February ordinance. Best probably confused the times. Furthermore, as Eicke understood it, the energy for the later move came from Best, who, according to Eicke's August 1936 complaint to Himmler, had "stated on various occasions that the situation in the camps is disgusting and that it is high time the camps were returned to command of the Gestapo."[31] Gestapo concern over the camps seems to have been as much a matter of Best's conceptions of propriety as of Heydrich's power plays.

To return to the Ministerial Council meeting of June 27, 1935 and the events leading up to the actual decree, the minutes of the meeting indicate more of the nature of the possible compromise among Goering, Frick, and perhaps Guertner to curb Himmler. After some discussion of Gestapo affairs, the council expressed its general consent to the draft as presented at that time by Himmler, who must have been forced to submit to the compromise. Himmler and Frick had worked out the details, and after June 27 the draft underwent only minimal changes. Most significantly, the Council "confirmed that *for the present* the specially created instrument of the Gestapo for the combatting of the state enemies *cannot be dispensed with."* However, they counterbalanced the acknowledged necessity for a "taut, pervading authority" with the expressed desire that its "absolutely necessary connection with the agencies of the general administration (*Oberpraesidenten, Regierungspraesidenten, Landraeten*) be preserved."[32]

This was, however, still a compromise and not yet a complete defeat for Himmler, for the conservative ministers, who included not only Frick and Guertner but also Popitz and Schacht, had accepted the continued existence of the extraordinary police, the Gestapo. They accepted the argument that such police were essential to combat the threats against Germany. They abandoned their position that the state of emergency was over and that the Gestapo and the camps were no longer needed. In return, Goering accepted resubordination of the field posts to the governors. The last minute on the proposed law indicated that Frick had draft proposals on procedures for remedies against Gestapo measures; however, knowledge of their nature awaits further evidence, for they never saw application.[33]

Although Goering proceeded within the month to circulate the draft to the ministers for specific comments, setting a deadline of August 3 for its decree, action hung fire until February 1936.[34] The reasons for the delay are not documented. Himmler apparently counterattacked, and Goering may have had second thoughts. As before, Goering continued to play a vacillating role in the power struggle through the spring of 1936. The draft law and opposition pressure encouraged him to continue asserting administrative control over the Gestapo field offices, but he would soon reverse the process. His inconsistent orders undoubtedly confused and frustrated responsible officials trying to control the Gestapo; they certainly remain a confusing factor today. The complications arising from the highly legalistic struggle between Frick and Himmler must certainly have discouraged this flamboyant personality from becoming actively involved. Frick had apparently convinced him that he could and should prevent the Gestapo from slipping through his fingers into Himmler's, and Goering might have tried to reassert his and Frick's administrative control. On the other hand, torn by Himmler's arguments for the necessity of maintaining the "sharp instrument" for combating Communism and other threats to the new order, Goering vacillated. When Himmler and Frick had recourse to Hitler, he withdrew further from the competition, to avoid being on the wrong side, and directed his attention to paths of less resistance—the more glamorous Luftwaffe and the more lucrative economic sphere.

From June 1935 through spring 1936, Goering and Himmler felt opposition from the ministers around them, from the administrators, bureaucrats, and officials of Prussia, from the judiciary, and from influential private sources, exerting great pressure to reform the SS, Gestapo, and camp system. Goering's governors pressed him to resubordinate the Gestapo field posts and decried the delay in issuing the new law. Powerful *Gauleiter* like Erich Koch added to this pressure in their dual roles in Party and state. The camps came under renewed attack. At the Reich level, Guertner tried to preserve the case against the Saxon Gestapo official Vogel for his role in camp excesses prior to June 30, 1934.[35]

By October, such pressure produced mixed results, but Himmler's overall defenses seemed more firm. For instance, in response to suspicion about the frequency of death due to unnatural causes in the camps, in October the Gestapo published guidelines requiring camp commandants to report immediately to the Public Prosecutor's Office every case without clear medical evidence of death due to natural causes. A clear concession to the demand for propriety and due process in the camps, the guidelines would discourage excesses without creating outside controls and would strengthen official apologies for the system.[36] In contrast to such concessions, the political police continued to violate Frick's April 1934 directives on protective custody by using such custody for the preventive detention of enemies of the state, like KPD officials who might return to their old work.[37] In such cases, the conservative opposition found protests awkward.

Real measures of the emerging constellation of power appeared, however, in Saxony and Bavaria. In Saxony, Hitler quashed the case against Vogel in September. In Bavaria at an October 8 meeting of the Ministerial Council, Wagner deflected Epp's efforts to tighten control over the BPP by responding that Himmler was in control and that he could intervene only if Frick, as Reich minister, had the authority.[38] The answer to that question came shortly.

On November 1, under pressure from all these attacks, Himmler turned to Hitler for support. Undoubtedly he employed all of his appeals about the necessity of the Gestapo and the camps for the internal defense of national security. In Hitler, impatient with internal administrative details and increasingly preoccupied with preparations for "national defense," he found a responsive ear. On November 6, he forwarded the results to Goering, Frick, and Guertner. On the issues of Gestapo field post subordination to the governors, specifically Koch's case in East Prussia, Hitler "decided that no change should be made in position of the Koenigsberg Gestapo." On Guertner's demand that in protective custody cases prisoners have access to legal assistance, Hitler prohibited the consultation of lawyers. And on Guertner's call for more stringent measures to avoid deaths in the camps, Hitler responded. "In view of the conscientious direction of the camps special measures are not considered necessary."[39] Himmler had won most points of contention.

Meanwhile, in legislative and judicial matters the tide had also turned decisively in Himmler's favor. A significant expansion of police powers had come in June 1935 with passage of an ordinance on criminal punishment. The new law destroyed the principle of punishment only for crimes under the law. Henceforth, one could be punished for any act that went against the "public" sense of propriety. In this way, the police and the leadership of state and Party became the only real judges of what constituted a crime. As another aspect of the *voelkisch* concept of law, essentially any violation against "the living law of the Germanic racial community," that is, the Nazi weltanschauung, became a crime. These new crimes would now be punished by analogy with the most similar law. In this way, crimes of "racial defilement" were prosecuted even before the September 1935 passage of the Law for the Protection of German Blood and German Honor.[40] The broad interpretation of protective custody powers had given the Gestapo this de facto authority for some time; now it was established in law.

The judiciary showed itself equally adaptive to the growing totalitarian mood of law and order. In December 1935, the Prussian Court of Appeal (Kammergericht) upheld sentences against juveniles for activities in a Catholic youth movement. In the spirit of the "camouflaged enemy" argument and the philosophy of totalitarian solidarity for national defense, the judges ruled that such organizations in which undue emphasis was placed on religious beliefs undermined the NS drive to build an indivisible national community and, therefore, indirectly assisted Communist subversion.[41]

While such measures harmonized with arguments emanating from Gestapo and SD sources, courts were also rendering decisions directly undermining the conservative opposition. On October 7, 1935, the Hamburg Administrative Court went as far as an SS jurist could ask. Beyond ruling that political police orders were immune to test in administrative courts, it decided that the courts could not even test whether or not such orders lay within the political authority of the state once the state had assumed that they did. This was the kind of freedom the Gestapo needed in Prussia, where the court decision of the previous fall had not eliminated the court's right to test political orders to determine if they were really within the purview of the political police.[42]

In light of all this, it seems unlikely that the law finally passed because Himmler had to accept it under pressure from the ministers, governors, and *Gauleiter*. Most of that pressure had been deflected with Hitler's support in November, and only the threat of court review remained a serious opposition trump in Prussia. All parties involved had accepted the law in its final form, but Himmler's victories had apparently encouraged him to counterattack with proposed executive directives for the law that became a bone of contention in December. This may have been a tactical maneuver, however, for he backed down by the time he and Goering met to settle details with Hitler in January, guaranteeing Himmler's position.[43] By then, Himmler had turned a potential defeat into a desirable compromise.

Although his opposition may have forced Himmler to negotiate and to accept the draft during the summer of 1935, by February the law represented a renewed expression of the spirit of compromise and common front that had existed prior to June 1934. Himmler accepted a role for Frick in the basic policy and personnel matters of the Gestapo for the sake of harmony and propriety and in return for freedom from attack through the courts. Because he probably held to the Ministerial Council's expressed desire for close cooperation between police and administration, he could accept the apparent subordination of the field posts to the governors. In both cases, he could count on Goering's values to prevent too much interference by Frick or other bureaucrats. Given these realities and Himmler's increased strength by the beginning of 1936, the law now gave far more than it took away.[44] Best, as their legal expert, may have steered Himmler and Heydrich in this direction, more legally and administratively proper than they might otherwise have chosen. In any case, on February 10, 1936, the law became effective.

Goering, "in understanding with" Frick, immediately bolstered the new law with a number of specific directives, and throughout February and March, earnestly involved himself in an effort to ensure close coordination between the field posts and the governors. For his part, Heydrich dutifully ordered his field post leaders to observe the new relationships. Of course, he thought it proper to exploit every loophole. For instance, although Goering ordered the Gestapo Office to forward to the governors informational copies of all directives sent to the field posts, it had been easy to convince him that orders relevant to Abwehr police work should be excluded from this directive for the sake of national security. Furthermore, Heydrich widened the loophole by distinguishing between orders that fell under Goering's directive and "personal assignments" sent to individual field post leaders. According to Heydrich, the governors need not receive the latter. He thus left himself the freedom, for reasons of security or other priorities, to violate the procedures as he saw fit, while simultaneously ensuring tranquility by ordering his subordinates to adhere to the guidelines.[45]

For his part, Goering predictably set clear limits as to how far he would allow administrative interference in Gestapo work. The new arrangement was not to disrupt Gestapo business. "The Gestapo must . . . remain a tightly organized, forceful instrument in the hands of the state government." The governors could intervene only in cases of special political interest, and he repeated the old formula limiting their authority to give directives only insofar as they did not contradict those of the Gestapo Office. In such cases, the Gestapo Office would mediate.[46]

An added effect of the new Gestapo law was to heighten the authority of the Gestapo to use local regular police for executing Gestapo business where Gestapo personnel were unavailable or of inadequate strength. Consequently, on March 19, when the Prussian Supreme Administrative Court acknowledged that the Gestapo law removed review of Gestapo actions from its purview, it ruled that the same immunity applied to the actions of county and local police acting for the Gestapo.[47]

Nevertheless, the Prussian court would still not go so far as to renounce its right to judge the validity of Gestapo authority in cases not clearly within political police competence. On this issue, there would be an ongoing battle in professional legal publications over the legal philosophy of the NS state. In support of SS-police desires, the more radical interpretations argued that the legislature, executive, and judiciary should not stand against one another as checks and balances but represented merely different activities of the same organism. The judiciary could not contest what the executive had undertaken as its political responsibility. Against these arguments and the compliant decisions of the courts, the conservatives would fight rear-guard actions, mostly in vain.[48] Arguments for national solidarity and an escalating concern over national security decisively shaped the attitudes of those who counted.

Meanwhile, Goering began reneging on his compromise with Frick, influenced by Himmler and his supporters, who appealed to Goering's concern about Gestapo freedom and efficiency at the expense of close coordination with the administration. On April 2, he weakened the effectiveness of the governors' control by removing them from participation in the system of political situation reports, contending that their involvement endangered national solidarity and security by increasing the chances of leakage. A release of pessimistic or negative reports might affect public morale or provide the enemy with propaganda detrimental to the regime. He also repeated the line that the Party and, by implication, the ideologically oriented Gestapo and SD were better attuned to the mood of the nation than the bureaucracy.[49]

If any doubts remained that the apparent conservative gains of the previous months were nullified, an article by Best published on April 15 should have dispelled them. He proclaimed an interpretation of the February law that reasserted the total independence of the Gestapo Office. Goering was its chief; Himmler, his deputy, was responsible for its activity, and no other ministry could interfere. A special secret police had to be separate from the general administration, bound by legalistic procedures. Henceforth, the Gestapo operated according to "special principles and requirements." In this interpretation, Best fell back on the older Gestapo law of November 30, 1933, as a precedent. Despite its abrogation, he asserted that it had proven itself in practice, and therefore was a part of the new law. Consequently, the Gestapo remained "an independent branch of the interior administration," not a department of the Interior Ministry.[50]

As for the Gestapo field posts and cooperation with the rest of the government. Best's interpretations stood the law on its head, as one historian put it. Best stated that at the intermediate level, relations between the Gestapo and the inner administration were a two-way street.

When the Gestapo needed help in political police work, it had the power to issue orders to local authorities. When a governor felt the need for political police action in his district, he had the authority to issue orders to the local Gestapo field office. This kept simple problems at lower levels and avoided excessive red tape. He then quoted Goering's directive that the governors could not counter orders from the Gestapo Office, and that in cases of conflict the latter had the final word. Although he claimed the new arrangement met the wishes of the administration for input into Gestapo activity, in fact his interpretation essentially subordinated the administration to the Gestapo and made appeal against it dependent on Goering's approval.[51]

In one last twist, Best proclaimed the separateness of the concentration camps from state control. He declared that the Gestapo administered the camps *through* the inspector of the concentration camps (Eicke) *attached* to the Gestapo Office.[52] Again, the dual authority of an SS official serving as an authority for the state so confused the chains of authority as to destroy any hope of direct control.

In a paean of triumph, Best proclaimed the emerging police state in terms designed to appeal to all right-thinking citizens:

With the establishment of the National Socialist Fuehrer State, Germany for the first time has a system of government which derives from a living idea its legitimate right to resist, with all the coercive means at the disposal of the state, any attack on the present form of the state and its leadership. National Socialism's political principle of totalitarianism, which corresponds to the ideological principle of the organically indivisible national community, does not tolerate within its sphere the development of any political ideas at variance with the will of the majority. Any attempt to gain recognition for or even to uphold different political ideas will be ruthlessly dealt with, as the symptom of an illness which threatens the healthy unit of the indivisible national organism, regardless of the subjective wishes of its supporters.

Proceeding from these principles, the National Socialist Fuehrer State has created for the first time in Germany a political police which we regard as modern, i.e., as meeting our present-day needs; an institution which carefully supervises the political health of the German body politic, which is quick to recognize all symptoms of disease and germs of destruction—be they the result of disintegration from within or purposeful poisoning from without—and to remove them by every suitable means.[53]

Best then described how the new political police must be ideologically attuned to detecting the enemy and must function as a fighting formation. In this way he fused his article with the companion piece by Heydrich, who elaborated on the necessity of the close union between political police and SS.[54]

Himmler and his people were now ready to proclaim openly their goal of an SS-police system independent of regular, restricted state authority. They had explicitly flouted all that Frick and the conservative opposition had sought, and the opposition's inability to answer effectively contributed to Himmler's forthcoming victory. In Hitler's survival-of-the-fittest system, they now had little hope of blocking unification of the police under Himmler.

18

Himmler's Triumph

During early 1936 the "sales campaign" reached new levels as a variety of sources delivered it to a wide spectrum of German society—but always with the same monotonous uniformity. For instance, the broad outline of the message for the general public appeared in the January 23 issue of the *Voelkischer Beobachter*, describing the Gestapo as the indispensible organ for the defense of the state against its enemies. The article employed the increasingly familiar theme of the camouflaged enemy to reassert the need for a *special* political police. Assured that due process provided sufficient guarantees against the Gestapo's abusing its power, the good citizen had nothing to fear from the Gestapo and should ignore the rumors spread by those domestic and foreign enemies who had good reason to be apprehensive.[1]

One new element, however, was publicity for the SD. As part of an effort to reduce hostility and fear of it as a Cheka that spied on Party and *Volk*, the article depicted the SD as a supplement to the Gestapo in combating the enemy. Going a step further, the state protection corps emerged in the propaganda as an ideologically guided elite, created by SS presence in the Gestapo.[2] Hencefoth, Gestapo and SD (soon Sipo and SD) would be described as an exemplary team—the union of political police and SD, of state and Party—in common cause against the enemy.

In March, in a speech before the State Council in Berlin, Himmler elaborated extensively. Guertner had spoken before him, apparently giving a "law and order" line about how punishment was the ultimate deterrent for crime. With due respect for this argument, and after a careful show of honoring Frick for pre-1923 work in Munich, Himmler proceeded to rub the noses of the conservative opposition in their "errors" of the past few years. He charged them with failure to see their true enemies as incorrigible, being either of racial stock inherently hostile to a great Germany, or fanatical adherents of an ideology born of that hostility. Instead, the opposition had insisted on emptying the concentration camps, believing the internees had learned their lessons. The result, he proclaimed, was the rebirth of an almost impenetrably secret

Communist movement. The opposition was even so misguided as to talk of dissolving the political police. Now that the period of open struggle had passed, they would absorb its work in the regular criminal police.[3]

Himmler decried this course as suicidal. Not only was the best prevention the rooting out and elimination of the racial and ideological roots of opposition, but it could be done only by a special police force, free of bureaucratic encumbrances, free to strike at this enemy like a combat unit. He described Germany's struggle as one that would last perhaps a century, as long as the enemy operated freely from neighboring states, and as long as they had command posts in Moscow and Wall Street. He claimed that from the beginnings in 1933-34, five years were needed to build a proper political police apparatus that combined the technical knowledge of the police and civil service with the ideological insight and soldierly qualities of the Movement. Again, in answer to criticism of the SD, he described it as the instrument of "ideological intelligence," essential as a supplement to executive police work against political enemies. He concluded by alluding to the creation of a "corps" for the struggle, a corps to be formed in the fusion of Gestapo, SS, and SD. Omitting reference to any other police, he insisted that such a corps was vital as the model for future generations in the ongoing struggle of the German nation.[4]

Of course, these same themes would soon be presented in the companion articles by Heydrich and Best in the April 15 issue of *Deutsches Recht*. The essence of the newly proclaimed state protection corps remained carefully limited to a fusion of the SS with the *political* police, although the argument easily and obviously extended to the rest of the police. In his March speech, Himmler offered his audience a choice between the conservative opposition, with its "fatal errors," and himself and the SS—the only ideologically reliable agency for the job. He warned of two dangers inherent in any political police: becoming flaccid and withering into ineffectiveness, or becoming like the Cheka. Since one could not dispense with a political police, these dangers could only be avoided through proper leadership.[5] Given the world view of the conservative opposition and the mood of the times, such arguments must have been persuasive enough to split and weaken them. Himmler undoubtedly presented the same arguments to Hitler.

On the other side of the contest, Frick also had successes in bolstering his claim to command of a national police. Not only was he Reich minister of the interior, but through his alliance with Goering and the acquisition of the Prussian Interior Ministry, he also directed all the uniformed police of the superstate. He had created a Reich police force for the Saar as well. However, his constant complaints to Hitler about

Himmler's disobedience revealed his weaknesses and impotence. Frick's demand of the previous spring that Hitler either *give* him all political police power or *let* it be assumed by Himmler, who already claimed it, was undoubtedly the most self-defeating gesture he could have made.[6] Himmler appeared to have the necessary strength, will, and understanding to guarantee internal security under any conditions. Frick desired a return to more "normal" systems and was weak against determined opposition. In his shifting tactics, he had conceded Himmler's basic arguments about the continued emergency status and the necessity for the sort of repressive measures he himself opposed. After the fateful sparring of late 1935, Himmler had emerged on top.

At some point afterward, apparently in May, Frick learned that Hitler had decided to give Himmler command of the new national police. By June 8, Frick's ministry obediently began the paperwork for such a Fuehrer order,[7] and Himmler was secure enough in his victory to propose the terms under which he would assume command.

In presenting his viewpoints to Hitler on June 6, Himmler insisted that the title "Chief of the German Police" was most appropriate, since it incorporated both the command and administrative authority desired. He preferred this to "Commander of the German Police" (*Befehlshaber*), which could be interpreted as limiting him to command authority only.[8] Obviously, he was alerting Hitler to efforts that would be made to limit his command, and he was confident of Hitler's support for his relatively unlimited authority. Himmler also intended to preserve the division between the regular police and the special political police. He wanted two separate divisions (*Abteilungen*), the regular police (old Abteilung III) continuing under Daluege's leadership, and the Gestapo, a new division, expanded under Heydrich to include all aspects of political police work, even those sections of Frick's ministry that elaborated political police affairs at the ministerial level.[9]

If Frick had been forced to accept the logic of Himmler's appointment on the basis of the NS world view, he continued to resist for both personal and objective reasons. He not only distrusted Himmler personally, but his tactics and arguments indicate that he understood reasonably well the threats inherent in Himmler's approach to police work. Despite repeated defeat, both he and his close associates, like State Secretary Hans Pfundtner, continually tried to limit Himmler's power.[10] They apparently had no knowledge of the full extent of Hitler's intentions to support Himmler, for as late as June 8, Frick's legal division submitted drafts of decrees giving limited authority to Himmler. As a matter of fact, they still envisioned a relative victory for themselves. One Ministerial Councilor proposed that Himmler be "Inspector of the German Police," directly subordinate to the Minister of Interior, who would be responsible for the details relevant to the execution of the proposed decree. Himmler's deputy inspector was to be Daluege,[11] undoubtedly expected to assume the real working responsibilities. Apparently, Frick's supporters also hoped to reincorporate the political police into the rest of the police. In other words, they expected to eliminate all intermediate authorities between Frick and Himmler and to subordinate Himmler and all German police directly under Frick. Daluege could guarantee a certain degree of cooperation from below.

This bubble burst abruptly on June 9, when Heydrich gave Pfundtner Himmler's version of the Fuehrer decree. For the first time, Frick became fully aware of the scope of Himmler's victory. Himmler would be titled "Reichsfuehrer SS and Chief of the German Police"; he would be "personally" subordinate to the Interior Minister and would hold the rank of Reich minister participating in cabinet meetings. From the ministry, he would assume responsibility for national defense and military affairs as far as they concerned *Abwehr* work, matters pertaining to foreigners, to border affairs and to the churches, and all the work of the former police division (Abteilung III). "In his own capacity," he would regulate and represent the ministry in these affairs, and he would manage the organization of the police. Heydrich explained that Hitler desired the new title for Himmler to make him comparable to the commander in chief of the Army or the Navy. As if to apply pressure, the draft decrees that Heydrich offered were dated for Hitler's signature on June 15.[12]

Pfundtner dealt cautiously with Heydrich, avoiding any sort of confrontation. He contested only issues directly affecting his own competence. He got Heydrich to agree that Pfundtner would retain authority over legislation concerning affairs under Himmler's future police responsibilities, and they agreed that some matters affecting foreigners required further consideration. Pfundtner promised to return with Frick's responses the next day. He immediately notified Frick, suggesting some changes in the draft and some tactics for fighting back. Basically, however, he simply gave in.[13]

Tactically, Pfundtner suggested that Frick consult with Goering, since the matter also concerned him.[14] Undoubtedly, Pfundtner suspected that, as in the past when Himmler tried for such a power play, Goering might be goaded into limiting it. Frick obviously thought otherwise. By now, aware of Goering's diminished interest in police affairs and his general predilection for seeing things Himmler's way, especially if Hitler supported it, Frick preferred to keep Goering out of the problem until he had arranged what he could with Himmler.[15] As for Himmler's proposed drafts, Frick evidently saw much more danger in them than Pfundtner, so much so that he rushed immediately to Hitler to reverse whatever he could. The fact that he got an instant audience indicates that he retained some influence, and that the Fuehrer still valued Frick's opinions on police affairs.

Although all interpretations of this meeting have minimized the concessions Frick got from Hitler, they had potential significance. By this time, with Himmler's command of the police a foregone conclusion, his title, Chief of the German Police, had become inconsequential. The real issue was Himmler's relationship to Frick's ministry, and on this Frick scored a point. Hitler either denied or reversed Himmler's claim to standing as a Reich minister, instead he would be a state secretary within Frick's ministry.[16] This left Frick some possible control over Himmler. Unfortunately, Hitler always refused to be bothered with administrative details, leaving it up to a trial of strength between Frick and Himmler. The compounding of such details to his advantage was Frick's only hope of success. Himmler's strength lay in his position as chief of all police with very broad powers, and Frick could only try to limit them without nullifying what Hitler intended. To limit Himmler, Frick had to consolidate into the machinery for control a number of concessions from Himmler over administrative details. Hitler had given Frick no more support than a vague limitation to the effect that Himmler's position was "within" Frick's ministry and, therefore, without ministerial standing.

As the only documented case study of Hitler's alleged support for Himmler on his road to complete police power, this affair warrants a few observations. First, this incident of support proves nothing about previous developments. Although it clearly stands as the culmination of a growing acceptance of Himmler for the role, it indicates nothing about whether any such role was a foregone conclusion in Hitler's mind even a few months previously—much less in 1933 or 1934. Most important, it provides a clear measure of just how ambiguously Hitler did indeed support those like Himmler who often came away from an audience claiming full support or claiming Hitler's approval of a very specific move—in this case, the exact status of Himmler as chief of police.

Apparently, in seeking approval from Hitler, the best course was to propose a very general scheme designed to appeal to a specific aspect of the Fuehrer's vaguely expressed goals, then to take whatever expression of approval Hitler gave and proclaim it to the other parties. A skillful player elaborated to his advantage the sort of relevant details that Hitler preferred to ignore. The final outcome depended on who else had access to Hitler or had the power to ignore some or all of the pronouncement. A successfully ignored clause provided the crucial measure of how seriously Hitler took the matter relative to his other problems of rule. If a decree was involved, as in this case, a good strategist proclaimed Hitler's support for a draft and tried to buffalo the other involved parties into approving as much as possible of the draft so it could be signed quickly by the Fuehrer. After that, the real issue was who had the power either to enforce or to nullify the decree.

In this case, the concessions Frick won from Hitler have two possible interpretations. Either they show how far Himmler was willing to exaggerate claims of Hitler's support and, on his own initiative, to build what he wanted, or they show how Hitler's support could quickly become vague in detail, subject to modification, and by no means unlimited. The entire incident, however, portended an unusually thorough victory for Himmler in the coming years. Not only did Himmler have the necessary power (the machinery of SS and police) to enforce every concession he won and to erode those given the opposition, but, at that moment, the issue of the police held such significance for Hitler that he was compelled to make a rare decision.

If, as posited, Hitler had only begun to support the expansion of Himmler's police power—the creating of an SS and police system—as late as spring 1936, the reason must lie in the development of his foreign policy goals. After securing his domestic power in 1934, Hitler turned increasingly away from details of internal affairs to concentrate on international pursuits. Nevertheless, with mounting international tension during 1935-36 and the emergence of a more aggressive military and foreign policy, he must also have become more concerned about internal security. In his few public pronouncements on domestic security, the only primary concern he had expressed was the prevention of internal collapse at moments of international crisis—the nationalist version of the 1918 defeat. As such crises became increasingly part of his plans for the future, he became more willing to risk an imbalance in his divide-and-conquer system in order to create a strong mechanism of "internal defense" by giving one man the necessary authority to build it. Encouragement from Blomberg and perhaps other conservative powers who shared this concern for security was undoubtedly significant. Finally, the expansion of a reliable, yet radical NS police would help Hitler balance an expanding conservative military establishment. The contemporary expansion of Goering's authority over industrial affairs in the Four Year Plan fits the same formula.[17]

Meanwhile, having gained some approval from Hitler to continue his influence in police affairs, Frick tried to reshape a few concessions on details into some semblance of control. One point of immediate defeat was Himmler's compound title, Reichsfuehrer SS and Chief of the German Police. Hans Lammers, the chief of Hitler's Chancellory involved in these transactions, speculated that Himmler proposed the title. If so, it was an afterthought to the proposals he presented to Hitler on June 6. Lammers claimed to have objected because Himmler's Party title equaled the rank of *Reichsleiter* directly under Hitler, and, therefore, equated to a Reich minister. As chief of police, he should have been equivalent to a state secretary subordinate to the Minister of Interior. More significant, the fusion of these titles would confuse chains of command and frustrate efforts at control. Perhaps at this time Hess and Schwarz also objected, since on later issues, according to Schellenberg, they raised similar objections to fusions of Party and state by Himmler. Frick hoped to eliminate the title from the draft decree, but to no avail. Hitler decided the title should be preserved.[18] Having bought Himmler's plan for the fusion of the SS and police, he preferred having the chief of police immediately accessible to himself.

To counter this defeat, Frick did succeed in inserting behind "Reichs-fuehrer SS and Chief of the German Police" the phrase "*in* the Ministry of Interior." In other alterations to the drafts of the proposal, he changed Himmler's *personal* subordination to *direct* subordination, eliminated the chief's rank as a Reich minister, made his attendance at cabinet meetings possible rather than mandated, and tried to limit significantly the responsibilities Himmler would assume from the ministry.[19]

On June 12, after Heydrich received the proposed changes, he and Pfundtner met as the first of an ever-widening circle of negotiators. By June 24 they had concluded the basic details of the final settlement, and all involved accepted the last of the decrees. Throughout the process, Heydrich, representing Himmler, conceded a number of minor points—even a few major ones—only to introduce new demands, often negating the concessions. Frick and his negotiators were slowly worn down and finally recommended concessions on Heydrich's most adamant positions. Throughout the process, the fact that men like Pfundtner and Daluege would acquire expanded powers from the overall reorganizations undoubtedly weakened their determination. Pfundtner seems unbelievably naive about the significance of some of the concessions he recommended to Frick and a bit overwhelmed by "necessary" concessions to Himmler in the name of national security.[20]

On June 17, Hitler signed the decree appointing Himmler. Its form reveals some of the results of the struggle:

I. To ensure a unified concentration of police responsibilities in the Reich, there will be appointed a chief of the German Police *in* the Reich Ministry of the Interior, to whom will be transferred *concurrently* [*zugleich*] the direction and executive authority for all police matters within the competence of the Reich and Prussian ministries of the interior.[21]

As an obscure compromise, Frick won the inclusion of the office of the chief *in* the Ministry of the Interior. Himmler won the inclusion of the word *zugleich* for reasons of his own. Apparently, he felt it gave him an independent claim to authority, despite his inclusion in the minis-try.²² The next clause held more compromises:

II. (1) The deputy chief of the Secret State Police of Prussia, Reichsfuehrer SS Heinrich Himmler, is named to chief of the German Police in the Reich Ministry of the Interior.

(2) He is *personally and directly* subordinate to the Reich and Prussian Minister of the Interior.

(3) For his sphere of competence, he represents the Reich and Prussian minister of the interior *in the latter's absence.*

(4) He carries the title: *The Reichsfuehrer SS* and chief of the German Police *in the Reich Ministry of the Interior.*²³

The fusion of personal and direct subordination was a compromise between the separate terms proposed by Himmler and Frick. From Frick's point of view, as long as "directly" was included, a clear bureaucratic-administrative relationship existed. From Himmler's, the term "personally" corresponded more with NS concepts of the fuehrer principle, which preferred personal to bureaucratic relationships. Furthermore, in the reality of NS power relations, a personal relationship was like that of feudal lord and vassal. Though ostensibly subordinate to his lord, the vassal was absolute in his own domain (sphere of competence), and his lord should not interfere therein. Himmler would soon show that he interpreted his "subordination" to his personal and direct superior in that manner. Given Himmler's parallel subordination to Hitler as Reichsfuehrer SS, his inclusion *in* the Ministry of the Interior gave him the authority of that ministry without subordinating him to it.²⁴

The third clause of the decree stated that Himmler would "take part in meetings of the Reich cabinet insofar as his sphere of competence will be affected."²⁵ Frick hoped thus to control his access to cabinet meetings, but in fact Himmler would show that his definition of police responsibilities went far beyond anything Frick would dream.

Even before its publication, Heydrich revealed some repercussions of the decree. On June 15, he and Pfundtner met to settle details about the wording of Himmler's appointment, of the related press notice, and of Frick's order for the execution of the decree. He announced that Daluege would not be named as Himmler's deputy; instead, only in Himmler's absence would Daluege act as deputy. At the same time, Heydrich explained how the police would be divided, with all uniformed police under Daluege, whom Hitler would promote to general of the Police. Henceforth, this branch of the police would be known as Order Police (Ordnungspolizei, or Orpo). Then came a surprise for everyone:

the birth announcement of Sipo. All criminal police or detectives would be fused with the Gestapo and its border police under Heydrich's command as Security Police (Sicherheitspolizei, or Sipo). Not only would the Gestapo remain a special, separate police, but Heydrich also gained its potential replacement, the Criminal Police.

Himmler planned a press release accompanied by an explanatory article by Gunter d'Alquen in the *Voelkischer Beobachter*. He wanted the public to see these developments as a necessary and desirable improvement in "law and order" and "national security," with all involved— Hitler, Frick, Himmler, Daluege, and Heydrich—as one happy team, completely in accord over what was best for the nation.[27]

At the June 15 meeting, Himmler also dodged another of Frick's attempts to bring him under control. In the letter of appointment, Frick wanted Himmler named to office "under call to the status of an official of the civil service" (*unter Berufung in das Beamtenverhaeltnis*), thus establishing Frick's authority over him. Consistent with the NS spirit, however, Himmler refused. He would remain an agent of the Movement in the service of the state, and the encumbering phrase had to be removed.[28]

Subsequently, negotiations over the wording of Frick's order for the execution of the decree became heated. As a definition of Himmler's competence within the ministry, the wording of Frick's order for the decree offered a last opportunity to limit Himmler. In previous negotiations, they had agreed that, aside from absorbing the Police Division (Abteilung III) of the ministry, Himmler would demand few changes in the old arrangements. On June 22, however, Heydrich revealed that Himmler had increased his demands to absorb numerous sections and desks of the ministry and to consolidate his absolute control over police affairs. Only on the key issue of military and national security affairs did Frick's people retain a significant compromise—subject, of course, to erosion. Himmler had responsibility for the *Abwehr* aspect of these affairs; the legislative aspect remained for the rest of the ministry.[29]

Although Himmler's victory was already apparent, its full impact emerged only with time. As if to herald these developments, in the July 15 issue of *Deutsches Recht* Werner Best presented an "official" definition of Himmler's new position. He justified the union of SS and police under one leader with some of the arguments used for extraordinary Gestapo powers. Again, he trotted out the parallel between the Wehrmacht as executive against the outside and the police as executive of the interior— an "*innere* Wehrmacht." Most significant, he proclaimed in this fusion of SS and police a permanent identity essential to the further reconstruction of the Reich and the security of the nation's future.[30]

Himmler's new title replaced the old ones; *Reichsfuehrer SS und Chef der Deutschen Polizei im Reichsministerium des Innern* marched off behind his name, often as an impressive string of initials, RFSSuCdDPiRMdI. Significantly, in typing this title, his subordinate offices often rendered it as "<u>RFSSuCdDPiRMdI</u>." The end of the double underlining made it clear to all subordinates where the real seat of power lay as far as they were concerned.[31] The tail of Himmler's title, "in the RMdI," originally a sop to the defeated Frick, soon provided a mantle of legality for Himmler and Heydrich, and even for Hitler himself. Himmler and his police became subordinate to Frick in title only as Himmler pursued an increasingly independent course. The police gradually evolved from an agency of the state into an instrument of the sovereign Fuehrer.

As the German historian Hans Buchheim described what happened, the appearance of maintaining the police under the old agencies of the state fitted well with the NS pattern of "revolution." They never really abolished the old institutions; they just hollowed them out and allowed them to dry up while the new institutions of the Third Reich, such as the SS-police, grew up through and around them.[32] The change occurred gradually and carefully, to provide camouflage and to prevent the old institutions from absorbing the revolutionary body.

The official state position within the ministry was at best a bogus legality. For internal use, Himmler's police offices issued orders openly under the heading "Reichsfuehrer SS and Chief of the German Police." When he made proposals to the cabinet, however, or when he had to deal officially with state agencies outside his offices, he had the use of the official label "Reich and Prussian Ministry of the Interior."[33] Although Himmler's relationship to Frick originated in an awkward compromise, he soon realized its value as camouflage. Thus began a wide range of changeable state, semistate, and SS titles used against rivals as "covers" and as "confusion factors" that would proliferate in the future.

Of course, whenever Himmler's departments issued a legal draft or any directive using the authority of the Ministry of Interior, Frick was supposed to sign it. This provided his one chance to impose some control, unless Himmler, as was often the case, already had Hitler's approval, and could therefore force the issue. Needless to say, despite the established channels, Heydrich's offices found occasions to bypass Frick. Whenever this happened, Frick issued one of his usual ultimatums demanding adherence to proper procedures, and Best's office dutifully circulated it with a cover letter ordering compliance.[34] Of course, compliance was for the subordinates; Heydrich or Himmler resorted to breaches as necessary.

Meanwhile, Frick gradually lost official contact with Hitler. His constant complaints about Himmler's uncontrollability must have undermined Hitler's confidence and all hope of appeal against violations and abuses. Increasingly, Frick had to submit his complaints through channels at the Chancellery. At Nuremberg, Hans Lammers, head of the Chancellery, recalled that Hitler finally told him, "Tell Herr Frick that he should not restrict Himmler as chief of the German Police too much; with him the police is in good hands. He should allow him as much free rein as possible!" According to Frick, in 1937 he ceased entirely to report directly to Hitler in his official capacity. Thereafter, he only dined with him occasionally or encountered him at group meetings of Party and state leaders.[35]

Needless to say, Frick found equally frustrating all efforts to assert his "personal and direct" authority over Himmler. Later, he claimed that when Himmler became chief of the police, he had asked him to appear at least once every fortnight to report on events in the police. Himmler never came. Within less than a year, Frick had surrendered all hopes of control, even through his power to sign the ministerial decrees on the police. Himmler's monopoly on access to Hitler had made Frick a rubber stamp, so in May 1937 Frick declared Himmler's rulings valid *as ministerial decisions*.[36]

Before this final surrender, the opposition lost one last hope for a barrier against a full victory by Himmler. The centralization of police command had not settled the complex problem of financing, for police personnel remained under the state budgets. Shortly after he became chief, Himmler pushed for legislation to create a Reich police budget, but counterproposals from the Ministry of Finance produced another round of negotiations and a repetition of the June "compromise." In March 1937, all involved parties finally issued the necessary legislation, and with the advent of the new fiscal year on April 1, they completed creation of a centralized Reich police force, with the minor details requiring a few more years for settlement.[37]

As before, the resultant compromise imposed minimal limitations on Himmler. In fact, by taking away state (*Land*) control of police finances, it ended a significant fragmentation of his power, reducing all limiting influences to two main ministries' budgets and to Schwerin von Krosigk, the Reich minister of finance. Despite Hitler's general support for Himmler, the ministries and von Krosigk could use financial arguments and technicalities to block Himmler's complete budgetary control over the police.[38]

In the end, Himmler would triumph over all such arrangements, but only after a certain degree of hindrance. As Buchheim so aptly put it:

Although the police were now constitutionally and organizationally divorced from the authority of the government, this did not mean that all legal, official, technical and organizational links with the previous system were severed, particularly for matters of minor political importance. Time was required for the official character of the police and its internal and organizational regulations to be adapted to the very different forms and rules operative in the SS. Many aspects of police administration therefore remained unaffected but they were allowed to continue only on a "subject to cancellation" basis and only as long as established practice did not run counter to the aims and actions of the political police.[39]

19

The Formation of Sipo and SD

On June 26, 1936, after assuming his position as chief of police, Himmler created the two major divisions he had announced during negotiations. He united all uniformed police into the Order Police (Ordnungspolizei), with General of the Police (and SS General) Kurt Daluege as their chief. SS Lieutenant General Heydrich became chief of the Security Police, or Sipo, consisting of all detective police, both political and criminal,[1] thus reestablishing the former link between the plainclothes detective forces. But instead of the criminal police reabsorbing the political police and returning them to subordination under the state administration as Himmler's opponents had desired, the criminal police assumed more of the extraordinary status of the political police.

Although the terms "security police" and "order police" had long been employed in Germany, the new designations did not derive from traditional usage. One historian suggested that Heydrich chose the title Security Police because it paralleled Security Service (SD) and because he desired to fuse the two.[2] This may be correct; however, the two terms referred to new distinctions between the two branches of the police. The Order Police maintained order among the citizens, while the Sipo provided security against their enemies. This meant that within their usual realm of activity, the Order Police retained their basically *reactive* function, while Sipo assumed the new *preemptive* function that distinguished NS police work from that of liberal states. (More about that later.)

Having achieved his goal of command of all police, Himmler removed himself from the detailed work of a police chief. As before, he continued the struggle to expand his police powers, and he provided guidance in the fusion of SS and police; however, expanded SS interests in the economy, in political policy (including foreign policy), and in the future Waffen-SS demanded a growing share of his time. Consequently, his two police lieutenants assumed the active roles of chiefs of police. For Heydrich, the process of becoming in fact the chief of political police was now completed. Himmler clearly signaled his less direct involvement when he failed to create any office to administer his functions as

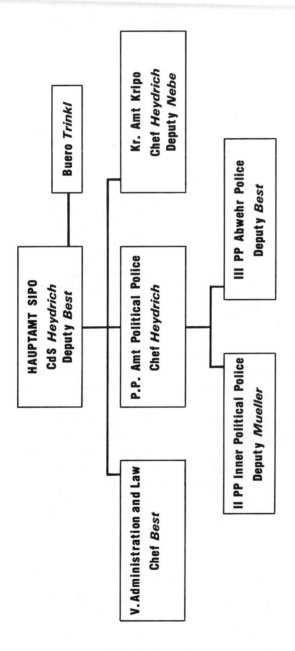

Further subdivisions within the SIPO Main Office varied somewhat over the years. They were designated by capital letters or Arabic numerals; for instance:

- Under AMT Administration and Law subdivision V 5 was Training.
- Under AMT Political Police II A was Communism and other Marxist Movements, and III L was Espionage.
- Under AMT KRIPO Kr. I was Organization.

Figure 2. Hauptamt Sipo

chief of German Police. Instead, he had two adjutants for liaison with his two chiefs, and he acted through the Orpo and Sipo Main Offices.[3]

The designation of the Orpo and Sipo Main Offices (*Hauptaemter*) as ministerial offices was an affront that Frick's people refused to acknowledge. "Main office" was an SS term, not a proper ministerial designation. The ministry always spoke of the Chiefs of Orpo and Sipo, refusing to use the term "main office." Nevertheless, Himmler created the two main offices as his ministerial offices, and so they were.[4]

In Main Office Sipo, Werner Best served as Heydrich's deputy. In addition to being the ministerial office for Sipo affairs, the Main Office was also the administrative center for Sipo as a Reich police. Essentially, it fused the relevant components of the Gestapo Office with a few sections from the Prussian State Criminal Police Office. Heydrich retained his staff of Gestapo adjutants, Schupo Captains Pomme and Suchanek, and SS Lieutenant Neumann for liaison with Himmler. Trinkle now headed a Main Bureau (*Hauptbuero*). The heart of the main office was Office V for Administration and Law, with Best as office chief, expanding his role to the entire Sipo.[5]

The other two offices of the main office were Political Police (*Amt PP*) and Criminal Police (*Amt Kr.*). Essentially, they consisted of the appropriate specialists to represent the Gestapo Office and Criminal Police Office in ministerial work. In the Political Police Office, Heinrich Mueller was deputy for domestic political police affairs and Best for *Abwehr* police affairs. Arthur Nebe was deputy in the Criminal Police Office.[6]

The elevation of Heinrich Mueller to Heydrich's deputy for domestic political police affairs signaled his rise in the Gestapo. Effective July 1, 1936, he became head of Division II of the Gestapo Office, responsible for action against the internal enemy. Best remained in charge of Division III, *Abwehr* police; this division of labor in the Gestapo lasted until the war. Mueller had thus risen to the number three position in the Gestapo and was responsible for all political police work in the Reich. On September 20, the Gestapo Office officially assumed the work of the commander of the Political Police of the States. It was de jure as well as de facto central headquarters for a unified Reich political police force.[7]

The proclamation of a Reich-wide Gestapo preceded this act by almost a month. On August 28, a uniform system for designating all political police posts as Gestapo posts was ordered. The central authority of the political police in each non-Prussian state was designated as Gestapo, State Police (Superior) Post ——— . The name "superior post" paralleled that developed in Prussia and was applied in the states large enough to have a system of political police field posts rather than just one central office: Baden, Bavaria, Wuerttemberg, and Saxony. The designations of "posts," "outposts," "border commissariats," and "border service posts" were also applied uniformly after the Prussian pattern.[8] Although the geographic borders of each state's political police sphere still determined the territories of the field posts, that small deference to the states gradually vanished in a rationalization of a Reich-wide Gestapo.

Although these changes sounded the death knell for *Land* limitations on Heydrich's full command over a centralized political police, which had been evolving since late 1933, the inclusion of the criminal police marked a more radical transition. Of course, the criminal police had been purged like other branches of government and infected by infiltration and conversions to Nazism, but for the most part it had undergone relatively little change as a result of the Nazi takeover. Detective work was highly specialized, and crime fighting had been a Nazi priority. This explains why detective and administrative personnel had a certain immunity from the purge; however, it makes all the more perplexing the Nazis' delay in reforming the criminal police organizationally and operationally. The lack of police centralization had been a problem since the nineteenth century. Prior to Himmler's great change, the only significant NS reform had been Frick's conversion of the State Criminal Police Office in Berlin into a central office for the Prussian Criminal Police, and that was not done until January 1935.[9]

If Frick had intended to build a Reich Criminal Police as a replacement for the Gestapo when "normality" returned, he had a ready-made corps amenable to such a goal. Although the regular detectives may have disdained political work, being pleased to have it separated from themselves, a rivalry and hostility had developed between them and the Gestapo on which Frick could have capitalized. The rivalry involved methodology and the detectives' claim to the use of sophisticated, scientific techniques only. The Gestapo's advocacy of forceful interrogation in special cases had become a point of controversy. Whatever the real differences between their methodologies, however, they were unimportant compared with the differences as perceived by the professional detectives, for these distinctions were the essence of their self-image as criminal detective policemen. They saw themselves as scientific specialists, immune to ideological contamination and above—and distinctly separate from—the Gestapo and its crude methods and dirty work.[10]

The rivalry between the Gestapo and criminal police had grown since Heydrich took over the Gestapo and Nebe acquired the Prussian Criminal Police. It found expression in arguments over whose methods were more effective. By May 1936, Heydrich was ready for a maneuver designed to win his case. Since April 1933, a number of children had been mysteriously murdered in North Prussia and Mecklenburg. In March 1935, Adolf Seefeld had been apprehended for the crimes and convicted for eleven of the murders, but much mystery still surrounded his methods. Under the pretext that he was possibly a Communist agent, the Gestapo interrogated him and extracted a story of how he had poisoned these victims, as well as confessions of many other murders. Although the account of one of the criminal police witnesses to the affair raises doubts about accuracy, such details would have seemed puny compared with the success of the Gestapo's "thorough" work.[11] Heydrich could substantiate his claim that his police had the proper approach. The release of the report on May 23, 1936, came notably close to the timing of Hitler's decision to make Himmler chief of all police; perhaps it provided the finishing touch, at least for public consumption.

The failure of Frick and Nebe to nationalize the criminal police has never been explored. Perhaps Frick preoccupied himself with other problems; perhaps his people failed to realize how little time they had or how total Himmler's plans were for the police. In any case, the extent and the rapidity of the reform following June 1936 gave Himmler and Heydrich claim to being the only men in the Reich thoroughly determined and capable enough to build the police force Germany allegedly needed. This claim gave them an appeal to all professional policemen, including the regular detectives, and they would exploit it.

For Heydrich, acquisition of the criminal police meant the addition of over nine thousand men to his command—almost six thousand in Nebe's Prussian Criminal Police, the rest from the other states.[12] This more than doubled the size of Heydrich's forces, for at this time the total political police establishment numbered probably less than seven thousand.

Within a few months, the reorganization of the criminal police had advanced sufficiently to establish centralized command. Nebe's Prussian State Criminal Police Office was physically and operationally removed from the Berlin Police Presidency and charged with the technical leadership of the criminal police of all states. Although the detective forces would remain administratively and financially components of their respective state or community establishments until the completion of the reforms in 1937, for technical operations they were subordinate to Nebe's office, with training guidelines issued under the authority of the chief of Sipo. The large number of cooperative centers (*gemeinsame Laenderzentrale*) that had been created to coordinate the states in combating specific types of crime now became official Reich centers (*Reichszentrale*), most of which Nebe consolidated into his headquarters. In another centralization, for the first time in the history of the criminal police in Ger-

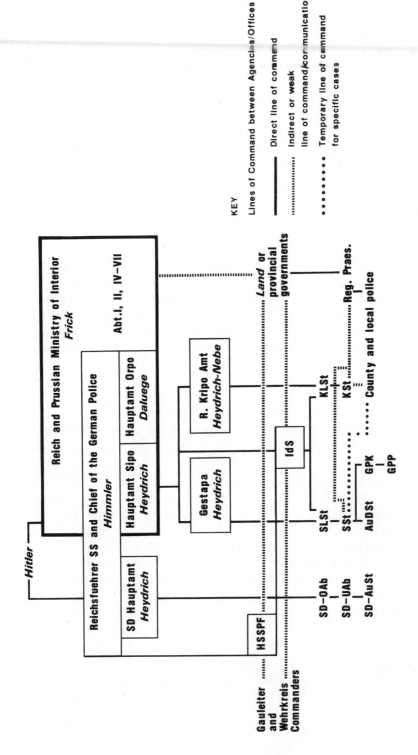

Figure 3. Sipo and SD Command Structure after Reforms, 1936-1937

many a single office coordinated the work with foreign police and international police organizations.[13] Such reforms became part of Himmler's and Heydrich's claims to legitimacy as police chiefs.

Although the term Reich Criminal Police (Kripo) appeared only after the consolidation of the following year, the uniform designation "State Criminal Police" (Staatliche Kriminalpolizei, as opposed to Landeskriminalpolizei), was applied in each state (*Land*). In the command structure of field posts, the reorganization of the Kripo proceeded more thoroughly and rationally than the immediate reorganization of the political police under the new Reich Gestapo. In the Gestapo, the political police of most states retained their separate field post systems directly under the Gestapo Office. In contrast, the Kripo often consolidated the posts of several states into regional jurisdictions with similar crime problems, coordinated under the direction of a superior post. For instance, the Kripo Superior Post Halle had jurisdiction that included three Prussian posts for the Province Magdeburg and the posts for the states of Anhalt and Thuringia. The jurisdiction of superior Post Bremen included the posts for the city-state, for the *Land* Oldenburg, and for the two Prussian districts of Aurich and Stade, all North Sea coastal areas.[14] Once inertia had been broken and reform begun, the less politically sensitive issue of criminal police jurisdictions was more easily rationalized than jurisdictions of the political police.

The need to coordinate police work that cut across Orpo and Sipo lines contributed to the creation of a new office of police authority. The criminal policemen in the field posts held a unique position that encouraged their sense of autonomy within Sipo. Although Nebe's Berlin Office provided their central command in technical matters, the criminal policemen in the field retained their old subordination to the administrative structure of each of the states or the Prussian provinces and districts. This subordination remained unchanged even after further centralization of the police in 1937, so they never acquired the fully extraordinary status of the Gestapo. They remained subordinate to the local police presidents and directors in the cities where they were headquartered and, as such, remained partially under Order Police authority as well as under Sipo command. Such an arrangement was necessary to retain the local coordination of crime fighting, especially cooperation between the detective force and the uniformed police. To square the problems that could arise from such overlapping jurisdictions and to ensure a uniform application of Sipo directives to Gestapo and Kripo, inspectors of Sipo were established. Paralleling the newly created inspectors of the Order Police, they were part of a general organizational system to coordinated Reich central with regional authority, and police with administrative and military authority.[15]

Effective October 1, 1936, inspectors of Sipo were established for each Prussian province and the states of Baden, Bavaria, Saxony, and Wuerttemberg. (The smaller states would be incorporated later.) Their responsibilities included ensuring Sipo cooperation with regional and local state officials, with the *Gauleiter* and other Party regional officials, and with the military district officials within their jurisdiction. The occasional differences among the state boundaries and those of Party *Gau* and military districts often made their work difficult. Of course, the inspectors had to effect cooperation for the sake of efficiency; however, they were also to guarantee Sipo independence from top to bottom. The inspectors' "personal and direct subordination" to the provincial governors or state ministers of interior not only duplicated Himmler's "subordination" to Frick, but Heydrich also reinforced that parallel with an order that, although they should conform to the assignments of these ostensible superiors, he would have the final authority in cases of conflict with policies of the chief of Sipo. Finally, Heydrich charged them with ensuring the organizational assimilation of Gestapo and Kripo posts.[16] The inspectors had to wean Kripo away from local police officials and state authority while securing cooperation with them.

Of course, the inspectors became involved in later power struggles among Heydrich, Daluege, and local officials, and their significance vis-à-vis the military officials increased as the war approached. Historians must be cautious, however, about reading too many later objectives into the act of their creation. In later power struggles the inspectorates as originally established proved inadequate for subsequently developed objectives and had to be redesigned. Meanwhile, the posts were filled only gradually, but always by high-ranking SS and SD officers,[17] and despite all their gains, Himmler and Heydrich still suffered some restraint. Their various apparatuses, even the Gestapo, worked under many of the same restrictions that any society places on its institutions. A sense of propriety still pervaded all orders and daily business, and during the years immediately following 1936, the agencies could violate social norms only under "extraordinary" conditions. Neither the Gestapo nor Sipo and SD was the almost unlimited instrument of terror they would become. Their development was just beginning.

At this time, the Gestapo had instructions to proceed with tact and foresight, to avoid the public eye, and to coordinate carefully all actions that might lead to conflict with other authorities. Relations with the Party became increasingly delicate again, especially as tension between SS and Party mounted. Himmler had to remain constantly on guard against creating solid Party opposition while continuing the SD and police function of safeguarding inner security. The threat of attack against protective custody remained. In December, the Gestapo received orders to use protective custody only in emergencies, for "excessive use of protective custody must discredit this strongest weapon of the Gestapo and give encouragement to the wide spread efforts to abolish protective custody."[18]

Having won his fight for control of the police, Himmler illustrated his new propriety by denying the SS any executive action. In September 1936, he ordered the SS to refuse all further executive orders from Party or state officials and to refer them to the proper police authority.[19] This was, of course, propriety achieved by mirrors. What he denied his SS was now done by his police.

Some members of Sipo and SD generated internally and spontaneously part of the pressure responsible for the image of propriety. Having achieved their goals of a powerful, centralized police establishment, they developed a greater awareness of where Himmler was headed, and they sought to retard the development of completely uncontrolled institutions under irresponsible or dangerous men. This seems to be the proper context for Heydrich's traditionally attributed drive to reabsorb the concentration camps under Gestapo authority. With him, it would have been largely an amoral power play, but Werner Best strongly encouraged such a move for other reasons.

The February 1936 law had placed the camps in Prussia under the Gestapo, but Himmler's tactics and the new Reich police structure put all this in limbo. If this were not enough incentive for Best, continued irregularities in the camps undoubtedly disturbed his sense of propriety, and the rumors that "disgusting things went on in the camps" embarrassed him as the one legally responsible. Now that the threat of the previous winter (that external control might be imposed) had passed and Himmler was semiautonomous lord of police and camps, Best apparently expected the more proper state control of the camps through police officials to be restored. His agitation became so great by August that Eicke complained to Himmler about it. Best's hopes were futile, however, and on August 2 Eicke's staff established itself at Oranienburg, far removed from the Gestapo Office. Eicke's separate command over the camps would continue, for he ran them more to Himmler's liking than Best's police bureaucrats and lawyers would have done.[20]

Another impetus for an appearance of propriety grew from the reality that Himmler's extraordinary police powers existed without legislative foundations. They were grounded primarily on Hitler's will, which might change in the face of determined opposition. The basis of the new Reich Gestapo and its power was application of the Prussian Gestapo Law (February 1936) to the entire Reich, without enactment of a new Reich law, justified solely by the Nazi principle that the will of the leadership made law.[21] Of course, this interpretation was supposedly only a stopgap measure until a future codification of Reich police law could solve all such problems, but both Hitler and Himmler resisted such codification, for laws could interfere with their plans and be used by the opposition to curb their power.

Meanwhile, to control such pressure for codification, the propagandists of Sipo and SD continued to push their arguments about the necessity for extraordinary police power, given the preeminence of national security and order over individual needs.[22] In October, when Himmler spoke before the constituent assembly of the Committee for Police Law, he sought to head off any effort to repeal his achievement. He reminded them how, when they had come to power, they had found the police a hated and impotent force.

> Then we National Socialists set to work . . . , not without right, for we bore that within us, but certainly without law. From the outset, I had taken the position that it was a matter of indifference to me if our actions were contrary to some paragraph [of the law]; in the fulfillment of my mission, I did basically in my work for the Fuehrer and Nation that which suited common sense. It was entirely irrelevant if other people moaned about the "violations of the law" in those months and years in which the life or death of the German nation was on the line. There was naturally talk abroad—with much support from numerous circles at home—of the condition of lawlessness in the police and, therefore, the state. They called it lawless because it did not suit what they understood as law. In reality, through our work, we laid the foundations for a new law, the law of destiny of the German nation.[23]

Himmler then described this new police and this new law as the foundations for the emergence of a new Germany and for the future defense of the nation against its enemies. To play its role, the police had to emerge with the image of "friend and helper of every fellow-countryman," and they had to establish a deeply rooted sense of right and wrong in the people themselves. He charged the committee with codifying, in simple sentences, the national cultural principles he claimed to have salvaged in his SS and police work. As further insurance against trouble, he stacked the committee with his SD jurists and propagandists.[24]

Regardless of the limitations that remained, the foundations of the police state were securely laid. Himmler had tied the SS and police together, and the Sipo and SD had come into being. To be sure, the two were still ostensibly separate organizations—Sipo, under Main Office Sipo, remained a state police agency, and the SD, under the SD Main Office, was an SS-Party organization—but they had a common head, SS-General Reinhard Heydrich, who bore a joint title like Himmler's:

chief of Sipo and SD. More important, the overlap of personnel between SD and Gestapo (soon to include Kripo) tied the leading posts of the police with the SD, while a steady influx of SD members would enter Sipo from below. Sipo and SD was a de facto entity that would acquire semiofficial status in 1939 with the creation of the Reich Security Main Office. Although most leading members of Sipo and SD sought to deny its unity and to treat the overlapping membership as a matter of mere form, the entity became in many ways a growing reality. The third component of this entity was the Kripo.

The sudden addition of the criminal police to Heydrich's realm was the most significant departure from the status quo. Arthur Nebe, head of the Prussian State Criminal Police Office, was a Nazi but not an SS-man. His close allies, the Daluege-Frick faction, had expected him to stay under Daluege's command. Needless to say, his subordination to Heydrich created significant opposition, and the fact that Himmler made such a decisive move indicates the importance to him and Heydrich of having closer personal control over the Kripo. They derived two main benefits from the inclusion: greater respectability for Sipo and SD, and ideological consistency in police work. Since the criminal police were widely considered to be a purely professional police force, highly skilled and relatively free of SS penetration and control, Kripo enhanced the image of Sipo and SD. On the one hand, the subordination to Heydrich of this significant body of policemen accelerated the process of creating the new police force. On the other, the fact that others considered Kripo relatively free of SS influence made the criminal police a useful cloak to cover interference in more normally impenetrable areas. For instance, the military thought of the Kripo as reliable long after their own cooperation with the Gestapo had gone sour.[25] Whether Himmler and Heydrich perceived such roles in advance is problematic, but Kripo obviously contributed to the Sipo image.

This sort of double-edged value accrued in the person of Authur Nebe as well. He was drawn into the SS and SD, effective December 2, 1936, as an SS major, remaining only one step behind Heinrich Mueller until they acquired parity in 1939. Himmler and Heydrich undoubtedly recognized Nebe's stance as a veritable double agent, yet they kept him because he had the respect of the criminal police and would have been a logical choice for any NS chief of detectives. He would provide effective leadership and expertise. More important, Hitler favored him, and his retention was perhaps a compromise with Frick and Daluege. Whatever opposition there was to the inclusion of Kripo in the Sipo would be somewhat cooled, for his presence would give the opposition hope that the Kripo would not become another tool for Heydrich. Nebe's position and his highly vaunted cooperation with the "resistance" perpetuated the myth that the criminal police were free of SS control. In fact, as he stayed on, not only did he provide camouflage, but he also cooperated, making his removal unnecessary, even undesirable. Like most other leaders trapped in the mesh of Sipo and SD relationships, Nebe and other Kripo leaders passed the supreme Nazi test as commanders of the mass murder squads on the eastern front. They clung tenaciously to their myth of separateness, and Nebe played his mostly ineffectual double role until his elimination after the July 1944 attempt on Hitler.[26]

Beyond all this, the primary reason for the union of Kripo with the Gestapo under one command lay in Himmler's version of NS ideology. In his mind, one could not separate questions of race, genetics, and criminality. Habitual criminality was a mark of inferiority, of foreign elements in the blood. A good German might succumb to criminal behavior, but often he could be salvaged. On the other hand, anyone with excessively "polluted" blood was subhuman—a threat to society and an element conductive to further genetic deterioration. The internal conspiracy that Himmler saw against Germany fomented a high rate of crime and the seduction of good Germans to commit criminal and immoral acts. Not only would crime and immorality undermine the moral fiber of the nation, but "related" homosexuality and abortion would reduce the manpower pool of national strength. The Jews and other "subhumans" lay behind all of this, just as they fostered communism, socialism, and liberalism to undermine solid German institutions.

The SS adopted the biological school of criminology almost as second nature. Of course, they distorted it beyond any claim to science. Heydrich assured that it became the sole orientation of crime fighting, and Nebe apparently accepted the basic theory also, despite his alleged resistance to any infection from Himmler's "Nordic cult."[27] From this point on, official statistics on criminals emphasized their racial and national origins, with recidivists drawing special attention. Political and criminal offenses were seen as inseparable—both fostered by the common enemy. An effective fight against this enemy and all of its manifestations had to be conducted by one office; it could be coordinated properly in no other way. Since such views were widely held in Nazi circles, proclaimed in *Mein Kampf* and repeated even by moderate Nazis,[28] they provided a convincing argument for the union.

The imagined interrelationship of crime and political offenses justified the logical extension of the extraordinary powers of the political police to the regular detectives: Both fought the common enemy of the nation in a time of emergency; both required emergency powers, since the execution of justice for any crime had to be swift and severe. The Kripo could make protective custody arrests on its own authority and often served as the executive arm of the Gestapo in localities without

Gestapo personnel. Capital punishment had been more freely applied in Germany since the advent of NS rule; now it would be directed at habitual criminals, with the extermination of the "criminal element" as the goal [29] This step could be taken and *publicly* proclaimed several years before the Final Solution could be *secretly* launched to strike at the "root" of the problem in exactly the same way. Severe punishment and even destruction of the "criminal element," a ubiquitous theme in most cultures, was an easy step to take in Nazi Germany. Exterminating "the criminal element" became one of many steps in the escalation that led to the boundless mobilization of Germany and its police against the "enemies of the *Volk*."

This proffered freedom and "efficiency" in the prosecution of crime undoubtedly had its appeal to many professional detectives. The process of their incorporation into the SS and SD began relatively late, continually lagged behind progress in the Gestapo, and was never as complete. Even so, it occurred, and the professional criminal investigation detectives joined their Gestapo counterparts in fusion with the SD. Each component of Sipo and SD could retain its supposedly separate mission, its self-image, and its nominal separateness from the other components, but they were welded together into a unit. In fulfilling their missions diligently, each made its contribution to the functioning of the police state. Despite their insistence that they did not support the work of the other components, whom they often rejected, even opposed, they were all trapped in the meshes of a machine that coordinated their efforts; all were drawn into the extralegal and heinous acts of Sipo and SD to preserve their roles and their self-created images.

Himmler and Heydrich had won; the SS–police state had come alive. The individual parts adapted themselves to survive within it, and, in doing so, carried on and ensured the growth of the NS police state toward the *Staatsschutzkorps*—police state terrorism and the execution of racial policies that resulted in genocide. In subsequent years Sipo and SD would become intensely involved with the "Jewish problem," less out of design than through functional pressures. Rivalry between Gestapo and SD would compel each to compete with the other. At the same time, both felt the need to assert its more "legitimate" authority over the uncontrollable NS elements prone to embarrassing excesses, and its more ideologically appropriate authority over bureaucratic agencies. As an unintended result of the Kristallnacht, in 1938 the Gestapo became the official vehicle for the first Final Solution—forced emigration. But the responsible Gestapo office came under SD-trained personnel, specifically Adolf Eichmann. This office would then be responsible for resettlement from all over Europe to the ghettos in Poland and then the ultimate Final Solution: transportation to the extermination camps.

Closely related was the responsibility of Sipo and SD for the Einsatzgruppen, which conducted the mass shootings of more than one million victims on the Eastern front. This in turn grew from involvement in foreign intelligence and the escalation of Hitler's plans for expansion. In the Austrian *Anschluss*, the annexation of the Sudetenland, and the establishment of the Protectorate over Bohemia and Moravia, Sipo and SD created the prototypes of the Eistazgruppen. Here, as later, they played the role of establishing the German police and security apparatus and of securing the areas being absorbed. After Sipo and SD agents executed the Gleiwitz canard, Einsatzgruppen entered Poland, where their role in the emasculation of the potential Polish resistance and the terrorizing of Jews presaged their future mission in Russia. Wherever Germany conquered, Sipo and SD extended its field network with its machinery for police state terrorism and the execution of Nazi racial programs. Another building block in the criminal edifice of the Third Reich was the domestic euthanasia program, in which Sipo personnel played key roles. Though terminated in the Reich proper, this program grew into the extermination of "useless eaters" in the Eastern territories. In both euthanasia and genocide, Sipo and SD experts facilitated technical developments.

As the war proceeded, the fully totalitarian police state finally emerged, with Sipo and SD at its heart. Under the pretext of national survival in the face of a world of enemies, Sipo and SD would purge Germany of all its threats—racial, criminal, moral, religious, and intellectual. After 1938, the previously "normalized" concentration camps filled faster than expansion of facilities could handle. Without intention, they evolved into supplements to the newer extermination camps, for death by exposure, malnutrition, and disease was hardly a desirable process *inside* Germany.

Whether any specific aspect of the Nazi police state evolved functionally or was assigned as a conscious step toward Hitler's goals, there was a component of Sipo and SD to assume executive responsibility for it. It is hard to conceive of the Third Reich and its horrors without Sipo and SD—the union of SS and police, preconceived only abstractly by Himmler in the early years and only begrudgingly accepted by everyone else as it gradually evolved to meet later demands.

Conclusion

This study has proposed some revisions of our understanding of how the SS and police came into being. Granted that prior to 1934 Himmler had ambitious dreams, they were nothing more specific than creating centralized police and intelligence services under SS leadership that possessed a clear ideological understanding of what needed to be done. The exact nature of that link between SS and police emerged only after 1934. The formation of Sipo and SD in 1936 marked not only a major step in the achievement of those dreams, but also the emergence of Heydrich as a driving force in the ongoing process. Prior to this time, Heydrich and his SD had played roles more secondary than previously believed, roles more appropriately compared to those of craftsmen executing, with some independence and bumbling, the vague designs of the architect who was Himmler.

Further revision include a more gradual evolution toward an irreversible police-terror system than previously supposed, and new insights into the process by which this happened. Foremost among the new perceptions is the openness with which Himmler's people argued for the essential components of the police state. The system was not imposed too quickly and secretly for anyone to resist—it was offered, and in many ways accepted, as the answer to widely felt fears and concerns.

The foundations were firmly laid in 1936, not in 1933-34, when the system was merely nascent. Until 1936, although Himmler frequently had powerful support for specific steps along the way, he created his system largely with his own resources and on his own initiative against significant opposition. Although Hitler frequently preserved from attack some parts of the system that Himmler had already built, there is little evidence that Hitler supported any significant expansion prior to naming him chief of the German Police in 1936. On the contrary, there is more evidence of Hitler's ambivalence and reluctance to increase Himmler's weight in the delicately balanced distribution of power. The initial processes of Himmler's rise to power prior to 1934 occurred piecemeal and at levels well below those concerning Hitler; after 1934, Hitler's attention turned increasingly from domestic to foreign affairs, leaving him even less inclined to attend personally to the growth of the police state.

Given the premise that Himmler did not build his SS-police system with Hitler's support, an explanation of how he overcame his opposition becomes a more serious problem. The answers lie in a combination of factors, not the least of which were the mistakes of more powerful opponents like Roehm. To his credit, however, Himmler had abilities as a planner, organizer, salesman, and political strategist. He could attract and exploit valuable lieutenants to do what he could not do. Above all, he combined his abilities with an evolving plan for a police-state structure that ideally suited the logic of Hitler's NS world view. Many rivals succumbed to this logic, especially as Himmler and his lieutenants applied it in the power struggle the evolved around them.

The base of Himmler's power was the SS, which Hitler had proclaimed quite early to be the special security and police force within the Movement. Although there is no indication the the Fuehrer had any preconceived role for Himmler's SS in a future police state, its mission within the Movement led members of the Party Reichsleitung to see the SS and SD as potential checks on the SA and other elements opposing centralization. Even at his weakest, Himmler often had Reichsleitung support for specific expansions of his power and for defense against powerful attacks. At the same time, his relationship with Roehm was sufficiently close that the latter rarely opposed and in fact often supported Himmler's expansions, at least initially.

Most significant, Himmler evolved a plan for a new institution with a revolutionary ideological mission, while his competitors tried merely to seize the existing instruments of power, as much for personal advancement as for any other reason. Although Himmler's personal power was inseparable from the system he built, his system was conceived as a logical fulfillment of Nazi ideals. By pursuing a rationalization of power, he had a "moral" advantage over those who would keep it fragmented. In the struggles of bureaucratic empire building, champions of rationalization have advantages. Since Himmler's rationalization program had a revolutionary quality from the NS perspective, he had a further advantage over conservative rationalizers like Frick. Furthermore, in the process of clarifying their goals, Himmler and his lieutenants would have been more likely to acquire that sixth sense that successfully competitive executives must have. Such a sense of direction helps to exploit every opportunity, often subconsciously, but usually to more advantage than opponents without clearly formulated goals.[30]

A further advantage lay in the early vagueness of the grand scheme. Without a detailed preconception of his future system, Himmler avoided an overly ambitious frontal assault like Roehm's, which produced a united opposition. Evolving his goals piecemeal, he pursued limited, achievable objectives for which he often had support as powerful as his opposition. In 1933, when he began his campaign, he focused only on the political police establishments of the smaller states.

Penetration of, involvement in, and use of state bureaucratic police powers were consistent with the revolutionary goals Himmler evolved, but they were contrary to conceptions of Second Revolutionaries like Roehm. Their fear of contamination by the establishment denied them weapons in the power struggle.[31] In contrast, the more conservative NS bureaucrats entrenched themselves in state offices and disdained Party radicalism. Not only did they thus deny themselves allies, but their brand of opposition increased Himmler's awareness of the need to replace conservative bureaucrats with SS-men holding proper ideological perspectives. Ironically, the nature of his opposition helped shape his image of a state protection corps as a synthesis of the extremes, preserving the advantages that each forfeited, and transcending them both in its radicalism.

From 1933 to 1935, Hitler clearly revealed his predilection for unlimited police powers to eliminate enemies and to maintain "order," thus supporting Himmler and encouraging Goering to move in directions that paralleled Himmler's. In so doing, Hitler constantly undermined the more conservative elements who would have limited the scope of the emerging police state, so that they gradually abandoned their most effective arguments and strategies. This, however, was the limit of Hitler's role in the matter, for before 1936 he apparently preferred the contradictory goal of efficient, unlimited police power without concentration in the hands of one lieutenant. Only the mounting international tension of 1935-36 and preparations for a more aggressive foreign policy forced him to act. By then, related concern over counterespionage had increased Blomberg's support for Himmler's system. The very fact that Himmler recruited Blomberg's intercession on his behalf is the strongest proof that he had to work to win Hitler's support as late as 1935.

Though Hitler and ideological consensus were clearly central to everything that happened, if this reinterpretation of the development of the police state stands, then the intentionalist arguments about all developments for which the police state was central require revision to include functionalist perspectives to such a point that intentionalism may cease to be a valid concept in any but the most abstract sense.

As for arguments about the role of ideological consensus, Graf is certainly correct in arguing for a continuity between Wilhelmine attitudes and the police of Weimar and NS Germany. There was indeed an ideological consensus at work that bound together police, NS, and conservative allies. Graf is also correct in pointing to the Papen coup of 1932 as a decisive turning point—not, however, in labeling it *the* decisive turning point—rather than as one in a series of steps. The next such step was the NS "power seizure," putting the police under Nazi command, while people like Diels maintained the continuity and laid foundations for the next step. That came with Himmler's acquisition of the Gestapo, properly labeled by Aronson as a decisive turning point, perhaps the most decisive. Nevertheless, Graf again is correct in emphasizing that little immediate change occurred. What followed was indeed a gradual transition. The next major step was Himmler's 1936 acquisition of command over all German police, at which point the building process had created a solid foundation.

Through each of these steps, many problems weakened conservative opposition. More than anything, however, the conservatives were defeated by their own beliefs and values. Whether they were Nazis like Frick or non-Nazis like the generals, or Guertner and Schacht, they shared in more moderate form many of the same basic assumptions as Himmler. They could not refute his law-and-order and national security arguments, while he exploited the conflicts of interest among them over what to preserve and how. Meanwhile, their own drives to repress perceived enemies prevented them from mounting adequate resistance against his arguments for radical enforcement. They thus sacrificed whatever humane conservative values they may have held, and contributed directly to the construction of one or more aspects of the police state. The inherent logic of the anti-liberal, anti-Marxist, racist, nationalist, survival-of-the-fittest world view that they shared overwhelmed them just as it did the mass base of Nazi power they disdained.

Although "ideological consensus" does explain the development of the evils of the Third Reich, it was not such a consensus in detail that all involved moved intentionally toward either the SS-police state essential to the fulfillment of these evils or toward those evils themselves. It was rather an "ideological conjunction" that sabotaged resistance. Police states are not all the same, but ideological compulsions to curb basic rights or to repress minorities or ideas lead all who hold them down the same slippery slope.

This reassessment of Hitler's role in the formation of the police state does not exonerate him or anyone else from responsibility. It merely puts in more accurate perspective the nature of the leader's responsibility in complex modern societies. It should no longer be stated that Hitler ordered the creation of this system or that he preconceived the system and set Himmler to work on it. Himmler, nevertheless, created *his* system with the intent of appealing to Hitler, and it did. Giving the Four Year Plan to Goering and the police to Himmler were logical correlations of his foreign policy goals. Regardless of the need to balance all against all, regardless of what Hitler thought of Himmler and lieutenants like Heydrich, Himmler offered the security instrument most suitable to the future Hitler foresaw. The division of the conservatives, marked most notably by Blomberg's call for a security system like Himmler's, must have facilitate Hitler's final decision.

This study has suggested that the membership of the separate agencies in Sipo and SD were bound together in an uneasy union, but in such a way as to drive them not only to fulfill their missions but also to contribute to the further growth of police state terrorism and ultimately genocide. Each had a mission and an organizational image that its members embraced precisely because they proclaimed their separateness from and transcendence above those they disdained in Sipo and SD, in other parts of the SS, or in the Movement in general. The ethos of each separate branch thus enabled its members to do their jobs self-righteously, while denying any connection between themselves and the less respectable work of others. Consequently, then and ever since, members of each branch have denied that Sipo and SD constituted any real union of its components. When they were required to contribute to—even participate directly in—the work of other branches that they disdained, they could dismiss such contamination as temporary and an unfortunate but necessary evil if they wanted to remain with their chosen branch and fulfill its mission, which would contribute to a better Germany.

The special union that Sipo and SD represented offers insights into how its members came to play the roles that they did. Especially since so many of its members came from the so-called better elements of society, there is a need for better explanations than a takeover by sadists or authoritarian personalities. With the foundations laid by this study, it should be possible to explore more fruitfully the more pressing questions raised by the Nazi experience, at least as far as how it came to be that its horrors were performed by professional policemen, lawyers, academics, civil servants—the full range of ordinary German citizens who belonged to Sipo and SD.

Appendix

Table of Comparative Officer Ranks

SS	German Army	U.S. Army	German Police
Reichsfuehrer	Generalfeld- marschall	General of the Army	Chef d. Deutsch. Polizei
ObstGruppen- fuehrer	Generaloberst		Generaloberst d. Polizei
Oberguppen- fuehrer	General	General	General d. Polizei
Gruppenfuehrer	Generalleutnant	Lieutenant General	General leutnant d. Polizei
Brigadefuehrer	Generalmajor	Major General	Generalmajor d. Polizei
Oberfuehrer		Brigadier General	
Standartenfuehrer	Oberst	Colonel	Oberst d. Schupo Reichs Kriminaldi- rektor
OSturmbann- fuehrer	Oberstleutnant	Lieutenant Colonel	Oberstleutnant d. Schupo Oberregierungs-u. Kriminalrat
Sturmbann- fuehrer	Major	Major	Major d. Schupo Reg- u. Kriminalrat
Hauptsturm- fuehrer	Hauptmann	Captain	Hauptmann d. Schupo Kriminalrat
Obersturmfuehrer	Obertleutnant	First Lieuten- ant	Oberleutnant d. Schupo Kriminalkommissar Kriminalinspektor
USturmfuehrer	Leutnant	Second Lieu- tenant	Leutnant d. Schupo Kriminalsekretaer Kriminal-Oberassis- tent

Sturmschar-fuehrer	Stabsfeldwebel	Sergeant Major	Meister
			Kriminalsekretaer
			Kriminal-Oberassistent
Hauptschar-fuehrer	Oberfeldwebel	Master Sergeant	Hauptwachtmeister
Oberscharfuehrer	Feldwebel	Tech Sergeant	Revier-Oberwachtmeister
			Kriminal-Oberassistent
Scharfuehrer	Unterfeldwebel	Staff Sergeant	Oberwachtmeister
			Kriminalassistent
Unterscharfuehrer	Unteroffizier	Sergeant	Wachtrmeister
			Kriminalassistent Anwaerter
	Obergefreiter		Rottwachtmeister
Rottenfuehrer	Gefreiter	Corporal	Unterwachtmeister
Sturmmann	Oberschuetze	Private First Class	
SS-Mann Anwaerter	Schuetze	Private	Anwaerter

Notes

Orpo	Ordnungspolizei; Order Police (uniformed)
OSAF	Oberst SA Fuehrung; Highest SA Command
PD	*Polizei Direktor* or *Direktion*; police commissioner, chief or headquar
PK	Partei Korresdondcnz; Party correspondence files
PLPA	Politische Landespolizeiamt; State Political Police Office
PPKdL	*Politische Polizei Kommandeur der Laender*; political police commander of the states
PPras	*Polizei Praesident* or *Praesidium*; police president, commissioner, or headquarters
Pr	Preussisches; Prussian
PrFM	Preussisches Finanz Ministerium; Prussian Finance Ministry or minister
R	Reichs; imperial/national
RdErl	*Runderlass*; decree
Reg	*Regierungs*; government
RegBez	*Regierungsbezirk*; governmental district
RPras	*Regierungs-Praesident*; district governor or officer
RR	*Reigierungsrat*; government councilor
RFSS	*Reichsfuehrer SS*; Reich commander of the SS
RK	*Reichskanzlei*; Reich chancellery or chancellor
RKM	Reichskriegs Ministerium; Reich War Ministry or minister
RPL	Reichspropagandaleitung; Reich Propaganda Command or Office
RStH	*Reichsstatthalter*; Reich territorial governor (of a *Land*)
RuSHA	Rasse und Siedlungs Hauptamt; Race and Settlement Main Office
RWM	Reichswehr Ministerium; Ministry or minister of National Defense
SA	Sturmabteilung; Storm Troopers, Brown Shirts
Schupo	Schutzpolizei; State Police (uniformed)
SD	Sicherheitsdienst; Security Service (of the Reichsfuehrer SS)
Sipo	Sicherheitspolizei; Security Police (plainclothes detectives)
SS	Schutzstaffel; Protection Squadron
SSO	SS officers files
S(L)St	Staatspolizei (Leit)Stelle; Gestapo (Control) Post
StSek	*Staatssekretaer*; state secretary
StVCuI	*Stellvertretender Chef und Inspekteur*; deputy chief and inspector (of the Prussian Gestapo)
StVdF	*Stellvertretender des Fuehrers*; deputy of the Fuehrer
u.	*und*; and
UAb	*Unterabschnitt*; subregion (SA, SS, SD)
VO	*Verordnung*; decree
WM	Wehrmacht; Armed Forces

Publications

AHR	*American Historical Review*
APSR	*American Political Science Review*
CEH	*Central European History*
DAL	*Dienstaltersliste der SS*
GVtP	*Geschaeftsverteilungsplan*

IMT	*International Military Tribunal, Trial of the Major War Criminals before the*
JCFH	*Journal of Central European History*
JCL,C&PS	*Journal of Criminal Law, Criminology and Police Science*
JMH	*Journal of Modern History*
JPS&A	*Journal of Police Science and Administration*
KDAL	*Dienstaltersliste der hoeheren Kriminalbeamten* (Prussia)
MBliV	*Ministerialblatt des Reichs- und Preussischen Ministeriums des Innern*
NCA	*Nazi Conspiracy and Aggression* (Red Series)
PrGS	*Preussische Gesetzsammlung*
RGBl	*Reichsgesetzblatt*
TWC	*Trials of the War Criminals* (subsequent trials-Green Series)
VB	*Voelkischer Beobachter*
VfZ	*Vierteljahrshefte fuer Zeitgeschichte*

Archives

BA	Bundesarchiv (Koblenz)
BA-MA	Bundesarchiv-Militaerarchiv (Freiburg)
BDC	U.S. Document Center, Berlin
By	Bayerisches
GlStAnwalt	Generalstaatsanwalt bei dem Kammergericht, Berlin
GStA	Geheime Staatsarchiv Berlin-Dahlem (also Hauptarchiv)
HA	Hauptarchiv der NSDAP (Hoover Institute Microfilm)
Hess	Hessisches
HStA	Hauptstaatsarchiv
IfZ	Institut fuer Zeitgeschichte
LC	Library of Congress (Washington, D.C.)
NA	National Archives (Washington, D.C.)
NSach	Niedersaechsisches
PA	Politischesarchiv des Auswaertigen Antes (Bonn)
Sach	Saechsisches
StA	Staatsarchiv

Introduction

1. A detailed analysis of relevant literature is found in the bibliographical essay under "Subsequent Literature."

2. See Pierre Aycoberry's analysis of the significance of Hans Buchheim's contribution resulting from his early *Gutachten* on SS-police-KL systems, *The Nazi Question: An Essay on the Interpretation of National Socialism, 1922-1975* (New York: Pantheon Books, 1981), p. 209.

3. The reader can both achieve an overview of the debate and trace its evolution through historiographical essays such as Aycoberry (originally in French, 1979), especially pp. 208-15; Hans Mommsen, "National Socialism—Continuity and Change," and Karl D. Bracher, "The Role of Hitler: Perspectives of Interpretation," in *Fascism: A Reader's Guide*, ed. Walter Lacquer (Berkeley: Univ. of California Press, 1976); Klaus Hildebrand, *The Third Reich* (London: George Allen & Unwin, 1984; originally in German, 1979), pp. 136-40; with further elaboration by Tim Mason, "Intention and Explanation: A Current Contro-

versy about the Interpretation of National Socialism," and Mommsen, "Hitlers Stellung in nationalsozialistischen Herrschaftssystem," and Hildebrand, "Monocratie oder Polycratie? Hitlers Herrschaft und das Dritte Reich," in Gerhard Hirschfeld and Lothar Kettenacher, *"The Fuehrer Staat": Myth and Reality* (Stuttgart: Klett-Cotte, 1981); John Heiden and John Farquharson, *Explaining Hitler's Germany: Historians and the Third Reich* (Totowa, N.J.: Barnes & Noble Books, 1983); Ian Kershaw, *The Nazi Dictatorship: Problems and Perspectives of Interpretation* (London: Edward Arnold, 1985); Mommsen, "Flight from Reality: Hitler as Party Leader and Dictator in the Third Reich," *Syracuse Scholar* 8 (1987): 51-59; and on the most recent twist, Konrad H. Jarausch, "Removing the Nazi Stain? The Quarrel of the German Historians," *German Studies Review* 11 (1988): 285-301.

4. See Kershaw, *Nazi Dictatorship,* pp. 5-10.

5. For example: Andreas Hillgruber, *Hitlers Strategie, Politik und Kriegsfuehrung, 1940-1941* (Frankfurt a.M.: Bernard & Graefe, 1965); Klaus Hildebrand, *The Foreign Policy of the Third Reich* (Berkeley: Univ. of California Press, 1973); Karl D. Bracher in *Die Nationalsozialistische Machtergreifung* (Cologne: Westdeutscher Verlag, 1960), and *The German Dictatorship* (New York: Praeger Publishers, 1970); and Eberhard Jaeckel, *Hitler's Weltanschauung: A Blueprint for Power* (Middletown, Conn.: Wesleyan Univ. Press, 1972).

6. For example: Hans Mommsen, *Beamtentum im Dritten Reich* (Stuttgart: Deutsche Verlagsanstalt, 1966); Peter Diehl-Thiele, *Partei und Staat im Dritten Reich* (Munich: Bech, 1969); and Edward N. Peterson, *The Limits of Hitler's Power* (Princeton: Princeton Univ. Press, 1969).

7. Heiden and Farquharson, *Explaining Hitler's Germany,* p. 47.

8. Raul Hilberg, *The Destruction of the European Jews,* 3 vols. (New York: Holmes & Meier, 1985). Although he has avoided taking a clear position in the debate, Hilberg describes "the machinery of destruction, moving on a track of self-assertion, engaged in its multipronged operation in an ever more complicated network of interlocking decisions. . . . We know that the bureaucracy had no master plan, no fundamental blue-print, no clear view of its actions. How then was the process steered? How did it take on *Gestalt?*" 3:998.

9. Kershaw, *Nazi Dictatorship,* especially p. 61, n. 2, for one complete chain of published exchanges during 1980-81; and Jarausch, "Removing the Nazi Stain?" on the more recent *Historikerstreit.*

10. Kershaw, *Nazi Dictatorship,* p. 80.

11. For an interesting elaboration of this "dialectical" perspective in developmental psychology, Michael Basseches, *Dialectical Thinking and Adult Development* (Norwood, N.J.: Ablex Publishing, 1984), especially pp. 9-15, 20-30. The potential of this approach for psychohistorical analysis remains wholly untapped, yet highly relevant to the Nazi experience.

12. For example, Christopher Graf, *Politische Polizei zwischen Demokratie und Diktatur* (Berlin: Colloquium Verlag, 1983).

1. Factionalism in Pursuit of Power

1. The early history of the Nazi Movement found excellent summary in Dietrich Orlow, *The History of the Nazi Party: 1919-1933* (Pittsburgh: Univ. of Pittsburgh Press, 1969); and a pioneer study of Hitler's position and of factionalism can be found in Joseph Nyomarkay, *Charisma and Factionalism in the Nazi*

Party (Minneapolis: Univ. Minnesota Press, 1967). For elaborations of internal ideological differences prior to 1933, see, Barbara Miller Lane, "Nazi Ideology: Some Unfinished Business," *CEH* 7 (March 1974): 3-30) Lane and L. Rupp, *Nazi Ideology before 1933* (Austin: Univ. of Texas Press, 1978); and Simon Taylor, *Prelude to Genocide: Nazi Ideology and the Struggle for Power* (New York: St. Martin's Press, 1985). The most widely accepted interpretation of Hitler's own ideology is Jaechel, *Hitler's Wetanschauung*. Michael H. Kater, "Hitler in a Social Context," *CEH* 14 (September 1981): 243-72, explores the social aspects of Hitler's charismatic technique.

2. Arguments over the deliberateness of Hitler's style and its effects on his control are central to the debate. For a clear review of the problem and related literature, Hiden and Farquharson, *Explaining Hitler's Germany*, pp. 64-66.

3. Robert Koehl, "Feudal Aspects of National Socialism," *APSR* 54 (December 1960): 921-33.

4. In addition to Nyomarkay and Orlow, Jeremy Noakes, "Conflict and Development in the NSDAP, 1924-1927," *JCH* 1 (October 1969): 3-36, provided a deeper study of the Strasser faction. In contrast, Lane, "Nazi Ideology," forced a serious reconsideration of what in fact constituted the differences between the factions. More recently, Udo Kissenkoetter, *Gregor Strasser und die NSDAP* (Stuttgart: Deutsche Verlags-Anstalt, 1978); and Peter D. Stachura, *Gregor Strasser and the Rise of Nazism* (London: George Allen & Unwin, 1983) have fleshed out these analyses. On factionalism in Bavaria: Geoffrey Pridham, *Hitler's Rise to Power: The Nazi Movement in Bavaria, 1923-1933* (New York: Harper & Row, 1973).

5. Recent studies of the early SA: Richard Bessel, *Political Violence and the Rise of Nazism: The Storm Troopers in Eastern Germany, 1925-1934* (New Haven: Yale Univ. Press, 1984); Conan Fischer, *Stormtroopers: A Social, Economic and Ideological Analysis, 1928-35* (London: George Allen & Unwin, 1983); Mathilde Jamin, *Zwischen den Klassen* (Wuppertal: Hammer Verlag, 1984); and Erich G. Reiche, *The Development of the SA in Nuernberg, 1922-1934* (Cambridge: Cambridge Univ. Press, 1986).

6. OSAF, GRUSA VII, "Schutzstaffel (SS)," 12 April 1929, U.S. National Archives Microfilm Publications, Microcopy T-580, *Captured German Documents Microfilmed at the Berlin Document Center*, Roll 87, Folder 425 (hereafter cited as T-580/roll no./folder no.). "Die wichtigsten Daten aus der Geschichte der SS," from *SS Handbuch*, n.d., probably Waffen-SS in orgin, U.S. National Archives Microfilm Publications, Microcopy T-175, *Records of the Reichsfuehrer SS and Chief of the German Police*, Roll 232, frame 2720313 (hereafter cited as T-175/roll no./frame no.). Hitler on the origin and purpose of the SS: *Secret Conversations, 1941-1944* trans. Norman Cameron and R.H. Stevens (New York: Farrar, Strauss & Young, 1953), p. 138. For the official history of the SS, Gunter d'Alquen, *Die SS, Geschichte, Aufgabe und Organization der Schutzstaffel der NSDAP* (Berlin: Junker & Duenhaupt Verlag, 1939), pp. 6-7. On the early SS, Hans Buchheim, "The SS—Instrument of Domination," in Helmut Krausnick et al., *Anatomy of the SS State* (New York: Walker & Company, 1968), pp. 140-42; Heinz Hoehne, *The Order of the Death's Head* (New York: Coward-McCann, 1969); Peter Hoffman, *Hitler's Personal Security* (Boston: MIT Press, 1979), pp. 15-22; and Robert L. Koehl, *The Black Corps* (Madison: Univ. Wisconsin Press, 1983), chaps. 1-3. One of the most significant folders of primary sources on the formative years of the SS is T-580/87/425.

7. Rundschreiben Nr. 1, Munich, 21 September 1925, and Richtlinien, n.d., T-580/87/425.

8. GRUSA VII, 12 April 1929, T 580/97/425; and Hoehne, *The Order*, pp. 25-28. For detail on early SA-SS relations, Andreas Werner, "SA und NSDAP." (Inaugural dissertation, Friedrich-Alexander-Universitaet, 1963), pp. 400-402, 495-99, 585-87; and Bessel, *Political Violence*, pp. 65-66.

9. On Himmler's positions, *Dienstaltersliste der Schutzstaffel der NSDAP, Stand von 1. Oktober 1934* (henceforth *DAL*) T-175/204/2673857; and d'Alquen, *SS*, pp. 7-8.

10. SS Befehl Nr. 1, Munich, 13 September 1927, T-580/87/425.

11. The early biographies of Himmler are uneven and dated: Willie Frischauer, *Himmler* (New York: Belmont Productions, 1962); Roger Manvell and Heinrich Fraenkel, *Himmler* (London: William Heinemann, 1965); Josef Wulf, *Heinrich Himmler* (Berlin: Arani Verlag, 1960). Interesting short sketches can be found in Joachim C. Fest, *The Face of the Third Reich* (New York: Pantheon Books, 1970), pp. 111-24; and Hoehne, *The Order*, pp. 29-50. An interesting effort at psychoanalysis of Himmler is Peter Loewenberg, "The Unsuccessful Adolescence of Heinrich Himmler," *AHR* 76 (June 1971): 612-41, who identifies symptoms of an obsessive-compulsive character and schizoid personality in the adolescent diaries of Himmler. Finally, Bradley F. Smith, *Heinrich Himmler: A Nazi in the Making, 1900-1926* (Stanford: Hoover Institution Press, 1971), has made extensive use of available sources to produce a most satisfactory account of the development of Himmler's character.

Werner T. Angress and Bradley F. Smith, "Diaries of Heinrich Himmler's Early Years," *JMH* 31 (September 1959): 206-24; and Helmut Heiber (ed.), *Reichsfuehrer!* . . . *Briefe an und von Himmler* (Stuttgart: Deutsche Verlags-Anstalt, 1968), provide some primary insights, as does the occasionally questionable Felix Kersten, *Memoirs*, who, as confidant and masseur, saw aspects of Himmler that normally would be revealed only to a psychoanalyst. A useful firsthand description is Werner Best, "Betr.: Heinrich Himmler," September 18, 1949. On Himmler's reactions to the Final Solution, Kersten, pp. 119-20; and Raul Hilberg, *Destruction of European Jews* 1:332-33.

12. Hoehne, *The Order*, pp. 41-43. Interestingly, it took Himmler almost two years, 1925-27, to work his way through *Mein Kampf*. Transcript of Himmler's "Gelesene Buecher" notebook, Library of Congress, Himmler File, container 418.

13. Angress and Smith, "Diaries," pp. 210, 216.

14. Smith, *Himmler*, p. 165.

15. Oberst Walter Nicolai, *Geheime Maechte, International Espionage und ihre Bekaempfung im Weltkreig und heute* (Leipzig: K.F. Koehler, 1923), pp. 11-13.

16. Ibid., pp. 20, 89, 121, 184. The significance of such ideas to Himmler at this time is indicated by his rejection of Georg Popoff's *Tscheka* as "a bad book," because "the word Jew is not mentioned in connection with the Cheka, which is almost completely Jewish . . . " Smith, *Himmler*, p. 165.

17. Wilhelm Hoettl, *The Secret Front*, pp. 30-45, is a source of this rumor.

18. Kersten, *Memoirs*, p. 54.

19. Kissenkoetter, *Gregor Strasser*, pp. 59-60, revealed Himmler's heretofore unsuspected role in building the Party's Propagandaleitung and propaganda work before Goebbels. For Goebbels's account of Himmler and his continued role in running the RPL for several months after Goebbels's takeover, Elke Froehlich (ed.), *Die Tagebuecher von Joseph Goebbels: Saemtliche Fragmente*, 4 vols. (Mun-

ich: K.G. Sauer, 1987), 1: 20.XI. & 22.XI.29; 23.III., 28.IV., 2.V., 12.V., 24.V., & 29.VII.30.

20. On attention to details and his tendency to drive himself, Angress, Smith, "Diaries," p. 215; for an example of Himmler's attitude on discipline, letter, Himmler to Kaltenbrunner, July 14, 1944, T-175/59/2574386; on loyalty to Hitler and manipulation, Kersten, *Memoirs*, pp. 53-54, 244-47.

21. Ibid., pp. 28-29.

22. Smith, *Himmler*, p. 171.

23. On the appeal to Hitler, *Hitler's Secret Conversations*, pp. 87, 352. Fest identified a passage in one of Hitler's Reich Party Congress speeches in 1938 as an attack upon "pseudo-academic folkish occultism," which might have been directed specifically toward curbing Himmler and his ilk, *Face of the Reich*, p. 113. Albert Speer relates several occasions upon which Hitler disdained Himmler's mystical and romantic preoccupations, *Inside the Third Reich* (New York: Macmillan, 1970), pp. 94-95, 122.

24. On Party tensions, especially in Berlin in 1930, Martin Broszat, *Hitler and the Collapse of Weimar Germany* (Leamington Spa, UK: Berg Publishers, 1987), pp. 11-25; Taylor, *Prelude to Genocide*, pp. 89-106; and Bessel, *Political Violence*, pp. 62-63. The Berlin SA or Stennes faction's version of this and the subsequent conflicts can be found in Walter Jaehn, *Wie es zur Stennes-Aktion kam!*, printed by Walter Stennes, *Documents of the Hauptarchiv der NSDAP*, Microfilm of the Hoover Institution on War, Revolution and Peace, Roll 4, Folder 83 (hereafter cited as HA/4/83).

25. Nyomarkay, *Nazi Party*, pp. 119-21; and Bessel, *Political Violence*, pp. 63-65.

26. Hoehne, *The Order*, pp. 66-68; and Koehl, *Black Corps*, pp. 34, 45-46. On the SS as spies and headquarters guards, Jahn, *Stennes-Aktion*, pp. 3-4.

27. Letter from the Partei- und OSAF, Stabschef Wagener to OSAF-Stellv., 3 October 1930, and Hitler's announcement of intentions for SS independence, Partei- und OSAF, 7 November 1930, T-580/85/403. SS Befehl Nr. 20, Munich, 1 December 1930; and SA Befehl Nr. 1 (Gleichzeitig fuer SS), 16 January 1931, T-580/89/449.

2. The Roots of the SD

1. The *Lebenslauf* of Alfred Riechers (b. 2.3.95), Berlin Document Center/ SS Officers Files (hereafter, BDC/SSO), claims entry into the "gesamten Nachr. Abtlg. in die SA" in 1922-23, and after the Party Verbot in 1923, membership in the "geheimen Nachr. Dienst" of the Movement. Saxon KR Erich Vogel (b. 13.7.89) worked from September 1926 for the NSDAP "im Nachrichtendienst," informing the Party confidentially, especially regarding government and police measures (BDC/SSO).

2. Kissenkoetter, *Strasser*, pp. 59-60. Lebenslauf, BDC/SSO Dr. Otto Rasch (b. 7.12.91), claims service in the Gau ND at Dresden since 1930. The PL of Gau Hannover-Sued-Braunschweig during 1930 issued monthly reports, well informed on enemy organizations; BA/Schu 209, Monatl. Rundschreiben d. GPL, Nr. 10, 15.12.30. RPL, Abtl. ND, 19.12.31, makes a reference to independently working Gau Nachrichtenstellen, N.Saech. HStA Hannover, 310 I/A/37 II.

3. On Strasser, Orlow, *Nazi Party, 1919-1933*, pp. 211, 306 n.; on Stennes, clipping from *VB*, 15 April 1931, "Das Berliner Polizeipraesidium schuetzt durch

Befehlsausgabe die Stenees-Revolte," T-175/357/2866878; and Jaehn, *Stennes-Aktion*, HA/4/83.

4. Warnings about spies and especially KPD agents in SS Befehle Nr. 27, 6 June 1931, and Nr. 53, 10 October 1931, T-580/87/425; Gau-Muenchen-Oberbayern, Propaganda Abtlg. (N.D.) to all Bezirks-und Ortsgruppenleiter, 13 October 1931, HA/71/1533; and OSAF, Ic Nr. 7459/31, re "Nachrichtendienst," 9 December 1931, HA/16/306. T-175/375/EAP 173-b-16-05/398 is a Polizeipraesidium Berlin collection of materials on KPD efforts to penetrate and undermine the SA, 1930-32. The propaganda played cleverly on factionalism in the NSDAP and appealed to the socialistic elements in the SA. Frames 2866846-55 provide insight into exploitation of a turncoat, Lt. a.D. Scheringer.

5. The early history of the SA intelligence service can be pieced together from scattered documents in Folder 1773, HA/27A and 28A; see especially Nr. XVI a 315/31., Der Oberstaatsanwalt bei dem Landgerichte Muenchen I to the General staatsanwalt bei dem Oberlandesgerichte Muenchen, 12 February 1931, re "Riester, Herbert . . . wegen Vorbereitung zum Hochverrat," HA/28A/1773. According to Beilage I of Andreas Werner, *SA und NSDAP* (inaugural dissertation, Frierdrich-Alexander-Univ., 1964), in April 1931 Riester's Ic was under Wilhelm Weiss's Nachrichtenstab, directly subordinate to Roehm.

6. 12 February 1931, "re Riester," HA/28A/1773. Examples of Riester's reports precede and follow this document.

7. Der OSAF, Stabsbefehl and Verfuegung Ic Nr. 3274/31, both of 9 June 1931, HA/16/306.

8. On the development of RPL propaganda machinery and the monthly reports, Orlow, *Nazi Party, 1919-1933*, pp. 204-5. For examples of these developments from December 1930 in such *Gaue* as Schwaben, Weser-Ems and Hannover-Sued-Brauschweig, BA/Schu 209.

9. The surviving Goebbels's diary entries contain no references to his RPL ND before 5 October 1932. Until shortly before that date, all entries indicate that Franke was running the RPL for him and much to his satisfaction. Goebbels's rapid about-face against Franke in late 1932 indicates he probably paid little attention to the actual workings of the RPL organization until serious problems arose. *Tagebuecher von Goebbels*, 1: 12.X.30., 17.XII.30.; 2: 15.I.31., 26.II.31., 6.III.31., 17.V.31., 19.IX.32., 5.X.32., 2.XIII., 13.XIII. & 14.XII.32., 11.I & 24.I.33. Both Gau Sachsen, PL, Rundschreiben Nr. 16/31, 22 May 1931, (BA/Schu 208I/Bd.1/137-38) and Gau Weser-Ems, 2 July 1931, to all B.-u. OGL (BA/Schu 209) refer to the May directive of RPL for the establishment of an ND. The key passage of the directive is quoted in an unidentified report (perhaps police report) L. Nr. 101, Muenchen, 9 June 1931, HA/28A/1773. An example of early control problems can be seen in correspondence with GPL Hannover-Sued-Braunschweig from 2 February to 31 March 1931, N.Saech.HStA Hannover 310 I/B/2 II. On the transfer, BDC/SSO Arthur Schumann (b. 30.8.99). An example of his continued problems with the GPL can be traced in N.Saech.HStA Hannover, 310 I/B/2 II.

10. Verfuegung Ia Nr. 4690/31 or OSAF, 10 August 1931, and attached organizational chart, HA/16/306; and for a sample report, der OSAF, Ic Nr. 7459/31, re "Nachrichtendienst," 9 December 1931, in the same folder.

11. Clippings of the *Muenchener Post* for 25 and 28-29 November 1931, along with numerous other related clippings, police reports, and court documents related to the trial can be found in HA/28A/1773. Aronson (*Heydrich*, p. 45) has discovered that the forger Johann Loedel was an SS-man. However, his speculation that the affair might have been engineered by Himmler to destroy com-

petition is too strained. To begin with, the affair dates back as far as September 1931, before Himmler's Ic was of any significance, and Himmler would hardly sabotage such vital Party work, especially since his relations with Roehm remained so warm. More likely, Loedel's involvement reveals the extent of cooperation between the SA and SS at this time.

12. Clipping of *Muenchener Post*, 28-29 November 1931, "Der Geheimdienst der Nazipartei," HA/28A/1773.

13. LC/Himmler File/container 418, entries 304 and 306.

14. Der OSAF, S.A. Befehle Nr. 3 and Nr. 4, 25 February 1931, T-580/93/457. This bodyguard, or Sicherheitsdienst, had no direct relation to the later SD; they existed simultaneously as separate branches of Himmler's staff, this Sicherheitsdienst being designated Ig, while Heydrich's nascent SD was Ic. (Nachrichtensammelstelle, n.d., re "Referate bei der Reichsfuehrung der SS . . . ," BA/R-58/1151/466). The real lineal descendants of this Sicherheitsdienst were the SS Leibstandarte Adolf Hitler and the later Reichssicherheitsdienst, the plain-clothes police bodyguard unit.

15. Himmler recalled these early developments in two separate speeches: "Rede des Reichsfuehrers SS vor dem Staatsraeten im Haus der Flieger," 5 March 1936, pp. 36-37, BA/NS-19/H.R./2; and "Wesen und Aufgabe der SS. und der Polizei," from *Nationalpolitischer Lehrgang der Wehrmacht vom 15. bis 23. January 1937*, 1992(a)-PS, IMT, 29: 206-34. *Anlage zum Stabsbefehl vom 12. Mai 1931*; and RFSS, SS Befehl-C-Nr. 28, 9 June 1931, HA/28A/1773.

16. The most reliable, well-documented biography is Aronson, *Heydrich*, the major source for the following paragraphs. The only first-hand account not hostile to him is that of his wife, Lina Heydrich, *Leben mit einem Kriegsverbrecher* (Pfaffenhofen: Verlag W. Ludwig, 1976). The journalistic Edouard Calic's *Reinhard Heydrich* (New York: William Morrow, 1985) provides more insight—unfortunately undocumented—into the family environment.

17. Aronson, *Heydrich*, pp. 17-25, based on interviews with family and friends. A good summary of the allegations of Heydrich's Jewish ancestry can be found in Fest, *Face of the Reich*, pp. 335-36 n. 11, and they are a major element of Wighton's analysis of Heydrich. Aronson proves that none of Heydrich's grandparents were Jewish, as alleged; however, broadly based beliefs can never be laid to rest. Calic, *Heydrich*, p. 33, alleges Heydrich had a gift subscription to the *VB*.

18. Lina Heydrich, *Leben*, pp. 99-100. Schellenberg, *Memoirs*, pp. 31-34, 244-45. On Hitler's lament, *Secret Conversations*, p. 415.

19. Aronson, *Heydrich*, pp. 25-35, based on interviews with family and crew mates.

20. Ibid., pp. 35-37; and BDC/SSO, Heydrich: NSDAP Nr. 544,916.

21. Aronson, *Heydrich*, p. 63. Every study of Heydrich has stressed his apolitical posture, and the source has always been the same—Lina Heydrich (repeated in *Leben*, p. 28). Wighton, *Heydrich*, pp. 35-36. Despite his lack of documentation, Calic's assertions to the contrary cannot be ignored, *Heydrich*, pp. 35-51.

22. Aronson, *Heydrich*, p. 37. The exact dates for this sequence of events are unclear and vary greatly from source to source. Heydrich's membership in the SS became official July 14, SS Nr. 10,120 (BDC/SSO, Heydrich). Lina Heydrich, associating Heydrich's trip to Munich with her birthday, set its date on June 14, followed by a return to Hamburg where he joined the SS and served until August, when he joined Himmler's staff (*Leben*, pp. 26-27).

23. Aronson, *Heydrich*, pp. 37-38, quoting Eberstein.

24. RFSS to SS Sturmfuehrer Reinhard Heydrich, 10 August 1931, BDC/SSO, Heydrich.

25. Police Report Nr. /48, "Fuehrerbesprechung der SS-Muenchens am 26 8 31 im Braunen Haus," IIA/72/1546.

26. RFSS, SS-Befehl-D-Nr.43, 4 September 1931, HA/28A/1773.

27. Aronson, *Heydrich*, p. 56.

28. Lina Heydrich, *Leben*, pp. 28, 32-33.

29. NSDAP, Reichsleitung, re "Nachrichtendienst," 26 November 1931, HA/89/1849.

30. BDC/SSO, Alfred Riechers (b.2.3.95), *Lebenslauf*, 5.9.33, indicated simultaneous leadership in SA Ic and Gau ND. A police report, Nachrichtensammel stelle im RMdI, re "Nationalsozialistischer Nachrichtendienst," 2 March 1932 (BA/R-58/1151/483), describes a Gau ND working with the SA observer net.

31. Peter D. Stachura, " 'Der Fall Strasser': Gregor Strasser, Hitler and National Socialism, 1930-1932," in Stachura, ed., *The Shaping of the Nazi State* (London: Croom Helm, 1978), pp. 90-94, 101-4.

32. Aronson, *Heydrich*, p. 56; and Wighton, *Heydrich*, p. 45, both citing Lina Heydrich as the source. Lina Heydrich, *Leben*, pp. 27-29, 32-33. For Heydrich's promotions, BDC/SSO Heydrich. On full responsibility for Ic, apparent police report, "Besprechung in der Reichsfuehrung der SS," 22 December 1931, HA/28A/1773.

33. Herbert Mehlhorn, who became a PI agent in 1932, remembers that the PI was fully titled the Pressinformationsdienst des Reichstagsabgeordneten Himmler and therefore shared Himmler's immunity from police measures, 6 December 1965, "Antwort auf Aronson Fragebogen vom 20. November 1965," p. 2. By mid-January 1932, the Bavarian police had material for developing a fairly accurate breakdown of Himmler's staff—for example, VI/N 112/32 to the BayMdI, 15 January 1932, HA/28A/1773, which was forwarded to the Berlin central office and distributed throughout the Reich (Nachrichtensammelstelle, re "Referate bei der Reichsfuehrung der SS der NSDAP," n.d., BA/R-58/1151/466). The joint Roehm-Himmler-Franke order for cooperation turned up in Bavarian police files, HA/89/1849. The tendency to visualize a centralized "Nazi Intelligence Service" appears in the previously cited Nachrichtensammelstelle report of 2 March 1932 (see n. 30). For an example of the greatest police confusion, a cover letter Nr. VI/N 316/32 from the PD Muenchen to the Bay. MdI, 4 February 1932, HA/28A/1774, where the author states that direction of the intelligence services has been entrusted to Count Du Moulin by the SS-Fuehrung.

34. References to the Nawroth-Weichardt case spread through several Hauptarchiv folders, but see especially Nachrichtensammelstelle, 18 March 1932, re "Nachrichtendienst der NSDAP," HA/28A/1774, and Polizeiamt, Oldenburg, Abt. Exekutive, to PD Wilhelmshaven, 27 February 1932, HA/71/1533.

35. Schellenberg, *Memoiren*, pp. 37-38. He got the story from Himmler.

36. Aronson, *Heydrich*, p. 56.

37. See n. 33 for this and similar examples.

38. *Muenchener Post*, 24 June 1931, headline articles "Das Braune Haus der Homosexuellen," clipping in HA/28A/1773.

39. T-175/467/EAP 173-b-22-05/6 contains police records of the colorful activities of Emil Danzeisen, the head of the vigilante team. Hoehne describes the entire comedy delightfully in *The Order*, pp. 71-75.

40. PrMdI, to RMdI, 6 April 1932, imparting the results of the raids and

other investigations, Politische Archiv des Auswaertigen Amtes, Bonn, Referat D, Polizei 5, Band 2, s.Band 3 (hereafter cited as PA/Provenance/volume number/ page number, if any).

41. OSAF, Verfuegung, 31 March 1932, IIA/77/1566. It was not then dis- solved in favor of Heydrich's service but continued as a decentralized rival. Ic affairs were lumped together with various press and publicity duties under Josef Seydel on the SA staff. Der OSAF, Verfuegungen, 31.3.32 and 5.4.32, LC/ Misc.NSDAP/Container 823, folder u.

42. Letter of Bormann to Hess, 5 October 1932, HA/17/319. On Bormann's role, Joachen von Lang, *The Secretary, Martin Bormann* (New York: Random House, 1979), pp. 63, 66-68, 72. On Roehm's funding of the SD, Heydrich, *Leben*, p. 36.

43. "Bericht ueber den Ausbau der Unterabteilung Nachrichtendienst," n.d. (but by contents post–April 1932), BA/Schu 457, reveals the status of the or- ganization and its work. Gau Hessen-Nassau-Nord, "Neuorganisation nach der Dienstvorschrift vom 15. Juli 1932," indicates the date by which the elevation to Hauptabteilung status reached the *Gau* level (Hess.HStA Wiesbaden/Abt. 483/ 1254). "Information ueber den Gegner," for February 1932, HA/89/1849; for July, N.Saech.HStA Hann. 310 I/B/3 II; for August, 310 I/C/3.

44. On *Muenchener Post* exposé, see n. 12. For Werner Best on Hitler, 24 November 1974 (letter to Kahn) "Auslandsnachrichtendienst des SD," p. 3.

45. On the "Strasser era," Kissenkoetter, *Strasser*; Orlow, *Nazi Party, 1919- 1933*, pp. 256-85; Stachura, "Der Fall Strasser"; and Max H. Kele. *Nazis & Workers* (Chapel Hill: Univ. of North Carolina Press, 1972), pp. 175-76. Goebbels's only diary mention of Schumann and HAbtl. ND came on 5 October 1932, as part of a reorganization growing out of his dissatisfaction with Franke's work (see n. 9). On the move to APA, BDC/SSO Schumann, *Lebenslauf*, n.d.; and Hans-Adolf Jacobsen, *Nationalsozialistische Aussenpolitik 1933-1938* (Frankfurt a.M.: A. Metz- ner, 1968), p. 58.

46. Werner Best confirmed the results, "Beantwortung der Fragen (Aron- son) vom 3 December 1964," p. 1.

47. On PID camouflage, Heydrich, "Der Anteil der Sicherheitspolizei und des SD an den Ordnungsmassnahmen im mitteleuropaischen Raum," T-175/ 247/2738889. On the emergence of the SD, SS-Amt, 22 July 1932, to Heydrich, BDC/SSO, Heydrich, which gives the date as July 19. Several unofficial sources indicate the transformation in fact predated official orders by several weeks; for instance, see BDC/SSO, Dr. August Simon (b. 14.12.98).

48. BDC/SSO, Hans Kobelinski, Stammrollen-Auszug.

49. Himmler's concept of a *Staatsschutzkorps* was more fully developed by the mid-1930s and described to all SS- and SD-men as their mission—the model for the SS and police system. Unfortunately, there is no written evidence of the level to which this concept had developed in the early 1930s. Walter's *Geheime Maechte* (p. 41), read by Himmler in 1926, emphasized the necessity of a national police for national security and the requirement for determined and forceful political leadership over security agencies. The juxtaposition of his readings and his initial contacts with the SS implies the extent to which his thoughts on the SS and the police state system must have grown together over the next decade. Aronson cites a balanced spectrum of oral sources to trace the kernel of the *Staatsschutzkorps* concept as far back as 1932-33 (*Heydrich*, pp. 107, 134, and 169: Heydrich's wife, Freiherr v. Eberstein, and Werner Best, respectively).

50. Hoettl, *Secret Front*, pp. 21, 45; and Schellenberg, *Memoirs*, p. 21. Fest,

Face of the Reich, p. 104; Wighton, *Heydrich*, p. 48; Deschner, *Heydrich*, pp. 87-88, and apparently Buchheim, "The SS," pp. 166-67 (no sources cited), built upon such references to attribute to Heydrich a preconceived plan supported only by a he-did-it-therefore-he-planned-it argument. Aronson, *Heydrich*, p. 107. In a letter written to her parents in March 1933 when Heydrich won his first police position, Lina Heydrich indicated that he did not like such work and viewed it as temporary, *Leben*, p. 39.

3. The Weimar Police

1. John Coatman, *Police* (London: Oxford Univ. Press, 1959), pp. 78-84, and David H. Bayley, "The Police and Political Development in Europe," in Charles Tilly (ed.), *The Formation of National States in Western Europe* (Princeton: Princeton Univ. Press, 1975), provide good brief sketches of the development of the police in Germany; Raymond B. Fosdick, *European Police Systems* (New York: Patterson Smith reprint, 1969 [1915]) has a thorough study of police in the Wilhelmine era; Eugene Raible, *Geschichte der Polizei*, (Stuttgart: Richard Boorberg Verlag, 1963); Claus Kaestl, "Reich und Laenderpolizei in der Weimarer Republik", *Die Polizei* 53 (October 8, 1962): 302-5, and Horst-Adelbert Koch, "Zur Organisationsgeschichte der Deutschen Polizei, 1927-1939," *Feldgrau* 5,6 (1957-58), are good for the problems of federalism in the Republic. For a sketchy comparison of the German with other more centralized European systems, Morris Plascowe, "The Organization of the Enforcement of the Criminal Law in France, Germany and England [sic; meaning Italy]," *JCL&C* 27 (September 1936): 305-327; and Bayley. For the separate *Land* forces, Hsi-Huey Liang, *The Berlin Police Force in the Weimar Republic* (Berkeley: Univ. of California Press, 1970); Albrecht Funk, *Polizei und Rechtstaat: Die Entwicklung des staatlichen Gewaltsmonopols in Preussen, 1848-1918* (Frankfurt a.M., 1986); Siegfried Zaika, *Polizeigeschichte, Die Exekutive im Lichte der historischen Konfliktforschung* (Luebeck: Schmidt-Roemhild, 1979) for Prussia; Lothar Danner, *Ordnungspolizei Hamburg* (Hamburg: Verlag Deutsche Polizei, 1958); and Johannes Schwarze, *Die bayerische Polizei und ihre Funktion bei der Aufrechterhaltung der oeffentlichen Sicherheit in Bayern von 1919-1933* (Neue Schriftenreihe des Staatsarchivs Muenchen, 1977); and Raible for Wuerttemberg.

2. "Tableaux de Repartition des Effectifs de la Police Allemande," attached to a note from the Allied Military Committee of Versailles to the Conference of Ambassadors, 25 July 1928, *Records of the Department of State Relating to Internal Affairs of Germany, 1910-1929*, NA Microcopy 336, roll 43, folder 862.20, document 520, frames 492-93 (hereafter M-336/43/862.20/492-93); and U.S. Department of Justice, Bureau of Investigation, *Uniform Crime Reports* 1 (August 1930): 32, for statistics on American cities.

3. Gordon, *The Beer Hall Putsch*, pp. 121-24, for an example in Bavaria.

4. Juergen Siggemann, *Die kasernierte Polizei und das Problem der inneren Sicherheit in der Weimar Republik: Eine Studie zum Auf- und Ausbau des innerstaatlichen Sicherheitssystems in Deutschland 1918/19-1933* (Frankfurt a.M.: Rita G. Fischer Verlag, 1980).

5. Correspondence from the Interallied Military Commission of Control at Berlin and reports of the limitations on the police are contained in M-336/38/362.105, especially frames 68-110, and M-336/43/862.20; Kaestl, "Reich und Laenderpolizei," pp. 303-4. For insight into German arbitration with the commission and the results, Siggemann, *Kasernierte Polizei*, chap. 3; and Carl Severing, *Mein*

Lebensweg, 2 vols. (Koeln: Greven Verlag, 1950) 1:296-97, 312-17. "Tableaux de Repartition des Effectifs de la Police Allemande," M-336/43/492-93, for 1928; and Koch, "Deutsche Polizei," 0.109, for 1932 statistics on state and municipal police.

6. Overall ratio, Kaestl, "Reich und Laenderpolizei," p. 303. Berlin ratios based on Albert C. Grzesinski, *Inside Germany* (New York: E.P. Dutton, 1939), p. 124; Germany, *Statistischesreichsamt, Statistisches Jabrbuch fuer das deutsche Reich,* 1930, p. 5. Prewar ratio, Fosdick, *European Police*, p. 401. Ratios for 1935, Daluege report, "Die deutsche Polizei," BA/R-43 II/391.

7. *The Statistical History of the United States from Colonial Times to the Present* (Stamford, Conn.:, 1965), pp. 7, 77 for 1920 and 1930 (unfortunately, police statistics include privately employed policemen); for France, Etienne-Felix Guyon, *L'organisation de la police en France* (Paris: Éditions de la vie universitaire, 1923), p. 101. Contemporary statistics are based on International Police Association, *International Bibliography of Selected Police Literature* (London, 1968). On urban police: U.S., F.B.I., *Uniform Crime Reports*, 1930, 1:32; and U.S. Bureau of Census, *Statistical Abstract of the United States: 1964* and *1970* (Washington, D.C., 1964 and 1970), pp. 98-99, 151.

8. There are numerous brief histories of the early German criminal police: Frank Arnau, *Das Auge des Gesetzes, Macht und Ohnmacht der Kriminalpolizei* (Duesseldorf-Wien: Econ Verlag, 1962), pp. 50-59; Coatman, *Police*, pp. 82-84; of special interest for its interpretation, *Organisation und Meldedienst der Kriminalpolizei, Schriftenreihe der Reichskriminalpolizeiamt Berlin Nr. 1* (Berlin, 1939), T-175/451/2967014-18; and perhaps the most thorough are Wolfgang Ullrich, *Verbrechensbekaempfung, Geschichte, Organisation, Rechtsprechung* (Berlin: Luchterhand Verlag, 1961), pp. 20-165; and Manfred Teufel, "Die geschichtliche Entwicklung der Kriminalpolizei," *Das Polizeiblatt* 34 (June-July 1971): 87-92, 102-6.

9. Herbert Jacob, *German Administration since Bismark,* (New Have: Yale Univ. Press, 1963), pp. 90-91; *Reichsgesetzblatt (RGBl.)*, 1922, pp. 585-90, 593-95; records of Reich agencies are in BA/R-43 II/2689; and similar files on efforts to establish Reich agencies exist in the archives of most former *Laender* and free cities.

10. Teufel, "Die geschichtliche Entwicklung," pp. 102-3.

11. Coatman, *Police*, p. 85; Ullrich, *Verbrechensbekaempfung,* pp. 226-34; and RMdI, "Aufzeichnung ueber eine Vereinheitlichung der Kriminalpolizei und Politischen Polizei der Laender durch das Reich," 12 May 1933, T-580/94/462.

12. An excellent brief sketch of the development of political police among the German states, with special emphasis on the Hapsburg lands, can be found in the first two chapters of Donald E. Emerson, *Metternich and the Political Police* (The Hague: Martinus Nijhoff, 1968). For the Gestapo official training version of the history of the political police, "Politische Polizei," T-175/277/5487511-15.

13. Polizeirat Henning, "Das Wesen und die Entwicklung der politischen Polizei in Berlin," *Mitteilungen des Vereins fuer die Geschichte Berlins* 43 (1925): 90-91; Paul Kampfmeyer, "Die Politische Polizei," *Sozialistische Monatshefte* 35 (1929): 26-28; and Graf, *Politische Polizei*, pp. 5-6. For a tentative explanation of why political police work had little urgency in Germany prior to the late nineteenth century, Bayley, "Police and Political Development in Europe," pp. 362-64.

14. Henning, "Politischen Polizei in Berlin," pp. 90-91; and Kampfmeyer, "Politische Polizei," pp. 25-26. Both of these articles typify the effort to convince the public of the need for political police, but perhaps Bernhard Weiss, *Polizei und Politik* (Berlin, 1928) is the most famous example.

15. For more detail on the Prussian *Staatskommissariate*, Graf, *Politische Pol-*

izei, pp. 8-9. RMdI, "Denkschrift ueber Organisation des Reichskriminalpolizeiamts," under a cover letter of 28 March 1923, pp. 32-33, BA/R-43 I/2689/53; and RMdI to "saemtliche Landesregierungen mit Ausnahme von Preussen," 12 May 1920, StA Detmold, L 75/IV/7/2.II. On Prussian resistance, RMdI to Reichskanzler, 10 November 1920, BA/R-43 I/2689/27-29.

16. Some of the initial efforts of the commissioner survive in records of a meeting with representatives from Bremen, Luebeck, and Hamburg, "Bericht ueber die Besprechung in Hamburg am 21.6.1921, den Nachrichtendienst betreffend," StA Bremen, 3-P.1.a. Nr. 1141. Vertretung der Reichsregierung Muenchen to Reichskanzlei, 15 April 1923, BA/R-43 I/2689/58. For a brief analysis, Ilse Maurer and Udo Wengst (eds.), *Staat und NSDAP, 1930-1932: Quellen zur Aera Bruening* (Duesseldorf: Droste Verlag, 1977), pp. xiv-xvii.

17. "Die Politische Polizei" in Berichtsformen, dated Breslau, 14-25 June 1930, Polizei Institut Hiltrup, PG 4-23-7 PR, pp. 1-11; *MBlPriV.,* 1928, 1198-1201. For details on the evolution of the Prussian system, Graf, *Politische Polizei,* pp. 11-15.

18. Shlomo Aronson, *Beginnings of the Gestapo System: The Bavarian Model in 1933* (Jerusalem: Israel Univ. Press, 1969), pp. 1-2; and James H. McGee, "The Political Police in Bavaria, 1919-1936," unpublished doctoral dissertation, University of Florida, 1980.

19. Grzesinski, *Inside Germany,* pp. 124, 257. "Geschichte der schaumburg-lippischen Polizei seit Beginn des 19. Jahrhunderts," N.Saech.StA Bucheburg, L4/9191/4b. Kurt Daluege, "Die deutsche Polizei," under cover letter of November 1935, BA/R-43 II/391.

20. BA/R-58/212 contains a material on a Nachrichtenkonferenz held in Berlin, 28-29 April 1930, at which the work of the new central office was described; see also Maurer and Wengst, *Staat und NSDAP,* pp. xvi and 13-51.

21. T-175/R589/EAP 173-b-16-18/40 covers the establishment of I^4; see especially correspondence from Severing (II 1000/38) to Prussian offices, 11 November 1931, frames 62-65; and Groener to non-Prussian state governments, 18 January 1932, frame 76. Correspondence of LKPA (I), 10 January 1932, BA/R-58/669; 21 April 1932, T-175/357/2867425-26; and 24 October 1932 and subsequently, BA/R-58/423, illustrate the problems faced by I^4.

4. Plans, Preparations, Penetrations

1. One complete record of such early plans for the police is a *Denkschrift,* November 1931 ("Geschrieben unter der Regierung Bruening fuer den Reichsorganisationsleiter I der NSDAP"), based on conferences between its author, the Leiter der Mecklenb.-Schwerinschen Landespolizei, a.D., Petri, and Gregor Strasser, BA/R-18 (Rep. 320)/104/7-39 (hereafter Petri *Denkschrift*).

2. The few relevant passages in *Mein Kampf* (Boston, 1962) are pp. 367-68, 391-94, 402, 534-35, 537-38.

3. Since little scholarly attention has been devoted to the SA's attitude toward the police, this is basically an impressionistic interpretation based on such as the following. SA-man Wilfred Bade's (*Die S.A. erobert Berlin: Ein Tatsachen Bericht,* Munich, 1933, p. 201) reference to their "war" against the police is a typical attitude. Nazi Old Fighter hostility against policemen is exemplified in Wilhelm Kube's letter to Reichsgeschaeftsfuehrer Bouhler, 4 November 1930, protesting preferential treatment for former policemen in the SA, which was, in

turn, illustrative of the other side of the ambivalence (HA/77/1565). The PrMdI
report of 6 April 1932 on evidence gathered in raids on Nazi headquarters shows
the extent of SA work vis-à-vis the police in preparation for a coup (TA/Kel.D/
Po 5/Bd.2, sBd.3).

4. Orlow, *Nazi Party, 1933-1945*, pp. 7, 12-14.

5. Gordon, *Beer Hall Putsch*, pp. 261, 303-305; McGee, "Political Police in
Bavaria," pp. 31, 41-43, 51-54, 154, 159-61. "Personal Data and Career History
of Dr. Wilhelm Frick" (summary of interrogation, 6 September 1945) and interrogation of 1 October 1945, a.m., pp. 2-8, 19-20, NA/RG 238; and Hitler, *Mein
Kampf*, pp. 367-68.

6. Kaestl, "Reich und Laenderpolizei in der Weimarer Republik," p. 304;
for Severing's attitude, *Mein Lebensweg*, 2:229-30; Hitler's attitude was expressed
in a personal letter of 2 February 1930, published in Fritz Dickmann, "Die Regierungsbildung in Thueringen als Modell der Machtergreifung," *VfZ*, 14
(1966): 460-64.

7. Hitler letter, p. 461.

8. A remark by Frick to pro-Nazi representatives of the Saxon Policeman's
League quoted in SPB letter to Strasser, 12 June 1932, BA/Schu 456. See also
RMdI, re "Politik in der Schutzpolizei," 17 June 1933, in which he supports
Goering's similar position on the limitations of the role of Party organizations
in the police, StA. Hambg., Senatskommission fuer Reichs- und auswaertige
Angelegenheiten III B 1 Fasc. la Bd. VI, reprinted in Timpke, *Gleichschaltung
Hamburg*, p. 191.

9. "Der Nationalsozialismus in der hamburgischen Polizei," *VB*, 14 October 1932.

10. As examples, see correspondence from Ortsgruppe Gross-Essen of the
ehem. Polizeibeamter Preussens, 21 July 1931, HA/28A/1774; and Nationale Ar-
beitsgemeinschaft, Gruppe Dresden, 25 July 1932, BA/Schu 456.

11. By 1932, Nazi success with discharged policemen concerned the KPD
AM-Command, *Information Nr. 6*, T-175/357/2867576-77.

12. Ehem. Polizeibeamter Preussens, Ortsgruppe Gross-Essens, 21 July
1931, HA/28A/1774. On Himmler's travels, PD Muenchen, to StMdI Muenchen,
re NSDAP and Polizei, 19 September 1931, HA/28A/1774.

13. BDC/SSO and NSDAP files, Paul Scharfe (b. 6.9.76),.

14. Aside from Scharfe's BDC/SSO file, there are four documents in HA/
77/1565 providing insight into Ig: 18.11.31, Ig re "Offizierssaebel bei der Preuss.
Schutzpolizei"; 27.11.31, Ig re "den ehemaligen Kommandeur der Berliner
Schutzpolizei Kaupisch"; 9 March 1932, Ig to "die NS Korrespondenz"; and
22.3.32, RFSS to SS Abschnitt IV. HA/28A/1773 contains typed reports, apparently of a police spy, dated Munich, 1 October 1931. One report is on Scharfe's
appointment.

15. Cf. BDC/SSO Scharfe with SSO Heydrich. SSO Erwin Schulz (b.
27.11.00), a political police officer in the Nachrichtenstelle Bremen; he had had
clandestine contact with the SS since early 1931, but did not become a member
of the SD until 1935, when it became the official holding organization for SS
men in the Gestapo. SSO Dr. Wilhelm Harster (b. 21.7.04) of the Stuttgart Political
Police; he was drawn into the SS in 1933 but not transferred to the SD until 1935.
SSO Christian Sachs (b. 3.8.03); this SS-man was even in Heydrich's BPP without
being drawn into the SD until at least 1935. Cf. SSO Dr. Emanuel Schaefer (b.
20.4.00), who became head of the Political Police in Breslau in early 1933; although

he immediately established clandestine contact with the SD, he did not join until 1936.

16. Ig, "die NS Korrespondenz," 9 March 1932; and Ig re "Offizierssaebel bei der Preuss. Schutzpolizei." 18.11.31; HA/77/1565.

17. Summarized in Tonnis Hunhold, *Polizei in der Reform, Was Staatsbuerger und Polizei von einander erwarten koennten* (Duesseldorf & Vienna: Econ Verlag, 1968), pp. 25-33.

18. For example, McGee, "Political Police in Bavaria" (1980); Siggemann, *Kasernierte Polizei* (1980); and Graf, *Politische Polizei* (1983).

19. Examples of political police analyses of the Nazi threat are "Ueber die Entwicklung der Nationalsozialistischen Deutschen Arbiterpartei seit Anfang 1929" by RR Kuntze, BA/R-58/212; "Kann ein Nationalsozialist Polizeibeamter sein?" under cover letter of RMdI, 3 June 1930, BA/R-58/1150; and "Denkschrift des Preussischen Polizeiinstituts ueber Kampfvorbereitung und Kampfgrund-saetze radikaler Organisationen," early December 1931, BA/R-134/59, excerpts in Maurer and Wengst, *Staat und NSDAP*, especially pp. 234-35, analyzing the SS as more reliable than the SA, indicating strong police and military sympathy for the NS Movement, and mentioning police plans based on assumed SA support against a Communist uprising. On attitudes about I^4, see the correspondence in T-175/368/2881206-8, 2881825; and T-175/R589/71-75. "Generaleubersicht ueber die staatsfeindliche Zersetzungstaetigkeit in Reichswehr und Schutzpolizei in der Zeit vom 1. Januar bis zum 30. Juni 1932," T-175/R589/78-79. Even left-liberal political leaders, who were acutely aware of the NS threat, were frustrated in their efforts to reveal that threat by their own inability to describe it in terms other than criminal putsch activities; for example, "Staatsamt fuer auswaertige Angelegenheiten Nr. 10698 in das RMdI," 8 December 1932, StA. Hambg., Senatskomm. f. Reichs- und auswaertige Angelegenheiten VI B 1 Fasc. 11, printed in Timpke, *Gleichschaltung Hamburg*, pp. 181-90. See also Graf, *Politische Polizei*, pp. 29-48.

20. On the Papen coup, Graf, *Politische Polizei*, pp. 29-91; much the same argument was made earlier by Koehler, "Crisis in the Prussian Schutzpolizei."

21. For some changes in the decrees prohibiting Nazi membership for policemen: Runderlass of the PrMdI, 29 July 1932, *MBliV.*, p. 773; "Verbot der Mitgliedschaft von Polizeibeamten zur N.S.D.A.P. in Hessen aufgehoben," *VB*, 7 October 1932. "Uebersicht . . . vom. 1.10-31.12.32," T-175/R589/107-118. For insight into the efforts of most *Laender* to forbid NS in the police and how the shift of mood in the RMdI undermined such efforts, "Staatsamt fuer auswaertige Angelegenheiten," Nr.10698 to RMdI, 8 December 1932. On Schnitzler, see Gestapa IB to Reg.viz.Praes.Egidi, 17 March 1934 and subsequent documents, GStA/Rep.90, Abt.P/Nr.5/pp. 10-15.

22. James M. Diehl, *Paramilitary Politics in Weimar Germany*, (Bloomington: Indiana Univ. Press, 1977); on SA tactics in particular, Bessel, *Political Violence*.

5. Prussian Beginnings

1. Papen's version, *Memoirs* (1953), pp. 293-95.

2. Stefan Martens, "Hermann Goering: Der 'Zweite Mann' im Dritten Reich?" *Francia* 12 (1984): 478.

3. Perhaps the first scholarly versions of these developments were Hans

Buchheim, "Die organisatorische Entwicklung der politischen Polizei in Deutschland in den Jahren 1933 und 1934," *Gutachten des Institut fuer Zeitgeschichte* 1 (1958): 294-307; and Karl D. Bracher, Wolfgang Sauer, und Gerhard Schulz, *Die nationalsozialistische Machtergreifung* (1962), especially Schulz's Part Two. More journalistic versions, most recently Hoehne, *The Order*, chap. 5, must be handled cautiously because of untested reliance on sources like Diels, Gisevius, Lina Heydrich, and Orb. The more scholarly, detailed, and accurate account came with Aronson, *Heydrich*, chap. 3, extensively supplemented by Graf, *Politische Polizei*, chap. 4.

4. A clear statement of Goering's views on the police as an instrument of his legitimate state authority and of the limited role he saw in the police for NS organizations in RdErl.d.PrMdI, Nr. 24/33. 4 May 1933, StA Hamburg, Senatskommission fuer Reichs- und auswaertige Angelegenheiten VI B 1 Fasc.la, Bd.VI., printed in Timpke, *Gleichschaltung Hamburg*, pp. 192-94. R.J. Overy, *Goering: The Iron Man* (London: Routledge & Kegan Paul, 1984), describes Goering as radical and revolutionary, but his classification is not based on a comparison with more radically revolutionary Nazis. His description (as on pp. 12-21) is largely consistent with that in this text. See n. 12. Graf's interpretation of Goering's and others' contributions to the ultimate SS and police system as part of a coordinated and intentional building process overemphasizes commonly held goals at the expense of equally significant differences.

5. Goering testimony, *IMT*, 9:255.

6. Graf, *Politische Polizei*, pp. 111-20; and Jacob, *German Administration*, pp. 129-31.

7. For some of the political intricacies of personnel appointments in Prussia, especially in 1933, Orlow, *Nazi Party, 1933-1945*, pp. 35-36. For specific examples, Gauleitung Pommern to Daluege, 4 February 1933, T-580/223/75; and SA der NSDAP, der Gruppenfuehrer Schlesien an Gruppenfuehrer Krueger, Berlin, 26 February 1933, BDC/SSO Friedrich W. Kruger. Cf. Graf, *Politische Polizei*, pp. 111-20, for a different emphasis, but also for examples that lend themselves equally to this interpretation.

8. Graf, *Polizei*, pp. 112-16, especially for details on Daluege's role.

9. Martin Brozat, "The Concentration Camps, 1933-45," in Krausnick et al, *Anatomy*, pp. 400-401, and Graf, *Politische Polizei*, pp. 254-59, provide analyses of background and development of Schutzhaft, especially in Prussia.

10. Graf, *Polizei*, pp. 259-63. The text of the *Verordnung des Reichspraesident* of 28 February 1933 can be found in *RGBl.*, 1933, I:183; and the Prussian *Verordnungen* of 2 and 3 March in *Pr.GS.*, 1933, pp. 33; and *MBliV.*, 1933, 1:233.

11. Unpublished *Verordnung* of 22 February 1933, "Einberufung und Verwendung von Hilfspolizei," Nr. 40/33 with attachment; and OSAF re "Einberufung und Verwendung von Hilfospolizei in Preussen," 27 February 1933, BA/Schu 267.

12. On the Hilfspolizei and its reign of terror, Bracher, Sauer, Schulz, *Machtergreifung*, pp. 438-42, 468-69, 866-75.

13. Aronson's masterly analysis of the distinctions between Goering's early Gestapo as an instrument of the state authority and Himmler's SS-police is delineated in *Heydrich*, chaps. 3 and 4, and will be elaborated on in the following pages. See also Diels, *Lucifer ante Portas*, p. 168.

14. BDC/SSO Rudolf Diels (b. 16.12.00); and Graf, *Politische Polizei*, pp. 318-19.

15. Graf, pp. 51-64, 103-106, 319; BDC/SSO Diels; Franz von Papen, *Vom*

Scheitern einer Demokratie, 1930-1933 (Mainz: Hese & Koehler Verlag, 1968), p. 233; and Walter Hofer et al, *Der Reichstagsbrand* (Munich: K.G. Sauer, 1978), 2: 20-26. Heiden, *Der Fuehrer*, pp. 471-72; Koehler, *Inside the Gestapo*, pp. 14-15 (who even claims Diels was the key intermediary between Papen and Hitler); and, if one can overlook his penchant for manufacturing sensational quotations, Willi Frischauer, *The Rise and Fall of Hermann Goering* (London: Odhams Press, 1950) is useful for his access to some of the inside stories that are part of the "history" of any organization. For Diels's version, *Lucifer ant Portas*, pp. 13, 106, 129-31, 289-90.

16. Goering testimony, *IMT*, 9:256.

17. Guenter Plum, "Staatspolizei und innere Verwaltung, 1934-1936," *VfZ*, 13:191, n.3, has set the acquisition of IA as prior to 17 February. On 24 February a directive from Grauert established the LKP-Amt fuer die politische Polizei as the political intelligence center for Prussia and announced its pending removal from the Polizeipraesidium and direct subordination to the PrMdI, NSaech.HStA Hannover, 122a/VIII/430. Graf, *Politische Polizei*, pp. 120-22.

18. Plum, "Staatspolizei," p. 192.

19. BDC/SSO Arthur Nebe (b. 13.11.94).

20. (Goering) Der PrMdI, 21 February 1933, ordered a purge (BA/Schu 465); cf. Gritzbach, *Goering*, pp. 33-35; and Goering testimony, *IMT*, 9:256, 414. On choices in personnel, Diels, *Lucifer ante Portas*, pp. 123-25; and Gisevius, *Bis zum Bittern Ende*, 1:56-57; and cf. Hofer, *Reichstagsbrand*, 2:34-45; and Graf, *Politische Polizei*, pp. 110-21, 169-88 for the first thorough analysis of early Gestapo personnel.

21. Gesetz ueber die Errichtung eines Geheimen Staatspolizeiamts, 26 April 1933, *PrGS*, 1933, pp. 122-23; and Neuorganisation der politischen Polizei, RdErl 26 April 1933, *MBliV*, 1933, 1:503-507.

22. Diels, *Lucifer ante Portas*, p. 169.

23. RdErl 26 April 1933, MBliV, 503. Emphasis added.

24. Aronson, *Heydrich*, p. 175 for chart of SSt as of 1 February 1934. Wolf Heinrich Graf von Helldorf for Potsdam, *Fuenftausend Koepfe*, pp. 186-187,; Paul Hinkler for Altona, ibid., p. 199; Adolf Kob for Koenigsberg, ibid., pp. 239-40; Fritz von Pfeffer for Kassel, BDC/Mappe Polizei/SSt Lists, 1935; Otto Brien for Koeslin, Thevoz, *Pommern 1934/35*, 1:21, 284; Fritz-Karl Engel for Stettin, ibid., p. 286-87; Dr. Joachim Hoffman for Stettin, ibid., p. 225; BDC/SSO Emil Apel (b. 20.1.76) for Koblenz; SSO Hermann Heerdt (b. 31.12.00) for Frankfurt a.M.; SSO Rudolf Loeffel (b. 6.7.87) for Schneidemuehl; SSO Wilhelm Markotzke (b. 16.8.97) for Elbing; NS Hans Moebus (b. 5.10.95) for Frankfurt Oder; SSO Hans Nockemann (b. 16.11.03) for Aachen; SSO Dr. Emanuel Schaefer (b. 26.4.00); Theodor Bilo for Wilhelmshaven, *KDAL*, 1935, p. 86; and on Karl Draeger, apparently first appointee for Frankfurt a.M., *KDAL*, pp. 46, 74, and Hess.HStA Wiesbaden, 483/714.

25. The police role in fomenting the Red scare, Hofer, *Reichstagsbrand*, 2:53, 337-41. Their preparedness for action and plans to expand arrest powers (pp. 47-52) were appropriate given their fears, however, and do not *prove* that the fire was the preplanned pretext. Diels's version (*Lucifer*, pp. 51-52, 131, 136-52) conforms mostly with the evidence; for example, Pr.MdI an Kommissar z.b.V., Daluege, 28 February 1933, BDC/SSO Diels, warns of imminent Communist action, as though they had convinced each other, at least momentarily, of a real threat.

26. Graf, *Politische Polizei*, pp. 255-84, summarizes the early evolution of

Schutzhaft and the camps; Daluege to Diels, 27 March and 4 April 1933, BDC/ SSO Diels, provides insight into their cooperation and goals.

27. Goering's justifications for this phase of his life can be studied in his contemporary speeches, his own book, such sources as Gritzbach, *Goering*, pp. 35-39, for example, and his testimony, *IMT*, 9:255-61. Diels's constant clashes with Daluege are a major theme of *Lucifer ante Portas*.

28. The most thorough, although unfortunately undocumented, history of the Forschungsamt is in D.C. Watt's introduction to David Irving (ed.), *Breach of Security* (London: William Kimber, 1968), pp. 15-22. David Kahn, *Hitler's Spies* (New York: Macmillan, 1978), p. 55, uncovered the complex status of the For-schungsamt. Graf, *Politische Polizei*, p. 298, on Gestapo personnel taken into Forschungsamt.

29. BDC/SSO Kobelinski.

30. Fragments of the records of Sonderabteilung Daluege are widely scat-tered, one example being BA/Schu 278; and for an example of Daluege's use of this agency in his work with Diels, Daluege to Diels, 27 March 1933, BDC/SSO Diels.

31. Aronson, *Heydrich*, pp. 80, 107, n. 94; but cf. Lina Heydrich, *Leben*, pp. 37-38. On Daluege-Heydrich cooperation, SDdRFSS an RFSS, 3 February 1933, re RGO-Streikversammlung, Berlin, T-580/223/75. Some allege that at this time Heydrich and Daluege engineered the Reichstag fire: Hofer, *Reichstagsbrandt*, 2: 243-45, 361-62, 400, 403; and Calic, *Heydrich*, pp. 82-107. See chap. 8, n. 5. Hey-drich's parting shot at Daluege, March 5, 1933 (BDC/SSO Heydrich). Hofer's dismissal of this note as manufactured to cover Heydrich's involvement makes no sense, since it would provide him with no alibi for February 27. Lina Hey-drich's often cited story that Heydrich fled Berlin at this point because Goering threatened to have the Gestapo arrest him (Hoehne, *The Order*, p. 77) seems questionable. Her confusion over the timing of the order becomes apparent in her book (*Leben*, pp. 44-45), where she also dates the order as following the birth of their first son, 17 June 1933. Since the latter date should have been more prominent in her mind, the order probably belongs to the summer months. Diels's only reference to such an arrest order also indicates a later date (*Lucifer ante Portas*, p. 236).

32. PrMdI, "Ergaenzende Durchfuehrungsbestimmungen," 21 April 1933, p. 3, T-580/97/467.

33. PrMdI, re Hilfspolizei, 7 June 1933, BA/Schu 267.

6. Himmler in Bavaria

1. On the complexities of the seizure of power in Bavaria, Peterson, *Limits of Hitler's Power*, pp. 157-66; Pridham, *Hitler's Rise to Power*; Falk Wiesemann, *Die Vorgeschichte der nationalsozialistischen Machtuebernahme in Bayern 1932/1933* (Ber-lin: Duncker & Humblot, 1975); and Ortwin Domroese, *Der NS-Staat in Bayern von der Machtergreifung bis zum Roehm-Putsch* (Munich: R. Woelfle, 1974).

2. Praesidium des Bayr. Regierung von Oberfranken und Mittelfranken to das StMdI, re Politische Polizei, 17 February 1933, HA/28A/1774.

3. Weisemann, *Vorgeschichte . . . in Bayern*, pp. 204-5.

4. Aronson, *Beginnings*, pp. 1-2, previously the definitive study of the es-tablishment of the BPP and the closely related SS concentration camp, Dachau; James H. McGee, "The Political Police in Bavaria, 1919-1936," unpublished doc-

toral dissertation, University of Florida, 1980, has now replaced Aronson as the in-depth study of the BPP in its Weimar era origins. See also Domroese, *NS-Staat in Bayern*, for a more general overview.

5. On relations between PD Muenchen and PD Nuernberg-Fuerth, PD Nuernberg-Fuerth to PP, LKPA (I) Berlin, "Bekaempfung der staatsfeindlichen Zersetzungstaetigkeit in Reichswehr und Polizei," 16 January 1933, BA/R-58/670. StMdI to saemtl. Min., 26 March 1933, ByHStA, Abt.II, Akten Siebert. McGee, "Political Police in Bavaria," pp. 205-9, 256-57.

6. Lina Heydrich, *Leben*, pp. 39-40, 45, including the text of a letter she wrote to her parents on 13 March 1933, indicating Heydrich's attitude and the move to Berlin.

7. OSAF, re "Sonderkommissare in Bayern," 20 March 1933, T-580/49/272, elaborating earlier orders of 12 and 14 March; and StMdI, re "Sonderkommissare in Bayern," 18 March 1933, T-580/49/272, in which Wagner gave governmental sanction to Roehm's orders.

8. Himmler had been using SA and SS as auxiliaries from the very beginning, and as early as 12 March, he announced his intentions to make then official, "Unterredung mit dem Muenchener Polizeipraesidenten . . . ," *VB*, 13 March 1933. Der Kom.StMdByIM, "Einberufung und Verwendung von Hilfspolizei in Bayern," 27 March 1933, BA/Schu 267.

9. Aronson, *Beginnings*, pp. 13-14; OSAF, re "Sonderkommissare in Bayern," 31 March 1933, T-580/49/272, as a counterbalance to Wagner's order, commanded the Sonderkommissare to assert themselves.

10. Copy in message form of KfdByStMdI to ByPD and Staatspolizeiaemter, 15 March 1933, BA/Schu 267.

11. AO des StMdI, 1 April 1933, T-580/107/Ordner 17.

12. Ibid.; and Aronson, *Beginnings*, pp. 12, 18-21. Bavaria was not among the early, desperate supplicants for Reich support of its KL (Saechs.Md auswaertige Angelegenheiten to RMdI, 5 April 1933; and RMdI re "Schutzhaft," 13 May 1933, StA Hambg., Finanzdeputation IV/II C 5a II A 7bb, and Senatskommission f.R-u. auswaertige Angelegenheiten I A 1a 14, Bd.IV, printed in Timpke, *Gleichschaltung Hamburg*, pp. 239-44).

13. Aronson, *Beginnings*, p. 13; Peterson, *Limits*, pp. 239-46; E.G. Reiche, "From 'Spontaneous' to Legal Terror: SA, Police, and the Judiciary in Nuernberg, 1933-34," *European Studies Review* 9 (1979): pp. 237-64; and "Der neue Polizeipraesident uebernimmt sein Amt," *VB*, 15/16/17 April 1933.

14. Hans-Guenther Ricardi, *Schule der Gewalt: Die Anfaenge des Konzentrationslager Dachau, 1933-34* (Munich: Verlag C.H. Beck, 1983), pp. 36-37, 44-56.

15. Niederschrift, Ministerratssitzung vom 7. April 1933, p. 11, ByHStA, Abt.II, MA 99-525; and der StKfdMdI an den StKfdMdJ, Frank, 13 March 1933, T-580/49/271.

16. OSAF re "Sonderkommissare in Bayern," 31 March 1933, T-580/49/272, reinforced the sharp delimitation between Sicherheits and politische Hilfspolizei and ordered the careful management of conflicts. Presumably this extended to the camps for political prisoners.

17. Domroese, *NS-Staat in Bayern*, pp. 36-38; Peterson, *Limits*, p. 167; Pridham, *Hitler's Rise*, pp. 134-35; and Niederschrift, Ministerratssitzung vom 7 April 1933, p. 11, ByHStA, Abt.II, MA 99-525.

18. Broszat, "Concentration Camps," pp. 429-30; Ricardi, *Schule der Gewalt*, pp. 88-113.

19. Broszat, "Concentration Camps," p. 431; Aronson, *Beginnings*, pp. 21-

22; and Charles W. Sydner, *Soldiers of Destruction: The SS Death's Head Division, 1933-1945* (Princeton: Princeton Univ. Press, 1977), pp. 3-9.

20. Aronson (*Beginnings*, pp. 28-32) successfully established the real relationship between Heydrich and the camps.

21. Ibid., pp. 29-30.
22. Domroese, *NS-Staat in Bayern*, pp. 133-53; Peterson, *Limits*, pp. 160-68; for example, RKfBy, re *Verbot von Eigenmaechtigkeiten*, 8 April 1933, T-580/49/272.
23. Peterson, *Limits*, pp. 165-79.
24. Ibid., pp. 160, 163-79.
25. Ibid., pp. 166-67; and Aronson, *Beginnings*, pp. 10-14.
26. "Gutachten ueber die Zulaessigkeit der verwaltungsgerichtlichen Nachpruefung staatspolizeilicher Massnahmen in der Ostmark," p. 4, BDC/Schu 464; and Pridham, *Hitler's Rise*, p. 314.
27. Aronson *Beginnings*, pp. 47-48.
28. Ibid., p. 29; and Peterson, *Limits*, p. 168. For an example, Niederschrift, "Ministerratssitzung vom 16 Mai 1933," ByHStA, Abt.II, MA 99-525.
29. StMdI Wagner to PPK Bayern, re "Schutzhaft," 17 May and 22 May 1933, T-580/107/Ordner 17.
30. Peterson, *Limits*, p. 172.
31. Ibid., pp. 174-75; Aronson, *Beginnings*, pp. 13-14 and see Niederschrift, n. 28.
32. Aronson, *Beginnings*, pp. 16-17.
33. "Ministerratssitzung vom 26 July 1933," p. 3, T-580/49/272.
34. Peterson, *Limit*, p. 176, referring to an October 20 debate in a special meeting of the government commissars.
35. Aronson, *Beginnings*, p. 32, describes how Heinrich Mueller of the BPP was already applying this logic as early as March to quash exposures of concentration camp conditions.
36. Ibid., pp. 38-40 on the case of the priests, and Heydrich's techniques.
37. The history of these cases is related in Aronson, pp. 48-52; Broszat, "Concentration Camps," p. 414; and Ricardi, *Schule der Gewalt*, pp. 192-93, 209-19. On determination to control the BPP, Niederschrift, "Ministerratssitzung vom 21 November 1933," pp. 11-12, ByHStA, Abt.II MA 99-525.

7. The Vortex of Intrigue

1. Frick's earliest pressures applied to the pre-*gleichgeschaltet Laender* are described in Bracher, Sauer, Schulz, *Machtergreifung*, p. 428. Within the first week of power, the author of the Petri Denkschrift (see chap. 4, n. 1), submitted his plans to Frick, Ld.Mechlenb.-Schwerinschen Lapo a.D. to RMdI, 7 February 1933, BA/R-18/104/1-5. A similar proposal, "Denkschrift ueber die Vereinheitlichung der Polizei," was forwarded by Reg.Praes. Bachmann from Thueringen in April. Cover letters Thuer.MdI to RMdI, 20 April 1933, ibid., pp. 43-77 (hereafter Bachmann Denkschrift).

2. Extensive analysis of Frick's program and methods can be found in Bracher, Sauer, Schulz, *Machtergreifung*; David Schoenbaum, *Hitler's Social Revolution* (Garden City, N.Y.: Doubleday, 1966), especially pp. 195-98; Peterson, *Limits*, chap. 2; and Jane Caplan, "The Politics of Administration: The Reich Interior Ministry and the German Civil Service, 1933-1943," *The Historical Journal*, 20 (1977): pp. 707-36; and "Bureaucracy, Politics and the National Socialist State,"

in Peter D. Stachura (ed.), *The Shaping of the Nazi State* (London: Croom Helm, 1978), pp. 234-56. Gisevius, *Bis zum bittern Ende*, 1, is an apologetic but useful account of the failure of right opposition to coordinate well with Frick before it was too late.

3. Caplan, "Politics of Administration," pp. 719-24.

4. RMdI, re Schutzhaft, 13 May 1933, StA Hambg., Senatskommission f. Reichs- u. auswaertige Angelegenheiten IA la 14 Bd.IV, printed in Timpke, *Gleichschaltung Hamburg*, pp. 242-44; and Niederschrift, "Polizeibesprechung im RMdI am 11. Mai 1933," NSaechStA Bueckabg., L4/12525.

5. Niederschrift, 11 May 1933. Petri and Bachmann had included Goering when submitting their proposals for Reich centralization (see n. 1). RMdI to Herrn PrMdI, 12 May 1933, T-580/94/462:.

6. RMdI to P.MdI, 12 May 1933.

7. Daluege began correspondence with Frick about Reich centralization on the very date the Goering received Frick's letter, Zipfel, "Gestapo und SD in Berlin," p. 269, n. 19, citing Schriftwechsel Frick-Daluege, BDC. Unfortunately this author and others have failed to relocate this correspondence, Graf, *Politische Polizei*, p. 158, n. 139. On the Reich-wide activities of the Gestapo as a base for Goering's aspirations, ibid., pp. 166-68. Diels, *Lucifer ante Portas*, p. 246.

8. RMdI to Herrn PrMdI, "Aufzeichnung ueber eine Vereinheitlichung der Kriminalpolizei und politischen Polizei der Laender durch das Reich," 24 May 1933; and Goering to MR Fischer, 6 June 1933, T-580/94/462. Versammlung d.RStH beim Reichskanzler, 6 July 1933, ByHStA/Abt II/Epp 148. Unfortunately Epp's notations are vague and Goering's position is not clear, but a strong position of opposition would surely have been noted.

9. See n. 7.

10. Beantwortung des Fragebogens (Aronson), B.1.

11. Fried. Krupp Aktiengesellschaft, Friedrich-Alfred-Huette Direktion to Grauert, 6 July 1933, refers to previous concerns expressed in February over the powerlessness of the regular police against Communist sabotage, GStA/77/28/13.

12. On the Adolf-Hitler-Spende, see Arthur Schweitzer, "Business Power in the Nazi Regime," *Zeitschrift fuer Nationaloekonomie* 20 (October 1960): pp. 436-39.

13. Ernst Poensgen to Graf Schimmelmann, 13 June 1933; Schimmelmann to Poensgen, 16 June; and Poensgen to Schimmelmann, 21 June GStA/77/15.

14. Poensgen to Schimmelmann, 13 and 21 June 1933, GStA/77/15; and on Poensgen, Erich Stockhorst, *Funftausend Koepfe* (Blick + Bild Verlag, 1967), p. 327. For other examples of Daluege's collections, Nachlasse Daluege, T-580/229/107-109, Firmenspenden fuer die SS, 1933-34.

15. Poensgen to Schimmelmann, 13 June; and Schimmelmann to Poensgen 16 June, 1933, GStA/77/15.

16. Letters, Poensgen to Grauert and Schimmelmann, 21 June 1933, GStA/77/15.

17. Gauleiter Hessen-Nassau-Sued to the Oberste Leitung der P.O., 10 May 1933, BA/Schu 465.

18. Orlow, pp. 61-66, 70-75; and Klein, *Germany's Economic Preparations*, pp. 35-36.

19. Peterson, *Limits*, p. 90, citing BA/R-43 I/1461,391. Other copies of Frick's proposal have survived in the files of the Foreign Office, where he was seeking von Neurath's support, PA/Ref.D/Po 5 N.E. Nr. 10/Bd.1.

20. AA to RMdI, 15 May 1933, with note by Neurath of 9 May, PA/S-17/ Bd.1; and "Die Hilfspolizei in Genf," V.B., 31 May 1933. RMdI to ByStMdI, re "Hilfspolizei," 12 May; and StSek i d Reichskanzlei to Epp 25 May BA/R-43 II/ 395/20-21.

21. Testimony of Paul Korner, IMT, 9:149-50.

22. Diels, Lucifer ante Portas, pp. 190-93; and Reitlinger, SS, p. 47.

23. Graf, Politische Polizei, pp. 195-208, 269-84.

24. This may explain Gisevius's rather confused references to the "field police" and Goering's use of them, To the Bitter End, pp. 114-15.

25. RdErl.d.PrMdI, 4 May 1933, StA Hambg., Senatskommission f. Reichs- u. auswaertige Angelegenheiten, VI B1 Fasc.la Bd.VI, printed in Timpke, Gleich-schaltung Hamburg, pp. 192-94. "SA., S.S. und Schutzpolizei," V.B., 13/14 May 1933.

26. PrMdI, re "Hilfspolizei," 21 April 1933, T-580/97/467; and 7 June 1933, BA/Schu 267.

27. Daluege to Diels, 4 April 1933, BDC/PK Diels.

28. Diels, Lucifer ante Portas, pp. 189-90.

29. Diels to Daluege, 26 June 1933, T-580/94/462.

30. BDC/SSO Diels. The exact dates of Diels's honorary entry into the SS and his promotion are obscured by typical personnel file contradictions. Diels claims it occurred in October, after Daluege's raid on his home, Lucifer ante Portas, p. 238.

31. RdErl.d.MdI, "Aufloesung der Hilfspolizei," BA/Schu 267. On 13 July (RMdI, IA 5001/9.6), Frick had already called for the end or the severe curtailment of Hilfspolizei and required further justification for continued Reich supplements after August 15, Staatsamt f. auswaertige Angelegenheiten to RMdI, re "Kosten fuer die Hilfspolizei," 19 July 1933, StA Hambg., Senatskommission f. Reichs- u. auswaertige Angelegenheiten, VI B1 Fasc. la Bd.VI, printed in Timpke, Gleich-schaltung Hamburg, pp. 212-13.

32. PrMdI, 25 September 1933, with "Geschaeftsanweisung fuer die Leitung der Konzentrationslager," GStA/90, Abt.P/104/90-91b; PrMdI, re "Vollstreckung der Schutzhaft," 14 October 1933, T-580/49/271; and AA/Ref.D 4798 to alle Be-rufsvertretungen, 20 September 1933 with "Uebersicht ueber die Zahl der am 31.Juli 1933 in Schutzhaft befindlichen Personen," NA/RG-238/NG-093.

33. OSAF ordered a complete severance of the SA from the auxiliaries; SA members could serve only as individuals, not in uniform or as SA units, Bericht of a Police Captain Timm to Polizeiherrn, Hamburg, 24 August 1933, StA Hambg., Inn. Verwaltung A III 1b, printed in Timpke, Gleichschaltung Hamburg, pp. 214-16. OSAF, re "Feldjaegerkorps in Preussen," 7 October; PrMdI re "Auf-stellung eines Feldjaegerkorps in Preussen," 13 October, GStA/90, Abt.P/197/7-11; and Anlage I zur Staatssekretaerbesprechung am 7.9.33, raised the projected number to 2,301, GStA/77/28. PrMdI to SSt, 30 August (Hess.HStA Wiesbaden, 483/714), indicates that preparations for forming the Feldjaegerkorps were carried out in coordination with the Gestapo, which may have played a role in the selection of its personnel. On background and evolution of Feldjaegerkorps, Koehl, Black Guard, p. 78.

34. Diels, Lucifer ante Portas, pp. 235-36. Diels's version is supported by Martha Dodd, to whom he gave a similar account at that time: Martha Dodd, Through Embassy Eyes (1939), p. 52; and by Graf, Politische Polizei, pp. 141, 145, 148.

35. Diels boasted in his comments on a speech by Daluege, 11 September 1933, BDC/PK Diels; and GeStapa to SSt, 2 October, T-175/337/2943179. For one example of the use of SS men, I.AdI.3., 19 July, BA/R 58/1238.

36. PrMdI to Herren Regierungspraesidenten, 19.10.33, with attachment, RMdI to Herren Reichsstatthalter und die *Laendersregierungen* 6 October, BA/ Schu 267.

37. Gisevius, *To the Bitter End*, p. 107-8.

38. "Entwurf eines Gesetzes ueber die politische Polizei," n.d.; evaluations submitted to Pfundtner and Frick, 20 October 1933; and a memorandum of the same date from Pfundtner to Frick re a conference with Grauert over the proposal, BA/R-18/642/13-16, 21-25, 45-47. There are contradictory renditions of what Frick was proposing in this draft law: see Aronson, *Heydrich*, p. 172; Plum, "Staatspolizei und Innere Verwaltung," p. 193; and cf. Schulz, *Machtergreifung*, p. 537, n. 96; and Graf, *Politische Polizei*, pp. 159-60.

39. Aronson, *Heydrich*, pp. 172-73; Plum "Staatspolizei," p. 193, n. 12; and cf. Schulz, *Machtergreifung*, p. 538; and Graf, *Politische Polizei*, pp. 142-43, 159-61.

40. Pfundtner to Frick, 20 October 1933, BA/R-18/642/21-22. In fact, Goering was being as cooperative with the RMdI on police matters as Grauert's polite wording indicated. He soon agreed to a more thorough supervision and control of his police budget. See memo, apparently from Pfundtner to Frick re conference with Goering, Popitz and others over Polizei- und SA-Kosten, 27 October, BA/ R-18/646/27-31.

41. Martha Dodd, who had contact with both Diels and Goering, noted that Goering was distrustful perhaps even afraid of Diels, *Through Embassy Eyes*, p. 53; and Gisevius, *To the Bitter End*, p. 51.

42. Diels, *Lucifer ante Portas, passim*; and Gisevius, *To the Bitter End*, pp. 58-61.

43. In the "Namentliches Verzeichnis der bei der (Pr.GeStapo). . . beschaeftigen maennlichen Personen," 25 June 1935, BDC/Mappe Polizei, and similar reports for the SSt, BDC/Sammelliste 49/1-12, 20-164, the 1 October date is the most conspicuously frequent entry date for Gestapo personnel, usually SS members, recruited from nongovernment positions. One surviving memo from Diels to Goering summarized developments, GeStapo to MPraes, 24 March 1934, GStA/90, Abt.P/1, Heft 1/95-97. Pfundtner's notes on the Staatssekretaerbesprechung of September 7, 1933 (GStA/77/28), An1.I, indicate that 122 *Beamten* and 600 *Krim. Angestellte* augmented the allotted ranks of the Gestapo.

44. Orb (p. 127), in an apparent mistake, identifies a Johst as Himmler's liaison officer from the BPP. The Gestapo Geschaeftsverteilungsplan, 22 January 1934, (GStA/90, Abt.P.2, Heft 2/107) lists SS Lieutenant Sohst as liaison officer to RFSS. Orb contends that Johst (Sohst) was commander of the "SD-Rollkommando," and that he was able to infiltrate three other SD men into the Gestapo office staff. Sohst's personnel file, BDC/SSO Walter Sohst (b. 23.9.98), is very sketchy on his early SS career (entry 1.9.32), and there is no indication when he joined the SD. Orb's reference to the SD-Rollkommando may be a confusion with SS-Kommando Gestapo. Sohst had served in Berlin as some sort of liaison officer (for Himmler with Daluege, or between the Berlin and Munich SD) since 1 November 1932.

45. BDC/SSO Daluege; Aronson, *Heydrich*, p. 82, and see especially a copy of Daluege's letter to Himmler, 3 October 1933, reprinted as Document 12, p.

320. For some time, Himmler had been reducing the size of Gruppe Ost till it was limited to Berlin and the District of Potsdam, SS-Uebersichts-Karte, Stand 15.XI.33, T 175/200/2741055.

46. Gisevius, To the Bitter End, pp. 49-51; and Gisevius testimony, IMT, 12:169.

47. Diels, Lucifer ante Portas, pp. 236-38, 244, 247-48, 289. Wighton, Heydrich, p. 59, also identifies Daluege as the author of the order to search, but contends (without citing any source) that it was Heydrich who persuaded him to issue the order. This and Hoehne's assertion that Himmler was part of this cabal (The Order, p. 88) seem anachronous. Hoehne's cited source, Gisevius, does not refer to his liaison with Himmler until the following winter (To the Bitter End, p. 140-41), and on this point, Diels is not reliable. Delarue's (Gestapo, p. 77) contention that Diels was dismissed because generals had turned Hindenburg against him seems to be based solely on an offhand reference by Gisevius (To the Bitter End, p. 51) that does not warrant such a definitive statement. Graf's version (Politische Polizei, pp. 143-45) of Daluege's maneuverings against both Diels and Himmler seems more plausible; he has also cast more light on Daluege's tactics and dates his shift to Himmler as February 1934 (pp. 213-15).

48. Diels's version (Lucifer ante Portas, pp. 238-239) is not fully substantiated by Ambassador Dodd, Ambassador Dodd's Diary, 1933-1938 (New York: Harcourt, Brace, 1941), p. 65. Gisevius's version mentions no arrest orders, merely refers to his transfer and flight (To the Bitter End, pp. 51-52). Koehler refers to the transfer and to Diels's work in the Polizei Praesidium as though there were no flight (Inside the Gestapo, p. 108). On November 18, Diels was made Polizeipraesident "vertretungsweise," which could either have been the change of assignment he had promised Frick, or Goering's first move to make amends after Diels's dismissal. As for the dates of the flight, Gisevius places Diels's absence between mid-September and the end of October (p. 62), but is apparently off by two months. Dodd says two weeks early in December, after Goering had threatened him late in November (p. 65). Diels says he fled in October and is very definite about returning on December first. Wighton's version that he fled after his new appointment (Heydrich, p. 60) is one likely possibility. In Gestapo documents at least as late as 7 November, Diels still appears as head of Gestapo. Of course, this does not prove he was physically present. The first document carrying the name of his successor, Hinkler, is dated 18 November, the date of Diels's transfer. Since some time would be required for Hinkler to move in, Diels's removal (and possibly his flight) must have occurred some time between 7 and 18 November. On 29 November, Hinkler was dismissed and Diels, who was officially addressed as being in the Berlin Polizei Praesidium, was named Inspector of the Gestapo (PrMPraes to StSekdMdI, 29 November 1933, BA/R43 II/395). Of course, he may not have actually returned to Berlin till December 1 as he contended, and Koehler's references to his work in the Polizei Praesidium may be to events that occurred later, for Diels then held both positions simultaneously (ibid.). See Graf, Politische Polizei, pp. 140-42, for similar conclusions.

49. BDC/NS, PK, SA, OPG, Paul Hinkler (b. 25.6.92). See especially his letters of 12 October 1933 and later to Daluege, and a letter of illegible authorship to Frick, 21 January 1931. On Luegenabwehrstelle, NSaech.HStA Hann., 310 I/B/211, letter to Hinkler, 13 April 1932. For more details on Daluege-Hinkler relationship, Graf, Politisich Polizei, pp. 243-45. According to Koehler, Rosenberg had been an early intriguer for political police power but was set aside by Goering

(Inside the Gestapo, p. 21). Schumann's office remained in rivalry with the SD (see chap. 8, especially n. 24).

50. Diels, *Lucifer ante Portas*, p. 246. Diels quoted Hitler as saying, "This Hinkler is half crazy and we can't use him." NA/Interrogation, 9 October 1945, p. 12.

51. On Roehm's joining the cabinet, "Gesetz zur Sicherung der Einheit von Partei und Staat," 1 December 1933, *RGB1.*, 1016. Diels, *Lucifer ante Portas*, pp. 246-47; and on Gestapo-SD cooperation, Pol.Praes.Berlin to StSek, 6 April 1934, GSta/90, Abt.P/3/62.

52. *SS Personalbefehl Nr.10*, 24 November 1933, p. 4, T-611/3/429.

53. Schulz, *Machtergreifung*, chapter 4; and Peterson, *Limits*, pp. 102-105.

54. *PrGS*, p. 413.

55. Ibid.; Diels, *Lucifer ante Portas*, pp. 246, 248-49; and Gisevius, *To the Bitter End*, pp. 52-54.

56. Because it caused such considerable administrative confusion, the November Law was probably drawn up in haste and without adequate consultation with the ministry personnel affected. Many weeks were needed to restructure channels and responsibilities. See note to Grauert, 7 December 1933, GSta/77/30/5-6; and PrMPraes., St.M.P. 161, 29 January 1934, GSta/90, Abt.P/104/22-23. When Grauert tried to reassert some of his lost authority, Goering slapped him down with remarks about how he intended the new law to circumvent bureaucratic *Verwirrung*, PrMPraes., Cd Gestapo, St.M.P. 172, 29 January 1934, GSta/90, Abt.P/1, Heft 1/14-15.

57. On Diels-Daluege relationship, Daluege to Himmler, 18 February 1934, BA/NS-19/236. Koehler (*Inside the Gestapo*, pp. 23-24) contends this independence was the nature of the Diels-Daluege power relationship from the very beginning, and that is why Daluege became hostile to Diels. If this were true before the November decree, then only de facto. PrMPraes. to StSekdMdI, 29 November 1933, BA/R43 II/395.

8. The SD Emergent

1. On the "Strasser era" and his resignation, Kissenkoetter, *Strasser*; Orlow, *Nazi Party, 1919-1933*, pp. 256-94; and Stachura, *Strasser*.

2. Orlow, *Nazi Party*, pp. 292-94; Peter Heyes, " 'A Question Mark with Epaulettes'? Kurt von Schleicher and Weimar Politics," *Journal of Modern History*, 52 (March 1980): pp. 35-65; and Goebbels, *Tagebucher*, 2: 2. & 3.IX., 9.XI., 8., 10. & 13.XII.32.

3. Hans J. Koehler, *Inside Information* (London: Pallas, 1940), p. 207, is typical of this tradition; and Wighton, *Heydrich*, p. 42. Strasser allegedly complained that Himmler, Goering, Goebbels, and Roehm dominated the circle around Hitler at his expense, Hans Frank, *Im Angesicht des Galgens* (Munich: Friedrich Alfred Beck Verlag, 1953), p. 108. Kissenkoetter (*Strasser*) ignores Himmler in the account of Strasser's fall, and Stachura (*Strasser*, p. 106) merely gives Frank's quote.

4. Leffler recalls that toward the end of 1932, Hess inspected the small central office, promised a supplement of 1,000 RM, but could only deliver 500, Auszug, Bericht Leffler, p. 3 (made available to the author by Aronson).

5. Untitled order, der RFSS, 27 January 1933, BDC/SSO Heydrich. Hofer,

Reichstagsbrandt, 2: 243-45, 361-62, 400, 403; and Calic, *Heydrich*, pp. 82-107, both stem from allegations originating in the Berlin SA and remain strained and unconvincing. Acceptance, Gordon A. Craig, *Germany, 1866-1945* (Oxford: Oxford Univ. Press, 1980), pp. 573-74.

6. "1. SS-Standartenfuehrer Heydrich scheidet als Stabsfuehrer des Sicherheitsdienstes aus dem Stabe des Reichsfuehrer-SS aus. 2. SS-Standartenfuehrer Heydrich wird als SS-Standartenfueher z.b.V. dem Stab des Reichsfuehrers-SS zugeteilt." RFSS, 27 January 1933, BDC/SSO Heydrich.

7. Hoehne, *The Order*, pp. 176-77, erroneously citing Aronson; and cf. Aronson, *Heydrich*, pp. 139-40.

8. Heydrich's Reports from Berlin, SDdRFSS to RFSS, re SS-Befehl, 26 January 1933; and SDdRFSS to RFSS, re "RGO-Streikversammlung, Berlin," 3 February 1933, Daluege Nachlasse, T-580/223/75. That Leffler joined the SD in Berlin, "Generalstaatsanwalt, Braunschweig, Anschuldigungsschrift gegen Selle," 7 October 1933, BA/R-43 II/1323/85. Leffler's replacement in Brunswick, Klare, reported to Leffler in Berlin in July, Leffler statement (1323/45). Klare's SD Ausweis was signed by Kobelinski (Vernehmung Bonewald, 1323/18); and Kobelinski also handled SD correspondence in the Kaufmann case in June (see n.10).

9. Kaufmann to Oberste Leitung der PO, 21 June 1933, "Bericht ueber die Spitzeltaetigkeit des SS-Sicherheitsdienstes . . . ," BA/Schu 457. In fact, Funke was officially assigned to SD South, effective April 3, BDC/SSO Ferdinand Funke (b. 22.4.95). Funke's file is thin, especially on this period. He may only have had Mitarbeiter status in the SD prior to April.

10. Quoted in Kaufmann, "Bericht."

11. Ibid. At least part of Kaufmann's intelligence was accurate, for Funke remained in the SD until April 1937, BDC/SSO Funke.

12. The subsequent narrative is compiled from the often contradictory sources assembled for the Selle and Leffler trials to be found in BDC/USchla Leffler and BA/R-43 II/1323, a Reichskanzlei file on Klagges.

13. The most complete narrative by Leffler was a series of Meldungen for Heydrich, 18, 20, and 21 September and 23 November 1933 (USchla Leffler), which must be contrasted with affidavits by Leffler and the others involved (in USchla Leffler and BA/R-43 II/1323). Leffler's report, "An 1," April 1933, re "Braunschweig" and reports to him from Klare are also in USchla Leffler.

14. Bonewald's affidavit, 18 July 1933; and Jeckeln's response to an inquiry from Himmler, 8 September 1933, and an undated note on the fate of Klare and others, USchla Leffler.

15. SD evidence is in Uschla Leffler, as are Leffler's reports. On Bonewald and Klare, see OPG, 20 February 1934, Begrundung, p. 6. Cf. Aronson, *Heydrich*, p. 166, who interprets Himmler's degradation of Klare as a tactical retreat to placate Klagges and Jeckeln. On Buch, Orlow, *Nazi Party, 1933-45*, pp. 67, 150-51, 166-67.

16. OPG, 20 February 1934, "Beschluss und Begrundung," BDC/USchla Leffler.

17. In SDdRFSS to Schwarz, 19 July 1933 (T-580/93/457), Heydrich still signs himself "der Stabsfuehrer." BDC/RuSHA Josef Strohmeier (b. 30.6.05), contains RFSS, SS Gericht to *CdSD*, Heydrich, dated 2 August; and Strohmeier's marriage request of 22 July was personally signed by Heydrich.

18. The Daluege Nachlasse (T-580/229,230/107-110) contain correspondence relevant to Daluege's fund raising in 1933-34. On the complaints, KL Salzwedel to GL, 4 July 1933; NSDAP, RL to RFSS, 17 July; and PI 10125, re "Geldsamm-

lungen angeblich im Auftrage des Staatssekretaers Daluege fuer den SD des RFSS," n.d., received at SD on 25 July 1933, BDC/SSO Daluege.

19. On the rumors, StVdF to all Gauleiter, 13 November 1933, T-580/94/462

20. Aronson, Heydrich, p. 167, and Best, Beantwortung der Fragen (Aronson), p. 1 (made available by Aronson), which supports this interpretation of OPL's need for and use of the SD.

21. OPG, 20 February 1934, "Begrundung," pp. 2-5, BDC/USchla Leffler, which also describes the change of mission.

22. StVdF to all Gauleiter, 13 November 1933, T-580/94/462. Unfortunately, Hitler's order has not survived in writing and is only known through this directive.

23. Ibid.

24. On the APA and its problems, Louis de Jong, "The Organization and Efficiency of the German Fifth Column," in The Third Reich (London: Weidenfeld & Nicholson, 1955), pp. 883-84; and Jacobson, NS Aussenpolitik, pp. 64-65, 634. The vagueness of the relevant documents leaves it unclear whether Hess's November order called for the complete absorption of Schumann's ND or just Abtl. III, Inland. In any case, the entire ND had succumbed to SD expansion by the summer of 1934, but the transition was not peaceful. Some of Schumann's lieutenants sought to sabotage the process, and they and he were expelled from the SD and SS by December 1934, BDC/SSO Schumann (b. 30.8.99).

25. BDC/SSO Heydrich.

9. Toward Command of a Reich Political Police

1. On the plots, "Mordanschlag gegen Adolf Hitler geplant," V.B., 21 March 1933; Fritz Tobias, Der Reichstagsbrand (Rastatt: Grote Verlag, 1962), pp. 135-36; and Hoehne, The Order, pp. 80-81, who erroneously credits Himmler with a similar revelation made by his predecessor in the Munich P.D. James J. Weingartner, Hitler's Guard (Carbondale: Southern Illinois Univ. Press, 1974), pp. 4-7.

2. Weingartner, Hitler's Guard, pp. 2-7; and Hoffmann, Hitler's Security, pp. 19, 21, 44-48.

3. Weingartner, pp. 5-7; and Gisevius, To the Bitter End, pp. 140-41, for one example of use of the Leibstandarte for liaison with Nebe and Gisevius. Heiden, Der Fuehrer, p. 742, reported that such guard groups were all coordinated by a black cabinet responsible for keeping the Movement in line. Its membership included Hess, Himmler, and Major Walter Buch. Even if such a control committee existed, when it would have come into being is unclear.

4. Sk.f.d. Polizeiwesen in Hessen, re "Die Einrichtung von Kommandos (z.b.V.) . . . als politische Hilfspolizei," 24 June 1933, BA/Schu 462; Pfundtner report to Frick re "Politische Bereitschaften in Wuerttemberg," 31 May 1934, BA/R-18/642/49-51; and Buchheim, "The SS," pp. 142-43.

5. Buchheim, "Die organisatorische Entwicklung der politischen Polizei in Deutschland in den Jahren 1933 und 1934," Gutachten, pp. 294-301.

6. Hoehne, The Order, p. 90; Deschner, Heydrich, pp. 83; Domroese, NS-Staat in Bayern, pp. 145-46; but cf. Frick interrogation, 9 October 1945, pp. 9-10 (NA/RG 238).

7. Hoehne, The Order, p. 90; Aronson, Heydrich, pp. 167-68, 171-72; Domroese, NS-Staat in Bayern, p. 144; and Broszat, "Concentration Camps," p. 415.

8. Himmler definitely gave Reichsstatthalter Murr of Wuerttemberg the impression that Hitler favored the tie between SS auxiliaries and political police, Pfundtner to Frick, 31 May 1934, BA/R-18/642/51; and Frick interrogation (see n. 6). In later official versions, Himmler always took credit for having done it *on his own initiative,* "Rundfunksprache des RFSS . . . anlaesslich des Tages der Deutschen Polizei 1937," T-175/89/2612030; and Werner Best, "Die Geheime Staatspolizei," *Deutsches Recht* 6 (15 April 1936): p. 127. In sharp contrast, he always noted that Hitler named him CdDP in 1936. See Peterson, *Limits,* p. 128, that Himmler's "salesmanship, and not Hitler's particular backing, won the battle." Gunter d'Alquen (letter 24.7.78) contends that neither Hitler, Hess, nor anyone but Goering supported Himmler's expansion to KdPPdL (apparently he refers to Goering's appointment of Himmler over the Gestapo in spring 1934).

9. Braunsch. MdI to RFSS, 1 June 1933, BDC/SSO Friedrich Jeckeln (b. 2.2.95). Best (letter 28.5.78), who reorganized the Hessian political police, knew of no such guidelines and doubts they existed. D'Alquen (le 24.7.78) conjectures that Klagges used or created a rumor as pretext for consulting Himmler and appointing Jeckeln.

10. Henning Timpke (ed.), *Dokumente zur Gleichschaltung des Landes Hamburg 1933* (1964), facilitates analysis of the NS power seizure in Hamburg. He assembled relevant materials from the Staatsarchiv Hamburg and devotes considerable space to the police and concentration camps. See pp. 34-41, 177, and on Simon, Doc. 36, pp. 187-88.

11. Ibid., pp. 174-75; and Doc. 58, anonymous (KPD) "Rundschreiben ueber die Behandlung der Schutzhaeftlinge," p. 256.

12. Ibid., pp. 171-72; and Doc, 41, CdO IV/W, "Einsatz von Hilfspolizei," 17 March 1933; Doc. 42, Die Polizeibehoerde Hamburg, "Einberufung und Verwendung von Hilfspolizei," 16 March; Doc. 43, "Richtlinien ueber die Ausbildung"; and Doc. 44, "Verteilung der Hilfspolizei," pp. 202-11.

13. Ibid., p. 175.

14. Ibid., pp. 178-179. Kaufmann praised the kommando as late as 21 July, Doc. 39, Kaufmann to Kosa, 21 July 1933, p. 196; but as early as 5 July Polizeisenator Richter was calling for decisive action to limit excesses, Doc. 38, Protokoll of meeting between Richter and leading police officials, 5 July 1933, p. 195. On Kommando procedures, Doc. 48, Meldung of SA Rottenfuehrer Paul Winkler, 12 November; and Doc. 49, "der Praesident der Gesundheits- und Fuersorgebehoerde to the Innere Verwaltung," 14 December, pp. 219-26. Doc. 58, anonymous Rundschreiben, pp. 255-56, and p. 257, n. 3. Doc. 68, State Police report on the KPD, 27 October 1934, p. 301, refers to a previous report in which Streckenbach used the Kommando's reputation to gain its dissolution.

15. Timpke, pp. 229-31; Doc. 50 on the creation of Wittmoor, pp. 236-38; and Doc. 51, der Polizeipraesident to der Finanzdeputation, 11 April 1933, pp. 240-41.

16. See pp. 93-94.

17. BDC/PK Karl Kaufmann (b. 10.10.00), especially K. to H.H., 22 November 1926 and 7 June 1927.

18. Timpke, *Gleichschaltung Hamburg,* pp. 31, 37, 42.

19. BDC/SSO Dr. Hans Nieland (b. 3.10.00), especially SS-OAb Nord to RFSS, 21 March 1934 and Timpke, *Gleichschaltung Hamburg,* p. 177.

20. Timpke, pp. 177-78; Timpke unfortunately gives no documentation for these relationships.

21. BDC/SSO Bruno Streckenbach (b.7.2.02), especially RStH in Hamburg, *Beurteilung* on Streckenbach, 27 April 1937.

22. Timpke, *Gleichschaltung Hamburg*, p. 176. Contrary to Timpke and Aronson (*Heydrich*, p. 171), who see Streckenbach as Kaufmann's choice for a compromise with Himmler, Ramme (*Sicherheitsdienst*, p. 272) states that he was appointed on Himmler's personal order (unfortunately, no source is cited). The tradition that Hitler's support won Himmler his appointments (which is repeated by Timpke, pp. 175-76) has some circumstantial support in the fact that both Hitler and Himmler visited Hamburg on November 6 (Timpke, p. 316), a few weeks before Himmler's appointment. Unless more evidence becomes available, however, it would seem the matter was already settled with Streckenbach's earlier appointment. Unfortunately, Streckenbach died (28 October 1977) before clarifying the Hamburg situation for this writer.

23. On Kaufmann's honorary rank, *DAL*, 1934, p. 2. BDC/SSO Ahrens (b. 29.4.96). BDC/SSO Streckenbach, *Beurteilung*, 27 April 1937, which states he actually commanded the local SD; unfortunately, no dates for this can be established. Ahrens only had a short membership in the SD, until August 1934.

24. Timpke, *Gleichschaltung Hamburg*, pp. 231-32; Doc. 53, 28 SS-Standarte to RStH, 24 August 1933; Doc. 54, SS-Gruppe West to SS-Gruppe Nord, 17 August; and Doc. 55, "Ansprache des kommissarischen Praesidenten des Strafvollzugsamts vor den Haeftlingen des Konzentrationslagers Fuhlsbuettel am 4. September 1933," pp. 245-49.

25. Timpke, pp. 231-33; Doc. 56, der Landesjustizverwaltung und Strafsvollzugsbehoerde to RStH, 28 September 1933, pp. 250-51; and Doc. 58, anonymous "Rundschreiben ueber die Behandlung der Schutzhaeftlinge," pp. 254-60.

26. Timpke, pp. 233-34; and Doc. 57, minutes of a meeting of Polizeibehoerde Hamburg re Fuhlsbuettel, 10 November 1933, pp. 252-53.

27. Timpke, p. 179; and Doc. 68, Streckenbach report of 27 October 1934, p. 301, referring to a previous report of February.

28. According to the *Staatsanzeiger* in Stuttgart, 11 December 1933, the appointment came first in Mecklenburg and Luebeckk; clipping, HStA Stuttg., E151a/Bue 1452/41. BDC/SSO Friedrich Hildebrandt (b. 19.9.98), especially letter to RFSS, 26 March 1934. Significant documentary material relevant to Himmler's appointment in Luebeck is unavailable at Luebeck (letters Archiv der Hansastadt Luebeck, 17 January and 15 February 1977). Related material is not in the Landesarchiv Schleswig-Holstein either (letter LA Schleswig-Holstein, 16 March 1977). StA Schwerin holds "luckenhafte Bestaende" on the political police and NS penetration of Mecklenburg (letter StA Schwerin, 10 July 1975), but the author has not been allowed access.

29. Buchheim, "Entwicklung," pp. 297-98; and BDC/SSO Ludwig Oldach (b. 21.9.88.). Since one Friedrich Oldach had formed SD-UAb Mecklenburg-Ost in March 1933, there may have been a family connection that allowed the SD to facilitate penetration: BDC/RuSHA Friedrich Oldach (b. 28.2.06).

30. Herbert Schwarzwaelder, *Die Machtergreifung der NSDAP in Bremen 1933* (Bremen: Carl Schuenemann Verlag, 1966), pp. 101-105; and Inge Marssolek and René Ott, *Bremen im Dritten Reich: Anpassung—Widerstand—Verfolgung* (Bremen: Carl Schuenemann Verlag, 1986), pp. 113-16.

31. Peter Fricke, "Anfaenge und Organisation der Nachrichtenstelle bei der Polizeidirektion Bremen," unpublished Bericht fuer gehobenen Archivdienst

(Breman, 1966), pp. 3-4, StA Bremen, b.411U; and Schwarzwaelder, *Machtergreifung Bremen*, p. 107.

32. BDC/SSO Erwin Schulz (b. 27.11.00); see especially Personalangaben 22 March 1943. In 1933 Schulz established Party membership as soon as possible, but strangely did not become an SS-man until 1935.

33. On the excesses, tensions, and competition, Schwarzwaelder, *Machtergreifung Bremen*, p. 107-108; and Marssolek and Ott, *Bremen*, pp. 121-27. On May visit, Fritz Peters, *Zwoelf Jahre Bremen, 1933-1945* (Osterholz-Scharmbeck: H. Saade, 1951), p. 25. BDC/SSO Theodor Laue (b. 1.3.93), Lebenslauf, 4 February 1937.

34. Auszug, Senatorenbesprechung, 28 November 1933, StA Bremen, 3-P.I.a/Nr.1152/1; Buergermeister to RFSS, 14 December 1933, ibid., 2; Telegraph RFSS to Buergermeister, 18 December, ibid., 4; Auszug, Senatorenbesprechung, 22 December, ibid., 5; and Peters, *Bremen*, p. 42. In May, at the request of Bormann, Leffler produced SD reports incriminating Markert as a Freemason. Perhaps Himmler gained his allegiance by providing "protection." BDC/OPG Dr. Richard Markert, CdSHA to OPG, 9 May 1934. Himmler's role in the Bremen power struggle was terribly convoluted, for he apparently maintained links with both sides to the end, Marssolek and Ott, *Bremen*, pp. 177-78.

35. BDC/SSO Schulz; *TWC*, 4:518; and Marssolek and Ott, *Bremen*, pp. 176-77.

36. N.Saech.StA Oldenburg, 136 Registratur, Oldenb. StMdI indicates that the folder relevant to Himmler's appointment was turned over to the Gestapo.

37. Himmler had been wooing Murr since at least the summer, NA/Berger testimony, 17 October 1945, pp. 2-3. According to Best (le 28.5.78) relations were "nicht sehr eng aber korrekt." Paul Sauer, *Wuerttemberg in der Zeit des Nationalsozialismus* (Ulm: Sueddeutsche Verlagsgesellschaft, 1975), pp. 58-60; and Wuertt. IM, re "Errichtung der Dienststelle fuer die politische Polizei im Innenministerium," 28 April 1933, HStA Stuttg., E130b/Bue 1064/449.

38. Sauer, *Wuerttemberg*, p. 59: Wuertt.IM, 28 April 1933, Bue 1064/449; and on Murr's recollections, Pfundtner to Frick re conference with Murr, 31 May 1934, BA/R-18/642/49-51. From this record, unfortunately, it cannot be established when or how Himmler claimed Hitler's support for the Bereitschaften, if indeed he did.

39. "Weitestgehende Einfluss," Auszug aus dem *Staatsanzeiger*, 11 December 1933, HStA Stuttg., E151a/Bue 1452/41.

40. BDC/SSO and RuSHA Robert Zeller (b. 15.7.95), in which the Lebenslauf, 24 June 1936, and correspondence indicate the Himmler-Murr-Zeller relationship. By 1936, after he had served Himmler's purposes, Zeller was being edged out of the SS. HStA Stuttg. E151a/Bue 1139/1,4,5, reveal some of Murr's interest in the political police; and RStH to saemtl. Min., 6 December 1933, shows its reduction, Bue 1139/48.

41. Wuertt. IM, re "RR Dr. Stahlecker," 24 May 1933, HStA Stuttg., E151a/Bue 1452/14; M.Praes., re "Personalakten," ORR Dr. S.," 6 June 1934, E130b/Bue 1065/51; and BDC/SSO Dr. Walter Stahleccker (b. 10.10.00). Although Murr tried to establish S. as an old Party member, 1921-23 (Murr to Schwaz, 28 July 1934), this claim was successfully denied by the same local Party opposition leaders. Best (le 28.5.78) on Murr-Stahlecker-Himmler relationship; and Min.Praes. to RMdI, re "Leitung d. Wuertt. PP," 30 May 1934, HStA Stuttg., E130b/Bue 1065/48.

42. RStH to StMin., 9 December 1933; "Auszug aus dem *Staatsanzeiger*," 11 and 12 December 1933, HStA Stuttg., E151a/Bue 1452/40-42.

43. Sauer, *Wuerttemberg*, pp. 60-61; and the details of the financial crisis are revealed in HStA Stuttg., E1F1a/Duc 1132 and 1454.

44. Sauer, *Wuerttemberg*, pp. 62-63; F.d.SS OAb Suedwest to RFSS, 5 June 1934, BDC/SSO Wilhelm Murr (b. 16.12.88), whom Himmler made an SS general in September 1934. The dispute over Stahlecker can be traced in HStA Stuttg., E151a/Bue 1452/57ff., and E130b/Bue 1065/41ff. Wuertt. IM to PLPA, re "RR Dr. Harster," 19 May 1934, E151a/Bue 1452/20.

45. The records of RStH Robert Wagner are not at the Karlsruhe archive, and the relevant Baden IM records were burnedd in 1945 (letter from Generallandesarchive Karlsruhe, 11 June 1975). Horst Rehberger, *Die Gleichschaltung des Landes Baden 1932/33*, (Heidelberg: Carl Winter Universitaetsverlags, 1966), pp. 97, 100, 104, 142. On Pflaumer, Stockhorst, *Fuenftausend Koepfe*, p. 322; and BDC/SSO Pflaumer, GL Baden on OSAF, 20 April 1933, and SS-Gruppe-Sued on RFSS, 12.5.33, indicating that Jeckeln, still in Munich, served to build the Himmler-Pflaumer link. On 22 May 1933, Kurt Wuhrle, Pflaumer's new personal secretary, was drawn into the SS and promoted to *Sturmfuehrer* in October. Best letters of 28.5 and 21.7.78. On Wagner, Pflaumer and Berckmueller, Johnpeter H. Grill, *The Nazi Movement in Baden, 1920-1945* (Chapel Hill: Univ. of North Carolina Press, 1983), pp. 261, 571, n. 46. BDC/RuSHA Berckmueller, Karl (b. 10.10.95), forced to withdraw from SS in 1937 for failure to establish Aryan heritage.

46. "Denkschrift ueber den Aufbau einer Geheimen Reichspolizei und eines Geheimen Reichspolizeiamts," with cover letter, 19 December 1933, BA/R-18/642/36-44. "Denkschrift ueber die Vereinheitlichung der Polizei," with cover letters of 20 April 1933 BA/R-18/104/41-77, carried proposals from Thuringia for unification under Frick.

47. Denkschrift, 19 December 1933, pp. 38-44. Support of the Murr-Himmler opposition is a later example.

48. Gisevius, *To the Bitter End*, p. 182.

49. The pre-1933 establishments for Lippe can be studied in StA Detmold, L-75/IV/7/2, and for Schaumburg-Lippe, in N.Saech.StA Bueckebg., L4-9174; L4-9703 contains material on the extent of cooperation with Prussia. On the Lippe political police, Lipp.LReg., to RStH, 5 January 1934, StA Detmold, L-76/C7a; and Hans-Juergen Sengotta, "Der Reichsstatthalter in Lippe 1933 bis 1939," unpublished dissertation, Technische Universitaet Hannover, n.d., p. 128.

50. BDC/SSO Otto Helllwig (b. 24.2.98); and LPD to GeStapa, 8 December 1933, StA Detmold, L80Ie/P/2.II.

51. SS Ab.XVII to Riecke, 16 February 1934, StA Detmold, L-76/B,9a,I; and Lipp.LReg. to RStH, 5 January 1934, L-76/C,7a. From this last letter, it is not entirely clear that Meyer initiated the exchange over Himmler's appointment; cf. Sengotta "Reichsstatthalter," pp. 128-30.

52. On Meyer, BDC/SA; and Riecke, Stockhorst, *Fuenftausend Koepfe*, p. 346. SS Ab.XVII to Riecke, 16 February 1934; Riecke to RStH, 23 February; RR Wolff to RMdI, 28 February; RMdI to RStH, 8 March; RFSS to RStH, 14 May; RStH to RR Wolff, 18 May; Lipp.LReg. to RFSS, 1 June, StA Detmold, L-76/B,9a, I. RMdI to Reg.d.Landes Schm.-Lippe, 30 May, indicates a similar course of events there, N.Saech.StA Bueckebg., L4-10193/1.

53. 20, 20, 21, and 23 December respectively, Buchheim, "Entwicklung," 295-301.

54. BDC/SSO Dr. Alfred Freyberg (b. 12.7.92). On 10 October 1975, the Historisches Staatsarchiv Oranienbaum responded "liessen sich in den hier ver-wahrten Bestaenden . . . zu Ihrem Thema bisher nicht ermitteln."

55. BDCC/SSO Wilhelm Lueper (b. 12.10.93); and SSO Wilhelm Otto Sens (b. 14.4.988).

56. BDC/SSO Karl Rudolf Werner Best (b. 10.7.03); Aronson, *Heydrich*, pp. 150-51; Best's "Beantwortung des Fragebogens" (Aronson), A-1, A-5; and Best, "Himmler," pp. 1-2.

57. NA/RG-238 Vernehmung des Werner Best, 19 September 1946, p. 18; Aronson, *Heydrich*, p. 170; and Beantwortung, A-1-4.

58. Hess.HStA Wiesbaden, 483/678 contains material on the SS and SD personnel in Stapo Darmstadt, 1933-36, and their absorption into the SD; see especially documents 17 December 1935 through 16 April 1936. In SD-Dienststelle Stapo Darmstadt to SD-OAb Rhein, 19 February 1936, Berges made an offhand reference to relations with Dr. Schulze.

59. BDC/SSO Walter Ortlepp (b. 9.7.00); and Buchheim, "Entwicklung," 301. The Historisches Staatsarchiv Gotha (letter 10 August 1975) has no holdings on this topic. BDC/SSO Max Rausch (b. 14.10.98).

60. BDC/SSO Horst Boehme (b. 24.8.09); and SSO Herbert Mehlhorn (b. 24.3.03). The story of Saxony also suffers from lack of surviving documentation (letter, St. Archivverwaltung, DDR, 27 June 1975).

61. BDC/SSO Fritz Schilegel (b. 25.3.94), in which as early as June 6, in an otherwise politely worded letter, Schlegel seems to have informed Himmler that, despite the intrigues of rivals in the local SS, he had the support of Mutschmann and could not be toppled from his police position; Schlegel to RFSS, 14 September 1933; and RFSS to Schlegel, 2 October. Antwort Dr. Mehlhorn to Aronson's Fragebogen of 20 November 1965, pp. 3-6 (provided by Aronson).

62. Antwort Mehlhorn, p. 5; Schlegel to RFSS, 21 December 1935, BDC/SSO Schlegel; and Best (le 21.7.78) who states that Mutschmann retarded Himmler's influence, which increased only after 30 June 1934.

63. By early January, Himmler had purchased letterhead stationery listing all his KdPP titles *except* Braunschweig and the Lippes; see n. 69.

64. RStH to Klagges, 19 January 1934, N.Saech.StA Wolfenbtl., 12A Neu/16075.

65. D'Alquen le 24.7.78.

66. Braunschwg. MdI to RFSS, 27 January 1933; and "Pressnotiz fuer die Brnschwg. Tageszeitungen," N.Saech.StA Wolfenbtl., 12A Neu/16075. BDC/SSO Friedrich Jeckeln (b. 2.2.95).

67. Best, "Beantwortung des Fragebogens" (Aronson), B,1.

68. Best, "Himmler," p. 3. Cf. Aronson, *Heydrich*, pp. 169-72, for differences and similarity of overall interpretation; and Peterson, *Limits*, p. 128.

69. The earliest record of this office found by the author is PKK . . . , Zentralbuero, to Brnschwg. MdI, 22 March 1934, N.Saech.StA, Wolfbtl. 12A Neu/16074. The January creation date is inferred from the stationery created for this office. The letterhead lists all *Laender* in alphabetical order except Braunschweig, obviously inserted after the initial design.

70. BDC/SSO Guenther Patschowski (b. 3.3.03).

71. BDC/SSO Emanuel Schaefer (b. 20.4.00), especially Lebenslauf and SD-F.d.SS-OAb Suedost, Personal-Bericht, 12 July 1937.

72. Orb, *Nationalsozialismus*, pp. 128-29.

73. Pr.M.Praes., ST.M.P., 70/34, 1 January 1934, and GeStapo-IB 3/34-P, 19

January, GStA/90, Abt.P/5/24-25, re Patschowski's transfer; and "Geschaefts-verteilungsplan," 22 January 1934, ibid./2, Heft 2/100, 105.

10. Acquiring the Prussian Power Base

1. NA/Frick interrogation, 9 October 1945, p. 10. Kaufmann to Ley, "Bericht ueber die Spitzeltaetigkeit der SS-Sicherheitsdienst . . . ," 21 June 1933, p. 3, BA/Schu 457.

2. The development of his RMdI budget shows he participated in the building of the "inner political instrument of power." The 1932 budget for protection of *Volk* and State, 182,500 RM, was increased to 660,000 RM for his first year in office, and he created an allocation of 3 million marks for support of protective custody actions. For 1934, he sought to raise the allocation to 8 million. *Haushalt d. RMdI f.d. Rechnungsjahr 1933*, pp. 28-29, 80-81, and 1934, pp. 32-33, NA/RG 238/NG-4214, NG-4213, respectively.

3. Diels, *Lucifer ante Portas*, pp. 251-52, 255-57: GeStapa, re "Entlassung von Schutzhaeftlinge," 5 January 1934, T-580/49/271; and article in the *Berliner Lokalanzeiger*, 10 March 1934, "Deutsche Staatspolizei ist Volkspolizei," *IMT*, 42:301-302.

4. "Deutsche Staatspolizei . . . ," *IMT* 42:302; and Daluege, "Bericht der Polizei-Abteilung des Preuss. Ministerium des Innern ueber ihre Arbeiten im Jahre 1933 . . . ," p. 4, 1 February 19334, BA/R43 I/2290/30.

5. PrMPraes., Gestapo, re "Aufstellung einer staatlichen Wachttruppe fuer die Konzentrationslager im Reg.Bez. Osnabrueck," 18 December 1933, GStA/ Rep 90, P/104/12-13; "Geschaeftsverteilungsplan," GeStapa, 22 January 1934, GStA/90, P/2, Heft 2/92; and Orb, *Nationalsozialismus*, p. 118. Cf. Diels, *Lucifer ante Portas*, pp. 189-90.

6. Diels, *Lucifer ante Portas*, pp. 287-90; and for more accurate details, Thevoz, *Pommern*, 1: 21-24, 29-38, 2 (Quellen): Docs. 38, 51. BDC/SSO Fritz Herrmann (b. 15.6.85); and SSO Daluege, Herrmann to Daluege, 19 June 1933, and subsequent correspondence.

7. Graf, *Politische Polizei*, pp. 195-208; Daluege to Himmler, 23 March 1934, BA/NS-19/236; and Hoehne, *The Order*, p. 188, citing reports of some of Diels's coconspirators.

8. RMdI to Laenderregierungen, 9 January 1934; and StMdI, der PPK Bayerns, 25 January 1934, HA/84/1722; Aronson, *Heydricch*, p. 183-84; and Broszat, "Concentration Camps," p. 413.

9. "Gesetz ueber den Neuaufbau des Reiches, von 30. Januar 1934," *RGBl*, p. 75; Peterson, *Limits*, pp. 105-107; and Schulz, *Machtergreifung*, pp. 597-601. On Goering's reaction, Diels, *Lucifer ante Portas*, p. 67.

10. Diels, *Lucifer ante Portas*, pp. 67, 252-53.

11. See p. 74 above.

12. PrMdI, to the O- und RPraes., 17 January 1934, and a second version to the internal staff, GStA/90,P/1, Heft 1/10, 13; PrMPraes., CdGeStapo, to all SSt and RPraes., and to Grauert, 29 January, GSTA/90, P/1, Heft 1/14-16; Gisevius, *To the Bitter End*, pp. 134-37; and Gisevius testimony, *IMT*, 12:171-72.

13. Gisevius, *To the Bitter End*, pp. 140-41. Gisevius estimated the date as mid-February, but most of his early memoirs were at least a month off.

14. Ibid., p. 141.

15. Ibid., p. 139.

16. BDC/SSO Dr. Hermann Behrends (b. 11.5.07), SSO Kobelinski; and Peis, *Man Who Started the War*, pp. 33-40.

17. BDC/SSO Behrends· Orb, *Nationalsozialismus*, p. 87; and Daluege to Himmler, 23 March 1934, BA/NS-19/236. See also PPraes to StSekretaer, 6 April, GStA/90,P/3/62.

18. Daluege-Himmler correspondence, 22 February 13, 19, and 23 March, 7 April 1934, BA/NS-19/236; and Graf, *Politische Polizei*, pp. 213-15, who has uncovered more documentation of charges and countercharges between Diels and Daluege.

19. PrMPraes., GeStapo, re "Anordnung von Schutzshaftmassnahmen," 11 March 1934; and GeStapa, 19 March, T-175/422/2949639-43. Compare Aronson, *Heydrich*, p. 184; and Peterson, *Limits*, pp. 129-30.

20. "Besprechung mit dem RStH," 22 March 1934, ByHStA, Abt II, RStH Epp, 148. Saech.MdI, 8 March 1934, in Reimund Schnabel, *Macht ohne Moral* (Frankfurt: Verlag Roederberg, 1957), p. 65. Broszat, "Concentration Camps," pp. 415-16; RStH an ByMPraes., betr.: "Schutzhaft," 20 March; and StMdI an RStH, 13 April, BA/R43,II/398/134-38, 140-44.

21. "VO zur Durchfuehrung des Gesetzes ueber die Geheime Staatspolizei von 30. November 1933," 8 March 1934, *PrGS*, p. 143; RdErl.d.MPraes., 8 March 1934, *MBliV*, p. 469: and RdErl.d.MPraes., 14 March 1934, *MBliV*, p. 471.

22. GeStapa, re "Nachwuchs der politischen Polizei," 15 March 1934, T-175/422/2950062-64.

23. On Diels's awareness, Diels, *Lucifer ante Portas*, p. 294. GeStapa, to MPraes. CdGeStapo, 24 March 1934, GStA/90,P/1, Heft 1/95-97, with a notation of "ja," signed Goering.

24. RMdI, re Schutzhaft, 12 April 1934, T-175/422/2949912-15. As an apparent oversight, the decree initially undermined Epp's more stringent efforts to curb Schutzhaft abuse in Bavaria, StMdI to RStH, 13 April, BA/R43,II/398/ 140-44. That was corrected when the decree was subsequently modified to give the RStH final authority, RMdI, re "Schutzhaft," 26 April, BA/R43,II/398/147.

25. Schulz, *Machtergreifung*, pp. 602-608; and Neufeldt, *Ordnungspolizei*, pp. 8-10.

26. PrMdI to ORR Nebe, GeStapa, 30 April 1934, GStA/90,P/5/99; and BDC/ SSO Nebe. For technical reasons, Nebe remained in a Gestapo pay slot until October 1934, but his new position was clearly free of any Gestapo control, PrMPraes. to CdGeStapo, 24 April, and PrMdI, 23 October, GStA/90,P/5/98, 104.

27. RMdI to Reg.dL.Schmbg.-Lippe, 30 May 1934; and LReg. to RFSS, 2 June, N.Saech.StA Bueckebg, L4/10193/1-2.

28. Goering allegedly expressed such a sense of conflict to Diels as early as January 1934, Diels, *Lucifer ante Portas*, p. 67. For an analysis of the advantage in bureaucratic struggles of a drive to unify power over mere bids for aggrandizement, Marshall E. Dimock, "Expanding Jurisdictions: A Case Study in Bureaucratic Conflict," in Robert K. Merton, *Reader in Bureaucracy*, (Glencoe, Ill.: Free Press, 1952), pp. 282-83.

29. Martha Dodd, *Through Embassy Eyes*, pp. 53, 134-38; for a contemporary reference by Goering to Diels's illness, and its effects on Gestapo work, PrMPraes., GeStapo, 19 March 1934, GStA/90,P/2, Heft 1/30; and on Goering's loss of confidence, interrogation of Goering, 13 October 1945, p.1, NA/RG-238. Cf. also Diels's version of Goering's comments at the time of his dismissal, Diels, *Lucifer ante Portas*, p. 295.

30. Diels, *Lucifer ante Pprtas*, pp. 279-85; and cf. Diels affidavit, PS-2460, *IMT*, 30:549.

31. Diels, *Lucifer ante Portas*, pp. 283-85, 295-96.

32. Koehler, *Inside the Gestapo*, pp. 99-110; and Orb *Nationalsozialismus*, p. 129, on Patschowski, the exposed plot, and claims that Heydrich personally confronted Goering with the evidence while Himmler capitalized on the coup by going straight to Hitler and proclaiming the Gestapo's failure as an example of the weakness caused by disunited political police. Nevertheless, Hitler is supposed to have encouraged Goering to resist pressure to drop Diels.

33. Aronson, *Heydrich*, pp. 187-88; and Lina Heydrich, *Leben*, pp. 46-47. Himmler stated publicly that he assumed the post after exhaustive discussions with Goering; Himmler speech of March 1936, BA/NS-19/H.R./3. Heydrich began his work in the Gestapo as early as April 1, well before the official takeover; PrMPraes., 20, 21, 24 September 1934, GStA/90/951/57, 59, 66.

34. D'Alquen, letter of 24 July 1978. In December 1933, Himmler's reading notes on a biography of Karin Goering indicate a warm regard for the man; Himmler's Gelesene Buecher, LC/Himmler File/Container 418.

35. British Ambassador, Phipps still classed Himmler as an ally of Roehm and saw his acquisition of the Gestapo as a victory of that faction against Goering; Phipps to Simon, dispatch No. 475, Berlin, 25 April 1934, *Documents on British Foreign Policy*, 2d series, 6:649.

36. Diels, *Lucifer ante Portas*, pp. 295-96; Wighton, *Heydrich*, p. 64; Peterson, *Limits*, p. 130. As late as April 28, the Bremen representative in Berlin reported that he had learned from reliable sources that Hitler had countermanded the appointment of Himmler because he had not been consulted and did not consider Himmler suitable; Br. Vertretung to Markert, 28 April 1934, StA Bremen, 3-P.l.a./1152/6. The British ambassador also picked up on a "wrangle . . . over the appointment of Herr Himmler," but mistakenly believed it was a Goering maneuver to block Himmler; Phipps to Simon, dispatch No. 477, Berlin, April 25, 1934, *Documents on British Foreign Policy*, 2d Series, 6: 652. Cf. Aronson, *Heydrich*, p. 187 for an interpretation of Diels's version to the effect that Hitler may have decided on a move against the SA, but needed Diels for the balance between the SA, Party, bureaucracy, and Reichswehr. Graf, *Politische Polizei*, p. 216, refers only to technical hitches in the paperwork.

37. Draft copy of PrMPraes. CdGeStapo, April 1934, GStA/90,P/1, Heft 1/33. Cf. Graf, *Politische Polizei*, pp. 208-20, who emphasizes continuity in the development of the Gestapo as more important than any single change during the process.

38. RdErl.d.MPraes., 8 March 1934, T-175/239/2728694; for notes on SS involvement in border patrol work, unidentified memo, e.o. II M391, 22 March 1934, PA/S-17/Bd.1.

39. "Anlagen I and II zur Staatssekretaerbesprechung am 7.9.1933," GStA/77/28.

40. Id.GeStapo to PrMPraes., 24 Marcch 1934, GStA/90,P/1, Heft 1/94, requests Goering's continued intervention against Frick; PPraes. (Berlin) to St-Sekretaer, 6 April, GStA/90,P/3/62-63, is an example of personnel politics in relation to Himmler's initial moves.

41. GeStapa, SA Verbindungsfuehrer, to PrMPraes., 13 April 1934; and GeStapo, Inspekteur to PrMPraes., 16 June, GStA/90,P/1, Heft 2/217-18b; subsequent correspondence between Goering and PrFM, July through November, 29-33, 66-71, 89-100.

42. For a written affirmation of the verbal agreement between Goering and Himmler, PrMPraes. to RFSS, 28 April 1934; and RFSS to PrMPraes., 1 May, GStA/90,P/2,Heft 1/40-40b.

43. PPraes. (Berlin) re "Die Organisation der Staatspolizeistelle Berlin," 4 April 1934, GStA/90,P/3/49-51; according to Werner Best, Richard Kube, Oberpraesident Brandenburg Berlin, worked effectively to limit Himmler's power in his province (le 21.7.78) (see nn. 26, 40).

44. For the titles and Frick's ridicule, Frick to Goering, 10 January 1935, T-175/70/2587696-97.

45. The political police of Schaumburg-Lippe came under his command on 2 June 1934, Buchheim, "Politische Polizei," p. 300; they actually became a field office of the Prussian Gestapo effective 1 April 1935, PPK d. Laender, 1 July 1935, T-175/250/2742171. Zentralbuero d. PPK, 2 May 1934, T-175/422/2949919.

11. The SD and Conservative Opposition

1. NSDAP, RL, Reichsschatzmeister to Reichskassenverwaltung, 26 January 1934; Heydrich to Schwarz, 14 May, T-580/93/457.

2. Ibid.

3. N.Saech.HStA Hannover, 310 I/A/122 II, provides a relatively complete picture of the development of this *Gau* ND through 1933. See especially "Sitzung des N.D. am 21.Mai 1933," n.d., n.a.; Pgl.Hpt.Abtl III., "Taetigkeitsbericht," n.d.; and NSDAP, Gau Sued-Hannover-Braunschwieg, H.A.III (N.D.) Rundschreiben Nr. 5/33, 28 June 1933.

4. StA Detmold, L 133/III2, contains numerous reports from early 1934. On *Gau* ND, Koeln-Aachen, BDC/OPG Brunkhorst, Johannes (b. 11.8.01).

5. Pr. MPraes.,GeStapo, re "Auskunfterteilung an Landesverrats- und Spionagesachen und Zusammenarbeit mit den Orgainisationsbeauftragten der Wehrmacht," 16 May 1934, T-175/405/2928199-200.

6. Cover letter to all Abwehrstellen des Heeres, with attachment: StSek.d.RK to Stabschef der SA, Roehm, 19 April 1934, PA/S-17/Bd.1.

7. NSDAP, StVdf, AO of 9 June 1934, T-580/93/457; and NSDAP, Reichsschatzmeister to Gauschatzmeister, re "Zuschuesse an den Nachrichtendienst," 27 June, *Rundschreiben des Reichsschatzmeisters vom 26 Juli 1926–31 Dezember 1934* (Munich, 1935).

8. BDC/SSO Hans U. Geschke (b. 16.5.07); SSO Dr. Walter Haensch (b. 3.3.04); and Ramme, *Sicherheitsdienst*, p. 53.

9. GeStapo, Inspekteur, re "Nachrichtendienst der Partei," 9 October 1934, quoting letter of the RFSS of 1 October re "Nachrichtendienst Deutschen Arbeitsfront," T-175/405/2928202-203.

10. BDC/SSO, Felix Schmidt (b. 17.6.01), Lebenslauf, 5 October 1943, and RuSHA report, 6 July 1944.

11. I.d.GeStapo, re "Nachrichtendienst der Partei," 25 June 1934; I.d.GeStapo, 6 August, specifying the inclusion of the ND of the Kampfring of the Deutsch-Oesterreicher under the ban, T-175/405/2928200-202.

12. GeStapa, "Rundschreiben an alle Abteilungen," 30 May 1934, T-175/414/2949981.

13. RMdI, re "Weitergabe von Nachrichten der politischen Polizei an die Presse," 9 April 1934, GStA/90,P/2, Heft 1/38; and PPK, Zentralbuero, same subject, 31 May, HA/84/1722. The lag between the two orders may simply have resulted from Heydrich's preoccupation with the problems of assuming control of the Gestapo.

14. Hans Frank, *Im Angesicht*, pp. 160-61.

15. Two surviving documents relevant to the initial developments of Kripo are Pfundtner to Nicolai and Daluege, 29 May 1934; and report to Frick, 28 May, BA/R-18/627/65-66, 71. Gisevius, *To the Bitter End,* p. 142.

16. ByStMdI, re "Schutzhaft," 2 May 1934, T-580/107/17.

17. The surviving documents of the former *Land* Wuerttemberg in the HStA Stuttgart provide a detailed study of how these financial controls were applied with varying degrees of success, E 151a/Bue 1452 and 1454. See also RMdF an RMdI re "Haushaltsfuehrung der Laender," 12 May 1934, E 140/Bue 3.

18. An extensive collection of relevant documents can be found in HStA Stuttgart, E 130b/Bue 1065, and E 151a/Bue 1452. Reference to Murr-Himmler collaboration in MPraes., re "Neubesetzung der Stelle des L.d.PLPA," 17 September 1934, E 130/Bue 1065/72/p.2.

19. "Niederschrift ueber die . . . Versammlung (19 Juni 1934)," GStA/90,P/1,Heft 1/62-63.

20. Neumann to Heydrich, 22 June 1934, GStA/90,P/1,Heft 1/, 58; drafts of decree, June 1934,. ibid., 50-53, 82-85; and Heydrich to Neumann, 26 June 1934, ibid., 59-60.

21. "Niederschrift . . . (19 June 1934)," GStA/90,P/1,Heft 1/62-81, especially p. 63 on his promise and desires.

12. The Roehm Purge

1. Perhaps the best English-language summaries are Nyomarkay, *Charisma and Factionalism*, and Orlow, *Nazi Party, 1933-1945*, chaps. 1-3, which emphasize not only the PO-SA clash but also tensions within the Party. Classic accounts remain Hermann Mau, "Die zweite Revolution," *VfZ* 1 (January 1953): 119-37; and Sauer, *Machtergreifung*, pp. 829-966. Schoenbaum, *Hitler's Social Revolution*, details the complexity of the socioeconomic conflicts of NS Germany. On the Second Revolutionaries versus economic and industrial power groups, Schweitzer, *Big Business*, pp. 246-52. A thorough English-language summary of the military clash with the SA is Robert J. O'Neill, *The German Army and the Nazi Party, 1933-1939* (London: Cassell, 1966), pp. 31-53; however, Wheller-Bennett, *Nemesis of Power*, pp. 304-28, remains a classic source; cf. n. 5.

2. Diels, *Lucifer ante Portas*, pp. 273-80; and Harry Wilde, "Der Roehm-Putsch," *Politische Studien* 10 (June 1959): 377. On Diels's rumors, Phipps to Simon, dispatch No. 477, April 25, 1934, *Documents on British Foreign Policy*, 2d series, 4:655.

3. Wheeler-Bennett, *Nemesis*, pp. 319-20; Nyomarkay, *Charisma and Factionalism*, pp. 128-33; and Bessel, *Political Violence*, pp. 132-33.

4. Specific acts contributing to the mounting tensions and rumors of coups and preparations for decisive "countermeasures" are revealed in the materials assembled in Nuremberg testimonies, statements of Karl Wolff (7-8 September 1952), Werner Best (1 October 1951), and in the materials assembled in the case against Dietrich (Munich, July 1956 and May 1957). It is always difficult to separate such witnesses' knowledge of factual happenings from their acceptance of traditions about Himmler and Heydrich, even in cases where they worked intimately with these men. Even more extreme are the often cited versions of Orb, *Nationalsozialismus*, pp. 219-308; and Hoettl, *Secret Front*, pp. 27-29. Cf. Gisevius, p. 173.

5. Sauer, *Machtergreifung*, pp. 950-60; Hoehne, *The Order*, pp. 97-112; and

Aronson, *Heydrich*, pp. 191-95. Heinrich Bennecke, *Die Reichswehr und der "Roehm-Putsch"* (Munich: Guenter Olzog Verlag, 1964) began the process of re- during 99 responsibility and increasing that of the military; Klaus-Juergen Muel- ler, "Reichswehr und Roehm-Affaire," Dokumentation, *Militaergeschichtliche Mitteilungen*, 1968, pp. 107-44; and *Das Heer und Hitler* (Stuttgart: Deutsche Ver- lags-Anstalt, 1969) have substantiated this view with significant evidence. Of course, claims that Heydrich had goaded the military to action with carefully planted false reports (Calic, *Heydrich*, p. 115) cannot be wholly dismissed, but require some supporting evidence before they are worthy of serious considera- tion. Bessel, *Political Violence*, pp. 132-33, relies on the impressions of involved parties to blame Himmler.

6. Gisevius, *To the Bitter End*, p. 171, quoting an order from Goering to this effect. BA/Schu 402 contains scraps of evidence mostly pertaining to the cleanup action that followed. The BDC personnel files include a few passing, usually vague references to individuals' roles in the purge.

7. Wheeler-Bennett, *Nemesis*, p. 321.

8. The pseudonymous Koehler claims to have personally collected from Papen's office extensive evidence of a pending right-wing coup, *Inside Informa- tion*, pp. 224-30. Unfortunately his details of the purge are not reliable. SD per- sonnel files (BDC/SSO) reveal cases of penetration of suspected groups. See von Papen, *Memoirs*, p. 325, on one agent in his offices. In the SA-Ic or ND, Hans- Ulrich Geschke (BDC/SSO; and Ramme, *Sicherheitsdienst*, p. 53, n. 75), and Dr. Walter Haensch (NA/RG-238/No-3261; and Ramme, *loc* cit.) were SD V-men. Theo Gahrmann (BDC/SSO/Personal-Bericht, 14.12.36); Dr. Karl Gengenbach (BDC/SSO/especially Befoerderungsvorschlag, 30.4.35); Wilhelm Maas (BDC/ SSO); and Otto Prast (BDC/SSO/Lebenslauf) are cases of SA-men in contact with the SD, although in every case, their SD connections cannot be established prior to June 1934. A major channel for penetration was the Wehrpolitisches Amt (until its dissolution in December 1934) whose chief, Friedrich Krueger, was a coconspirator with Himmler and worked especially closely with von Reichenau.

9. GeStapo re "Sauberungsaktion," 4 July 1934; and II 1 Sonderdezernat, 11 July 1934, T-175/422/2950059, -085; and Papen, *Memoirs*, p. 325. Lina Heydrich, *Leben*, pp. 47-49, records Heydrich's alleged attitudes and afterthoughts.

10. In conformity with this logic, many executioners of the purge, like Ernst Mueller, Heydrich's chief agent in Silesia, went on to play roles in the Austrian and Czechoslovakian predecessors of the *Einsatzgruppen*, and then in the mass murder squads themselves, BDC/SSO Mueller (b. 17.9.93).

11. According to Goering (PrMPraes. to Fuehrer u.RK, 29 August 1934, BA/ R43 II/398/197) 1,124 were arrested in Prussia and all but 35 had been released by the end of August. Other *Laender* made similar reports (ibid.) The most im- pressive, dispassionate, and detailed account of the behavior of Heydrich and his executioners is that of Kurt Gildisch who personally murdered Dr. Erich Klausener, head of Catholic Action, on the direct order of Heydrich; testimony from "Urteil des Schwurgerichts bei dem Landgericht Berlin," 18 May 1953, printed in Robert M.W. Kempner, *SS im Kreuzverhoer* (Noerdlingen: Delphi Pol- itik, 1987), pp. 325-29. Bessel, *Political Violence*, pp. 133-39, described events in Silesia and Pommerania, where most excesses occurred, relying on "Urteil des Schwergerichts beim Landgericht Osnabrueck vom 2. August 1957 gegen Udo von Woyrsch und Ernst Mueller."

12. Bennecke, *Die Reichswehr und der "Roehm-Putsch*," pp. 62-64, doubts that either he or Himmler dared take initiatives in Goering's Berlin; and Deschner, *Heydrich*, pp. 106-8, thinks Heydrich added only Erich Klausener to the list.

13. Kempner, *SS im Kreuzverhoer*, pp. 328-29, quoting the judgment on Gildisch, 18 May 1953, and p. 332, quoting interrogation of F.K. Freiherr von Eberstein, 6 July 1946, *IMT*; cf. *IMT* 20: 289-92.

14. BDC/SSO Ernst Mueller (b. 17.9.93), especially report of HSSPF Suedost, 21 October 1943. On replacing SStL, Klein, *Lageberichte*, I:50, citing le 9.7.34—GStAPKI, HA Rep. 90 Nr. 8 H.2.

15. For correspondence on police officials caught in the purge, PrMdI, Grauert to Koerner, 14 August 1934; PrMdI, Grauert to Goering, 8 August 1934, and GeStapa, Sond.Dez. to Goering, re "Beamtenhinterbliebenenenversorgung," 9 October 1934, GStA/90 P/4/13-14, 20-22, 26. BDC/SSO Anton Dunckern (b. 29.6.05); and SSO Mueller, report of HSSPF Suedost, 21 October 1943.

16. BDC/SSo, Geschke and Haensch; see n. 8.

17. A clear observation of this can be dated to Ernst K. Bramstedt, *Dictatorship and Political Police* (London: Kegan Paul, 1945), p. 74; and it was part of Nyomarkay's conclusions (*Charisma and Factionalism*, pp. 128, 138-41); however, the most explicit analysis is in Hermann Mau, "Die zweite Revolution," *VfZ* 1: 119-37.

18. As one example, in OAb Rhein the funds from contributing members suddenly tripled after June 30; Lonnie L. Lorance, "Financing the Local SS in Major Region Rhein, 1934-1936," p. 4, unpublished seminar paper, Univ. of Wisconsin, January 5, 1970. On SS contacts in and support from influential circles, Reinhard Vogelsang, *Der Freundeskreis Himmler* (Goettingen: Musterschmidt, 1972).

19. Aronson, *Heydrich*, p. 192; and more recently elaborated in extensive literature on the Army's involvement; for example, Christian Streit, "The German Army and the Policies of Genocide," and Juergen Foerster, "The German Army and the Ideological War against the Soviet Union," in Gerhard Hirschfeld (ed.), *The Policies of Genocide: Jews and Soviet Prisoners of War in Nazi Germany* (London: Allen & Unwin, 1986), pp. 1-29.

20. Orlow, *Nazi Party, 1933-1945*, pp. 116-118, 125-30ff.

21. Viktor Lutze's eyewitness accounts, T-175/33/2541892-93. Eyewitness verifications by Julius Schaub, Wilhelm Brueckner, and Robert Ley are cited by David Irving, *The War Path, Hitler's Germany, 1933-1939* (New York: Viking Press, 1978), pp. 39, 271, citing Sammlung Irving, IfZ.

13. The Conservative Counterattack

1. Gisevius testimony, *IMT* 12:175; and Frick interrogation, 9 October 1945, p. 11 (NA/RG 238).

2. Copy of RMdI, re "Dienstlicher Verkehr zwischen den Behoerden," 2 July 1934, GStA/90,P/1,Heft 1/110; and Aronson, *Heydrich*, pp. 217-18. The last digits on the office designation for the decree—that is, 22.6—indicate the date of initial action; and in RMdI to PrMPraes. re "Polizei," 13 July (StA Bremen 3-P.1.a/1178), Frick claims to have signed the decree on June 29, therefore denying any connection with the events of June 30.

3. On the Hitler-Frick relationship, NA/RG-238, Frick interrogation, 6 September 1945, p. 12.

4. Copy, PrMPraes.,CdGeStapo to RMdI, 5 July 1934, GStA/90,P/1,Heft 1/111; and Aronson, *Heydrich*, p. 218.

5. Frick's response, RMdI to PrMPraes., re "Polizei," 13 July 1934, StA Bre-

men, 3-P.1.a./1178. Saech.Erl. of 13.10.1934, referred to in BDC/SSO August Meier (b. 8.10.00). On some of the temporary restrictions against membership in the police and inconsistent enforcement. Lorenz, "General SS Membership," p. 18.

6. IdGeStapo, 24 May 1934, T-175/422/2949960.

7. Cited in StMdI, der PPK Bayerns, re "Die Zusammenarbeit der staatlichen Polizeibehoerden mit dem (SD) . . . ," 7 December 1934, T-580/93/457, which goes on to delimit SD and political police roles in more proper terms and to end SD executive action.

8. Broszat, "Concentration Camps," p. 432; Aronson, *Heydrich*, p. 220; and Sydnor, *Soldiers of Destruction*, p. 17. Himmler's objectives were revealed in IdGeStapo to PrMdI, 18 August 1934, GStA/90,P/104/49

9. See p. 104 above. Cf. Aronson, *Heydrich*, p. 221.

10. Himmler's agenda for conferences with Hitler, 27.4.34–23.8.34, T-175/94/2615274-79, the latter date being the first recorded discussion of the KL. Marginalia on the document cited in n. 8 indicates their ignorance, as do Frick's responses that followed.

11. Copy of PrMPraes., CdGeStapo. 6 July 1934, T-175/414/2950075-76. Cf. Plum, "Staatspolizei," 197, 208-10; and Aronson, *Heydrich*, p. 190.

12. Communication of July 6, n. 11. Emphasis added.

13. RMdI to PrMPraes., re "Staatspolizeistellen," 7 July 1934, GStA/90,P/1,Heft 1/140; RMdI, re "Berichterstaatung in politischen Angelegenheiten," 7 July, as Document 2 in Plum, "Staatspolizei," pp. 210-11; and Aronson, *Heydrich*, p. 219.

14. Copy of PrMPraes.,CdGeStapo., to RMdI, re "Staatspolizeistellen," 9 July 1934, GStA/90,P/1,Heft 1/141-141b.

15. PrMPraes. to PrMdI, 9 July 1934, GStA/90,P/1,Heft 1/107; Plum, "Staatspolizei," 197-98, 211-12 (Document 3); and Aronson, *Heydrich*, p. 219.

16. PrMPraes., 11 July 1934, GStA/90,P/1,Heft 1/104, 106-106b. This incident is an example of the "heated disputes" between Goering and Frick to which Gisevius referred in his testimony, IMT 12:172-73.

17. IdGeStapo, re "Organisationserlass vom 6.7.1934," 21 July 1934, with attachment from HAbtl III, 13 July, GStA/90,P/1,Heft 1/148-49.

18. PrMdI, re "dort. Erlass vom 6.7.1934" 13 July 1934, GStA/90,P/1,Heft 1/128-39. An example of a supporting complaint was that of Diels in his new capacity as RegPraes., RPraes., Koeln, "Immediatbericht ueber die politische Lage," 4 November 1934, Plum, "Staatspolizei," 213-14 (Document 5).

19. See n. 18; and Aronson, *Heydrich*, p. 219.

20. PrMdI to the Ober- und RPraes., 16 July 1934, GStA/90,P/1,Heft 1/144; Plum, "Staatspolizei," 212-13 (Document 4); and Aronson, *Heydrich*, p. 220.

21. RMdI to LReg., re "Anordnungen von Landesbehoerden in Angelegenheiten von politischer Bedeutung," 16 July 1934, HStA Stuttgart, E 151a/Bue 1452/76. For an account of efforts by Epp to carry through with such a curbing of the political police in Bavaria, Peterson, *Limits*, pp. 183-84.

22. On Dr. Walter Schaeffer's action in Breslau, Hoehne, *The Order*, p. 188, citing interview with Schaeffer; on the Hohnstein case, 784-787-PS, IMT 26:301-326; on the Dachau case, IMT 20:458; Frick's assembled evidence, T-175/240/2730237-303; and on the Frank-Guertner attack, Hans Frank, *Im Angesicht*, pp. 160-61; see p. 136 above.

23. Gisevius, *To the Bitter End*, pp. 185, 191-93, describes his role as liaison in this early, loose coalition of opposition. Aronson, *Heydrich*, p. 233.

24. Frank, *Im Angesicht*, p. 161.

25. Broszat, "Concentration Camps," p. 422. Copy of AA, 83-71 23/11 zu Eing. A 1094, 29 November 1934 (NA/RG-238/NG-093), in which Buelow-Schwante cites the number of internees in the Reich as only 3,200, only two-thirds of whom were in camps; a figure that was impressive compared with the previously cited 26,789 for 31 July 1933.
26. Broszat, "Concentration Camps," pp. 429-35; and Sydnor, *Soldiers of Destruction*, pp. 19-20, 23-24.
27. GeStapa, 31 July 1934, referring to Goering's order of 19 June 1934; and HAbtl III, 4 August, T-175/422/2950142-143. The quotation is from GeStapa, re "Gefaengnis Columbiahaus," 5 September; and GeStapa, re "Schutzhaft," 29 October, is a typical reminder about regulations, T-175/422/2949500-501.
28. "Ansprache des Reichsfuehrers-SS vor den Beamten und Angestellten des Geheimen Staatspolizeiamtes am 11. Oktober 1934," pp. 1-4, BA/NS-19/H.R./2.
29. Ibid., pp. 5-6.
30. Ibid., pp. 6-7.
31. Ibid., pp. 2-3.
32. Aronson, *Heydrich*, pp. 106, 254.
33. Copy of IdGeStapo to PrMdI, 18 August 1934, GStA/90,P/104/49-49b; and Aronson, *Heydrich*, p. 221.
34. Marginalia and markings on the MdI copy (n. 33); IdGeStapo to PrFM, 18 August 1934, GStA/90,P/104/49b.
35. Der PrFM, 25 August 1934, GStA/90,P/104/48-48b; Aronson, *Heydrich*, p. 221.
36. The marginalia on the note, some of which seems to be Goering's, indicates at least an initial reaction of complacency, although the careful reading of the attached copy of Himmler's proposal, again as indicated by reader's marks, should have aroused suspicions.
37. Copy, PrMdI to PrFM, 28 August 1934, GStA/90,P/104/51-51b. Cf. Gisevius's testimony, *IMT*, 12:181. Gisevius was apparently confusing events of the winter of 1933-34 with those of this time, and the only point that emerges clearly from his rendition is Himmler's freedom to shift camp finances to police purposes.
38. CdPr. Landespolizei, Amt PR, cover letter with draft of VO, 17 September 1934; draft of Himmler's response, IdGeStapo, re "Ordnungsstrafverfahren in der Vollzugspolizei," September 1934, GStA/90,P/1,Heft 2/186-93.
39. RMdI, re "GeStapa," 27 September 1934, GStA/90,P/1,Heft 2/183.
40. PrMPraes. to PrSt.Ministerium, 8 October 1934; PrMPraes., CdGeStapo to RMdI, 13 October 1934, GStA/90,P.1,Heft 1/182, 184.
41. PrMPraes., CdGeStapo to PrMdI, re "Ordnungsstrafverfahren . . . ," 31 October 1934, GStA/90,P/1, Heft 2/194-94b. Working copy of PrMPraes., CdGeStapo to IdGestapo, September, ibid., 168d-f(for an earlier draft from August, 168a-c); cf. Aronson, *Heydrich*, p. 222.
42. IdGeStapa, re "Form des dienstlichen Verkehrs des GeStapa mit dem Herrn Ministerpraesidenten," 10 September 1934, T-175/229/2767270-71.
43. Aronson, *Heydrich*, pp. 222-23. PrMPraes., CdGeStapo to RFSS, 15 October 1934, GStA/90,P/1,Heft 2/169-69b.
44. Ibid., 169b; "Geschaeftsanweisung fuer die GeStapo," GStA/90,P/1,Heft 2/172-75.
45. This was stated specifically in PrGeStapo, StVCuI, re "Inspektion der Konzentrationslager," 10 December 1934, BA/R-58/239.
46. PrMPraes., CdGeStapo, 30 November 1934, GStA/90,P/104/99-100b.

47. PrMPraes. to RFSS, 15 October 1934, GStA/90,P/1, Heft 2/169b; GeStapa, re "Schutzhaft," 29 October, T-175/422/2949501.
48. PrMPraes., CdGeStapo, re "Durchfuehrung der Geschaeftsanweisung fuer die GeStapo," GStA/90,P/1,Heft 2/176-78.
49. PrMPraes., CdGeStapo, 20 November 1934, GStA/90,P/1,Heft 2/244-46; cf. IdGeStapa, 30 November, carrying the above plus further instructions, T-175/239/272836-38; Aronson, *Heydrich*, p. 223.
50. RMdI to LReg. re "Haushalt der politischen Polizei," 16 July 1934, N.Saech.HStA Buckebg., L4/12525/36-37. On the continued struggle over Stahlecker's appointment, HStA Stuttg. E 130b/Bue 1065/59-77. RMdI to IMdL re "Kriminalpolizei," 18 September 1934, StA Detmold, L 80 Ie/P/2.II. RuPrMdI to Reg.dL, re den "Entwurf eines Reichspolizeiverwaltungsgesetzes," 1 December, StA Bremen, S-P.1.a./1183/2.

14. The Selling of the Police State

1. D'Alquen letter, 24.7.78, and Best letter 27.7.78, both of whom ridicule the idea that the police state was deliberately sold and describe an exchange of ideas that grew from an evolving debate.
2. Such classic studies as Hanna Arendt, *The Origins of Totalitarianism* (New York: Meridian, 1958), and Carl J. Friedrich and Zbigniew K. Brzezinski, *Totalitarian Dictatorship and Autocracy* (Cambridge: Harvard Univ. Press, 1965), made their contributions by emphasizing the similarities between the Nazi and Stalinist regimes. In the process, the particulars of each experience became lost in generalizations, despite the efforts of the analysts. Attempts to define totalitarianism or to design a model of totalitarian regimes generally emphasize a blueprint quality in the sense of direction of the leadership, or a deliberateness or inevitability in the process of development. Consequently, much that was inadvertent in the German or Soviet experiences is obscured. The later work of Arno J. Mayer, *Dynamics of Counterrevolution in Europe, 1870-1956* (New York: Harper & Row, 1971), has avoided many of the pitfalls of pursuing an heuristic concept by not trying to bridge the gap between the radical right and Stalinism.
3. Hoehne, *The Order*, pp. 275-9; and for a valuable case study, Ronald M. Smelser, *The Sudeten Problem, 1933-1938* (Middletown, Conn.: Wesleyan Univ. Press, 1975), especially chap. 8.
4. Gerhard L. Weinberg, *The Foreign Policy of Hitler's Germany* (Chicago: Univ. of Chicago Press, 1970), pp. 205-6, 232-33; and Orlow, *Nazi Party, 1933-1945*, p. 138.
5. Weinberg, *Foreign Policy*, p. 224.
6. Ibid., pp. 241-47, 251-53; and Orlow *Nazi Party*, p. 174.
7. Orlow, pp. 163-64; Peterson, *Limits*, p. 185; Hoehne, *The Order*, pp. 327-28; and Lucy S. Dawidowicz, *The War against the Jews, 1933-1945* (Toronto: Bantam Books, 1986), pp. 62-63, who also relates these actions to the mood of 1935. For an overview of historiography on the Holocaust, Kershaw, *Nazi Dictatorship*, chap. 5; and the most recent controversial addition, Arno J. Mayer, *Why Did the Heavens Not Darken?* (New York: Pantheon, 1988).
8. Orlow, *Nazi Party*, pp. 164-65; Peterson, *Limits*, pp. 135-43; and Hilberg, *Destruction of the Jews*, 1: 36-38.
9. Cf. Hoehne, *The Order*, p. 186, whose assertion to the contrary is not fully supported by his source, Broszat, "Concentration Camps," p. 425, and cf. p. 428.

10. Reinhard Heydrich, "Wandlungen unseres Kampfes," first delivered as a speech, then published as a pamphlet (Munich: Eher, 1935) and reprinted in *Schwarze Korps*, 1936 (copy in T-175/247/2738620-34).

11. Ibid.

12. Heydrich, "Die Bekaempfung des Staatsfeinde," *Deutsches Recht* 6 (15 April 1936): 121-23. The SD showed special interest in monitoring press reactions to this article, especially criticisms in the organs of the "camouflaged enemy." SD-Ab Wuerttembg., re "Abhandlung von SS-Gruppenfuehrer Heydrich ueber 'Die Bekaempfung des Staatsfeinde,' " 27 May 1936, StA Lundwigsburg, K 110/Bue 34.

13. BDC/SSO, Gunter d'Alquen (b. 24.10.10); and d'Alquen letter, 14.6.78. On origin and development of *Das Schwartze Korps* and Heydrich's role and use of it to distribute propaganda, William Combs, *The Voice of the SS: A History of the SS Journal 'Das Schwartze Korps'* (New York: Peter Long, 1986), pp. 21-26 and *passim*, e.g., pp. 48-49, 77-81.

14. d'Alquen letters of 14.6.78 and 24.7.78; Best letter, 27.7.78; and see n.1.

15. Hans Frank remembered the "Aufklaerungspropaganda ueber die Konzentrationslager, die Hand in Hand ging mit einer . . . Kritik an der Justiz, die als volksfremd, forschrittsfeindlich, reaktionaer, ueberheblich verdaechtigt wurde." *Im Angesicht*, pp. 161-62. He also related his own abortive attempt to mount a counter sales program for a "constitutional dictatorship," pp. 162-64, 169-73.

16. J.S. Conway, *The Nazi Persecution of the Churches, 1933-1945* (New York: Basic Books, 1968), provides a thorough survey. Especially relevant are pp. 108-15. On use and role of *Das Schwartze Korps*, Combs, *Voice of SS*, ch. 5.

17. On the delicate balance between the Church Struggle and Hitler's popular image, Kershaw, *Hitler Myth*, chap. 4.

15. The Military Factor, 1934-1936

1. The evolution of the Waffen SS is summarized in Stein, *Waffen SS*, pp. 1-8; see also O'Neill, *German Army*, p. 97.

2. An endless stream of semischolarly and polemical literature on the Abwehr, Admiral Canaris, and their role in the "resistance," began with an account from the Abwehr perspective by Karl H. Abshagen, *Canaris, Patriot und Weltbuerger* (Stuttgart: Union Deutsch Verlagsgesellschaft, 1950), which was elaborated by Ian Colvin, *Chief of Intelligence* (London: Victor Gallancz, 1951). A chain of Abwehr "memoirs" concentrated on espionage adventures, glossing over the political and moral issues or playing to the "resistance" theme: Paul Leverkuehn, *German Military Intelligence* (London: Wiedenfeld & Nicholson, 1954); and Oscar Reile, *Geheime Westfront* (Munich: Verlag Welsermuehl, 1962); *Geheime Ostfront* (1963); *Macht und Ohnmacht der Geheimdienste* (1968). Hoettl, *Secret Front*, and Schellenberg, in his memoirs, provided the SD perspective, but saw little advantage in challenging the popular view in any serious way. Karl Bartz, *Die Tragodie der deutschen Abwehr* (Salzburg: Pilgram Verlag, 1955), put Canaris in a more accurate, less heroic frame. Nevertheless, the glamorizing continued in Roger Manvell and Heinrich Fraenkel, *The Canaris Conspiracy* (London: Heinemann, 1969). Counterperspectives have consistently come from the DDR, first former Abwehr officer, Rudolf Bamler, "Der deutsche militaerische Geheimdienst bei der Vorbereitung und Durchfuehrung des zweiten Weltkrieges," in *Der zweite Weltkrieg 1939-1945* (Berlin, 1959); then Albrecht Charisius and Julius

Mader, *Nicht laenger Geheim* (Berlin: Militaerverlag der DDR, 1969); and Mader, *Hitlers Spionagegenerale sagen aus* (Berlin: Verlag der Nation, 1970). Other Federal Republic literature; Gert Buchheit, *Der Deutsche Geheimdienst* (Munich: Paul List Verlag, 1966); Sverre Hartmann, "Zwischen Staat und Oystem," *Deutsche Rund-schau* 81 (April 1955): 348-53; and Huelme, *The Order*, generally approached the touchy subject of Abwehr-Nazi relations through oral sources with little testing against the surviving, badly scattered documents. Finally, the most thorough evaluation of the Abwehr appeared in David Kahn, *Hitler's Spies* (New York: Macmillan, 1978).

3. O'Neill, *German Army*, pp. 96-97; and Gisevius, *To the Bitter End*, pp. 185-92.

4. On Himmler and Fritsch, O'Neill, *German Army*, pp. 99-101.

5. As summarized by Abshagen, *Canaris*, pp. 74-75.

6. Best, "Die deutsche Abwehrpolizei bis 1945" (manuscript), pp. 22-25; and Abw.A., re "Mitarbeit von Behoerden beim Abwehrdienst," 15 November 1929, T-77/1449/857-81. PPraes., LKPA to MdI, re "Besondere Dienststelle fuer die zentrale Beobachtung und Bekaempfung der Zersetzungstaetigkeit in Reichs-wehr und Schutzpolizei," 10 January 1932, BA/R-58/669. The monthly reporting on subversive efforts was taken over by Gestapa on May 15: PPraes., LKPA (I), 11 April 1933 and GeStapa, 15 May, T-175/399/2920945, 2920994.

7. Outlined in de Jong, "German Fifth Column," pp. 872-81, 884-85. For a more thorough study, Jacobsen, *Nationalsozialistische Aussenpolitik*.

8. Orb, *Nationalsozialismus*, pp. 128-29.

9. Best's descriptions of the competition emphasize as the prime source of friction the problems of overlapping jurisdictions and misapprehensions at the lower levels about professional rivalry, "Die deutsche Abwehrpolizei bis 1945" (manuscript), pp. 19-22.

10. GeStapa, Abtl.IV, re "Zusammenarbeit mit den Abwehrstelen der Reichswehr," 23 November 1933; and PrMPraes., GeStapo, re "Auskunfterteilung in Landesverrat- und Sionagesachen und Zusammenarbeit mit den Organisationsbeauftragten der Wehrmacht," 16 May 1934, T-175/403/2926107-108, 432/2961992-95.

11. Note to Reichsminister, 17 January 1934, and copy of letter to Botschaftsrat Smend, Rome, 4 February, PA/Inland II A/B.

12. Mimeo-letter stamped "Ausw.Amt II M 724, 29 May 1934," to alle Abwehrstellen des Heeres, and attachment, copy of StSekdRK to Stabschef der SA, 19 April, PA/S-17/Bd. 1.

13. Order signed RK and RWM, 24 October 1933, BA-MA/RW-S/195 (made available by David Kahn); and Abshagen, *Canaris*, p. 97.

14. LdGeStapa, 1 June 1934, and GeStapa, 16 June, T-175/422/2949989, 2950027; HAbtl.III-Abwehramt, re "Verteiler," 17 May, ibid., 2949943.

15. Buchheit, *Der deutsche Geheimdienst*, p. 43, 45-46; and Gisevius, *To the Bitter End*, pp. 142-44.

16. Gisevius, pp. 185-87. Under Diels, Patschowski had tried to eliminate all intermediaries between himself and Abwehr, GeStapa-Abtl.IV, 23.11.1933, T-175/432/2961992-93, but he apparently had to give in. On Sonderbuero Stein, Orb, *Nationalsozialismus*, pp. 257-59; and Buchheit, *Der deutsche Geheimdienst*, p. 168. This may be related to the "Abwehrkommissariat an die Staatspolizeistelle Berlin," mentioned in HAbtl.III, 13 July 1934, BA/R-58/239, for SSt Berlin was originally under PP Berlin. Buchheit speculates that "Stein" fled Germany in 1935, worked for the Poles, published an expose, *Inside the Gestapo*, under the

pseudonym Heinrich Pfeiffer (apparently he is referring to Koehler's book of the same title), and then another under the name Heinrich Orb. There are marked similarities between the Koehler and Orb books. See Buchheit, p. 455, n. 20a.

17. Orb names Josef Pospichil as one of these SD spies (p. 258). Unfortunately, nothing in Pospichil's personnel files (BDC/SSO, b. 20.12.99, and Mappe Polizei) indicates this role, and he was not posted to the Gestapo until June 1934, from "civil employ." This does not preclude the possibility of the roles Orb attributed to him as Sohst's deputy for Gestapo-SS liaison, which could have been counted as civil employ. The dissolution of the Stein office may have occurred in November 1934, when there was an influx of personnel into Gestapa from PPraes.Berlin, who then worked in HAbtl.III, Polizeiabwehr (BDC/Mappe Polizei, Namentlisches Verzeichnis . . . Gestapa, pp. 15-16). See also Buchheit, *Der deutsche Geheimdienst*, p. 168, who makes the Stein office an SD front.

18. GVtP GeStapa, October 1934, BA/R-58/840/26-49; on the "inner sanctum," Orb, *Nationalsozialismus*, p. 145, which is partially verified by the fact that all names are excluded from Habtl.III in the GVtP; and BDC/Mappe Polizei/ "Namentlisches Verzeichnis . . . Gestapa," pp. 14-18. Best, *Abwehrpolizei*, pp. 25-26, 32-34.

19. BDC/Mappe Polizei/Namentlisches Verzeichnis, pp. 1, 15-16; HAbtl. III, re III zbV, 4 May 1935, T-175/422/2950378; and SSO, Pomme (b. 14.2.99), especially Lebenslauf and RFSS, CdSHA to CdO re Pomme. Pomme's files deny Orb's contention that he was a secret "high SD member" (*Nationalsozialismus*, p. 63), but his lack of formal NS affiliation until 1937 coupled with his NS contacts from as early as 1929 did make him something of a Trojan horse. He may have been an SD V-man, but this should have been indicated in his file. Koehler, *Inside the Gestapo*, p. 33, described Pomme as Goering's man, forced on Heydrich, but successfully kept too busy to serve Goering's purposes.

20. Copy of Abw.Nr.108/11.34 IIIt, re "Aufgabenteilung zwischen Stapo-Abwehrstelle und M-Beauftragten," 26 November 1934, T-175/403/2926108-10.

21. Colvin, *Chief of Intelligence;* Mueller, *Heer und Hitler*, p. 161; and statements of Adm. Richard Protze to David Kahn, 24.8.1973 (made available by Kahn). Cf. Reitlinger, *S*, pp. 91-92, for the version that Heydrich exposed the operation to Blomberg.

22. A sensational, but relatively reliable, summary of the affair is in Brissaud, *Nazi Secret Service*, pp. 86-103, based on interviews with Protze, Jost, and Schellenberg, and some reference to the documents. Other factors such as SD rivalry may have influenced the timing of the exposure. Mueller, *Heer und Hitler*, p. 161, on Patzig-Canaris decision.

23. Reitlinger, *SS*, p. 92, is a typical example, although he suffers no illusions about Canaris's role in the resistance.

24. See n. 2.

25. To his wife, Heydrich allegedly expressed pleasure at Canaris's appointment and hopes for improved relations with Abwehr; Wighton, *Heydrich*, p. 88, quoting Lina Heydrich.

26. Canaris's political attitudes are revealed in Helmut Krausnick, "Aus den Personalakten von Canaris." *VfZ*, 10 (July 1962): 280-310.

27. Most of the sources in n. 2 provide a variety of views of the Heydrich-Canaris relationship: cf. Lina Heydrich, *Leben*, pp. 62-68. On Himmler: Aronson, *Heydrich*, p. 290, n. 18; Aronson also emphasizes Heydrich's special problems in the Navy, pp. 25-34.

28. Abshagen, *Canaris*, pp. 67-68; Hartmann, "Zwischen Staat und System,"

p. 348, quotes an alleged conversation between Patzig and Canaris; and Kahn, *Hitler's Spies*, p. 229, indicates that Raeder strongly opposed Canaris, but relented under Patzig's persuasion. Lina Heydrich claimed her husband expressed surprise at Canaris's appointment: Wighton, *Heydrich*, p. 88.

29. Brissaud, *Secret Service*, p. 131; and Colvin, *Chief of Intelligence*, pp. 15, 22.

30. O'Neill, *German Army*, pp. 97-99; and Wehrmacht publication, *Richtlinien fuer den Unterricht ueber politische Tagesfragen*, Nr. 2, 1935, BA-MA/Z 518z, summarizing Himmler's speech. During January, this and other Richtlinien (Nrs. 1 and 3) devoted space to dispelling "dangerous rumors" relating to military-SS hostility. GeStapa, Sonderbericht (Presse), "Vergiftung . . . ," December/January 1934/35, T-175/432/2962374-424 (although this was a "secret" report, several thousand copies were published for wide distribution).

31. Gisevius, *To the Bitter End*, pp. 185-87, 191-92, who blamed Major Bamler for betraying him to Heydrich, although it could just as well have been Canaris. Blomberg's decision was communicated in RWM to RuPrMdI, re "Verstaerkung der polizeilichen Spionageabwehr," 22 January 1935, GStA/90, P/1, Heft 2/310.

32. "Ergebnisse der Besprechung im Reichswehrministerium am 17.1.1935, 15-18 Uhr," GStA/ibid./313; on Bamler, Gisevius, *To the Bitter End*, p. 187; Best, "Abwehrpolizei," p. 19.

33. "Ergebnisse": Abshagen, *Canaris*, p. 98; and Schellenberg, *Memoiren*, p. 138, who also uses the label for a later accord. The "Ten Commandment" portion of the understanding became a part of Gestapo directives, "Erlasse betr. Abwehrstelle und M-Beauftragte" as of 15 October 1935, T-175/403/2926106-116. Best, "Abwehrpolizei," pp. 19-20, and other of his testaments give only a 21 December 1936 elaboration of the accord and are usually cited for details, which accounts for the tradition of giving December 1936 as the first date for the "Ten Commandments"; most recently, Hoehne, *The Order*, p. 229.

34. Best, "Abwehrpolizei," pp. 19-20. "Ergebnisse der Besprechung . . . " 17.1.1935, GStA/90,P/1, Heft 2/313-15.

35. Ibid., 315-16; and GeStapa, 6 February 1935, carrying Abwehr notice, Nr.101/2.35 geh. of 1 February 1935 re DAF, ND; and Abw., Nr. 1986/3.35 III 1g. to all Abwehrstelle, 30 March, T-175/422/2950238,-370. After Heydrich took over the Gestapa, one of his initial orders to Abwehrpolizei reasserted the exclusivity of the SD as the Party agency for Abwehr work, der MPraes., GeStapa, re "Auskunfterteilung . . . und Zusammenarbeit," 16 May 1934, T-175/432/ 2961995. Of course, this guaranteed neither Abwehr cooperation nor consent to SD involvement, for on the next day, he removed the SD from Abwehr police distribution lists (see n. 14). By August 1935, however, a local *Abwehrstellenleiter* like Hauptmann Lynker of Kassel would approach both Gestapo and SD posts on an equal basis in order to develop close cooperation, B/B. to Albert, 23 August 1935, Hess.HStA Wiesbaden, 483/171. Abw.3254/11.35ag., "Zeiteinteilung fuer die Besprechung vom 25.-30.11.1935, 21.11.1935," and "Abwehr-Arbeitstagung am 27. November 1935 im Dienstgebaeude des GeStapa," n.d., T-77/1449/650, 654-56, 665.

36. RWM to PrFM and RuPrMdI, 22 January 1935, GStA/90,P/1,Heft 2/309-312.

37. RKM u. Oberbefehlshaber d. WM to the F.u. Obersten Befehlshaber d.WM, 1 July 1935, BA/R 43 II/391/59-61.

38. PrGeStapo, der StVCuI, re "Zusammenarbeit der SSt mit Dienststellen der WM," 25 January 1935, T-175/403/2926103-104, in which Heydrich urged and

outlined the nature of cooperation, and ordered field posts to establish coordinating links with Abwehr posts. PrGeStapo, der StVCuI, to all SST, 30 January, ibid., 105, in which he established centralized reporting to Abwehr through Gestapo, not only to control the cooperation but to ensure it. Abwehr-Abtl., re "Ueberwachung von Truppen-Uebungsplaetzen usw.," 27 March 1936, ibid., 2926031-32, in which Bamler ordered local Abwehr posts to brief thoroughly SSt counterparts. Reile, *Geheime Ostfront*, p. 251, verifies that Gestapo and Abwehr representatives did work together well in field work and confirmed that Canaris, like Heydrich, did not observe the restrictions closely when he had important points to score (p. 252); Best, "Abwehrpolizei," pp. 20-21.

39. Extract from *Reichszollblatt*, 16 April 1936, T-175/423/2950964. Der PPKdL, PrGeStapo, der StVCuI, re "Dienstanweisung ueber die Zusammenarbeit der GeStapo mit den Polizeien auslaendischer Staaten," 3 December 1935, expands freedom beyond previous ordinances and seeks to tighten control over Gestapo agents, T-175/422/2950778-80. PrGeStapo, der StVC, re "Beantwortung von Anfragen auslaendischer Botshaften . . . durch die GeStapo," 11 May 1936, represents a significant increase in freedom, T-175/229/2767280. Deutsches Konsulat Luettich, to AA Berlin, 22 May 1936, reports one case of Gestapo kidnapping without providing details, NA/RG 238/NG-4261.

40. Habtl.III, re changes in GVtP Habtl.III, 4 May 1935, T-175/422/2950378-79; and GVtP GeStapa, Stand von 1. Oktober 1935, BA/R-58/840/56-57,64.

41. Orb, *Nationalsozialismus*, p. 145; no *Leiter* is listed for HAbtl. III in the October 1935, GVtP (see note 40). Der PPKdL, Pr. GeStapo, der StVCuI, 20 December 1935 re Best's assignment, BA/R-58/243/83; Best, "Abwehrpolizei," pp. 27-28, whose account seems to overemphasize his appointment as the turning point in Abwehr-Gestapo relations.

42. Best, pp. 19-20.

43. "Grundsaetze fuer die Zusammenarbeit zwischen der Geheimen Staatspolizei und den Abwehrdienststellen der Wehrmacht vom 21.12.1936," T-77/1449/484-87.

44. T-175/291/EAP 173-b-16-05/156 is a folder of IIA dealing with Czechoslovakia, with one of the earliest surviving reports dating from 19 January 1935 (2786937). The role of the Grenzpolizei is especially apparent. LdGeStapa, 16 May 1935, established the Dezernat II C3 for dealing with Austria, T-175/422/2950420. GeStapa, "Lagebericht ueber den Stand der polizeilichen Spionageabwehr in Preussen (Berichtsmonate Januar und Februar 1935)," 25 February 1935, reports on the operations of Czech and Polish intelligence services, T-175/405/2927348-54. BDC/SSO Puchta, Adolf (b. 25.2.08) for example of early Saxon Gestapo agent in Czechoslovakia and resultant problems.

45. PPKdL, PrGeStapo, StVCuI, "Dienstanweisung ueber die Zusammenarbeit der GeStapo mit den Polizeien auslaendischen Staaten," 3 December 1935, T-175/422/2950778-80; and PrGeStapo, StVC, re "Zusammenarbeit der GeStapo mit der jugoslavischen Polizei," 21 April 1936, GStA/90,P/1,Heft 2/286-91.

46. Abwehr-Abtl., re "Ueberwachung von Truppen-Uebungsplatzen usw.," 27 March 1936, T-175/403/2926031-32; RFSS-uCdSHA, Stabskanzlei, I/112, re "Staatspolizeiliche Ueberwachung von Wehrmachtsangehoerigen," 3 December 1936; and GeStapa, II 1B1, same title, 16 November 1936, T-175/414/2940057-59. Cf. Wheeler-Bennett, *Nemesis*, p. 342.

47. On inspection, O'Neill, *German Army*, p. 101; PPKdL, PrGestapo, GeStapa, re "Abwehrdienst in der SS-V.T.," 8 May 1936, T-175/423/2951012-14; and Weingartner, "Dietrich, Himmler, Leibstandarte," pp. 271-272, 279-81.

48. O'Neill, *German Army*, p. 100, citing correspondence between Infantry Regiment 40, and General Halder, April 1935, BA-MA/WK VII/1299; Wheeler-Bennett, *Nemesis*, pp. 341-42; and Mueller, *Heer und Hitler*, p. 166.
49. Abshagen, *Canaris*, pp. 116-22; and Colvin, *Chief of Intelligence*, pp. 40-43.

16. Persistent Opposition

1. PPKdL . . . , uIdGeStapo to Fuehrer u. Reichskanzler, re "Verband der Bayerischen Offiziers-Regiments-Vereine," 22 November 1934; StSekuCd-Reichskanzlei to PPKdL . . . , re same subject, 11 December, T-175/70/2587698-700.
2. RuPrMdI to PrMPraes. als CdGeStapo, re "Schriftsverkehr des Ge-Stapa," 10 January 1935, T-175/70/2587696-97.
3. Copy of RuPrMdI to StKanzlei des Freistaats Bayern, 30 January 1935, T-175/70/2587701-702.
4. Ibid., marginalia; Broszat, "Concentration Camps," pp. 423-24. Strangely, nothing in Himmler's notes of his November 20 meeting with Hitler seems to refer to the matter, T-175/94/2615267.
5. Frick Erl., see n. 3; on the use of Schutzhaft, Broszat, "Concentration Camps," pp. 446-48.
6. Peterson, *Limits*, p. 213; and Hjalmar Schacht, *Confessions of "the Old Wizard"* (Boston: Houghton Mifflin, 1956), pp. 314-16, containing a copy of his memo, in which he also conceded the need for the Gestapo against Communism.
7. On the Criminal Law Commission: Martin Broszat, *German National Socialism, 1919-1945* (Santa Barbara: Clio Press, 1966), p. 27; and Dennis L. Anderson, *The Academy of German Law, 1933-1944* (New York: Garland Publishing, 1987), pp. 87-94, 177-219. Dr. Friedrich Schack, "Die Generalermaechtigung der Polizei im kommenden Recht," (25 June 1935) T-175/249/2741312, quoting Drews.
8. Broszat, *National Socialism*, p. 27.
9. Copy of GeStapa, StVCuI to RJM, re "Kommunistische Bewegung," 28 March 1935, GStA/90,P/104/115-16. See also Aronson's analysis, *Heydrich*, pp. 238-41.
10. "Kommunistische Bewegung," ibid./116-19.
11. Ibid./119-20.
12. Ibid./121-25.
13. In his *Die Deutsche Polizei* (1941), Best described the legal bases, as he defined them, and some of the de facto bases of the SS and police system that he was so instrumental in constructing. See also Aronson, *Heydrich*, especially pp. 144-52, 238-42 on Best; and Karl O. Paetel, "The Reign of the Black Order," in *The Third Reich*, pp. 642, 648.
14. Gisevius, *To the Bitter End*, pp. 183-85; and Aronson, *Heydrich*, pp. 234-35, concerning his management of the case of the appeal for damages by the Jewish businessman, Wolmann, who had been a victim of the Stettin Gestapo under Hoffman.
15. Best, letter 21 July 1978; and PrGeStapo, StVCuI, re "Mitteilung grundsaetzlicher Veroiffentlichungen ueber die Politische Polizei," 3 April 1935, as cover letter for Dr. Walter Hamel, "Die Polizei im nationalsozialistischen Staat," *Deutsche Juristen-Zeitung* (15 March 1935), 326 ff., T-175/239/2728716-23.
16. Gisevius testimony, *IMT* 12:181-84, 256-58, 287-88.

17. Examples follow, nn. 19-21, 24, 26, 28.

18. Broszat, "Concentration Camps," p. 436.

19. Aronson, *Heydrich*, pp. 234-35, on the Wolmann case: PS-783-88, IMT 26:300-326, extensively documenting Guertner vs. RStH Saxony over Hohnstein KL case, 1935, involving SA and Saxon Gestapo excesses prior to June 1934.

20. Gisevius testimony, *IMT* 12:182-83, including Daluege's alleged reaction.

21. Ibid., pp. 183-84. Gisevius claims to have chosen this particular case for the appeal.

22. Ibid., p. 181; and Gisevius, *To the Bitter End*, p. 199. Gisevius's interpretation that Frick, in turning to Goering, had "lost his nerve" is a highly questionable evaluation of the political realities of the situation. Frick, who certainly was not strongly decisive, pursued his best available tactic, short of an open breach with the entire regime.

23. Ibid., pp. 193-96, citing Schacht through Herbert Goering as the source for the events at the council meeting. Although none of Gisevius's story has yet been substantiated with documentation, it is repeated here because of its consistency with general developments.

24. Mimeographed reprint of the 2 May 1935 decision of the Preussische Oberverwaltungsgericht, T-175/239/2728739-59; and Polizeiverwaltungsgesetz, 1 June 1931, *PrGS*, especially Sections 2, 8, and 45-54, pp. 77-78, 86-87. On the need for new legislation, cover letter by Best, 2 July 1935, and article by Dr. jur. Friedrich Schack, "Die Generalermaechtigung der Polizei im Kommenden Recht," T-175/249/2741311-15. Karl Llewellyn, "Remarks on the Theory of Appellate Decision and the Rules or Canons about how Statutes are to be Construed," *Vanderbilt Law Review* 3 (April 1950): 395-406.

25. Weakness of the German judiciary and judicial review, Arthur Taylor von Mehren, "The Judicial Process in the United States and Germany, A Comparative Analysis," *Festschrift fuer Ernst Rabel* (Tuebingen: Mohr, 1954), pp. 67-98, especially 87ff.: Werner Feld, "The German Administrative Courts," *Tulane Law Review* 36 (1962): 495-98; and Heinrich Nagel, "Judicial Review in Germany," *American Journal of Comparative Law* 3 (1954): 233-38. Sec. 14,1 of the Pr. Polizeiverwaltungsgesetz, 1 June 1931, *PrGS*, p. 79.

26. RMdJ to RuPrMdI, re "Misshandlungen von kommunistischen Haeftlingen durch Polizeibeamte," 14 March 1935, GStA/90,P/104/112-14; and Gisevius testimony, *IMT* 12:256, 258, 287-88.

27. Broszat, "Concentration Camps," p. 436.

28. Ibid., p. 435, quoting from a report to Himmler from Columbia-Haus Commandant, Dr. Reiner, 8 May 1935.

29. Ibid., pp. 435-36, citing Reiner report and records of RMdJ; RMdJ to RuPrMdI, 14 May 1935, GStA/90,P/104/112b.

30. PrGeStapo, StVCuI, cover letter and "Geschaeftsverteilungsplan der Abteilung I," 25 February 1935, T-175/422/2950251-61; compare GVtP, GeStapa, 1 October 1935, BA/R-58/840/53-54.

31. GeStapa to all SSt, re Lippe, 18 March 1935, T-175/239/2728799; GeStapa, PPKdL. re Schaumburg-Lippe, 1 July 1935, T-175/250/2742171; PrGeStpo, StVC, re "Die Ausuebung der politischen Polizei im Regierungsbezirk Sigmaringen," 29 January 1936, GStA/77/30/23-24.

32. One example from this time was BPP, re "Zusammenarbeit der SSt in Preussen mit den ausserpreussischen polit. Polizeien," 16 April 1936, T-81/184/334143.

33. Erl.d.Pr.MinPraes.-CdGestapo   vom   12.5.1934,   Dienstanweisung,

7.6.34, T-175/422/2950000-3. On Koch and clashes with the Gestapo and SS, Orlow, *Nazi Party, 1933-1945*, pp. 10-11, 54, 59, 124, 157; and Hoehne, *The Order*, pp 192-93 The local *Stapostellenleiter*, KR Cuno Schmidt had been a *Kriminalkommissar* in Koenigsberg since 1924. Although he did not officially enter the SS until 1936, "Namentlisches Verzeichnis . . . SSt Koenigsberg" (BDC/Sammelliste 49) listed him as a member in 1935, and his membership dated retroactively to 1 September 1934, one month prior to his affiliation with the Gestapo, BDC/SSO Cuno Schmidt (21.5.97), Lebenslauf 16.7.38, all of which hints at SS intrigues in Koch's domain.

34. Relevant documents and Dienstanweisungen dated 31 July, 17 August, 21 September 1934, 8 March and 10 April 1935 can be found in T-175/239/2728798, -800, -805-808. On Best and Buerckel, Orb, *Nationalsozialismus*, pp. 74-75; and on Buerckel, E.D.R. Harrison, "Gauleiter Buerckel and the Bavarian Palatinate," *Proceedings of the Leeds Philosophical and Literary Society* 20 (October 1986): 271-91.

35. Copy of PPKdL, re "Erfassung unzuverlaéssiger Vertrauenspersonen," 14 February 1935, T-175/422/2950632. One such report, "Zusammenstellung Nr. 4," October 1935, reveals what constituted unreliability, Hess.HStA Wiesbaden, 483/171.

36. Copy of PPKdL, PrGeStapo, StVCuI, to all SST., 14 June 1935, T-175/249/2741299; PrGeStapo, StVCuI, re "Einweisung von Schutzhaeftlingen in Konzentrationslager," 5 September 1935; same heading, re "Schutzhaft," 9 September; and same heading, re "Haftpruefungstermine in Schutzhaftsachen," 14 September, T-175/422/2949542-45.

37. BPP, re "Anzeigen politischen Art von Schuelern gegen Lehrer," 25 May 1936, T-580/106/14.

38. PPKdL, PrGeStapo, StVCuI, re "Zusammenarbeit mit der Deutschen Arbeitsfront," 23 October 1935; DAF, re "Zusammenarbeit mit dem GeStapa," 24 September, T-175/422/2950706-709; and BPP, re "Berichterstattung," 11 May 1936, T-580/106/14. Ronald Smelser, *Robert Ley* (Oxford: Berg, 1988), especially pp. 102-8 on growing rivalry.

39. Copy of GeStapa, re "Presseveroeffentlichungen ueber staatspol. Massnahmen," 20 September 1935, BA/R-58-243/54-55.

17. A Conservative Victory?

1. See, for instance, Peterson's description of Frick's behavior during the formulation of legislation on Jews in 1935, *Limits*, pp. 135-40, based primarily on Bernhard Loesener's account.

2. Diels, *Lucifer ante Portas*, pp. 85-86.

3. RuPrMdI, Abteilungsleiter III, re "Zusammenstellung ueber die verschiedenen Arten und Begriffe von Polizei," 13 June 1935, T-580/95/464.

4. The document in question is an undated memorandum by Frick (775-PS, abridged in *IMT* 26:289-91; complete but translated in *NCA* 3:547-50). As early as 14 March, Himmler informed Goering of a conference among Frick, Hitler, and himself, but recorded no subject: Himmler's conference notes, T-175/94/2615308. In his testimony, Gisevius (whose memory for dates is unreliable) stated that Frick's memo postdated his departure from the ministry in May 1935; *IMT* 12:182. Indeed on 8 May, Himmler and Goering discussed both the Schutzkommando and "Recht Umbau" (Gestapo law?); conference notes, T-175/94/2615310. By content, Frick's memo apparently predates 27 June (see n. 23). On

the formation of the RSD, PrMdI, MD Daluege, Herrn RFSS Himmler, 17 September 1934, T-175/R-78/2597185; and Peter Hoffman, *Hiter's Personal Security* (Cambridge, Mass.. MIT Press, 1979)), pp. 29-37

5. 775-PS, on Hitler's desires re the RSD. Hoffmann, "Hitler's Personal Security," *Police Forces in History,* 152-56.

6. As revealed in an untitled report to Daluege, signed Bracht, 9 March 1935, GStA/77/28/54-55.

7. "Auszug aus der Niederschrift ueber die Senatorenbesprechung" 25 June 1935, p. 220, re "Uebernahme der Schupo durch des Reich," 13 August 1935, and p. 257, re "Ueberfuhrung der Schutzpolizei auf das Reich," StA Bremen, 3-P.l.a., Nrs. 1220, 1223.

8. Blomberg to Hitler, 1 July 1935, BA/R-43 II/391/59-61.

9. Untitled, secret internal MdI memo, 12 October 1935, BA/R-18/5627/248.

10. Orlow, *Nazi Party, 1933-1945,* p. 151; police report on Lutze's investigations into June 30, Die Polizeibehoerde Hamburg, an GeStapa, 29 July 1935, T-175/33/2541891.

11. OSAF, Verfuegungen, 5 April 1935, BA/Schu 414. Pr.GeStapo, StVCuI, Bericht re "Unzulaessige Betaetigung einer nicht genehmigten Nachrichtenorganisation," 30 July 1935; and SAdNSDAP, OSAF, CdStabes to Schwarz, 6 May, BA/NS-10/78/67-68, 77.

12. Lutze to Schwarz, 6 May 1935; Schwarz to Lutze, 8 May; and StVdF, Stabsleiter to OSAF, re "Nachrichtendienst der SA," 7 June, BA/NS-10/78/74, 76, 77.

13. RuPrMdI to RMdF, re "Staerke und Aufgaben der statlichen Polizei," 21 September 1935, T-175/70/2587688-90; Staatssekretaer II, 13 November 1935, with drafts of "Verordnung zum Gesetz . . . ," and "Gesetz zur Ueberleitung der Staatlichen Polizei auf das Reich," BA/R-18/627/1-23.

14. Ibid., attached *Begrundung,* 25-49.

15. Gisevius, *To the Bitter End,* p. 185.

16. Akten-Notiz, 11 June 1935; Pr.GeStapo. StVCuI, 30 July 1935, with attached *Bericht* of 30 July; Bormann to Schwarz, 5 August; Schwarz to OPGd-NSDAP, 8 August; and Bormann to Adj.d.F., 15 November, BA/NS-10/78/60, 64-70, 75.

17. NSDAP, StVdF, *Rundschreiben* to all *Reichs-* and *Gauleiter,* 14 February 1936, T-580/93/457.

18. Heydrich on the DAF, GeStapa, 21 December 1935, T-175/337/2843180; Orlow, *Nazi Party, 1933-1945,* p. 126.

19. On October 18, in conference with Hitler, Himmler presented evidence of Lutze's drunken ravings about June 30, and argued his case against Frick's Gestapo proposals and for his control of the RSD, T-175/94/2615260, -63-64, and report on Lutze presented to Hitler on 18 October 1935, dated Stettin, 21 August 1935, T-175/33/2541892-98.

20. PPKdL to the Lippische Landesregierung, 15 October 1935, StA Detmold, L80 Ie/P/Nr.2, III.

21. Pfundtner to Herrn Minister, re "Reichssicherheitsdienst," 21 October 1935, BA/R-18/627/271-73; Hoffman, "Hitler's Personal Security," 153-54.

22. One such attack can be traced in OPraes. Ostpreussen to RuPrMdI, 7 September 1935; RuPrMdI to PrMinPraes., 23 September 1935; Himmler notes on Fuehrer conference, 1.XI.35, T-175/94/2615259; and RFSS to PrMinPraes., 6 November 1935 referring to Hitler's decision, T-175/71/2587790-93.

23. 775-PS, undated memorandum by Frick, *IMT* 26:291, referring to the

"vorgelegte Gesetz." In a 1949 testimony, Best mentioned, offhandedly, that he had been working with MR Dr. Ermert of the Ministry of the Interior on a newly conceived Prussian Gestapo Law during the spring of 1935. At the time, Himmler had expressed pleasure over the law, until Best drew his attention to some deficiencies that he did not elaborate on in his testimony. Unfortunately for the strength of the interpretation given here, Best did not indicate that the content of the law was subsequently altered. Best, "Heinrich Himmler," 18 September 1949, p. 4.

24. Draft "Gesetz ueber die GeStapo," presented at Ministerialrat am 27. Juni 1935, GStA/90,P/2.Heft 3/132b, 132e; and *PrGS*, 1936, 21.

25. Copy of PrGeStapo, StVCuI, re "Mitteilung grundsaetzlichen Veroeffentlichungen ueber Politische Polizei," 2 July 1935, T-175/249/2741311. Also on the pressure on Goering and Himmler for a new law, Plum, "Staatspolizei," 203.

26. Draft of *Gesetz*, GStA/90,P/2, Heft 3/132e-f; and "Verordnung zur Ausfuehrung des Gesetzes . . . , vom 10. Februar 1936," *PrGS*, 1936, 24.

27. Draft of *Gesetz*, 132f.

28. Reitlinger, *SS.*, p. 89, citing *IMT* (British version), 22:258; this is an error, as the correct page is 358, or 22:337 in the U.S. version. Neusuess-Hunkel, *Die SS*, p. 40, citing Gestapo law. Louis Saurel, *La Gestapo*, p. 62.

29. Gestapo training material, "Aufgaben der Gestapo," T-175/432/2962319. A more careful explanation of how this interpretation was derived through NS legal philosophy is ibid., 2962540-41. For a typical public explanation of the significance of the law, "Zehn Jahre Sicherheitspolizei und SD," *Die Deutsche Polizei* 2 (February 1943): 76. At Nuremberg, Goering's vague memory of legal details added to the confusion: interrogation, 8 October 1945, a.m., p. 8. Orb also added his authority to the error, *Nationalsozialismus*, p. 133.

30. VO zur Ausfuehrung des Gesetzes, *PrGS*, 1936, p. 23. Best, testimony, *IMT* 20:132-33; Crankshaw, *Gestapo*, 145; even Buchheim, "The SS," pp. 260-61, gives this some credence.

31. Best testimony, *IMT* 20:132-33. Buchheim, "The SS," p. 260, citing letter of Eicke to Himmler, 10 August 1936; and cf. Sydnor, *Soldiers of Destruction*, pp. 21-22.

32. Copy, St.M.I. 5998, "Ministerrat am 27. Juni 1935," GStA/90, P/2, Heft 3/132b-c. Emphasis added.

33. Ibid., 132a, 132c.

34. PrMPraes, St.M.I. 8269, *Schnellbrief*, 27 July 1935, ibid., 132d.

35. Plum, "Staatspolizei," 215-21, including notes, gives examples of the governors' complaints in June 1935; on Koch's attacks in September and the initiative it gave Frick to make demands see n. 10; Aronson, *Heydrich*, p. 242, cites a private complaint against the camps; and Broszat, "Concentration Camps," p. 423, on Guertner's actions.

36. Broszat, p. 436; compare Best's response to the complaint of Domkapitular Lichtenberg against the camps, Aronson, *Heydrich*, pp. 242-43.

37. Broszat, "Concentration Camps," pp. 446-47.

38. 778-PS, Meissner to Guertner, 9 September 1935, re Vogel case, *IMT* 26:326. Peterson, *Limits*, p. 185, citing *MinRat.*, 8.10.35, for Bavaria.

39. Himmler's notes on 1 November conference, T-175/94/2615258-59; RFSS to PrMinPraes., 6 November 1935, T-175/71/2587790, on the response to Koch's complaint; and Broszat, "Concentration Camps," p. 424, on the response to Guertner.

40. "Gesetz zur Aenderung von Vorschriften des Strafverfahrens und des

Gerichtsverfassungsgesetzes," 28 June 1935, *RGBl* 1:844-50; and Lawrence Preuss, "Punishment by Analogy in National-Socialist Penal Law," *JCL&C* 26 (1936). 847-56.

41. Broszat, "Concentration Camps," p. 426.

42. Plum, "Staatspolizei," 201-202; and Dr. U. Scheuner, "Die Gerichte und die Pruefung politischer Staatsshandlungen," *RVBl.* 57 (23 May 1936), T-175/239/2728813-39.

43. Cf. Plum, "Staatspolizei," 203. Himmler's notes for a conference with Goering, 10 January 1936, indicate the draft law was settled, but that control of the Stapostellen remained a bone of contention in counterdrafts for Ausfuehrungsbestimmungen, which Himmler put forth in mid-December. Since these notes were on the back of Hotel Deutsches Haus Berchtesgaden stationery, they probably preceded a meeting with Hitler, T-175/94/2615305-07. Himmler's December counteroffensive may have been encouraged by an early December conference with Hitler on Frick's proposals regarding the police; conference notes, ibid., 2615254.

44. This was certainly the spirit in which he described the effect of the law to the Staatsraeten on March 5, 1936, "Rede des RFSS . . . im Haus der Flieger," pp. 12-14, BA/NS-19/H.R.3.

45. PrGeStapo, StVC, re "Stellung der OPraes. zu den Organen der GeStapo," 18 February 1936, bearing a copy of PrMPraes., CdGeStapo, same subject, 10 February, BA/R-58/239; PrGeStapo, der StVC, re "Mitteilung allgemeiner Erlasse an die RegPraes.," 23 March, T-175/423/2950904; and PrMPraes., CdGeStapo, re "Ergaenzung der Dienstanweisung betr. die Berichterstattung und die Erteilung von Weisungen in der GeStapo," 25 March, T-175/414/2940045.

46. Copy of PrMPraes., CdGeStapo, re "Stellung der OPraes.," 10 February 1936, p. 2, BA/R-58/239.

47. Copy of "Beschlusses des Pr. Oberverwaltungsgerichts vom 19. Maerz 1936," T-175/239/2728762-65.

48. PrGeStapo, StVC, re "Beschwerde gegen politisch-polizeiliche Verfuegungen," 9 March 1936, sought to avoid further court tests by instructing county and local officials that the court decision of May 1935 and the February law denied court appeals against Gestapo action; appeal through the Gestapo itself was the only legal remedy. PrGeStapo, StVC, PPKdL, the cover letter, 12 June 1936, for Scheuner's article (see n. 42) presented the desired legal philosophy prohibiting court interference. PrGeStapo, GeStapa, re "Unanfechtbarkeit polizeilicher Verfuegungen staatspolizeilichen Inhalts," 30 September 1936, forwarded the decision of March 19, 1936, and attacked as "obviously devious" (*offensichtlich abwegig*) a rather weak and picky argument by one Tannert that due to a technicality, the court decision could not stand, T-175/239/2728758-59, -813-841, -760-61, respectively.

49. PrMPraes., St.M.I. 3490, 2 April 1936, as Document 8 in Plum, "Staatspolizei," 222-23.

50. Best, "Die Geheime Staatspolizei," *Deutsches Recht* 6 (15 April 1936): 125-28.

51. Ibid.; Plum, "Staatspolizei," 204, for a similar interpretation.

52. Best, "Geheime Staatspolizei," 128.

53. Ibid.; English translation rendered in Broszat, "Concentration Camps," pp. 426-27.

54. See p. 169 above.

18. Himmler's Triumph

1. "Die Gestapo," *VB*, 23 January 1936, pp. 1-2.
2. Ibid., p. 2.
3. "Rede des RFSS vor dem Staatsraeten im Haus der Flieger, 5.3.1936," BA/NS-19/H.R.3.
4. Ibid.
5. Ibid., p. 44.
6. Frick memorandum, n.d., 775-PS, *IMT* 26:291.
7. Cover letter, Medicus (Abtl.I) to Pfundtner, 8 June 1936, for three drafts of an appropriate Fuehrer Erlass, BA/R-18/628, Heft 3/919-25. On 27 May, the Mayor of Bremen notified his Senat that all police were soon to be unified under Himmler, "Auszug . . . Senatorenbesprechung," 27 May 1936, StA Bremen, 3-P.l.a., Nr. 1200/20; therefore, Frick must have known at least by then.
8. "Gesichtspunkte fuer eine Uebernahme der Leitung der deutschen Polizei durch den RFSS im Rahmen des RuPrMdI," stamped "Fuehrer vorgelegt," dated by hand, 6.6.36, and initialed by Himmler, BA/Schu 464.
9. Ibid. Referat III P (Politische Polizei) and III P. Log. (Lodges, Masonry and Orders) were to be included in Heydrich's new *Abteilung* Gestapo.
10. This is apparent from the surviving documents, from Gesevius's version, and the testimonies of other actively involved members of Frick's staff. Neufeldt, *Ordnungspolizei*, p. 13, citing "Auskunft des Herrn Ministerialdirigenten a.D. Dr. Medicus an das Bundesarchiv vom 16. Mai 1958," on file, BA.
11. Cover letter, Medicus to Pfundtner, 8 June 1936 (n. 7). By content, the last of the three drafts in the present file does not seem to have been one of the three original attachments, but a later replacement. Contrary to Medicus's cover letter, it differs in far more than the first sentence from the other drafts. Furthermore, it bears the designation, "Entw. H." indicating it is the draft presented by Heydrich on June 9.
12. Memo, Pfundtner to Frick, 9 June 1936, BA/R-18/628, Heft 3/911-17; and draft *Erlass* labeled "Entw. H.," ibid./925. Neufeldt, *Ordnungspolizei*, pp. 13-14, 17.
13. Memo, 9 June 1936, n. 12.
14. Ibid.
15. Ibid., 917, handwritten comments by Frick.
16. All previous versions of this incident have been based on the interpretation of GStA Berlin-Dahlem HA materials by Neufeldt, *Ordnungspolizei*, pp. 14-15. Frick's handwritten note on Pfundtner's memorandum, 9 June, BA/R-18/628, Heft 3/913, summarizes results of the meeting with Hitler.
17. Wilhelm Deist, *The Wehrmacht and German Rearmament*, (Toronto: Univ. of Toronto Press, 1981), pp. 49-53, has emphasized the coalescence of military, economic, and foreign policy into a more aggressive stage of development that matured precisely in spring 1936 (April, May, and early June).
18. Lammers testimony, *IMT* 11:60. On Hess and Schwarz, Schellenberg, *Memoiren*, p. 34. Notations on Heydrich's draft of the Fuehrer *Erlass*, 925.
19. Alterations noted on Heydrich's draft *Erlass*, 925, 857-59; and revised versions presented to him, copy a, 869, copy b, 937, and draft "Ausfuehrung des Fuehrererlasses," 871.
20. Records of negotiations are Pfundtner's memorandum to Frick, 12 June 1936, BA/R-18/628, Heft 3/865-68; the same, 15 June, ibid. 809-818; and the same, 25 June, ibid. 683-87.

21. "Erlass ueber die Einsetzung eines Chefs der Deutschen Polizei im RMdI," 17 June 1936, *RGBl.*, 487. Emphasis added.

22. Pfundtner memo, 12 June 1936, 865 (see n. 20 here).

23. *Erlass*, 17 June 1936, *RGBl.*, 487. Emphasis added.

24. Buchheim, "The SS," pp. 160-61; and Koehl, "Feudal Aspects of National Socialism," *APSR* 54 (December 1960): 921-33.

25. *Erlass*, 17 June 1936, *RGBl.*, 488.

26. Pfundtner memorandum, 15 June 1936, BA/R-18/628, Heft 3/809-811. That the formula Heydrich proposed for designating Himmler's deputy only during his absences was followed: RFSS, CdDP, re "Vertretung der RFSS als CdDP vom 10.11.36 ab," 6 November 1936, BA/R-18/628, Heft 2/383.

27. Ibid., Heft 3/809-813; drafts of the press notice, 819-29, 797-99; and *VB*, 18 and 19 June 1936.

28. Pfundtner memorandum, 15 June 1936, 815 (see n. 20 here); and drafts of the letter, 851, 853.

29. Ibid., 815; and memorandum, 25 June 1936, 683-87; drafts 657-63, 735-36; and cover letter, RuPrMdI, 25 June, with *Erlass*, 665-70. Neufeldt, *Ordnungspolizei*, pp. 17-18.

30. Best, "Der Reichsfuehrer SS und Chef der Deutschen Polizei," *Deutsches Recht* 6 (15 July 1936): 257-58.

31. On the printing of the title, Gestapo training material, "Politische Polizei," probable date 1938, T-175/277/5487516.

32. Buchheim, "The SS," p. 163.

33. RuPrMdI, Pol. O-V Nr. 1/36, 1 July 1936, T-175/229/2767283.

34. See, for example, Frick order of 25 January 1937, with cover letter by Best, 9 February, T-175/229/2767326-27.

35. Lammers testimony, *IMT* 11:60, and Frick's interrogation (6 September 1945), p. 13, NA/RG-238.

36. Frick interrogation (25 September 1945), p. 11, NA/RG-238. RdErl.d.RuPrMdI, 15 May 1937, *RMBliV*, 788-89.

37. Neufeldt, *Ordnungspolizei*, pp. 19-20, n. 19. "Gesetz ueber Finanzmassnahmen auf dem Gebiete der Polizei," 19 March 1937, *RGBl.* 1:325-27; and "Deutschen Polizeibeamtengesetz," 24 June 1937, *RGBl.* 1:653ff., essentially completing centralization.

38. Compare Jacob, *German Administration*, p. 145, where he contends that because police budgets were open-ended like the military's, they escaped Ministry of Finance or Interior control. Cf. Browder, "Sipo und SD," chap. 7, showing that the budget did provide some avenues for control or limitations by both ministries after 1937.

39. Buchheim, "The SS," p. 163.

19. The Formation of Sipo and SD

1. RFSSuCdDP, re "Einsetzung eines CdO und eines CdS," 26 June 1936, *RMBliV*, 947.

2. Neufeldt, *Ordnungspolizei*, pp. 25-26.

3. Ibid., pp. 23-24; and see n. 9.

4. RFSSuCdDP, 26 June 1936, see n. 3; and Neufeldt, *Ordnungspolizei*, p. 21.

5. RFSS, CdDP, re "Geschaeftsverteilungsplan des HA Sipo," 31 July 1936, BA/R-58/840.

6. Ibid.

7. PrGeStapo, GeStapa, re "Die Leitung der Abtl. I des GeStapa," 30 June 1936, BA/R-58/239; and RdErl.d.RuPrMdI, re "Beauftragung des GeStapa mit der Wahrnehmung der Aufgaben des PPKdL," 20 September 1936, RMBliV, 1343.

8. RdErl.d.RFSSuCdDP, 28 August 1936, re "Einheitliche Bezeichnung der Dienststellen der GeStapo im Reich," RMBliV, 1344-46.

9. RKPA, Organisation und Meldedienst der Reichskriminalpolizei (1939?), T-175/451/2967022-23.

10. Rudolf Augstein, "Das Spiel ist aus—Arthur Nebe," Der Spiegel (24 November 1949), p. 28.

11. Ibid.

12. "Verhaeltnis von Polizeistaerken zu Einwohnerzahlen," attached to RuPrMdI, IIA 1200-6/36, 17 February 1936, BA/R-18/629/77.

13. RdErl.d.RuPrMdI, "Neuordnung der staatlichen Kriminalpolizei," 20 September 1936, RMBliV, 1339-43.

14. Ibid.

15. RdErl.d.RuPrMdI, "Einsetzung von IdS," 20 September 1936, RMBliv., 1343; Buchheim, "The SS," pp. 184-85.

16. RdErl of 20 September 1936, and Anlage, "Dienstanweisung fuer die IdS," RMBliV, 1343-44. Note that the inspectors were not originally assigned to each Wehrkreis as is usually stated, but to governmental units. Compare Hoehne, The Order, pp. 206-207; and Ramme, Sicherheitsdienst, pp. 64-65.

17. Cf. Buchheim, "The SS," pp. 184-87; and the anachronous account in Hoehne, The Order, pp. 206-207. IdS, Stand 15.9.1938, T-580/93/457.

18. LdGestapa, re "Allgemeine Richtlinien fuer die Taetigkeit der SSt," 17 July 1936, T-175/423/2951277. On SS-Party tension, Orlow, Nazi Party, 1933-1945, p. 181. On subsequent compromises between Gestapo and Party, 1937-38, Browder, "Sipo and SD," pp. 173-74. Quote on protective custody restraint, Broszat, "Concentration Camps," pp. 444-45.

19. CdSSHA, re "Polizeiliche Massnahmen durch die SS," 18 September 1936, T-175/219/2757464.

20. Broszat, pp. 443-44. From his own memory, Best omits reference to all of this (IMT 20:132-33), thus misleading historians.

21. Explained in Gestapo training material, T-175/432/2962540-41.

22. For example, Best, "Die Reichsfuehrer SS und Chef der Deutschen Polizei," Deutsches Recht (15 July 1936), pp. 257-58; and Dr. Edgar Dockweiler, "Die Polizei in neuen Staat," Reichsverwaltungsblatt (29 August 1936), with cover letter by Best, 25 September 1936, T-175/239/2728724-35.

23. "Rede des Reichsfuehrers-SS Heinrich Himmler in der Konstituierenden Stizung des Ausschusses fuer Polizerecht . . . ," in Hans A. Jacobsen and Werner Jockmann, Ausgewaehlte Dokumente zur Geschichte des Nationalsozialismus, 1933-1945, (Bielefeld, 1961), C:1-3.

24. Ibid.; on the propagation by Hoehn and Best of the SS-police line during the committee's deliberations, see Hans Frank et al., Grundfragen des Deutschen Polizei Arbeitsberichte der Akademie fuer Deutsches Recht (Hamburg, 1937).

25. Leverkuehn, German Military Intelligence, p. 316.

26. BDC/SSO Nebe, Bierkamp and Mueller. Gisevius, To The Bitter End, passim; and Wo ist Nebe?, p. 26.

27. "Rede des RFSS . . . fuer . . . Heydrich," *Reinhard Heydrich*, p. 4; and Gisevius, *Wo ist Nebe?*, p. 27.

28. *Organization und Meldedienst der Reichskriminalpolizei*, T 175/151/150/021-20, which also cites *Mein Kampf*; "Rede des RFSS," 11 October 1936, *Ausgewachlte Dokumente*, C:2-3; and Frank speech, *Deutsches Recht* 2 (1933): 33-36.

29. *Organisation und Meldedienst . . .* , T-175/451/2967021-26.

30. For an analysis of executives' sixth sense in bureaucratic conflict, Dimock, "Expanding Jurisdictions," 282-91.

31. This weakness in Roehm's strategy was well analyzed by Aronson, *Heydrich*.

Selected Bibliography

The reader will find, scattered throughout the book (often at the beginning of sections), references to bibliographical notes relevant to the more general histories of Germany and the NS Movement, to specific historical problems, and to specialized literature peripheral to this study. The following bibliography is restricted to sources and literature on the general subject of the German police and security agencies, expecially the political and criminal police—the Abwehr and the SD.

Since much of the cited literature is, therefore, in the notes rather than bibliography, for the reader's conveninence a special Index to First Citation beginning on page 332 directs the reader to the first full citation of all published sources.

Research and Reference Materials

Bibliographies, Catalogs and Guides

Bernbaum, John A. "The Captured German Records: A Bibliographical Survey." *The Historian* 32 (August 1970): 564-75.

Boeninger, Hildegard R. *The Hoover Library Collection on Germany*. Stanford: Stanford Univ. Press, 1955.

Browder, George C. "Problems and Potentials of the Berlin Document Center." *Central European History* 5 (1972): 362-80.

Cline, Marjorie W., Carla E. Christiansen, and Judith Fontaine (eds.). *Scholar's Guide to Intelligence Literature*. Frederick, Md.: University Publications of America, 1983.

Grahm, Gerlinde, Helmut Loetzke, and Johanna Weiser. "Die Hilfe und Unterstuetzung der UdSSR fuer der Schutz und die Sicherung des staatlichen Archivfonds der DDR." *Archivmitteilungen* 25 (1975): 47-52.

Granier, Gerhard, Josef Henke, and Klaus Olenhage. *Das Bundesarchiv und seine Bestaende*. Boppard am Rhein: Boldt, 1977.

Gugenhaeuser, Max. *Geschichte des geheimen Nachrichtendienstes: Literatur-bericht und Bibliographie*. Frankfurt: Verlag fuer Wehrwessen, 1968.

Haase, Carl. *Die Archivalien zur deutschen Geschichte*. Boppard am Rhein: Harald Boldt Verlag, 1975.

Heinz, Grete, and Agnes F. Peterson. *NSDAP Hauptarchiv: Guide to the Hoover Institute Microfilm Collection*. Stanford: Hoover Institution, 1964.

Hewitt, William H. *A Bibliography of Police Administration, Public Safety and Criminology to July 1, 1965*. Springfield, Ill.: Charles C. Thomas, 1967.

Henke, Josef. "Das Schicksal deutscher zeitgeschichtlicher Quellen in Kriegs- und Nachkriegszeit: Beschlagnahme—Rueckfuehrung—Verbleib." *Viertel- jahrshefte fuer Zeitgeschichte* 30 (1982): 557-620.

Heulke, Hans-Heinrich, and Hans Etzler. *Verbrechen, Polizei, Prozesse: Ein Ver zeichnis von Buechern und kleineren Schriften in deutscher Sprache.* Part 2: Ma- terials appearing since 1900. Wiesbaden: Bundeskriminalamt, 1963.

International Police Association. *International Bibliography of Selected Police Litera- ture.* London: M&W Publications, 1968.

Jahrbuch der Bibliotheken, Archive und Dokumentationstellen der D.D.R. Berlin: an- nual.

Mady, J. "Fonds d'Archives concernant la deuxieme Guerre Mondiale conserves aux Archives Nationales." *Cahiers d'Histoire de la Guerre* (January 1949): 44- 46.

Marczewski, Jerzy. "Polish Research on the Role and Activities of the SS." *Polish Western Affairs* 23 (1982): 110-21.

Mommsen, Wolfgang. *Die schriftlichen Nachlaesse in den Zentralen Deutschen und Preussischen Archiven.* Koblenz: Schriften des Bundesarchivs, 1955.

Mork, Gordon R. "Note: The Archives of the German Democratic Republic." *Central European History* 2 (September 1969): 273-84.

Paetel, Karl O. "The Black Order. A Survey of Literature on the SS." *The Wiener Library Bulletin* 13 (1959): 34-35.

Robinson, Jacob, and Philipp Friedman. *Guide to Jewish History under Nazi Impact.* New York: Marstin Press, 1960.

Rothfeder, Herbert. *Checklist of Selected German Pamphlets and Booklets of the Weimar and Nazi Period in the University of Michigan Library.* Ann Arbor: Department of History, University of Michigan, 1961.

Schlachter, Gail (ed.). *The Third Reich, 1933-1939: A Historical Bibliography.* Santa Barbara, Calif.: ABC-CLIO, 1984.

———.*The Weimar Republic: A Historical Bibliography.* Santa Barbara, Calif.: ABC- Clio, 1984.

Stornfeld, Wilhelm, and Eva Tiedemann. *Deutsche Exil-Literatur 1933-1945: Eine Bio-Biography.* Heidelberg: Verlag Lambert Schneider, 1970.

U.S. Department of State, Historical Office. *A Catalog of Files and Microfilms of the German Foreign Ministry Archives, 1920-1945.* 3 vols. Stanford: Hoover Institution, 1962, 1964, 1966.

U.S. National Archives and Record Service. *Guides to German Records Microfilmed at Alexandria, VA.* Washington, D.C.: 1958–.

———. Pamphlets describing *Records of the United States Nuernberg War Crimes Trials.* Washington, D.C.: 1973–.

Weinberg, Gerhard L. *Guide to Captured German Documents.* Maxwell AFB, Ala.: Air University Human Resources Institute, 1952.

———. "Nazi Party and Military Records." *Michigan Alumnus Quarterly Review,* Autumn 1960: 55-58.

———. *Supplement to the Guide to Captured German Documents.* Washington, D.C.: National Archives, 1959.

Whitehouse, Jack E. *A Police Bibliography.* New York: AMS Press, 1980.

Wiener Library. *Catalogs of the Wiener Library of London.* London: Vallentine, Mitchell.

Wolfe, Robert. *Captured German and Related Records: A National Archives Conference.* Athens, Ohio: Ohio Univ. Press, 1974.

Ziegler, Janet. *World War II: Books in English, 1945-65*. Stanford: Hoover Institutution Press, 1971.

Biographical and Statistical References

Das deutsche Fuehrerlexicon. Berlin: Otto Stollberg, 1934.
Freiberg, Br., E. Eichler, and Th. Mommsen. *Dienstaltersliste der hoeheren Kriminalbeamten*. Berlin: Carl Heymanns Verlag, 1935.
Germany, Statistischesreichsamt. *Statistisches Jahrbuch fuer das deutsche Reich*. Berlin: Verlag von Reimar Hobbing in Berlin, 1880–.
National Council of the National Front of Democratic Germany. *Brown Book: War and Nazi Criminals in West Germany*. Dresden: Verlag Zeit im Bild, n.d.
Stockhorst, Erich. *Fuenftausend Koepfe: Wer war was im Dritten Reich*. Bruchsal/Baden: Blick u. Bild Verlag, 1967.

Documents

The unconditional surrender of Germany at the end of World War II has given historians a unique opportunity. For perhaps the only time in history, the extensive files of the political police and security agencies of a modern nation are accessible—materials that are usually destroyed or kept secret almost indefinitely. Nevertheless, the resultant collection of documents is a mixed blessing. On the one hand, they overwhelm with sheer quantity, while on the other, evidence is missing on an equally grand scale.

The records of the Third Reich were extensively damaged, some groups more than others. Those relevant to Sipo and SD fall on the side of extensive damage, but not so far as generally assumed. Given the nature of the organizations, there was significant deliberate destruction, both as a matter of routine security and as part of last-minute efforts. Fortunately, given the habits of modern bureaucracies, they could not eliminate every copy of many important documents.

The management of the captured documents has further mixed the blessing. The victorious Allies assembled records from all over Germany for the Nuremberg Trials, consequently destroying contexts. The physical relationships of documents within files is often as significant as the content of any single document. The significance of earlier drafts, related notes, responses, assembled information on the subject of the document, even such details as who possessed the document or who produced a note, can be destroyed with the context. However, Allied efforts to reorganize the documents for trials or for the denazification process also created new, equally useful contexts, bringing together related documents from different provenances.

Immediately after the war, the Allied governments removed from Germany much of the captured material, but they have allegedly returned almost all of it to German archives within the last three decades. Before its return, however, significant collections were microfilmed, making them more readily available to scholars around the world. The results of several such filming projects are listed below, the most extensive of which was that undertaken by the U.S. National Archives. German archivists redistributed to appropriate archives much of the material returned to Germany, and years of painstaking work have reestablished some of the original contexts and created newly valuable ones. In the Federal Republic, these archival holdings remain almost completely open to scholars.

Less is known about the materials captured by the Soviet Union or remaining in the hands of the East European governments. As in the West, the Soviets have allegedly returned the materials they held. Unfortunately, political tensions have severely limited scholarly access in the Soviet Union, Czechoslovakia, and the German Democratic Republic, especially in the sensitive area of political police and security agencies. The few documents made available from the Eastern side are significant and valuable pieces, leaving the student of Sipo and SD with the insecure feeling that much of what one needs for greater accuracy lies just beyond reach. The published papers from the National Archives conference, *Captured German and Related Records*, summarizes the history and problems of these materials, recently updated by Josef Henke's article.

The complex history of the documents has created several problems for this work. I began research with the readily available microfilmed publications and the holdings of the National Archives in Washington. When it became possible for me to work in the German archives, I reviewed much of the material that had been microfilmed, to benefit from any newly established contexts and to find the new documents that had been integrated into the old files. In initial research, I collected some documents from the microfilm. Subsequent work on the same folder in German archives gave other materials new significance, and they were collected then. It would be a herculean task to convert microfilm references to archival or vice versa; consequently, documents are referenced to the source from which I first collected them. Where documents have been published, however, preference has been given in citations to the more readily available published source. Similar problems have arisen since the National Archive began microfilming its Nuremberg Trial materials. Some testimonies and reports are cited from the original collection, others from microfilm.

The incompleteness of the surviving documents does not deny us a valid history of Sipo and SD, although overly abundant evidence in one area mixed with thin or nonexistent documentation in another does produce uneven pictures and a narrative with gaping holes. Such sources inevitably yield both relatively valid descriptions and analyses mixed with guesswork. The hope is that solidarity in some areas has educated the guesswork in others. Many of the gaps in the evidence have been filled, a process that will continue. The historian, like the detective, follows clues that lead from obvious sources to less apparent ones.

One obvious line of research required the scouring of regional and local archives, which provide details on grassroots aspects often unavailable in central archives. Beyond that, however, each local archive has documents created by central offices but surviving only in regional files. I have worked in many such local archives to find missing pieces; however, such work is endless, and much of what must be left for later may conceal significant new information.

Another endless but valuable line of enquiry leads through the surviving personnel files, especially those of the SS, which mix officially compiled data and evaluations with unofficial observations and personal contributions. Though most frequently used for biographical data, these records also contain a wealth of otherwise unrecorded insights into the organizations to which the men belonged.

Although the following list is incomplete, it includes all archives exploited for this book. References to relevant guides are given in parentheses.

The Archives of Former Reich Agencies

Ihe Bundesarchiv Koblenz (see Granier)

NS-1   Der Reichsschatzmeister, NSDAP
NS-6   Der Stellvertreter des Fuehrers
NS-10 Persoenliche Adjutantur des Fuehrers und Reichskanzler
NS-19 Personalstab des Reichsfuehrers SS
NS-26 NSDAP Hauptarchiv (see Heinz and microfilm)
R-18   Reichsministerium des Innern
R-43   Reichskanzlei
R-58   Reichssicherheitshauptamt, its subordinate agencies: Geheime
       Staatspolizei, Reichskriminalpolizei, Sicherheitsdienst des Reichs-
       fuehrers SS and predeccessors
       Subsequently subdivided into R-134, Sicherheitspolizei und poli-
       tische Nachrichtendienste (microfilm T-175)
Schu   Schumacher Sammlung, a miscellaneous collection taken from the
       holdings of the Berlin Document Center (microfilm T-580 and T-611)
Bundesarchiv-Militaerarchiv-Freiburg
RH-1   Oberbefehlshaber des Heeres-Adjutantur
RW-4   Oberkommando der Wehrmacht/Wehrmachtfuehrungsstab
RW-5   OKW-Amt Auslandsnachrichten und Abwehr (microfilm T-77)
RW-6   Allgemeines Wehrmachtamt, Abtl.-Ausland (microfilm T-77)
OKW-901   Reichsministerium, Wehrmachtabteilung, Geheime-Akten
           ueber persoenlicher, politischer Schriftwechsel
Z-518a   Richtlinien fuer den Unterricht ueber politische Tagesfragen
Politisches Archiv des Auswaertigen Amtes, Bonn (see U.S. Department of State,
Historical Office; microfilm T-120)
       Referat   Deutschland
       Referat   Inland II G (geheim)
       Referat   Inland A/B

Archives of the Former Laender

Bavaria: To avoid duplication of Aronson's and McGee's work and the microfilmed collections, I have made only cursory checks on the holdings of these
archives. (See Heinz and Hauptarchiv microfilm.) Subsequent to my research,
in 1977 the Hauptstaatsarchiv underwent reorganization, with all relevant holdings consolidated into Abteilung II.

Bayerisches Hauptstaatsarchiv, Munich, Abteilung I
    Bayerisches Innen Ministerium
    ———, Abteilung II
    Reichsstatthalter Epp
    Gesamtstaatsministerium, MA-99
    Akten des bayer. Ministerpraesident Siebert, MA-106
Bayerisches Staatsarchiv, Munich
    Polizeidirektion Munich

Bremen:
Staatsarchiv Bremen
    3-P.l.a.   Senatsregistratur, Polizeisachen im allge.

4,13-P.l.c.   Sicherheitspolizei, Kriminalpolizei, Geheime Staatspolizei
4,65   Polizeidirektion Bremen, Nachrichtenstelle
Senat des Inneres holds selected folders from the above.

Brunswick (Braunschweig):
Niedersaechsisches Staatsarchiv, Wolfenbuettel
   112 A Neu   Braunschweigisches Staatsministerium
   133 Neu   Polizeidirektion Braunschweig

Hamburg: The useful holdings of the Staatsarchiv Hamburg and the Archiv der Landesjustizverwaltung have not been exploited directly by me because of Henning Timpke's extensive publication of the relevant documents.

Hessia:
Hessisches Staatsarchiv Darmstadt
   G-12   Akten des Sicherheitsdienstes und der Geheimen Staatspolizei Darmstadt
   G-12(A)   Landespolizeiamt Darmstadt
   G-21   Hessisches Justizministerium
   N-1   NSDAP Akten
   R-1   Ersatsdokumentation ueber die Taetigkeit des hess. Innen Ministerium bezw. des Reichsstatthalter in Hessen, Ministerialausschreiben dieser Behoerde von 1907-1944 aus Landratsaemter, usw. This ambitious effort to reconstruct the destroyed state archives from the files of local offices was complete for the years 1933-36 at the time of my review.

Lippe:
Staatsarchiv Detmold
   L-76   Reichstatthalter und Staatsminister
   L80 Ie   Lipp. Regierung, Abtl. des Innern, Polizeiangelegenheiten, 1924-1949
   L-80 IeP Der Landespolizeidirektor und der Fuehrer der Landespolizei
   L-133   NSDAP, Kreisleitung Detmold und Lemgo

Oldenburg:
Niedersaechsisches Staatsarchiv Oldenburg
   136   Oldenburgisches Staatsministerium des Innern

Prussia:
Geheimes Staatsarchiv Berlin-Dahlem (Hauptarchiv Berlin, successor to the Prussian State Archive)
   77   Preussisches Ministerium des Innern
   90   Preussisches Staatsministerium (90, Abtl.P, holds the most relevant material)
   219   Landes Kriminalpolizeiamt Berlin (material from R-58, Bundesarchiv)
Hessisches Hauptstaatsarchiv Wiesbaden
   Abtl. 483   NSDAP Hessen-Nassau contains records of SD Gruppe West, later OAb Rhein, and Stapostelle Frankfurt a.M.

Niedersaechsisches Hauptstaatsarchiv Hannover
Hann. 112a   Oberpraesident der Provinz Hannover
Hann 310I   NSDAP, Gau Suedhannover-Braunschweig und Gau Osthannover

Schaumburg-Lippe:
Niedersaechsisches Staatsarchiv Bueckeburg
L4   Lfd. Regierungsregistratur-Rep. IV-

Wuerttemberg:
Hauptstaatsarchiv Stuttgart
  E-130 b II   Staatsministerium
  E-130 IV   Staatsministerium
  E-140   Reichsstatthalter in Wuerttemberg, 1933-1945
  E-151a   Ministerium des Innern, Abtl. I, Kanzleidirektion
  E-151b   ———, Abtl. II, Recht lund Verfassung
  E-151c   ———, Abtl. III, Polizeiwessen
Staatsarchiv Ludwigsburg
  E 188 c   Landespolizeidirektion Nordwuerttemberg—Personalakten
  K 100   Staatspolzeileitstelle Stuttgart, 1933-1945
  K 110   SD-Dienststellen in Wuerttemberg und
    Hohenzollern, 1933-1945

U.S. Archives

Library of Congress, Washington D.C. (see Weinberg)
Manuscript Division
The Deutsches Auslands-Institut Collection
The Himmler Files
The Rehse Collection (Hauptarchiv der NSDAP)

National Archives, Washington D.C. (see National Archives)
Aside from a complete collection of the American microfilming projects and miscellaneous research aids, this archive holds the materials collected for the International Military Tribunal in Nuremberg and subsequent American Trials, which are currently being microfilmed. All captured German documents belong to Record Group 238.

U.S. Document Center Berlin (see Browder)
Files on individuals, used for political and judicial purposes but available to scholars. The most significant:
  NS   Party Membership Files
  PK   Party Correspondence
  SSO   SS Officer's Files
  RuSHA   Rasse und Siedlungs Hauptamt Files on SS Personnel

Miscellaneous

Generalstaatsanwaltschaft bei dem Kammergericht Berlin

Holds materials assembled for the prosecution of NS criminals.
Institute fuer Zeitgeschichte, Munich
A valuable miscellaneous collection of relevant literature and documents,
made especially useful by an extensive indexing system.
Polizei-Fuehrungsakademie Hiltrup
A useful collection of literature, manuscripts, and miscellaneous documents.

Microfilmed Documents

Captured German Documents Microfilmed at the Berlin Document Center. T-580.
Captured German Documents Microfilmed at the Berlin Document Center. University
of Nebraska Microfilming Program at the Berlin Document Center. T-611.
Documents of the Hauptarchiv der NSDAP. Microfilm of the Hoover Insitiute on
War, Revolution and Peace. HA.
Miscellaneous SS Records: Einwandererzentralstelle, Waffen-SS, and SS-Oberabschnitte.
Microfilmed at Alexandria, Virginia. T-354.
*Records of the German Armed Forces High Command (Oberkommando der Wehrmacht/
OKW).* Microfilmed at Alexandria, Va. T-77.
Records of the National Socialist German Labor Party. Microfilmed at Alexandria,
Virginia. T-81.
Records of the Reichsfuehrer SS and Chief of the German Police. Microfilmed at Al-
exandria, Virginia. T-175.
Records of the United States Nurnberg War Crimes Trials: Interrogations, 1946-1949.
National Archives Microfilm Publications. M1019.
———. *USA v Otto Ohlendorf et al.* Case IX. National Archives Microfilm Pub-
lications. M895.

Published Documents

Anger, Walter (ed.). *Das Dritte Reich in Dokumenten.* Frankfurt a.M.: Europ Ver-
lag-Anst., 1957.
Boberach, Heinz (ed.). *Meldungen aus dem Reich.* Berlin: Hermann Luchterhand
Verlag, 1965.
Browder, George C. "Die Anfaenge des SD: Dokumente aus der Organisations-
geschichte des Sicherheitsdienstes des Reichfuehrers SS," *Vierteljahshefte fuer
Zeitgeschichte* 27 (1979): 299-324.
Dickmann, Fritz. "Die Regierungsbildung in Thuringen als Modell der Mach-
tergreifung: Ein Brief Hitlers aus dem Jahre 1930." *Vierteljahrshefte fuer Zeit-
geschichte* 14 (1966): 454-64.
Germany, Reichsministerium des Innern. *Ministerialblatt des Reichs- und Preus-
sischen Ministeriums.* Berlin: Carl Heymans Verlag, annual.
———. *Reichsgesetzblatt.* Berlin: Reichsverlagsamt, annual.
Historische Kommission des Reichsfuehrers SS. *Die Erhebung der oesterreischen
Nationalsozialistischen im Juli 1934.* Vienna: Europa Verlag, 1965.
International Military Tribunal. *Trial of the Major War Criiminals before the Inter-
national Military Tribunal.* 42 vols. Nuremberg: Secretariat of the Military
Tribunal, 1947-49.
Jacobsen, Hans Adolf, and Werner Jochmann (eds.). *Ausgewhaelte Dokumente zur*

Geschichte des Nationalsozialismus, 1933-45. Bielefeld: Neue Gesellschaft, 1961- .

Kompner, Robert W (ed.). SS in Kreuzverhoer. Noerdlingen: Delphi Politik, 1987.

Klein, Thomas. Die Lageberichte der Geheimen Staatspolizei ueber die Provinz Hessen-Nassau, 1933-1936. 2 vols. Cologne: Boehlau Verlag, 1986.

Krausnick, Helmut. "Aus den Personalakten von Canaris." Vierteljahrshefte fuer Zeitgeschichte 10 (July 1962): 280-310.

Mader, Julius. Hitlers Spionagegenerale sagen aus: Ein Dokumentarbericht ueber Aufbau, Struktur und Operationen des OKW-/genheimdienstes Ausland/Abwehr. Berlin: Verlag der Nation, 1970.

Meyer, Gertrud (ed.). Nacht ueber Hamburg: Berichte und Dokumente 1933-1945. Frankfurt a.M.: Roederberg-Verlag, 1971.

Mommsen, Hans. "Der Nationalsozialistische Polizeistaat und die Judenverfolgung vor 1938." Vierteljahrshefte fuer Zeitgeschichte 10 (January 1962): 68-87.

NSDAP, Reichsleitung. Rundschreiben des Reichsministers vom 26. Juli 1926–31. Dezember 1934. Munich: Reichsleitung, 1935.

———, Der Regierungsbildung der NSDAP. Organizationsbuch der NSDAP. Munich: Zentralverlag der NSDAP, annual.

———, Stellvertreter des Fuehrers. Anordnungen des Stellvertreters des Fuehrers. Munich: n.p., n.d.

Peter, Karl H. (ed.). Spiegelbild einer Verschwoerung. Stuttgart: Seewald Verlag, 1961.

Plum, Guenter. "Staatspolizei und innere Verwaltung, 1934-1936." Vierteljahreshefte fuer Zeitgeschichte 13 (April 1965): 191-224.

Poliakov, Leon, and Josef Wulf (eds.). Das Dritte Reich und die Juden. Berlin: Arani, 1955.

Prussia, Ministerium des Innern. Ministerialblatt fuer die preusische innere Verwaltung. Annual to 1934.

———, Preussischen Staatsministerium. Gesetzsammlung. Berlin: R. von Deckers Verlag, annual.

Schnabel, Reimund (ed.). Macht ohne Moral. Eine Dokumentations ueber die SS. Frankfurt a.M.: Verlag Roederberg, 1957.

Schumann, Heinz, and Gerhard Nitzsche. "Gestapoberichte ueber den antifaschistischen Kampf der KPD im frueheren Regierungsbezirk Aachen, 1934-1936." Zeitschrift fuer Geschichtswissenschaft 7 (1959): 118-130.

Thevoz, Robert, Hans Branig, and Cecile Lowenthal-Hensel (eds.). Die Geheime Staatspolizei in den preussischen Ostprovinzen. Pommern 1934/35. (Quellen). Berlin: G. Grotsche Verlagsbuchhandlung, 1974.

Timpke, Henning (ed.). Dokumente zur Gleichschaltung des Landes Hamburgs, 1933. Frankfurt a.M.: Europaische Verlagsanstalt, 1964.

United States, Office of U.S. Counsel for Prosecution of Axis Criminality. Nazi Conspiracy and Aggression. 8 vols. and 2 supplements. Washington: Government Printing Office, 1946-1948.

U.S. Government Printing Office. Trials of the War Criminals. 15 vols. Washington: Government Printing Office, 1946-49.

Vogelsong, Thilo. "Hitlers Brief an Reichnau vom 4. Dezember 1932." Vierteljahrshefte fuer Zeitgeschichte 4 (1959): 429-37.

Vollmer, Bernhard. Volksopposition im Polizeistaat: Gestapo- und Regierungsberichte 1934-1936. Stuttgart: Deutsche Verlags-Anstalt, 1957.

Contemporary Literature

Under this heading, the literature falls into two general categories: official publications of the Weimar and Nazi periods and public commentaries on the police; studies, exposes, and dramatizations of the NS police state by foreigners and émigrés. The former has obvious value. But aside from its insights into contemporary perceptions, the popular and polemical literature offers little. Some more reliable contemporary publications are included below, while the few reliable exposés will be found under "Memoirs."

Alquen, Gunter d'. *Die SS, Geschichte, Aufgabe und Organisation der Schutzstaffeln der NSDAP.* Berlin: Junker und Dunnhaupt Verlag, 1939. Official history of the SS.

Barek, Lothar. *Die Organisation des staatlichen Sicherheitsdienst in Baden.* Luebeck, Berlin: Deutscher Polizei-Verlag, 1931.

Best, Werner. *Die Deutsche Polizei.* Darmstadt: L.C. Wittich Verlag, 1941.

———. "Die Geheime Staatspolizei." *Deutsches Recht* 6 (April 1936): 125-28.

———. "Der Reichsfuehrer SS und Chef der Deutschen Polizei." *Deutsches Recht* 6 (July 1936): 257-58.

———. "Neubegruendung des Polizeirechts." Sonderdruck aus *Jahrbuch der Akademie fuer Deutsches Recht* 1937: 132-38.

Cantor, Nathaniel. "Recent Tendencies in Criminological Research in Germany." *Journal of Criminal Law and Criminology* 27 (March 1937): 782-93.

———. "Prison Reform in Germany—1933." *Journal of Criminal Law and Criminology* 25: 84-90.

Daluege, Kurt. *Nationalsozialistischen Kampf gegen des Verbrechertum.* Munich: F. Eher Verlag, 1936.

Ehrt, Adolf. *Bewaffneter Aufstand! Enthuellungen ueber den kommunistischen Umsturzversuch am Vorabend der nationalen Revolutions.* Berlin-Leipzig: Eckart, 1933.

——— and Julius Schweichert. *Entfesselung der Unterwelt: Ein Querschnitt durch die Bolschewisierung Deutschlands.* Berlin: Eckart, 1933.

Frank, Hans, et al. *Grundfragen der Deutschen Polizei: Arbeitsbericht der Akademie fuer Deutsches Recht.* Hamburg: 1937.

———. "Rede des Reichsjustizkommissare Staatsminister Dr. Frank bei der Gruendungskundgebung der Deutschen Rechtsfront in Hamburg." *Deutsches Recht* 2 (July 1933): 33-36.

Festgabe fuer Heinrich Himmler. Darmstadt: L.C. Wittich, 1941.

Gay, Willy. *Die preussische Landeskriminalpolizei.* Berlin: Kameradschaft Verlagsgesellschaft, 1928.

Gritzbach, Erich. *Hermann Goering, Werk und Mensch.* Munich: 1938. Trans. Gerald Griffen, *Herman Goering, the Man and His Work.* London: Hurst & Blackett, 1939. The only authorized biography.

Hartenstein, Wilhelm. *Der Kampfeinsatz der Schutzpolizei bei inneren Unruhen.* Berlin-Charlottenburg: Offene Worte, 1926. Official training material.

Henning (Polizeirat). "Das Wesen und die Entwicklung der politischen Polizei in Berlins." *Mitteilungen des Vereins fuer die Geschichte Berlins* 43 (1925): 88-92.

Heydrich, Reinhard. "Die bekaempfung der Staatsfeinde." *Deutsches Recht* 6 (April 1936); 121-23.

—. *Wandlungen unseres Kampfes.* Munich-Berlin: Eher, 1935.

Hoehn, Reinhard. "Die Wandlung im Polizeirecht." *Deutsche Rechtswissenschaft* 1 (1936): 100-123.

——— . *Die Wandlung in staatsrechtlichen Denken.* Hamburg: Hanseatische Verlagsanstalt, 1934.

Honig, Fredrich. "Recent Changes in German Criminal Law." *Journal of Criminal Law and Criminology* 26 (January 1936): 857-61.

Kampffmeyer, Paul. "Die politische Polizei." *Sozialistische Monatshefte* 35 (1929): 23-29.

Kempner, Robert M.W. "The German National Registration System as means of Police Control of Population." *Journal of Criminal Law and Criminology* 36 (January 1946): 362-87.

[Korrod, Walter?] *Ich kann nicht schweigen.* Zurich: Europa-Verlag, 1936. Allegedly by a leading person in NS Party who became disenchanted and spent time in Gestapo custody.

Koschorke, Helmut (ed.). *Die Polizei—einmal anders!* Mit einem Geleitwort des Reichsfuehrers SS . . . Geschrieben von der deutschen Presse zum "Tag der duetschen Polizei." Munich: Zentralverlag der NSDAP, 1937.

———. "Von der 'Knueppelgarde' zur Volkspolizei." *Jahrbuch der Deutschen Polizei—Leipzig,* 1936.

Landecker, Werner S. "Criminology in Germany." *Journal of Criminal Law and Criminology* 31 (January 1941): 551-75.

Leiser, Clara. "A Director of a Nazi Prison Speaks Out." *Journal of Criminal Law and Criminology* 28 (September 1938): 345-52.

Plascowe, Morris. "The Organization for the Enforcement of the Criminal Law in France, Germany and England" (sic; should read Italy). *Journal of Criminal Law and Criminology* 27 (September 1936): 305-27.

Preuss, Lawrence. "Punishment by Analogy in National-Socialist Penal Law." *Journal of Criminal Law and Criminology* 26 (January 1936): 847-56.

Prussia, Ministerium des Innern. "Landeskriminalpolizei." *Vorschriften fuer die staatliche Polizei Preussens.* Berlin: Kameradschaft Verlagsgesellschaft, 1927.

Reichssicherheitshauptamt. *Reinhard Heydrich: 7.Maerz 1904-4.Juni 1942.* Berlin: Ahnenerbe Stiftung Verlag, 1942.

———. *Nachruf fuer Reinhard Heydrich.* Berlin, 1942.

Schlierbach, Helmut. *Die politische Polizei in Preussen.* Emsdetten: H.& J. Lechte, 1938.

Schoenfleder, Roland. *Vom Werdern der deutschen Polizei: Ein Volksbuch.* Leipzig: Breitkopf & Haertel, 1937.

Schulze, Fiete. *Fiete Schulze—Briefe und Aufzeichnungen aus dem Gestapo-Gefaengnis in Hamburg.* Berlin: Dietz, 1959.

Schuster, V.J. (ed.). "Die Deutsche Polizei." Herausgabe im Auftrage des RFSSu-CdDPiRMdI. Berlin-Schoeneberg: Verlag Deutsche Kultur-Wacht, 1937.

Schwarz, Dieter [pseud.]. *Die Freimaurerei, Weltanschauung, Organisation und Politik.* Berlin: Eher, 1938. Foreword by Heydrich and allegedly written pseudonymously by him.

Schweder, Alfred. *Politische Polizei: Wesen und Begriff der politischen Polizei im Metternichschen System, in der Weimarer Republik und im nationalsozialistischen Staate.* Berlin: Carl Heymanns Verlag, 1937.

Sonderegger, Rene (ed.). *Moerdzentrale X: Enthuellungen und Dokumente ueber die Auslandstaetigkeit der deutschen Gestapo.* Zurich: Reso-Verlag, 1936.

Stephen, Otto (Polizeirat). "Polizei und Wehrmacht." *Die Polizei* 19 (20 July 1922): 143-46.

Miscellaneous clippings from *Die Polizei* and other police journals, aritcles from *Voelkischer Beobachter*, and clippings from other contemporary newspapers are found in the footnotes

Memoirs, Apologia, Inside Exposés

The problems inherent in such sources are exaggerated by the natural sensationalism of police and security work, especially in the Third Reich. Nevertheless, no historian can afford to ignore such potentially valuable information. The rule is to check carefully the validity of such evidence in detail and to employ it with great caution.

For this study, the books by Diels, Gisevius, Koehler, Orb, Peis (for Naujocks), and Lina Heydrich have been the most significant. Diels and Gisevius can be tested not only against the documents, but against each other. Strangely, Diels, despite obvious minimizing of his involvement in actions he would conceal, proves generally more accurate and reliable than Gisevius, a member of the resistance. It is mostly a matter of the difference in their positions. For two years, Diels was at the center of the development of the Gestapo; Gisevius was always on the periphery and, as a jealous opponent, had a jaundiced view. The ultimate value of all such self-justifying literature is its insight into the self-images of the key personalities who wrote them.

Alfred Naujock's memoirs, interpreted through Peis seem the most fictionalized and overdramatized of the six. Again, their prime value is the projected self-image. Nevertheless, some of Naujock's memories of the early SD are corroborated by other sources and are therefore worth quoting.

The two most useful—and most troublesome—sources are the books written under the pen names Koehler and Orb. Orb's book has traditionally been accepted as a reliable inside source for many studies of the Gestapo and SD. Koehler's has generally been ignored. Yet on comparison, it is obvious that the authors were either the same man or that "Orb" used "Koehler" extensively as a source. Koehler is occasionally more accurate on details when compared with the documents. However, many of Koehler's stories of cloak-and-dagger adventure, such as the Roehm purge, are contrary to most accepted and documented accounts and seem largely fictional. Both books appear to be the product of a man who was involved at some point directly in or with the Gestapo and the SD, who had extensive, detailed inside information and direct personal contacts, yet who was not above fabricating impressive-seeming details when he had none.

Gert Buchheit (*Der deutsche Geheimdienst*, p. 168) speculates that Koehler and Orb are the same, the former head of "Sonderbuero Stein" who fled Germany in 1935 after clashes with Himmler and Heydrich. Under the name Heinrich Pfeiffer, he worked for the Poles, then Hungary, and when war broke out moved to Switzerland, where the British declined his services "because he cost the Poles money and supplied only fraud." This could be accurate only if the Orb-Koehler descriptions of personal activities were largely fabricated for the period after early 1934, which may be the case; however, the Buchheit thesis is at odds with some of the apparently accurate passages in Orb and Koehler. With Koehler and Orb, the historian is torn between the almost certainly accurate inside information, the obviously fictional accounts, and much that has yet to be tested.

Her penchant for understatement is the least problem with Lina Heydrich's memoirs. Most problems derive from her confusion of time sequences and a need to deny unpleasant realities. Nevertheless, there are some surprisingly frank relations. Inconsistencies between her book and other versions of events she has given, to Aronson for instance, emphasize the need for carefully testing her every statement. Even so, she is valuable as the only intimate portrayal of Heydrich not simplistically negative.

Whenever possible, I have, of course, researched the original language editions of such sources, but I have also cited the more readily available English translations when the texts were adequate. In this respect, the Schellenberg memoirs presented unique problems. The English version was published first, postumously from an unrefined manuscript. The subsequent German edition is superior is some respects but not always, especially since some of the original manuscript was lost. Consequently, references to both versions are employed, depending on which is the richest and apparently most accurate. The most reliable source would be the original manuscript residing in the Institut fuer Zeitgeschichte.

To further complicate matters, many of these books appeared in several editions in the original language, each with different pagination. Over the years, I have used several of them; however, for the citations employed in this book, every effort was made to coordinate page references to the edition cited below.

Diels, Rudolf. *Lucife ante Portas: Es spricht der erste Chef der Gestapo.* Zurich: Interverlag, 1950(?) (There was also a Stuttgart edition in 1950.)

Dodd, Martha. *Through Embassy Eyes.* New York: Harcourt Brace, 1939.

Dodd, William E., Jr., and Martha Dodd (ed.). *Ambassodor Dodd's Diary, 1933-1938.* New York: Harcourt Brace, 1941.

Frank, Hans. *Im Angesicht des Galgens.* Munich: Friedrich Alfred Beck Verlag, 1953.

Friedensburg, Ferdinand. *Die Weimarer Republik.* Berlin: C. Habel, 1946. (Deputy Police President, Berlin, 1925-27.)

Gisevius, Hans B. *Bis zum bittern Ende.* 2 vols. Hamburg: Classen & Goverts, 1947. Trans. Richard and Clara Winston as *To the Bitter End.* Boston: Houghton Mifflin, 1947. (First German-language edition Zurich, 1946; also in English, London, 1948.)

———. *Wo ist Nebe? Erinnerungen an Hitlers Kriminaldirektor.* Zurich: Droemer, 1966.

Goebbels, Joseph. *Die Tagebuecher von Joseph Goebbels. Saemtliche Fragement.* Ed. Elke Froehlich. 4 vols. Munich: K.G. Sauer, 1987.

Grezesinski, Albert. C. *Inside Germany.* Trans. Alexander S. Lipschitz. New York: E.P. Dutton, 1939. (SPD police president of Berlin, 1925-26 and 1930-32.)

Heydrich, Lina. *Leben mit einem Kriegsverbrecher.* Pfaffenhofen: Verlag W. Lugwig, 1976. (Wife of Reinhard Heydrich.)

Hoettl, Wilhelm. *The Secret Front; the Story of Nazi Political Espionage.* Trans. R.H. Stevens. New York: Praeger, 1954. (Former member of the SD.)

Kersten, Felix. *The Kersten Memoirs, 1940-1945.* Trans. Constantine Fitzgibbon and James Oliver. New York: Macmillan, 1957. (Himmler's masseur and confidant.)

Koehler, Hansjuergen [pseud.]. *Inside the Gestapo.* London: Pallas Publishing, 1940.

———. *Inside Information.* London: Pallas Publishing 1940.

Leverkuehn, Paul. *Der Geheime Nachrichtendienst der deutschen Wehrmacht im*

Kriege. Frankfurt a.M.: Bernhard & Graefe, 1957. Trans. R.H. Stevens and Constantine Fitzgibbon as *German Military Intelligence.* London: Weidenfeld & Nicolson, 1954. (A former member of the Abwehr.)

Orb, Heinrich [pseud.]. *Nationalsozialismus, 13 Jahre Machtrausch.* Olten, Switzerland: Verlag Otto Walter, 1945.

Papen, Franz von. *Memoirs.* Trans. Brian Connell. New York: Dutton, 1953.

———. *Vom Scheitern einer Demokratie, 1930-1933.* Mainz: v. Hase & Koehler Verlag, 1968.

Peis, Guenter. *The Man Who Started the War.* London: Odhams, 1960. (Recollections of Alfred Naujocks, former member of the SD.)

Pruck, Erich. "Die Geheimepolizei im totalitaren Regime." *Politische Studien* 10 (May 1959): 313-19. (Former member of the Abwehr.)

———. "Heydrichs SD: Die nationalsozialistische Geheimpolizei." *Politische Studien* 10 (July 1959): 442-48.

Reile, Oskar. *Geheime Ostfront: Die deutsche Abwehr im Osten 1921-1945.* Munich: Verlag Welsermuehl, 1963. (Former member of the Abwehr.)

———. *Geheime Westfront: Die Abwehr, 1935-1945.* Munich: Verlag Welsermuehl, 1962.

———. *Macht und Ohnmacht der Geheimdienste.* Munich: Verlag Welsermuehl, 1968.

Schaefer, Karl. *20 Jahr im Polizeidienst (1925-1945).* Frankfurt a.M.: Decker & Wilhelm, 1977. (Former member of the Gestapo.)

Schellenberg, Walter. *The Schellenberg Memoirs.* Ed. and trans. Louis Hagen. London: Andre Deutsch, 1956. *Memoiren.* Cologne: Verlag fuer Politik und Wirtschaft, 1959. (Also in English in abridged form as *The Labyrinth.*)

Severing, Karl. *Mein Lebensweg.* 2 vols. Cologne: Greven Verlag, 1950.

Personal Correspondence and Unpublished Materials by Participants

As with memoirs, living sources confront the historian with a range of problems that are exaggerated by the nature of this subject. Former members of SS and police organizations are still subject to prosecution for crimes they might have committed. Nevertheless, their memories are invaluable sources that must be employed carefully.

I have established few contacts personally and am grateful for the assistance of colleagues who have forwarded the results of their correspondence. This has made it unnecessary to trouble the few cooperative living sources with duplication of effort.

d'Alquen, Gunter:
  Letters to the author, 14 June 1978 and 24 July 1978.
Best, Werner:
  Materials made available through Shlomo Aronson:
  "Die deutsche Abwehrpolizei bis 1945." Unpublished manuscript.
  "Betr.: Adolf Hitler," 17 March 1949, 15 pp.
  "Betr.: Heinrich Himmler," 18 September 1949, 14 pp.
  "Betr.: Wilhelm Canaris," 10 April 1949, 9 pp.
  Beanwortung des (Aronson) Fragebogens.
  Beanwortung der Fragen in (Aronson) Schreiben von 3.12.1964.

Material made available through David Kahn:
"Betr.: Auslandsnachrichtendienst des SD," 24.11.1974.
Letters to the author, a April 1977, 28 May 1978, 21 July 1978, 10 August
1980.
Hoettl, Wilhelm:
Material made available through Peter Black:
Protokoll eines Interviews mit Herrn Dr. Wilhelm Hoettl, am 14. and 15.
April 1977.
Letter, 8 November 1977.
Leffler, Paul:
"Auszug aus einem Bericht des Dipl.-Ing. Paul Leffler ueber den SD." Made
available by Best through Aronson.
Mehlhorn, Herbert:
"Antwort—Dr. Mehlhorn auf Fragebogen vom 20. November 1965." Made
available by Aronson
Neumann, Hans-Henrick:
Letter to author, 9 December 1986.
Patzig, Adm. Conrad:
Notes of conversations, 24 and 25 August 1973. Made available by Kahn.

Subsequent Literature

With the exception of Hitler and the military, no other figures of Nazi Germany
have produced more literature than the SS and police system, if its camps and
their atrocities are included. Today, one can dismiss as journalistic and sensational the vast bulk of that which deals extensively with persons and organizations in Sipo and SD. Even pioneer scholarship like Reitlinger's has become
dated by the extensive subsequent work.

Aside from the tangential insights in Reitlinger and the mass of literature
on the fate of the Jews, English-speaking authors had published no books of
value on the Gestapo and SD until recently. All serious scholarship in England
and America had been limited entirely to unpublished dissertations, scholarly
journals, or anthologies. The reading public had to rely on translations of Ger-
man- and French-language books. Unfortunately, the French-language literature
also makes few valuable contributions of knowledge, and, like the general literature from Britain and America, is listed below purely for bibliographical interest.

Among German scholars, Zipfel and those, like Buchheim, associated with
the Institut fuer Zeitgeschichte, removed the study of the Gestapo and SD from
the realm of journalism. The work of the Institut scholars has culminated in *The
Anatomy of the SS State*, while Zipfel, in addition to his own work, directed a
dissertation that has been the most significant single contribution. This dissertation by Shlomo Aronson, an Israeli, matured into the seminal biography of
Heydrich and history of the early Gestapo and SD.

Aronson's thoroughly documented biography is the base for the analysis of
Heydrich presented here. His book also provided significant leads for further
research into the pre-1933 history of the SD and was indispensable on the analysis
of the formation of the Bavarian Political Police. Beyond such specifics, the work
of Aronson and my own have overlapped so extensively that it is impossible to
determine where debt ends and originality begins. My doctoral dissertation was

completed early in 1968, and research for this book was well underway before a copy of Aronson's became available. Aronson's work then became the scale for measuring what would be a contribution to knowledge.

In an effort to distinguish between my debts and my contributions, the footnotes indicate where Aronson and others deserve credit for the initial discovery of documents and for interpretations that I share. Where there are differences in any way significant, the reader is asked to compare (cf.) the views.

Building from work like Aronson's and Buchheim's, Heinz Hoehne returned the effort to the realm of good popular literature. Although his book must be recognized as the best survey history of the SS in general, his efforts to condense our knowledge of Sipo and SD have frequently lost the fine edge of the scholars. Consequently, he has perpetuated, and even created, careless generalizations. Similar problems plague Deschner's biography of Heydrich, which, for the years covered by this book, adds little of significance beyond Aronson. Although Deschner maintained some of Aronson's modification of Heydrich's "evil genius" image, he returned him to the status of driving force behind Himmler and the focus of every development in Sipo and SD. Calic would carry us back to the even greater extremes, with Heydrich behind almost everything, including the Reichstag fire. Perhaps his book's only merit is that it requires the scholar to reconsider the extent to which Aronson and Deschner were convinced by the family's and wife's denials about Heydrich's basic convictions and the formative experiences that made him a Nazi at heart. Robert Koehl's long-awaited book on the SS has restored American scholarship to some prominence in this area. Written primarily for the scholar, it provides a survey of SS development that would lose most general readers, and it would have had more impact in the sixties, when first written. Today, it stands as a mix of many significant contributions with some dated perspectives.

At the level of more basic research, the first indication of movement in directions essential to further progress came from the staff of the Geheime Staatsarchiv Berlin-Dahlem. They commissioned a number of studies of local Gestapo posts, the only one to appear covering the area of Pommerania. Perhaps as an offshoot, two similar projects have appeared covering Frankfurt a.M. and Hessen-Nassau. This work, begun under Robert Thevoz, provided the first of the badly needed grassroots studies of the Gestapo, Kripo, and SD, of their operating procedures, and of their specific roles in major domestic and foreign actions and decisions. Most of all, we need analyses of their personnel. In this respect, the contributions of Boehnert and Ziegler provide quantitative and social analysis of the SS to compare with the more extensive work on the NS Movement in general and the SA.

One work on a specific involvement of the SD requires mention—Ramme's study of its role in the occupation of Poland. Although relevant more to the period following this book, Ramme's introductory chapter makes contributions to the general history of the SD. Especially interesting is his critique of the extant literature. Unfortunately, his own analysis errs to the opposite extreme of that for which he criticizes the "bourgeois historians." In his zeal to establish the links between the SD and industry and high finance, he converts circumstantial relationships into concrete connections without substantial evidence. The error here is more a matter of loose methodology than ideological dogmatism, however, for support for the police state from industrial and financial circles is another area where research is badly needed to advance understanding of the development and extent. As this book has indicated, regardless of their motives, between 1933 and 1936 Himmler's supporters, both within and without the Movement, tipped the balance in his favor. Perhaps recruiting and channeling the involvement of business and industry at all levels in an area where the SD played a crucial role.

The most recent major contribution has come, surprisingly, from the Internationallen Kimmittees zur Wissenschaftlichen Erforschung der Ursachen und Folgen des zweiten Weltkrieges—not from its unconvincing effort to expose Heydrich as responsible for the Reichstag fire, nor from Calic's journalism, but from the solid scholarship of Christoph Graf. His study of the evolution of the Prussian Political Police into the Gestapo appeared after this book was essentially completed. The independently developed parallels in analysis and in new insights that exist between Graf's and this book make them mutually reinforcing on most points. As with Aronson, the author gives credit to Graf for discoveries not already made by the author and directs the reader to compare interpretations when differences exist.

Unpublished Materials

Aronson, Shlomo. "Heydrich und die Anfaenge des SD und der Gestapo (1931-1935)." Doctoral dissertation, Free University of Berlin, 1967.

Browder, George C. "SIPO and SD, 1931-1940: The Formation of an Instrument of Power." Doctoral dissertation, University of Wisconsin, Madison, 1968.

Fricke, Peter. "Anfaenge und Organisation der Nachrichtenstelle bei der Polizeidirektion Bremen." Dienstlicher Bericht im Rahmen der Laufbahnpruefung fuer den gehobenen Archivdienst des Landes Bremen, 1966.

Houston, Wendell R. "Ernst Kaltenbrunner: A Study of an Austrian SS and Police Leader." Doctoral dissertation, Rice University, 1972.

Lorance, Lonnie L. "Financing the Local SS in Major Region Rhein, 1934-1936." Seminar paper, University of Wisconsin, Madison, 1970.

——"General SS Membership in Main Sector Rhein, 1934-1936." Seminar paper, University of Wisconsin, Madison, 1970.

McGee, James H. "The Political Police in Bavaria, 1919-1936." Doctoral dissertation, University of Florida, 1980.

Sengatta, Hans-Juergen. "Der Reichsstatthalter in Lippe 1933-1939." Wissenschaftliche Hausarbeit zur Erlangung der Befaehigung fuer des Lehramt an Gymnasium, Technische Universitaet Hannover, n.d.

Stokes, Lawrence D. "The Sicherheitsdienst (SD) of he Reichsfuehrer SS and German Public Opinion, September 1939–June 1941." Doctoral dissertation, Johns Hopkins University, 1972

Ziegler, Herbert F. "The SS Fuehrer Korps: An Analysis of Its Socioeconomic and Demographic Structure, 1925-1938." Doctoral dissertation, Emory University, 1980.

Books and Articles

Abshagen, Karl H. Canaris, Patriot und Weltburger. Stuttgart: Union Deutsche Verlagsgesellschaft, 1950. Trans. Alan H. Brodrick as Canaris. London: Hutchinson, 1956.

Angress, Werner T., and Bradley F. Smith. "Diaries of Heinrich Himmler's Early Years." Journal of Modern History 31 (September 1959): 206-24.

Arendt, Hannah. *Eichmann in Jerusalem: A Report on the Banality of Evil*. New York: Viking Press, 1963.

Arnau, Frank [pseud. for Heinrich Schmitt]. *Das Auge des Gesetzes. Macht und Ohnmacht der Kriminalpolizei*. Duesseldorf and Vienna: Econ Verlag, 1962.

Aronson, Shlomo. *The Beginnings of the Gestapo System: The Bavarian Model in 1933*. Jerusalem: Israel Univ. Press, 1969.

———. *Reinhard Heydrich und die Fruehgeschichte von Gestapo und SD*. Stuttgart: Deutsche Verlags-Anstalt, 1971.

Augstein, Rudolf, et al, "Das Spiel ist aus—Arthur Nebe." *Der Spiegel*, 3, 4 (1949-1950).

Bartz, Karl. *Die Tragodie der deutschen Abwehr*. Salzburg: Pilgrim Verlag, 1955. Trans. Edward Fitzgerald as *The Downfall of the German Secret Service*. London: W. Kimber, 1956.

Bayley, David H. "The Police and Political Development in Europe." In *The Formation of National States in Western Europe*, ed. Charles Tilly, pp. 328-79. Princeton: Princeton Univ. Press, 1975.

Beamten der Geheimen Staatspolizei, Die. Denkschrift des Bundes Deutscher Polizeibeamter e.V. Kassel, 1953.

Beneke, Paul. "Die Rolle der 'Gestapo.' " *Weg* 10 (1956): 353-58, 476-80.

Berkley, George E. "Criminalization, Democracy and the Police." *The Journal of Criminal Law, Criminology and Police Science* 61 (June 1970): 309-12.

Bewley, Charles. *Hermann Goering and the Third Reich*. New York: Devin-Adair, 1962. An apology for Goering that is occasionally well founded and severely critical of Gisevius.

Black, Peter R. *Ernst Kaltenbrunner: Ideological Soldier of the Third Reich*. Princeton: Princeton Univ. Press, 1984.

Blaudau, Kuno. *Gestapo-Geheim! Widerstand und Verfolgung in Duisburg 1933-1945*. Bonn: Verlag Neue Gesellschaft, 1973.

Boehnert, Gunnar C. "An Analysis of the Age and Education of the SS Fuehrerkorps, 1925-1939." *Historical Social Research* 12 (October 1979): 4-17.

———. "Jurists in the SS-Fuehrerkorps, 1925-1939." In *Der Fuehrerstaat, Mythos und Realitaet: Studien zur Struktur und Politik des Dritten Reiches*, ed. Gerhard Hirschfeld and Lothar Kettenacher. Stuttgart: Kett-Cotta, 1981.

Bracher, Karl D., Wolfgang Sauer, and Gerhard Schulz. *Die nationalsozialistische Machtergreifung: Studien zur Errichtung des totalitaren Herrschaftssystem in Deutschland 1933/34*. Cologne: Westdeutsche Verlag, 1960.

Brachmann, Botho. "Aktenbetreffe des Geheimen Staatspolizeiamts zur Widerstandsbewegung der deutschen Arbeiterklasse 1933-1939." *Archivmitteilungen* 11 (1961): 74-80.

Bramstedt, Ernst K. *Dictatorship and Political Police*. London: Kegan Paul, 1945.

Brissaud, Andre. *The Nazi Secret Service*. Trans. Milton Waldman. New York: W. Norton, 1974.

Browder, George C. "The SD: The Significance of Organization and Image." In George L. Mosse (ed.), *Police Forces in History*. London: SAGE Publications, 1975.

———. "The Numerical Strength of the Sicherheitsdienst des RFSS." *Historical Social Research* 28 (October 1983): 30-41.

Buchheim, Hans. *SS und Polizei im NS-Staat*. Duisdorf: Selbstverlag der Studiengesellschaft fuer Zeitprobleme, 1964.

Buchheit, Gert. *Der deutsche Geheimdienst: Geschichte der militaerischen Abwehr*. Munich: Paul List Verlag, 1966.

Calic, Edouard. *Reinhard Heydrich: The Chilling Story of the Man Who Masterminded the Nazi Death Camps.* New York: William Morrow, 1985.

Caplan, Jane. "Bureaucracy, Politics and the National Socialist State." In Peter D. Stachura (ed.). *The Shaping of the Nazi State.* London: Croom Helm, 1978.

———. "Civil Service Support for National Socialism: An Evaluation." In *Der "Fuehrerstaat," Mythos und Realitaet: Studien zur Struktur und Politik des Dritten Reiches,* ed. Lothar Kettenacher. Stuttgart: Klett-Cotta, 1981.

———. "The Politics of Administration: The Reich Interior Ministry and the German Civil Service, 1933-1943." *Historical Journal* 20 (1977): 707-736.

Charisius, Albrecht, and Julius Mader. *Nicht laenger geheim—Aufbau, System und Arbeitsweise des imperialistischen deutschen Geheimdienstes.* Berlin: Militaerverlag der DDR, 1969.

Colvin, Ian G. *Chief of Intelligence.* London: Victor Gollancz, 1951.

Crankshaw, Edward. *Gestapo: Instrument of Tyranny.* New York: Viking Press, 1957.

Danner, Lothar. *Ordnungspolizei Hamburg: Betrachtung zu ihrer Geschichte, 1918 bis 1933.* Hamburg: Verlag Deutsche Polizei, 1958.

Delarue, Jacques. *The Gestapo: A History of Horror.* New York: Dell Publishing, 1965.

Deschner, Guenther. *Reinhard Heydrich: Statthalter der totalen Macht.* Esslingen: Bechtle Verlag, 1977.

Desroches, Alain. *La Gestapo: Atrocités et secrets de l'inquisition Nazie.* Paris: Ed. de Vecchi, 1972.

Dicks, Henry. *Licensed Mass Murder: A Socio-Psychological Study of Some SS Killers.* New York: Basic Books, 1973.

Domroese, Ortwin. *Der NS-Staat in Bayern von der Machtergreifung bis zum Roehm-Putsch.* Munich: R. Woelfle, 1974.

Dulles, Allen. *Germany's Underground.* New York: Macmillan, 1947.

Emerson, Donald E. *Metternich and the Political Police: Security and Subversion in the Hapsburg Monarchy (1815-1830).* Den Haag: Martinus Nijhoff, 1968.

Fest, Joachim C. *Das Gesicht des Dritten Reiches: Profile einer totalitaeren Herrschaft.* Munich: R. Piper, 1963.

Frischauer, Willi. *Himmler, the Evil Genius of the Third Reich.* New York: Belmont Productions, 1962.

Freund, Michael. "Heydrichs Rolle." *Gegenwart* 13 (October 1958): 626-30.

Funk, Albrecht. *Polizei und Rechtsstaat: Die Entwicklung des staatlichen Gewaltmonopols in Preussens, 1848-1933.* Frankfurt a.M.: Campus Verlag, 1986.

Gordon, Harold. *Hitler and the Beer Hall Putsch.* Princeton: Princeton Univ. Press, 1972. (Contains an excellent chapter on the Bavarian police.)

———. "Police Careers in the Weimar Republic." In *Proceedings of the Citadel Symposium on Hitler and the National Socialist Era,* ed. Michael B. Barrett, pp. 160-69. Charleston, S.C.: Citadel Development Foundation, 1982.

Graber, G.S. *The Life and Times of Reinhard Heydrich.* New York: David McKay, 1980. (Simple, careless, gullible synthesis of previous literature, with no pretense of scholarship.)

Graf, Christoph. *Politische Polizei zwischen Demokratie und Diktatur.* Berlin: Colloquium Verlag, 1983.

Hartmann, Sverre. "Zwischen Staat und System. Ein Versuch zur Klaerung der Problems Canaris." *Deutsche Rundschau* 81 (April 1955): 348-53.

Heller, Karl H. "The Remodeled Praetorians: The German *Ordnungs-polizei* as

Guardians of the 'New Order.' " In *Nazism and the Common Man*, ed. Otis C. Mitchell, pp. 45-47. Minneapolis: Burgess Publishing, 1972.

Hoehne, Heinz. *Der Orden unter dem Totenkopf. Die Geschichte der SS.* Guetersloh: Sigbert Mohn Verlag, 1967. Trans. Richard Barry as *The Order of the Death's Head*. New York: Howard-McCann, 1969.

Hofer, Walter, et al. *Der Reichstagsbrand: Eine wissenschaftliche Dokumentation.* vol. 2. Munich: K.G. Sauer Verlag, 1978.

Hoffmann, Peter. *Hitler's Personal Security.* Cambridge: MIT Press, 1979.

Hunhold, Tonis. *Polizei in der Reform: Was Staatsbuerger und Polizei von einander erwarten koennen.* Duesseldorf: Econ Verlag, 1968.

Institut fuer Zeitgeschichte. *Gutachten des Instituts fuer Zeitgeschichte.* 2 vols. Munich: Selbstverlag des Instituts, 1958; Stuttgart: Deutsche Verlags-Anstalt, 1966.

Irving, David, ed. *Breach of Security: The German Secret Intelligence File on Events Leading to the Second World War.* London: William Kimber, 1968. (Dealing with the Forschungsamt and its reports, an exception to my negative comments about English-language literature that does not carry over to Irving's later work.)

Kaestl, Claus. "Reich und Laenderpolizeien in der Weimarer Republik." *Die Polizei* 53 (October 1962): 302-5.

Kahn, David. *Hitler's Spies: German Military Intelligence in World War II.* New York: Macmillan, 1978. (A greater exception to my negative comments about related American publications.)

Klein, Thomas. *Die Lagaberichte der Geheimen Staatspolizei ueber die Provinz Hessen-Nassau, 1933-1936.* 2 vols. Cologne: Boehler Verlag, 1986.

Koch, Horst-Adelbert. "Zur Organisationsgeschichte der deutschen Polizei 1927-1939." *Feldgrau* 5, 6 (1957, 1958).

Koehl, Robert L. *The Black Corps: The Structure and Power Struggles of the Nazi SS.* Madison: Univ. of Wisconsin Press, 1983.

Kohler, Eric D. "The Crisis of the Prussian Schutzpolizei, 1920-1932." In *Police Forces in History*, ed. George L. Mosse, pp. 131-50. London: SAGE Publications, 1975.

Kotze, Hildegard von. "Hitlers Sicherheitsdienst im Ausland: Belege zur Zeitgeschichte II." *Die Politische Meinung* 8 (1963): 75-80.

Krausnick, Helmut, et al. *Anatomie des SS-Staates.* 2 vols. Olten & Freiburg: Walter-Verlag, 1965. Trans. Richard Barry, Marian Jackson, Dorothy Long as *Anatomy of the SS State.* New York: Walker Co., 1968.

Lerner, Daniel, and Harold D. Laswell, eds. *World Revolutionary Elites.* Cambridge: MIT Press, 1965.

Levine, Herbert S. "A Jewish Collaborator in Nazi Germany: The Strange Career of Georg Kareski, 1933-37." *Central European History* 8 (September 1975): 251-81.

Liang, Hsi-Huey. *The Berlin Police Force in the Weimar Republic.* Berkeley: Univ. of California Press, 1970.

Lowenberg, Peter. "The Unsuccessful Adolescence of Heinrich Himmler." *The American Historical Review* 76 (June 1971): 612-41.

Mader, Julius. "Eichmann's Chef ist Bonner 'Gesandter Z. WV.' " *Deutsche Aussenpolitik* 8 (1963): 405-9. (Exposé and biographical sketch of Franz Six.)

Manvell, Roger, and Heinrich Fraenkel. *The Canaris Conspiracy.* London: Heinemann, 1969.

———. *Heinrich Himmler.* London: Heinemann, 1965.

Marssolek, Inge, and Rene Ott. *Bremen im Dritten Reich: Anpassung—Widerstand—Verfolgung.* Bremen: Schuenemann Verlag, 1986.

Mayer, Milton. *They Thought They Were Free. The Germans, 1933-45.* Chicago: Univ. of Chicago Press, 1955.

Neufeldt, Hans-Joachim, Juergen Huch, and Georg Tessen. *Zur Geschichte der Ordnungspolizei, 1936-1945.* Coblenz: Schriften des Bundesarchivs, 1957.

Neusuess-Hundel, Erminhild. *Die SS.* Marburg/Lahn: Norddeutsche Verlagsanstalt, 1956.

Pioch, Hans-Hugo. *Das Polizeirecht einschliesslich der Polizeiorganisation.* Tuebingen: Verlag J.C.B. Mohr, 1952.

Raible, Eugene. *Geschichte der Polizei.* Stuttgart: Richard Boorberg Verlag, 1963.

Ramme, Alwin. *Der Sicherheitsdienst der SS: Seine Stellung in der faschistischen Diktatur unter besonderer Beruecksichtigung seiner besatzungspolitischen Funktionen im sogenannten General Gouvernerment Polen.* Berlin: Deutsche Militaerverlag, 1970.

Reiche, E.G. "From 'Spontaneous' to Legal Terrorism: SA, Police and the Judiciary in Nuernberg, 1933-34." *European Studies Review* 9 (1979): 237-64.

Reitlinger, Gerald. *The SS, Alibi of a Nation, 1922-1945.* New York: Viking Press, 1957.

Richardson, James F. "Berlin Police in the Weimar Republic: A Comparison with Police Forces in Cities of the United States." In *Police Forces in History,* ed. George L. Mosse, pp. 79-93. London: SAGE Publications, 1975.

Rubehn. "Der Dienst in der Geheimen Staatspolizei." *Zeitschrift fuer Beamtenrecht und Beamtenpolitik* 6 (1958): 270-76.

Sauer, Paul. *Wuerttemberg in der Zeit des Nationalsozialismus.* Ulm: Sueddeutsche Verlagsgesellschaft, 1975.

Saurel, Louis. *La Gestapo.* Paris: Editions Rouff, 1967.

———. *Les SS.* Paris: Editions Rouff, 1966.

Schwarze, Johannes. *Die bayerische Polizei und ihre historische Funktion der Aufrechterhaltung der oeffentlich Sicherheit in Bayern von 1919-1933.* Munich: Neue Schriftenreihe des Stadtarchivs Muenchen, 1972.

Schwarzwaelder, Herbert. *Die Machtergreifung der NSDAP in Bremen 1933.* Bremen: Schuenemann, 1966.

Siggemann, Juergen. *Die kasernierte Polizei und das Problem der inneren Sicherheit in der Weimarer Republik: Eine Studie zu Auf- und Ausbau der innerstaatlichen Sicherheitssystems in Deutschland, 1918/19-1933.* Frankfurt a.M.: R.G. Fischer Verlag, 1980.

Smith, Arthur L., Jr. "Life in Wartime Germany: Colonel Ohlendorf's Opinion Service." *Public Opinion Quarterly* 1 (Spring 1972): 1-7.

Stokes, Lawrence D. "Otto Ohlendorf, the *Sicherheitsdienst* and Public Opinion in Nazi Germany." In *Police Forces in History,* ed. George L. Mosse, pp. 231-61. London: SAGE Publications, 1975.

Stolz, Gerd. "Die Gendarmerie in Preussen, 1812-1923." *Zeitschrift fuer Heereskunde* 40 (1976): 93-101, 148-59.

Sydnor, Charles W., Jr. *Soldiers of Destruction: The Death's Head Division, 1933-1945.* Princeton: Princeton Univ. Press, 1977. (Although primarily an example of the excellent American work on the Waffen-SS, contains a fine chapter on Eicke's early camps.)

Teufel, Manfred. "Die geschichtliche Entwicklung der Kriminalpolizei—unter besonderer Berucksichtigung der Verhaeltnisse in Baden-Wuerttemberg." *Das Polizeiblatt* 34 (June/July 1971): 87-106.

Thevoz, Robert, Hans Branig, and Cecile Lowenthal-Hensel. *Die Geheime Staatspolizei in der preussischen Ostprovenzen*. Pommern 1934/35 (Darstellung). Cologne and Berlin: G. Grote'sche Verlagsbuchhandlung, 1974.

Trefousse, Hans. "Failure of German Intelligence in the United States, 1935-1945." *Mississippi Valley Historical Review* 42 (June 1955): 84-100.

Ullrich, Wolfgang. *Verbrechensbekaempfung: Geschichte, Organisation, Rechtsprechung*. Berlin-Spandau: Luchterhand Verlag, 1961.

Wighton, Charles. *Heydrich, Hitler's Most Evil Henchman*. London: Odhams Press, 1962.

Zipfel, Friedrich. "Gestapo und SD in Berlin." *Jahrbuch fuer die Geschichte Mittel- und Ostdeutschlands* 10 (1961): 263-92.

———. *Gestapo und Sicherheitsdienst*. Berlin-Grunewald: Arani Verlag, 1960.

Index to First Citations of Published Literature Not in the Selected Bibliography

General Index

Note: The major figures, Hitler, Himmler, Heydrich, and Goering, are such ubiquitous characters that index entries under their names are limited to seminal relationships and particular points of interest. The same is true of the organizations: Gestapo, SS and SD, and NSDAP.

DATE DUE			
NOV 14 '03			

Lebanon Valley College Library
Annville, Pennsylvania   17003

Power Structure of the Third Reich

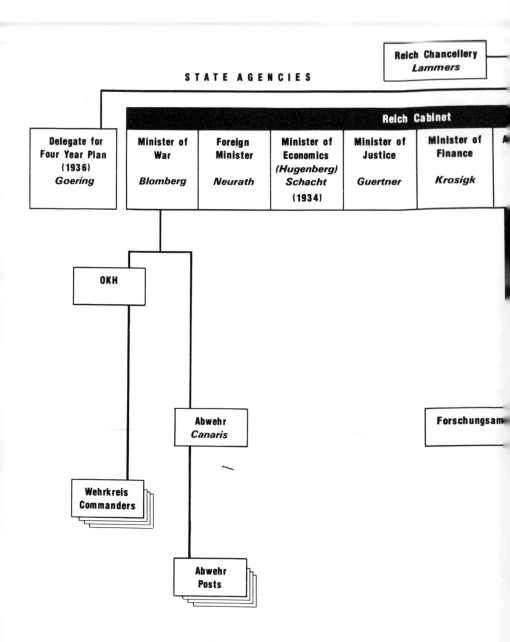

STATE AGENCIES

Reich Chancellery *Lammers*

Reich Cabinet

Delegate for Four Year Plan (1936) *Goering*	Minister of War *Blomberg*	Foreign Minister *Neurath*	Minister of Economics *(Hugenberg)* *Schacht* (1934)	Minister of Justice *Guertner*	Minister of Finance *Krosigk*

OKH

Abwehr
Canaris

Forschungsam

Wehrkreis
Commanders

Abwehr
Posts

This composite chart portrays the relationship of Sipo and SD to the power structure of the Third Reich as it existed in 1936. Dates in parentheses indicate additions to this structure after the NS acquisition of power in January 1933. Only agencies discussed in this book are listed. See the list of abbreviations beginning on page 252.